Praise for
Live Fast, Die Young

"The book is full to bursting with psychosexual tension, homoerotic innu-endo, mind games, power struggles, and the frantic chaos of creation that epitomized the film's long, rocky road to production."

—Thomas Leitch, *The Hollywood Reporter*

"*Live Fast, Die Young*'s real revelation is Ray, who emerges as the book's most compelling, tortured, and, arguably, talented figure."

—Chris Cronis, *Premiere* magazine

"The authors' movie love seeps through the prose, transcending the usual nuts-and-bolts approach. . . . They make a strong case that *Rebel* is more than just the residue of a star that burned too bright."

—Scott Von Doviak, *Fort Worth Star-Telegram*

"*Live Fast, Die Young*'s authors have feverishly documented every possible facet of *Rebel*, be it profound or provocative—or both. . . . They also achieve a delicate yet controlled balance between *Rebel*'s volatile realization and the dubious exploits that occurred offscreen. . . . For hardcore *Rebel* fans, this book is obviously a must."

—Frank Halperin, *Philadelphia City Paper*

"Behind-the-scenes conflicts, feuds, and power plays come to life thanks to the authors' thorough research and interviews."

—*Publishers Weekly*

"A riveting insider's account of the making of a film that was as dramatic and provocative as the film itself . . . highly recommended."

—*Library Journal*

"[Frascella and Weisel] satisfyingly balance scholarship and gossip."

—*Booklist*

The Wild Ride of Making
REBEL WITHOUT A CAUSE

LIVE FAST, DIE YOUNG

Lawrence Frascella
and
Al Weisel

A TOUCHSTONE BOOK
PUBLISHED BY
SIMON & SCHUSTER

NEW YORK

LONDON

TORONTO

SYDNEY

Dedicated to the memory of Gavin Lambert (1924–2005)
and Moss Mabry (1918–2006)

TOUCHSTONE
Rockefeller Center
1230 Avenue of the Americas
New York, NY 10020

This Touchstone Edition 2006

TOUCHSTONE and colophon are registered trademarks of Simon & Schuster, Inc.

For information regarding special discounts for bulk purchases,
please contact Simon & Schuster Special Sales at
1-800-456-6798 or business@simonandschuster.com.

Designed by Joy O'Meara

Manufactured in the United States of America

10   9   8   7   6   5   4   3   2   1

The Library of Congress has cataloged the hardcover edition as follows:
Frascella, Lawrence.
    Live fast, die young : the wild ride of making Rebel Without a Cause /
Lawrence Frascella and Al Weisel.
        p.   cm.
    Includes bibliographical references and index.
    1. Rebel Without a Cause (Motion picture)   I. Weisel, Al.   II. Title.
PN1997.R365F73 2005
791.43'72—dc22   2005050677

ISBN-13: 978-0-7432-6082-4
ISBN-10:   0-7432-6082-1
ISBN-13: 978-0-7432-9618-2 (Pbk)
ISBN-10:   0-7432-9618-4 (Pbk)

Contents

	Introduction	vii
CHAPTER ONE	Birth of a Rebel	1
CHAPTER TWO	Seducing Dean	15
CHAPTER THREE	Child Star	29
CHAPTER FOUR	The Script	42
CHAPTER FIVE	Gang Wars	60
CHAPTER SIX	The First Gay Teenager	78
CHAPTER SEVEN	Chateau Interlude	88
CHAPTER EIGHT	The Red Jacket	103
CHAPTER NINE	Starting Over	122
CHAPTER TEN	Meet the Parents	133
CHAPTER ELEVEN	A World of Their Own	153
CHAPTER TWELVE	Jim Kisses Plato?	171
CHAPTER THIRTEEN	Chickie Run	190
CHAPTER FOURTEEN	Last Good-bye	208
CHAPTER FIFTEEN	Crash	220
CHAPTER SIXTEEN	The Leading Lady	241
CHAPTER SEVENTEEN	The Erotic Politician	254
CHAPTER EIGHTEEN	Elegy for a Director	267
AFTERWORD	The *Rebel* Effect	288
	Notes	299
	Bibliography	347
	Acknowledgments	357
	Index	361

Introduction

Near dusk, on the evening of September 30,
1955, a telephone rang at the main gate of Warner Brothers Studios. When the guard on duty answered, a woman on the other end said that she was calling from Paso Robles War Memorial Hospital. Speaking calmly, without emotion, she told him that an actor who worked at the studio, James Dean, had been killed that evening in a car accident. Though Dean had starred in a mere three films and only one—*East of Eden*—had been released at that point, the guard knew who he was. The untamed young actor's reputation in the industry was growing much faster than his film résumé. And only a few days earlier, he had been stopped by security for speeding around the lot in his brand-new Porsche and told never to drive there again because he might kill somebody.

Immediately after hanging up the phone, the guard called Warners' publicity department, and word began to spread throughout town. "It was like a strange wind that came right through the streets of Hollywood," said screenwriter Stewart Stern about the news. And that wind blew quickly through Dean's favorite hangouts: Googie's diner, the Villa Capri, the Chateau Marmont. It cast a pall over that evening's black-tie functions: the Whisper Ball, sponsored by Jane Russell's new World Adoption International Fund, and the Deb Star Ball, a beauty pageant hosted by the town's makeup artists and hairstylists. At the Deb Star Ball guests thumbing through the official program were stunned to find a full-page ad that Dean had taken out thanking his makeup artist, which featured nothing but a close-up of Dean's eyes staring back at them. When the wire services got hold of the story, radio and TV stations around the country interrupted their programs to announce Dean's death to his growing legion of fans, young people who had responded enthusiastically to their first emotionally wrenching encounter with him in *East of Eden*.

Despite the immediate sense of shock and loss that accompanied the news, Dean's death might not necessarily have gone on to become such an enduring tragedy on the basis of *East of Eden* alone. After all, Dean's career had only just begun, and he wasn't the first young promising actor who would never get the chance to fulfill his potential. His sudden demise might have been just another sad story in a town full of sad stories, eventually fading away like a bad Technicolor print or a once-famous star of the silent screen. But the image of Dean was about to seep deeper into the public consciousness when, less than a month after his fatal accident, Warner Brothers released his second film—*Rebel Without a Cause*.

Almost immediately, Dean's image became inseparable from Jim Stark, the character he played in *Rebel*. With his white T-shirt, blue jeans and red jacket, Dean was instantly transformed into an adolescent ideal. His magnificent confusion, pained fragility, sexiness and even his narcissism made Jim Stark the template for teen rebellion. In fact, in many ways, *Rebel Without a Cause* invented the teenager.

Largely because of his work in *Rebel*, James Dean remains an undeniable force half a century after his death. But Dean's presence is not the only reason for the film's continuing relevance. *Rebel Without a Cause* asserted a romantic, mythic notion of adolescence that remains with us, that colors the way we see our own youth. And its preeminence resulted from the intense interactions of many fresh, raw-nerved personalities who came together at critical junctures in their lives and careers, including actors Natalie Wood and Sal Mineo and fledgling screenwriter Stewart Stern. Even the film's young supporting players—who portrayed the various gang members—contributed to the film's authenticity. But more than anyone, it was director Nicholas Ray who continually stoked *Rebel*'s fire.

The forty-three-year-old Ray was someone who revered youth, who viewed adolescence as a heightened human state and who refused to relinquish the teenager in himself. He was one of the great dark neurotic geniuses of American film. He raised the bar for emotional nakedness on screen, pushing his juvenile cast to reach ever more precarious heights of film acting. Ray had a dream vision of kids creating a world of their own. And under his direction, Ray's young cast coalesced into one large dysfunctional family, embarking on a journey rife with reckless behavior, deep devotion and betrayal.

Rebel Without a Cause is a film of sheer poetic expression that attempts to give shape to the internal feelings of kids alienated from the restrictions and contradictions of the adult world around them. At the time of its release, it frightened many parents with its violence, its upfront sexuality and its relentless desire to imbue teenagers with power—and glory. But in many ways, the behind-the-scenes story is more provocative than the already provocative film. James Dean stands defiantly at *Rebel*'s center, but the unbridled emotions that were channeled offscreen are the essential source of the film's dynamism and its endless ability to speak to the teenager in all of us.

LIVE FAST, DIE YOUNG

CHAPTER ONE

Birth of a Rebel

In the early 1950s, director Nicholas Ray was a regular at the classic Saturday night parties thrown by actress Betsy Blair and her husband, Gene Kelly—the kind of exclusive Hollywood soirees that would find Judy Garland singing at the piano, Leonard Bernstein playing charades or Greta Garbo sitting casually on the edge of the Kellys' kitchen sink. Blair remembers the tall, handsome, seductive Ray with great fondness. "He was always lively and iconoclastic and full of serious opinions," says Blair, who calls him "a Melville hero" for the way he chased dream projects and battled against the confines of the studio system. Blair knew Ray to be a compulsive womanizer, gambler and drinker, although "never a sloppy drunk." But one night in July 1951, after their weekly party broke up, Blair and Kelly looked out their front window and encountered a bizarre sight.

"There was a little slope in front of our house," says Blair, "and I remember Nick leaving and instead of getting into his car, he sank onto the grass, just sort of lying there. I was ready to go out and get him. But Gene said, 'Let's see if he gets up again.' And so we waited, fifteen to twenty minutes. I think Nick was actually planning to lie there all night. Eventually, we did go out and get him." Like everyone else in Hollywood, the Kellys knew that Ray had just filed for divorce from his second wife, the quintessential film noir blonde, Gloria Grahame, after a stormy three-year marriage, but they had no idea what precipitated the separation. "We didn't know in the beginning what had happened," says Blair, "just that they were fighting and breaking up and that he was desperate. And then, when I found out, it was hard to believe." The real story behind the breakup was shocking even by Hollywood standards.

Earlier that summer, everything seemed to be going well for Ray. In June 1951, he signed a lucrative contract with RKO Pictures, negotiated by his powerful new agents at MCA, making him RKO head Howard Hughes's right-hand man. That year, with the red-baiting McCarthy hearings getting under way in Washington and the Rosenbergs on trial in New York, having a protector like Hughes gave Ray—who had a history of leftist affiliations—a security and stability he rarely felt in his peripatetic career. Hughes kept him busy that summer doing uncredited patch-up work on such potential RKO disasters as *The Racket* and Josef von Sternberg's *Macao.*

One afternoon late in June, Tony, Ray's thirteen-year-old son from his first marriage to journalist Jean Evans, unexpectedly appeared on the doorstep of the Malibu beach house Ray was renting next door to his close friend, producer John Houseman. On vacation from military school, Tony had made the three-thousand-mile journey from New York all by himself, without telling anyone he was coming. Ray was not home when Tony showed up, so Grahame, who had met Ray's son only once, when he was ten years old, invited him inside. When Ray arrived home later that afternoon, he walked into the bedroom and stumbled on a sight almost too outrageous to believe. He found Grahame and his barely teenage son "in bed together," as Ray described it years later to his friend, writer Gavin Lambert.

Nicholas Ray was someone who always allowed himself—and those around him—an astounding amount of moral wiggle room. But this level of crisscrossing betrayal was too much to bear. Ray exploded in fury, smashing up the house and flinging Tony out into the street. Then Ray took off, refusing to spend another minute in the house with Grahame. Tony slept that night beneath a neighbor's porch.

Ray and Grahame had a famously tempestuous relationship. Ray claimed he married Grahame only because she was pregnant with his second son, Timothy, who was born five and a half months after the wedding. Ray said he spent their Las Vegas wedding night at the craps table, losing almost all his money because he "didn't want this dame . . . to have anything of mine." Their marriage had no chance of surviving the events of that afternoon in June 1951. Immediately, Ray filed for divorce and moved for a time into the Garden of Allah, a hotel once popular with screenwriters and silent-film stars. Seething with rage and paranoia, he forced Tony to make a tape recording detailing what happened, and threatened to make the tape public if Grahame tried to seek a large alimony settlement. In the end, Grahame did not ask for alimony and received only child support for their son Timothy. Ray never played the recording or made any mention in court of what happened that summer afternoon—which did not stop the story from becoming common knowledge. "In the circle emanating from Houseman's house we all knew," says actor Norman Lloyd, who was a friend of Ray's for many years, dating back to Ray's theatrical days in New York. Before long, the messy details of the scandal spread throughout the Hollywood community.

It's impossible to know what could have motivated Tony Ray and Gloria Grahame to engage in such a profound act of betrayal, devastating Nick's standing as a husband and father simultaneously. And Ray himself would never publicly venture an explanation. Even in private, he was reticent to discuss the events. "I remember asking him," says Gavin Lambert, " 'Do you think Tony did this in revenge for you neglecting him?' and all he said was 'Maybe.'"

Ray's marriage to Grahame may have ended with the scandal, but the relationship that began that afternoon in 1951 between the actress and Tony Ray did not stop there. In 1960, almost a decade later, they would stun Hollywood again by marrying each other, making Tony the stepfather to his half-brother Timothy.

Nicholas Ray survived the blow to his pride and it would not be long before he returned to the womanizing ways for which he was famous. Soon, Gene Kelly and Betsy Blair would find him back at their parties smooching with the likes of Marilyn Monroe. ("It was all very physical with him," Blair recalls.) But Ray would never get over the injury to his relationship with his son. And it would not be long before his rage turned to guilt, and even to an odd kind of curiosity, all of which funneled directly into his work.

Many factors contributed to Ray's passion for the story that would become *Rebel Without a Cause*. But his damaged relationship with Tony provided a key catalyst, a deeply personal underpinning to a film that would grow into a cultural phenomenon. Throughout the development of the script, Ray was "in anguish over his own role as a father," according to *Rebel* screenwriter Stewart Stern. "I think he hated himself to a large degree for failing as a father." Gavin Lambert concurs. "He should never have had kids," Lambert says. "He should never have been married. Nick had quite a few guilts. This was one of them. And it influenced his approach to the film."

Ray followed the dictum often attributed to one of his mentors, director Elia Kazan: "Turn trauma into drama." And indeed, Ray's art was fueled by personal trauma. In fact, much of his best work could be seen as autobiography. His troubled relationship with Grahame provided the raw material for one of his greatest movies, *In a Lonely Place* (which also starred Grahame), just as his disgust with the blacklist, which ruined the lives of many of his friends, would inform the plots of *Johnny Guitar* and the underrated *Run for Cover*. Using calamity to drive creativity is dangerous work. But Ray could pull it off. It was his gift, one to be envied, or so it seemed for a time. And eventually, Ray would find a way to channel all his alienation, confusion and curiosity into his most famous film, one that would ultimately transcend the personal realm to have a massive impact on generations to come.

BORN TO BE BAD

The sources of Ray's talents and genius are as mysterious as those of his *Rebel* star and cohort, James Dean, who, like Ray, sprung from the Midwest. Born Raymond Nicholas Kienzle on August 7, 1911, Nicholas Ray was raised in the small town of La Crosse, Wisconsin. Population: 50,000. His family was part of the first generation of Norwegians to settle in that part of the country and therefore, according to director Joseph Losey, who was also from La Crosse, "he was automatically on the 'wrong side of the tracks.' "

Ray's father was a contractor, and an alcoholic. His death, when Ray was sixteen, would have a devastating effect on his son. Late in his life, Ray would recount the night his father's mistress—whom Ray said he once tried to seduce, in an uncanny foreshadowing of his own problems with

Tony—took him to a hotel room where he found the dying man lying in his own vomit. "A boy needs a father at certain times in his life so that he can kick him in the shins, so he can fight for the love of his mother," Ray wrote. A father, said Ray, is "a gauge against which the boy can measure himself. Take that away and the spine is lost."

Troubled paternal relationships would remain a persistent motif in Ray's life, just as they would in his work. "Nick didn't have a father. A drunk is not a father," says his fourth and final wife, Susan Ray. "I think he was looking for that. And when people have a piece missing, they *magnetize* it in different forms." That was certainly true of Ray. It was one of the major contradictions in his character that despite a distinct contempt for authority, he entered into a series of intense mentor relationships throughout his restless early career.

Attractive, ambitious and serious-minded, Ray catapulted himself out of La Crosse when, at sixteen, he created a series of local radio programs that helped him win a scholarship to the University of Chicago. In the early 1930s, he moved briefly to New York, where he met and eventually married Jean Evans, a young writer who became a well-known reporter for the liberal newspaper *PM*. During this period, Ray was invited to take part in architect Frank Lloyd Wright's Fellowship at Taliesin, Wright's Utopian artists commune in Wisconsin—although Wright and Ray would soon have a falling-out, and Ray would leave Taliesin under a cloud of mystery. Ray returned to New York, where he joined the left-wing Theatre of Action and began a long, complex and often strained association with domineering director Elia Kazan. Kazan directed Ray in a play titled *The Young Go First* (the first of many ironic titles that would crop up throughout Ray's career). And under Kazan's tutelage, Ray was first exposed to Method acting, which would have a huge interlacing influence on his life and work.

In the year Tony Ray was born, 1937, Ray began working for the Department of Agriculture's Resettlement Administration, traveling throughout Depression-era America while writing and directing plays that starred coal miners, lumberjacks and farmers who dramatized their lives and recorded their music on his portable tape recorder. Ray's passion for American roots music led to a lifelong friendship with noted folklorist and ethnographer Alan Lomax. During World War II, and after Ray's separation from Jean Evans, producer John Houseman—who knew Ray from the

Theatre of Action—hired Ray and Lomax to produce a radio show for Voice of America, which Houseman was running for the Office of War Information (OWI). Called *Back Where I Come From*, the radio show introduced the public to such legendary folk and blues music talents as Woody Guthrie, Pete Seeger and Leadbelly.

But it wasn't until 1944 that Ray got his first taste of Hollywood. Kazan hired Ray as an assistant on his first film, *A Tree Grows in Brooklyn*. Kazan was impressed with the way Ray applied himself to studying filmmaking technique and the speed with which he was learning. Now, Kazan would have an even more acute influence on Ray's future. He showed Ray how to draw febrile, psychologically dense film performances from even the most resistant actors. And he also provoked Ray's pursuit of what he stubbornly viewed as the "truth"—a gritty, neurotic version of the truth.

Two years later, in 1946, Ray would finally make the move to Hollywood when Houseman, who had grown very close to Ray, hired him to be his assistant at RKO Pictures. In a remarkably short period of time, RKO head of production Dore Schary took a chance on Ray and gave him his first film to direct. *They Live by Night* (1948) was based on *Thieves Like Us*, a novel by Edward Anderson about two young Depression-era outlaws (which was readapted almost three decades later by another Hollywood iconoclast, Robert Altman).

From the start, Ray showed himself to be a director of maturity and sensitivity. He displayed a special affinity for the reckless romantic poignancy of youth, something for which he would soon become famous. He also proved to be bold and risk-taking. For the first scene of the film, Ray scheduled a dangerous and difficult helicopter shot. Fraught with the potential for disaster, the shot could have ended his film career before it began. But Ray's gamble paid off. "For a man who had not always shown himself emotionally secure or stable, Ray handled himself with courage and remarkable skill," said Houseman. "From the first day of shooting his authority on the set was complete and undisputed."

After Ray proved himself with *They Live By Night*, Schary pressured him into directing *A Woman's Secret*, an uneasy blend of film noir and "woman's picture." For Ray it was the beginning of a subtly destructive pattern in his career: bouncing between intimate projects and hackneyed studio affairs. Schary's girlfriend had already been cast to star in the film:

Gloria Grahame. Soon after shooting began, Ray started sleeping with Grahame and within the first month she was pregnant.

Stealing the girlfriend of the man who gave Ray his first directorial opportunity might have been career suicide if eccentric millionaire Howard Hughes had not suddenly swooped down at the end of 1948 to take over the studio. Schary was fired and Ray's position suddenly became more secure. Although he was no longer a young man—in fact, he was nearing his forties—there was something about Ray that motivated powerful figures to take him under their wing. Ray became Hughes's protégé. In between the lesser assignments Hughes gave to him, Ray continued to make the occasional fine film for RKO, such as *On Dangerous Ground* and *The Lusty Men*, small dark gems with surprisingly idiosyncratic themes. And during his RKO period, he also directed two films for the independent production company of his drinking buddy Humphrey Bogart: *Knock on Any Door* and *In a Lonely Place*. Through these films, Ray won the respect of a small coterie of Hollywood insiders, but he was not a well-known name to the industry at large. Then in 1953, the capricious Hughes sold all his shares of RKO—departing the studio as quickly as he had arrived—and Ray decided to strike out on his own. In many ways, independence—and the illusion of detachment from authority—was the state that suited Ray best. He had also been having a deeply conflicted reaction to his relatively easy success in Hollywood.

"Brought up in the Depression, one of a generation with a strong anti-Establishment bias, he had been taught to regard hardship and poverty as a virtue and wealth and power as evil," Houseman wrote about Ray in his autobiography. "When success came to him in its sudden, overwhelming Hollywood way . . . he was torn by deep feelings of guilt, for which his compulsive, idiotic gambling ($30,000 lost in one night at Las Vegas) might have been a neurotic form of atonement."

Despite his uncertain feelings about his success, Ray became concerned about his Hollywood status. After leaving RKO, Ray turned to another powerful ally, agent Lew Wasserman, head of MCA, an agency that was playing a pivotal role in the shift of power away from the studios to actors and directors. Wasserman put together two projects for Ray to direct, the Westerns *Johnny Guitar*, starring Joan Crawford, and *Run for Cover*, starring James Cagney. Although *Johnny Guitar* was a hit (and later became a cult classic), Ray later told Gavin Lambert that making the film was "an appalling experience" and that Joan Crawford was "one of the worst human beings he'd ever encountered." *Run for Cover,* meanwhile, was a box-office disaster.

After nearly a decade in Hollywood, Ray felt his career was falling behind that of his former mentor Kazan, with whom he carried on a private rivalry. By 1954, Kazan had already directed such award-winning films as *Gentleman's Agreement* and *A Streetcar Named Desire.* He was finishing up *On the Waterfront* and planning *East of Eden.* Ray's films had not been in the same league, in terms of prestige. Both *Johnny Guitar,* made for the low-rent Republic Pictures, and *Run for Cover,* made for the B-movie unit at Paramount, were low-budget programmers.

Ray had to find a way to break this downward pattern. As he explained to his agent Wasserman, he was weary of doing projects for "bread and taxes." He was desperate to do a film that he loved. Ray saw himself as an artist first. He needed a personal project—and he needed a breakthrough, something that would give him a little clout in Hollywood. And just when he craved it most, he found the perfect topic. It was screaming out from headlines across the country.

TEEN TROUBLE

Throughout the United States in the early 1950s, frightening reports of teen violence terrified parents and public officials. In Memphis, two boys shot a teenage girl who dared to resist their advances. In Kansas City, Missouri, nine teens looking for a cigarette nearly beat a man to death outside Union Station. In Illinois, young members of the military were revealed to be part of a secret gang who kept scorecards regarding the use of marijuana, switchblades, blackjacks and pistols.

Between 1948 and 1953, the number of juveniles charged with crimes increased 40 percent, a statistic that alarmed the country. "We have the spectacle of an entire city terrorized by one-half of one percent of its residents. And the terrorists are children," a Boston judge warned ominously in 1953.

The media fanned the public's fury with stories of the troubled teen and juvenile crime, stoking high anxiety in the form of moral outrage. In September 1954, *Newsweek* asked, "Our Vicious Young Hoodlums: Is There Any Hope?" and, in the same month, *U.S. News & World Report* published "Why Teen-Agers Go Wrong" (two articles Ray would cite in his initial *Rebel* proposal). The *U.S. News* article was actually an in-depth interview with Richard Clendenen, an expert on juvenile crime who was the executive director of the Senate Subcommittee to Investigate Juvenile Delinquency. This committee, headed by Senator Estes Kefauver, would haul in high-ranking members of the entertainment business for a series of very public grillings about the media's effect on adolescent behavior.

At the time, all rebellious teen behavior was seen as evidence of a mushrooming problem with juvenile delinquency. It didn't really matter whether teens were breaking laws, breaking taboos, or bending household rules. Every aspect of the emerging teen culture—with its new music, language and attitudes toward sexuality—was viewed as threatening and incomprehensible. But in many ways, teens were simply expanding their own boundaries, engaging in their own version of manifest destiny, dazzled by what critic Geoffrey O'Brien described as "the glitter of fulfillment" that lit up the country in the prosperous 1950s, when being a teen was still a new concept. The word *teenager* did not even enter the language until 1941. And as the number of teens doubled in the wake of the postwar baby boom, young Americans had simply begun to stake out their own culture separate from adults, although in the mid-1950s, this landscape was largely undefined. That would all begin to change with the arrival of one movie.

Nick Ray was inevitably attracted to what was happening with kids. It fed directly into his guilt over Tony. It spoke to his own issues with authority. And it justified his own natural affinity for young people, a tendency that seemed to get stronger as he got older. ("The celluloid strip is a bloodstream for me—and so is youth. It's what I live by," Ray would later say, in his self-mythologizing mode.) His growing passion rose to the surface one night in September 1954, after a screening of *Run for Cover*. Following the preview, Ray, Lew Wasserman and Wasserman's wife, Edie, had dinner in Ray's apartment at the Chateau Marmont. After watching *Dragnet* on television, Ray told Wasserman that he was frustrated with the direction his career was going. "I really have to want to do the next one," he said. "I have to believe in it or feel that it's important." Wasserman asked what Ray thought was important. "There are six films about *War and Peace* scheduled so I've given up on that," said Ray. "Well, what else is important?" Wasserman asked him. Ray paused for a moment, then finally said what was on his mind: "I want to do a film about kids. I want to do a film about the young people next door. . . . I've done the stuff with the depressed areas, the misfits. Now I want to do a film about the guy next door, like could be one of my sons."

Ray had already dealt with the subject of juvenile delinquency in 1949's *Knock on Any Door*—the movie that introduced the phrase "Live fast, die young, and have a good-looking corpse"—but he was dissatisfied with the film's approach. It did not rise above the socioeconomic view of the subject that Hollywood had been mining since 1933's *Wild Boys of the Road* and 1937's *Dead End*. Ray yearned to make a film that would stand with 1950's *Los Olvidados,* director Luis Buñuel's caustic, surreal and poetic account of lost Mexican youth. "I wish Buñuel had made *Los Olvidados* before I made *Knock on Any* Door," said Ray, "because I would have made a hell of a lot better film." It's no coincidence that a thirty-five-dollar rental receipt for a print of *Los Olvidados* appears among the *Rebel Without a Cause* materials housed at the Warner Brothers archives. Ray was intent on avoiding what he called "slum area rationalizations." Instead, he wanted to focus on middle-class kids, as he explained to Wasserman.

Wasserman may not have known the full scope of Ray's intentions—and, at the time, Ray seems to have had only the vaguest notion himself—but he knew that his client was serious. So he took the notion of a film about young people to Warner Brothers. Immediately, the studio bit. Ray's suggestion was the right one at the right time. Warner Brothers had just begun a campaign to find fresh, new faces. The studio was looking for ways to target the largely underexploited teen demographic, despite the chilling effect of the Kefauver hearings. In fact, the Kefauver hearings may have unintentionally focused Hollywood's attention on the emergence of a new type of adolescent audience, one that was looking for edgier product, and a more sizzling reflection of their experience.

The studio suggested that Ray consider adapting Dr. Robert Lindner's best-selling 1944 book *Rebel Without a Cause: The Story of a Criminal Psychopath,* a property that had been languishing at the studio for years. But Ray immediately dismissed Lindner's book. He thought the case was too extreme: "It was neither the psychopath nor the son of a poor family I was interested in now."

Warners then handed Ray two scripts with youth-oriented themes but, to the director's chagrin, they were set in economically deprived areas. Ray reacted in frustration: "No, I didn't mean that at all. Not at all." Finally, an exasperated Wasserman said to Ray, "Warners wants to know what you do mean. Will you go up and talk to them?"

Now it was up to Ray to convince the studio. Ray drove to the Warners lot and met with the head of production, Steve Trilling, often referred to as Jack Warner's "henchman." Trilling certainly had the look of a henchman right out of an old Warner Brothers gangster movie: grim, overweight and given to smoking cigars. For forty-five minutes, Ray shot from the hip, telling Trilling stories he had gleaned from newspaper clippings and his own experiences about kids from "ordinary families."

After he had performed for Trilling, Ray reported to Wasserman, who checked with the studio. Later that afternoon, Wasserman contacted Ray with some good news. "They want to know if you can put down on paper what you told them," Wasserman said. Ray was thrilled and said he would try. He called his secretary, Fae Murphy—who arrived at 7 p.m.—and they worked feverishly through dawn.

THE BLIND RUN

With the help of his secretary, Ray labored with the energy of an artist plugged directly into the Zeitgeist. He began his treatment with a burst of shocking imagery: "a man aflame" running toward the camera (a metaphor, perhaps, for the way Ray felt that evening), and a nearly pornographic scene of a sixteen-year-old girl, stripped to the waist, being whipped by three teenagers. These searingly graphic images would never appear in *Rebel,* and perhaps they were only meant to grab the attention of the Warners executives. In general, Ray's treatment had a lurid and exploitative tone. It lacked shape and depth. It was largely plotless. Still, he burst forth with some of *Rebel Without a Cause*'s key concepts that very night.

Ray already saw his film as being built around a teenage trinity: a heroic boy (who would grow into the iconic figure of Jim Stark), a girl named Eve (who would lose her biblical overtones to become Judy) and Demo (a teenage psychotic who would eventually evolve into the groundbreaking figure of Plato). He concocted a knife fight, which would become one of *Rebel*'s most memorable scenes. And Ray envisioned a suicidal car race—a "blind run"—that takes place in a tunnel with two cars speeding toward each other in the dark. This scene would later transform into *Rebel*'s race off the side of a cliff—the pivotal and influential "chickie run."

But the treatment's biggest break with convention appears as a side note in Ray's one-night downloading of ideas. "Youth is always in the foreground," he wrote, "and adults are for the most part only to be seen as the kids see them." These words signaled a remarkable change in the way this kind of material had always been treated and would ultimately represent *Rebel*'s most important leap forward.

At 9 a.m. on September 18, 1954, Ray's secretary finished typing up the seventeen-page treatment he had disgorged all night long. He called it "The Blind Run"—a title that foreshadowed the film's production, which would often feel like a headlong rush into the unknown. Ray called Wasserman, who immediately took the treatment out to Warner Brothers. Amazingly, by four that same afternoon, Wasserman phoned back, telling Ray, "You've got a deal. Go on out and pick your producer."

Ray chose thirty-nine-year-old David Weisbart to be his producer because he was the youngest on the Warners lot. Weisbart also "had two teenage children, which made me think he would bring a personal interest to the subject," said Ray. In addition, he had once worked with Kazan, as an editor on *A Streetcar Named Desire*. Weisbart would turn out to be the perfect producer for Ray. "He was a gentleman, one hundred percent mensch," says Dennis Stock, who was hired as the film's dialogue coach. "He was very unusual in Hollywood—he was civilized. There was no eccentricity in this guy. He was the guy who covered everybody's ass. Everybody trusted Weisbart. They knew that he was a real pro. Nick without Weisbart would never have made the film."

But when Weisbart first encountered Ray's treatment, according to Ray, "he was in a state of shock." As Ray later wrote, "His first reaction was as if he had swallowed a hot potato. (Later, of course, he knew he had.) This was not surprising. To begin with, he was faced with an original story—less a story at this stage than an idea and not the comfortable basis of an existing novel or magazine story or Broadway play. Also, the subject itself was potentially explosive."

Although Warners had given Ray the go-ahead to hire Weisbart and begin preproduction, the studio was wary. According to Gavin Lambert, "Warners was very dubious about it at first. It was a weird studio at that time. Jack Warner was a peculiar creature. On one level, he was ridiculous; on another level, very shrewd. He didn't really know in creative or technical terms what a good script was or what a bad script was. He had some kind of instinct about what would go down with an audience. And he liked prestige as well. They were both impressed with Nick and worried about him."

The studio insisted that Ray use the title of the bestseller they had previously offered him, Robert Lindner's *Rebel Without a Cause,* for which Lindner had been paid five thousand dollars. Ever since the studio optioned the book, Warners producer Jerry Wald had tried to turn it into a film. As far back as 1947, Marlon Brando was screen-tested for a possible role in a potential film version of *Rebel* (the same year Brando changed acting forever as Stanley Kowalski in Kazan's original Broadway production of *A Streetcar Named Desire*). But Ray continued to feel that Lindner's case "was too abnormal" for the film he wanted to make.

While working on *Rebel,* Ray did attend two of Lindner's lectures at the Beverly Hills Hotel. Titled "The Mutiny of Adolescence" and "Must We Conform?," the lectures defended adolescent rebellion in the face of creeping conformity. Afterward, Lindner walked up to Ray. The psychoanalyst was perplexed by the fact that Ray had completely thrown out his book. He pleaded with Ray to reconsider or at least hire him as a consultant. Although the content of Lindner's lectures must have struck a chord with the director, Ray rebuffed him.

It's no surprise that Ray refused to work from a preexisting source; he had something much more personal in mind, something more intimate to process. Nevertheless, Ray had no problem calling his film *Rebel Without a*

Cause, as long as he did not have to use a word of the actual book, which seemed to be fine with the studio.

In record time, Nicholas Ray secured a green light and a title. Now all he needed was a script and a cast. But that process would grow immensely complicated once Ray began to envision *Rebel* as a personal catharsis, and a challenge to the culture at large. As his idea expanded, Ray came to an inspired and potentially self-destructive decision. For the movie to be truly new, even the making of it had to be a unique experience, a rebel act, an emphatic and defiant break with the past.

CHAPTER TWO

Seducing Dean

During the early stages of *Rebel*, Nick Ray had nobody specific in mind for the lead role of Jim Stark. Handsome but relatively anemic actors such as Tab Hunter, John Kerr and Robert Wagner were suggested by Warner Brothers. In the past, Ray might have considered one of them; he had been known to make pragmatic concessions to the studios. But *Rebel* represented the promise of something unparalleled to Ray. He could not shake the feeling that he was about to embark on a major life adventure. He had so much faith in his new project, he even began chronicling the film's development in a diary, hoping someday to write a book about the making of *Rebel*—a book he never finished. Ray knew that both his film and his experience would fall short without a charismatic hero at its center. He needed an actor who could completely capture what he would call the "conflict of violent eagerness and mistrust created in the very young." As it turned out, that person was closer than Ray imagined. Right on the Warners lot, Ray would find an actor who "threw himself upon the world like a starved animal after a scrap of food," in Ray's own words. This actor would transform Ray's movie and, in many ways, the world around him.

Ray's office on the Warners lot was next door to that of his mentor and occasional rival, Elia Kazan, the man who had first brought him to Hollywood. One afternoon, Kazan invited Ray to see a rough cut of his new film, *East of Eden*, while he worked out the details of the scoring with composer Leonard Rosenman. When Ray entered the screening room, he was introduced both to Rosenman—who improvised at the piano during the screening—and to Rosenman's good friend, the movie's star, twenty-three-year-old James Dean. The thin, casually dressed, boyishly handsome Dean skulked in the background, a portrait of shaggy disinterest.

Although Ray hardly spoke to Dean that day, he was impressed by his sexy, feral, emotionally unfettered performance in *East of Eden*. But he did not know whether to credit Dean or Kazan. From his own experience, Ray was keenly aware of Kazan's abilities. He knew that the director could get a great performance out of almost anyone. And as far as the critical, often ungenerous Kazan was concerned, he viewed Dean as damaged goods and felt he had already squeezed everything he could get out of the actor. Toward the end of shooting *Eden*, Kazan had become fed up with Dean. He found him confrontational, undisciplined and self-indulgent. He felt it was necessary to keep Dean on a tight rein. But Kazan's attitude did not dissuade Ray from considering the young actor. In fact, it may have piqued Ray's interest. Dean's neurotic vitality, his narcissistic sexuality, his contempt for authority were qualities that attracted Ray. They were qualities Ray himself possessed. And they were just what he was looking for in a boy to play Jim Stark.

Ray began hearing stories about Dean, who had already gained a reputation on the Warners lot by keeping a loaded .45 under his pillow in the dressing room where he was actually living. Eventually, after a run-in with studio head Jack Warner himself, Dean was forced to leave the premises in the evenings. Dean exacted his revenge by ripping the nameplates off the Warner executives' office doors, switching some and dangling others from the ceiling.

Soon after the screening of Kazan's rough cut, Dean began dropping by Ray's office on the lot. One day, he asked Ray what he was working on and, for the first time, the director told him about *Rebel Without a Cause*. Although Dean remained tight-lipped, Ray could tell he was intrigued. But Ray could not have predicted that this muted, inconclusive meeting would mark the beginning of their long, strange courtship. "I didn't pick Jimmy for *Rebel*," said Ray. "We sniffed each other out, like a couple of Siamese cats."

"THE OPPOSITE DIRECTION"

From the beginning, Ray and Dean had more than temperament in common. Like Ray, James Byron Dean sprang from Middle America. From the age of nine, he had been raised by his aunt and uncle, the Winslows, in the sparsely populated farming town of Fairmount, Indiana, where he had been sent by his father, Winton, after Dean's mother died of cancer at the age of thirty. Dean later claimed it was his mother's idea to give her son the prescient middle name Byron after the Romantic poet famously described as "mad, bad, and dangerous to know."

Like Ray, Dean had a troubled relationship with his father. When Winton Dean shipped Jimmy to Indiana from Los Angeles, where the family had moved when Dean was five, he promised to join his son when he had saved enough money. He never did. "His father was a monster, a person without any kind of sensitivity," said composer Rosenman. "Jimmy was doing everything in his career to get his father to like and approve of him and his father never took the slightest interest."

Early on, Dean displayed a decided bent toward acting—and a tendency to use performance to vent and startle. During a statewide oratory contest—which he won—Dean read "A Madman's Manuscript" from Charles Dickens's *Pickwick Papers*. He began his reading with a scream. "I really woke up those judges," Dean said. He would go on to appear regularly in plays at Fairmount High.

When he was eighteen, Dean decided to explore acting more seriously. He moved back to Los Angeles to study acting at UCLA. He lived with his father, who remained distant and insisted Dean learn something substantial. "Why don't you become a lawyer?" Winton complained. "But no, it was acting with him all the way." Dean landed a Pepsi commercial where, in an attention-getting move, he ostentatiously slammed the top of a player piano. He also won a part in the television drama *Hill Number One,* playing John the Baptist, and got bit parts in three movies helmed by major directors: Sam Fuller's *Fixed Bayonets,* Douglas Sirk's *Has Anybody Seen My Girl?* and Michael Curtiz's *Trouble Along the Way.* But the restless, ambitious Dean could not see himself becoming a mere cog in the L.A. acting machine. So he took the advice of his acting teacher James Whitmore and headed to New York—where his future immediately snapped into sharper focus.

In Manhattan, Dean found a city that matched his sensibility. For the rest of his life, Dean would call New York home. In a revealing interview with a *New York Times* reporter, Dean compared New York's creative climate with that of Los Angeles. "Don't get me wrong. I'm not one of those wise ones who try to put Hollywood down. It just happens that I fit to [the] cadence and pace better here as far as living goes. New York is vital, above all, fertile. They're a little harder to find, maybe, but out there in Hollywood, behind all that brick and mortar, there are human beings just as sensitive to fertility. The problem for this cat—myself—is not to get lost."

The city that Dean discovered when he arrived in 1951 was pulsing with postwar energy. Several different kinds of revolutions were taking place, most pertinently for Dean in the theater, where a fierce, new, politically engaged generation of actors was making noise. The hub of all this new theatrical activity was the Actors Studio. Co-founded by Elia Kazan, Cheryl Crawford and Robert Lewis, the Actors Studio taught what became known simply as the Method, an approach to acting derived from the writings of Russian director and teacher Konstantin Stanislavsky. The Actors Studio trained students to build their characters from the inside, to use their own emotional lives as raw material. In a development that pushed acting ever closer to psychotherapy, actors were encouraged to draw on experiences from their memories, to have the courage to improvise and delve guiltlessly into their own neuroses and fears. The Method would advance what was viewed to be a more honest, naturalistic form of acting. But for a natural like Dean, even this technique ultimately proved too artificial and claustrophobic.

After the Actors Studio's most famous teacher, Lee Strasberg, ripped apart Dean's performance of a scene about a matador, which Dean had written, he stormed out, never to return. "I don't know what's inside me. I don't know what happens when I act—inside. But if I let them dissect me, like a rabbit in a clinical research laboratory or something, I might not be able to produce again," Dean said, revealing his tortured, volcanic relationship with his own acting gifts.

"Dean was scarcely at the Studio at all," Kazan later claimed, with undisguised disdain. "He came in only a few times. I remember him sitting in the front row, a surly mess. He never participated in anything."

Alienated as he was from the Actors Studio, Dean still remained under the spell of the Method and, especially, its most famous proponent, Marlon Brando. In many ways, there would not have been a Dean without Brando. Brando single-handedly widened the playing field for actors in terms of risk, sexuality and emotional exposure. In 1947, he stunned Broadway as Stanley Kowalski in Tennessee Williams's *A Streetcar Named Desire*, directed by Kazan. Brando's ferocious performance would have a monumental influence over the young actors that followed, including Dean, who had come to view acting as a mission. "He dropped his voice to a cathedral hush when he talked about Marlon," Kazan said of Dean.

Throughout his life and afterward, Dean was often accused of copying Brando. When Dean first came to New York, he did begin to consciously imitate his idol's acting tics and techniques—his mumbled line readings, his reckless physicality, his erotic bravado. But when it came to the similarities in their offstage behavior, it wasn't always easy to know how much was imitation and how much was the result of natural affinities. They both loved motorcycles, although Dean bought his first cycle—a small, 1.5-horsepower CZ—when he was fifteen, long before he lived in New York. Brando was an unpredictable prankster who would use strange and outrageous social behavior to gain the upper hand. Dean did the same. Brando wore Levi's, loafers and V-neck pullovers and so did Dean. Brando played the bongos and the recorder; he studied boxing and admired bullfighters. Dean did, too.

At one point, Dean even became a Brando stalker of sorts. He left countless messages with Brando's answering service—which Brando never returned. Brando became so concerned that he gave Dean the number of his therapist and insisted he go. "Be who you are, not who I am," Brando commanded him. Ultimately, Dean would take this advice to heart.

Dean landed his first Broadway role in a play entitled *See the Jaguar*—which ran only six days. But that was enough time for Dean to make an impression. His good reviews led to an avalanche of work in the often live TV plays that marked this period as the "Golden Age of Television." Dean appeared in sixteen television plays in 1953 alone, portraying everything from the man who shot Jesse James, in an episode of *You Are There,* to a psychotic janitor in *Death Is My Neighbor.* "He would do his homework on the set," says his co-star in *Death Is My Neighbor,* Betsy Palmer. "That's a very self-indulgent and attention-attracting thing. He would sit and talk and worry and they didn't know what the hell he was talking about. The director was saying, 'Come on, keep it going,' and he'd be doing all these inside things to make it interesting."

For a time, television was the perfect medium for Dean. "The movies were still portraying kids as bobbysoxers and cheerleaders, chewing gum and driving jalopies," said television playwright Rod Serling, who cast Dean in his first leading role in the teleplay *A Long Time Till Dawn*. "There was a post-war mystification of the young, a gradual erosion of confidence in their elders, in so-called truths, in the whole litany of moral codes. They just didn't believe in them anymore. In television, we were aware of this and more in touch with what was happening." It took a young medium to tap into the changes that were happening to America's youth. Television gave Dean the freedom to develop his craft, to uncover what director Arthur Penn calls his "quality of adolescent boil, that adolescent fury." Television became Dean's laboratory. He would move beyond his more dogged imitations of Brando—and also of actor Montgomery Clift. Soon Dean found his own voice, his own attitude and approach, his trademark ability to register heartbreakingly rapid flickers of humor and pain, boyishness and sexuality, fragility and heroism, celebration and anger.

Living in New York not only gave Dean the chance to improve his acting skills, it also expanded his worldview. Leonard Rosenman was a serious avant-garde composer when he was introduced to Dean by playwright Howard Sackler, who joked that Dean was "a tough kid. Sleeps on nails." But Rosenman saw through Dean's bravado. Seven years older than Dean, Rosenman thought the young actor was simply working to cover up his intense vulnerability. According to the composer, late one night Dean showed up at his apartment clad in black leather, looking "like a member of the Gestapo." He asked for piano lessons. Though Dean proved to be a poor student, Rosenman became one of his closest friends. Dean looked up to him as an intellectual mentor and tried to absorb his knowledge of music and culture. "I was reading some book by Kierkegaard at the time," said Rosenman. "Suddenly Jimmy was carrying around books by Kierkegaard and other philosophers though he never did get to read them. His desire for respect as an 'intellectual' was profound." But Rosenman also felt there was a darker side to Dean's drive to assimilate. "Jimmy had a severe identity problem," he said. "He had no real identity himself."

Tough and rebellious as Dean could be, he yearned most of all for the love and respect of the very people he challenged. He could be as charming as he was insufferable, and he knew when to turn on that charm to get what he wanted. He could be troublesome, but he seemed to know just how far he could go.

During this period, Dean composed a letter to the minister of the Wesleyan Church in Fairmount, the Reverend James DeWeerd, who had formed attachments with a number of young boys in town. In his letter to DeWeerd, Dean described the acting milieu and his place in it: "Their crazy world seems to be a continuous chase around the table. Nature has patterned itself that I must run in the opposite direction to complete the game." In many ways, Dean had written the defining statement of his life.

DEAN VS. KAZAN

In February 1954, Dean's theatrical career caught fire—for the briefest of moments. He was cast in a major Broadway production, garnering raves for his seductive work as a young gay Arab in Andre Gide's *The Immoralist*. The play seemed to be his biggest break yet. Then, on opening night, he handed in his two-week notice, stunning the New York theater world with his apparent career-killing move. What they did not know was that Dean had already signed on for the lead in the prestigious Hollywood version of John Steinbeck's novel *East of Eden*, to be directed by one of their own, Elia Kazan.

From the first, Kazan seemed to cast a contemptuous eye on Dean. After Brando turned down the lead in *East of Eden*, Kazan met with Dean to discuss casting him. An immediate power play ensued. Kazan found the actor dressed in blue jeans, slouching on the leather sofa in his waiting room with a pugnacious attitude and a belligerent expression on his face. Kazan decided to keep him waiting just to see how he would react. By the time Kazan actually allowed Dean into his office, Dean had softened. Yet when Kazan attempted to draw him into conversation, Dean was reticent. Instead of talking, Dean asked Kazan if he'd like to take a ride on Dean's motorcycle, an offer he would often make to break the ice—and get the upper hand. Kazan agreed to go for a ride but refused to surrender himself to the experience. He remained disdainful and merely felt Dean was showing off.

But despite his animosity toward Dean as a person, Kazan realized that the actor was not only right for the part of Cal, the angry adolescent desperately yearning for his father's love—Dean *was* Cal. "He had a grudge against all fathers," said Kazan. "He was vengeful; he had a sense of aloneness and of being persecuted."

To Dean, Kazan was the man who had turned his idol Marlon Brando into a star and, despite his initial belligerence, he was prepared to follow wherever the director might lead. Kazan indulged his new protégé, giving him as much time as he needed to prepare for a scene and patiently teaching him the basics of screen acting. Like Nicholas Ray, Kazan had a working method that was terribly intimate. Together they explored Dean's past, focusing on moments of mental and physical pain. Then just before a difficult scene, the director would remind Dean of one of these childhood traumas. It proved to be an effective technique.

But Kazan also began to resort to tricks to get a performance out of Dean. Once when a scene was not going particularly well, he got Dean drunk. When Dean was having difficulty pushing heavy blocks of ice down a chute, Kazan insulted his acting ability, making him so angry he began violently flinging down the ice. To Kazan, Dean needed to be coaxed and cajoled, manipulated and fooled into giving a great performance. "Directing him was like directing the faithful Lassie," Kazan said. "I either lectured him or terrorized him, flattered him furiously, tapped him on the shoulder, or kicked his backside. He was so instinctive and so stupid in many ways—and most of all I had the impression of someone who was a cripple inside. He was not like Brando. People compared them, but there was no similarity. He was a far, far sicker kid."

As Dean began to resent Kazan's treatment of him and what he called Kazan's "gimmicks," he grew more antagonistic—and Kazan exerted more control. By the time Kazan invited Nicholas Ray to view the rough cut of *East of Eden* in the fall of 1954, Kazan's relationship with Dean had completely deteriorated.

Although Kazan had been Ray's mentor, Ray was a very different man from his authoritarian friend, even as a director. "A director shows the way. He does not manipulate his actors," Ray once said. Although twenty years Dean's senior, Ray would prove to be unlike any role model Dean had ever encountered. Ray was the last person to play disciplinarian and he could easily match the young actor in rebelliousness, self-regard and the often destructive pursuit of something true. The fact that they were so much alike may have drawn them together—but it also made them wary. Ray and Dean were equally mistrustful and wounded creatures and neither was ready to commit to the other immediately.

SEDUCTION

Dean and Ray's mutual seduction shifted into higher gear late one night in the fall of 1954, soon after their initial meeting. Ray was startled by an unexpected knock at the door of his bungalow at the Chateau Marmont. Standing at his threshold was a Halloween trio of uninvited guests, denizens of a vaguely off-Hollywood demimonde. First, there was Maila Nurmi, better known as Vampira, the cult-horror actress who looked as if she had stepped out of a Charles Addams cartoon (and who would go on to star in Ed Wood's famous worst-movie-ever-made *Plan 9 from Outer Space*). Nurmi was joined by what appeared to be two James Deans. One was the real James Dean, while the other was a young actor named Jack Simmons, who had begun dressing and acting exactly like Dean after allegedly becoming his lover. As soon as Ray opened his door, Dean made a typically unorthodox and dramatic entrance, turning two complete backward somersaults into the room.

From the ground, Dean looked up at Ray and teasingly inquired, "Are you middle-aged?" Ray conceded that he was.

"Did you live in a bungalow on Sunset Boulevard, by the old Clover Club?" Dean continued.

"Yes," Ray said.

"Was there a fire in the middle of the night?"

"Yes."

"Did you carry a Boxer puppy out of your house in your bare feet and walk across the street with it and cut your feet?"

23

"Yes."

Dean seemed to approve. He had heard this story from Vampira and came to find out from Ray if it was true. Then as quickly as they appeared, Dean and his cohorts vanished, leaving Ray bemused and further intrigued.

After Dean's late-night appearance at his bungalow, Ray sensed distinct interest on Dean's part. But if Ray was persuaded that Dean might be the right person to play Jim Stark, convincing Dean to take the role was another matter.

As talk about his performance in *Eden* intensified, the people around Dean were advising him to hold out for a prestige picture, directed by a big-name Hollywood director—a William Wyler or, once again, Elia Kazan, directors whose credentials far exceeded Ray's (although Ray would later claim that "Kazan had told Dean there were only three directors in Hollywood he should work with: himself, George Stevens and me"). Dean was vying for the role of Jett Rink in Stevens's big-budget film version of Edna Ferber's hit book *Giant,* but the film was not ready for production. Director Vincente Minnelli wanted him to star as a neurotic sanitarium patient opposite Lauren Bacall—and Ray's ex-wife Gloria Grahame—in his MGM melodrama *The Cobweb.* But Dean's agent tried to use the salary he would be paid for *The Cobweb* as leverage to boost the actor's pay at Warners. When Jack Warner got wind of this strategy, he made a backroom deal with MGM to deny Dean the money his agent demanded and negotiations fell apart.

So on the heels of his first major role, Dean found himself floating in space. Meanwhile, the magazine press from *Look* to *Photoplay* continued to build him up—calling him a "smash," the "next success," a "face with a future" and, to what must have been Dean's satisfaction, "the most dynamic discovery since Marlon Brando"—all based on rumors about *East of Eden,* which had still not been released. With Dean-mania brewing, it became increasingly unlikely that Warners would allow their new star to take a role in *Rebel,* which was then planned to be a relatively low-budget, black-and-white film. It didn't help that Ray lacked a script—until, that is, Ray came up with a brilliant idea.

Ray decided to use his script problems to his advantage. He would involve Dean in the creative process. He would seduce him by making him feel that the project was just as much Dean's as it was Ray's. "I leveled with him all the time and made him feel a part of the entire project," Ray remembered. "He wanted to belong and I made him feel that he did." It also helped that Dean had ambitions of someday becoming a director.

Director George Cukor was known for the lavish pool parties he would throw on Sunday afternoons. Ray concocted his own modest version of this social flourish. Every Sunday, Ray's mostly East Coast friends were asked to drop by his small bungalow at the Chateau Marmont for jug wine, conversation and music. "Started at 1 p.m. with Bop, ended at 1 a.m. with Bach," columnist Army Archerd reported on one of Ray's Sunday parties. Ray invited Dean to come by, and the young man readily agreed, showing up week after week. Ray used every opportunity to discuss his plans for *Rebel*. "To work with Jimmy meant exploring his nature," wrote Ray in a revealing passage that also defines himself. "He wanted to make films in which he could personally believe, but it was never easy for him. Between belief and action lay the obstacle of his own deep, obscure uncertainty."

Ray describes their relationship the way one would describe a couple at the initial stages of a love affair. "It was exploratory on both sides," Ray said. "Was he going to like my friends, would he find their climate encouraging? Both of us had to know."

At Ray's parties, Dean could be charmingly seductive or boyishly shy. He was even given to naïve levels of enthusiastic gushing. One afternoon, he told playwright Clifford Odets that meeting him was "like meeting Ibsen or Shaw." Odets thought it was one of the most flattering remarks anyone had ever said to him. But Dean was just as transparent about those he disliked. During one gathering at Ray's bungalow, Dean met Irving Shulman, the author of the classic juvenile-delinquent novel *The Amboy Dukes*, who had been hired by Ray to flesh out *Rebel*'s screenplay. Ray thought that Dean and Shulman would hit it off because of their mutual interest in sports cars. But Dean was disappointed to discover that Shulman's car, an MG, had neither special carburetors for racing nor wire wheels. Shulman, meanwhile, resented the fact that Dean wanted to buy a German-made Porsche so soon after World War II. It wasn't long before their conversation sputtered to a halt and Dean withdrew into silence. Soon afterward, Shulman was off the picture. If Dean didn't want Shulman, neither did Ray.

Ray continued to court Dean rigorously, and while he could feel the actor coming around, he could not secure a final commitment. On screen and off, Dean was a master of the tease, and that would become apparent to Ray when Dean suddenly took off for New York to star in a television play. Ray was not about to let Dean slip out of his sphere of influence so, following Dean's tracks, he headed east.

When he arrived in New York, Ray dropped in at Dean's tiny fifth-floor walk-up apartment in a brownstone on narrow, tree-lined East 68th Street. He found Dean's place to be the perfect example of a 1950s bohemian pad. Amidst the unmatching furniture, there were piles of books scattered on the floor. Dean was known to surround himself with literature and a wide variety of books on topics as diverse as philosophy, Aztec culture and theater. According to Ray, there were "automobile posters, sailing shots, bongo drums and the score of *Harold in Italy* by Berlioz, which he was studying assiduously, partly, I think, due to the influence of Leonard Rosenman." Dean also owned many albums, by everyone from Bach to Bartok to Sinatra. Although he was most certainly a dilettante, Dean was as hungry for knowledge as he was for experience. "An actor would be selfish if he didn't learn everything life has to offer," he said. "He should try to learn what is valid in life and what isn't. It takes time, time when he could be goofing off, but it's worth it, when and if he finds it."

Dean's apartment also featured a small porthole window that looked exactly like a window that appeared in an old photograph of Marlon Brando at home. In his ever-active Brando fantasia, Dean liked to insist that his apartment was the very one his hero had once rented.

Hanging out together for days on end, Ray and Dean grew closer over dinners, drinks and long walks. Both Dean and Ray were prone to exaggerated mood swings and Ray shared Dean's "pathological desire for tension," as Leonard Rosenman described it. It soon became clear that they both had an intense, almost vampiric drive to meld into other people.

Ray and Dean also learned that they were both uplifted by the power of cinema. One afternoon when Dean was especially sullen and morose, they went to see Jacques Tati's classic comedy *Jour de Fête*. Within minutes, Dean began laughing so loudly he was asked to leave. Leaping gracefully over seats as he exited, he emerged on the street in a Tati reverie, impressing Ray with his perfect imitation of the French comedian's trademark walk.

Ray began to see that beneath Dean's cocky façade was a vulnerability and insecurity that began to more deeply inform his conception of Jim Stark. "The drama of his life, I thought after seeing him in New York," Ray recalled, "was the drama of desiring to belong, and fearing to belong . . . The intensity of his desires, his fears, could make the search at times arrogant, egocentric, but behind it was such a desperate vulnerability that one was moved, even frightened." Once again, in describing Dean, Ray may well have been describing himself.

Ray needed to return to Hollywood. But before he left, in a bold decision that reveals much about the director, he introduced Dean to his seventeen-year-old son Tony. Much of Ray's initial motivation in pursuing the *Rebel* project had begun with his attempt to deal with his emotional estrangement from Tony, and he now saw the perfect opportunity to involve his son. It's an example of the emotional density with which Ray worked— eagerly involving those around him in psychological games, all in the name of cinema. The director introduced Dean to Tony so that Ray might see Dean "through the eyes of his own generation," he later said. Tony might help his father to understand and evaluate Dean's power over his peers. And if they hit it off, Tony would certainly help strengthen the link between Ray and Dean.

Dean immediately bonded with Ray's son, and they attended several wild parties long on dancing, fevered conversation and percussion sessions in which everything from bongos to pot lids were pounded. "We knew he was Nick Ray's kid," says actor Bob Heller, who was Dean's acquaintance at the time. "We also knew he was schtupping his stepmother, Gloria." According to Heller, "Since Tony was not an original member of our group, he was left out of most of our ritual shenanigans. But he was Jimmy's friend so he was with us for a while. I don't think any of us knew or cared that he was pimping for his dad."

Despite his closeness to Tony, Dean stubbornly refused to commit to *Rebel.* He knew the studio was against it. He was unsure about Ray's ability to pull off the kind of top-line movie with which he wanted to be associated. So once again, Ray boarded the plane from L.A. to Manhattan.

Dean's mistrust of people was so great that Ray was at pains to penetrate it. According to Ray, "One day in a restaurant he wondered out loud, 'Where are my friends?' Four of his closest friends were with him at the table. Before they could answer he abruptly got up and walked out."

Finally, on what Dean knew was Ray's last night in New York, the director sensed that he had broken through. Their intense, prolonged courtship was nearing an end. They went out for Italian food. "Jim ordered the food with great ceremony," Ray remembered. "Taking pride in his knowledge of obscure dishes. I felt he had come to trust me." For Ray, these issues of trust were imperative because he was prepared to take his actor to the edge, which he knew *Rebel* required if it was to be as extreme and groundbreaking as he planned.

Ray felt a sense of great anticipation when Dean looked up at him and haltingly began to speak. "Something in his expression suggested he was about to impart a special confidence," Ray recalled. "He was restless, more so than usual."

But what Dean wanted to tell him had nothing to do with the movie. "I got crabs," he finally said. "What do I do?"

It would not have been surprising if, at that point, Ray simply chose to pack it in. But playing both Dean's permissive father and his partner-in-crime, which would become his double-edged role throughout their relationship, Ray entered a pharmacy and purchased Cuprex, a product he knew would solve Dean's problem. Outside, Dean thanked him and began to walk away. Then he turned around and smiled. "I want to do your film," Dean finally said, almost as if it were an afterthought. "But don't tell those bastards at Warners."

On January 4, 1955, Warner Brothers announced that James Dean would star in *Rebel Without a Cause*.

CHAPTER THREE

Child Star

News of the *Rebel* project spread quickly through Hollywood. It seemed as if every young actor in the business was vying for a part in the film—but none more than sixteen-year-old Natalie Wood. For nearly a decade, the brown-eyed, brunette Wood had been one of the most successful, hardest-working child actresses in Hollywood, and she had already earned a permanent place in movie history by playing the serious-minded little girl in the holiday classic *Miracle on 34th Street.* But as Wood began to move into her teenage years, she was no longer a precocious, pigtailed moppet, and it became more difficult for her to get parts. In the two years between turning fourteen and sixteen Wood had worked only sporadically. She had a small role as Bette Davis's daughter in *The Star,* a bit part as the young Virginia Mayo character in the Bible epic *The Silver Chalice* (which was so bad its star Paul Newman, making his feature film debut, took out an ad in *Variety* apologizing for it), and an ongoing role on a TV sitcom *Pride of the Family,* which was cancelled after one season. Wood was becoming desperate. She loved acting—and being a star. It was all she had ever known. She refused to abandon herself to obscurity, like so many former child actors had done. So when she heard about *Rebel,* she was eager to get her hands on the script. Before *Rebel,* films about teenagers were rare. And adding to the film's attractiveness was the fact that it starred James Dean, who had already left a strong impression on Wood when they briefly worked together in a television play titled *I'm a Fool.*

Wood managed to get a copy of an early version of the script through her agents at Famous Artists, which also represented Dean. Although the script, dated January 21, 1955, was only two-thirds finished, when she read it, she wept. As far as she was concerned, she was Judy. "I felt exactly the way the girl did in the picture toward her parents," Wood said. "It was about a high school girl rebelling, and it was very close to home. It was really about my own life." To Wood, *Rebel* was the opportunity that would propel her out of the ghetto of child stardom. She was determined to play the part of Judy and, well versed in the ways of Hollywood, she was prepared to do whatever was needed to land the role.

Natalie Wood had been acting since 1943, when she was five years old. She had lived her childhood through the movies. Her mother, Maria Gurdin, controlled every aspect of her life, which was entirely geared toward forwarding her career. But her Russian immigrant parents were nothing like the wholesome mothers and fathers she had on-screen. Her father was a weak, ineffectual alcoholic who couldn't keep a job, lurching between violent drunken outbursts and paralyzing bouts of depression, while her mother was a domineering and ruthless stage mother who filled her daughter's head with paranoid fantasies of the world outside her protection. Because her father was so often out of work, the responsibility for supporting the family largely fell on Wood's tiny shoulders.

Under her mother's tutelage, Wood stunned directors with her ability to master an accent or completely digest a script, to the point where she could feed older actors their lines. Playing a German refugee rescued by Orson Welles in *Tomorrow Is Forever,* her first major role, she mimicked a German accent perfectly and burst into tears on cue—though only after her mother told her a horrifying story about ripping the wings off helpless birds. Gurdin drove her daughter relentlessly. At the same time as she was making the most famous film of her juvenile career, *Miracle on 34th Street,* Wood was playing an English girl in the costume drama *The Ghost and Mrs. Muir,* and a farmer's daughter in the rural romance *Scudda Hoo! Scudda Hay!,* donning and doffing costumes and accents as she shuttled from one set to another. "I was playing so many parts, I had a hard time finding me," Wood would later say.

Her mother was capable of doing almost anything to ensure her continuing success. When Wood was eleven years old, Maria took part in a deception that would forever damage her daughter's trust in her. During the making of the hayseed drama *The Green Promise,* Wood was supposed to cross a rickety wooden bridge over a raging creek in the middle of a torrential downpour. The young actress did not know that the bridge was rigged to collapse as soon as she got to the other side—and no one, not even her mother, informed her. While they were shooting the scene, the bridge gave way too early. In the film, you can see the look of genuine terror on Wood's face. Luckily, Wood managed to grab onto the bridge's edge and pull herself up before the raging waters swept her away. But Wood had injured her wrist. Shockingly, Maria would not allow her to see a doctor, fearing that letting someone know about the accident might damage her career. The injury healed badly, leaving Wood's left wrist with a permanently protruding bone. For the rest of her life, she would cover her wrist with bracelets, never removing them in public. She would always blame Maria for her permanent scar.

As Wood grew into a teenager, she began to resent her mother's tight reins, but her indignation was offset by guilt at letting down her family, who depended on her income, and by a desire to please her mother. But Wood was finding her wilder tendencies harder to suppress. Steffi Sidney, whom Wood would meet again when they were both cast in *Rebel Without a Cause,* remembers encountering Wood at a fraternity party. "She was drinking zombies," remembers Sidney. "The next time I saw her she was passed out on a bed downstairs. I said, 'Who brought her because she's underage. Someone should take her home.'"

In 1954, the summer Natalie Wood turned sixteen, she and her friend Margaret O'Brien, another child actress who had made an indelible mark in Vincente Minnelli's *Meet Me in St. Louis,* were buying tickets for a movie when they heard that James Dean was in the neighborhood. Although *East of Eden* had not yet been released, Dean was already leaving a heat trail wherever he went. He had rolled his motorcycle up to Googie's coffee shop, one of architect John Lautner's 1950s-style space-age restaurants (which gave birth to the classic L.A. building style: Googie architecture). With its sharp angles, aerodynamic roof and boldly futuristic feel, Googie's had become a favorite hangout for Dean and his growing entourage. Wood and O'Brien could not resist the thought of a possible Dean sighting. They decided to head for Googie's, even though they had told their parents they were going to see a film.

Just as the starstruck teenagers were summoning up the courage to approach Dean's table, O'Brien's strict mother, who had just dropped them off at the theater, drove by and spied them through the window of Googie's. Enraged, she marched into the restaurant and dragged them out, right in front of Dean. Wood was embarrassed and angry. Mrs. O'Brien drove them back to her house and called Wood's mother. Unlike Margaret O'Brien, who accepted her mother's scolding for going somewhere without permission, Wood was already chafing under her mother's control and could not believe that they weren't even allowed to have a little harmless fun.

Furiously, Wood, who had an illegal driver's license, drove herself home in her pink Thunderbird, which had been sitting at the O'Briens' house. Preoccupied with confronting her mother, Wood took a curve too quickly. Her T-bird spun out of control, went over an embankment and hit a tree, which luckily kept the car from falling into a ravine. Wood emerged from the crash with only a few bruises. But the increasingly rambunctious actress would have a much worse accident within a year.

NATALIE REBELS

By the end of 1954, Wood had not worked for more than a year. Her days of child stardom seemed to be at an end. But she would take her first small, tentative step in a new direction when she accepted a role in a live television drama, based on a Sherwood Anderson story, called *I'm a Fool*. Wood played a young city girl who falls for a racetrack stable boy who is pretending to be wealthy and is lying about his identity. The producers had wanted a tall, blond actor named John Smith to play the stable boy, but instead they got stuck with their second choice—James Dean. Wood had no reason to believe that Dean might recall the embarrassing incident at Googie's, but the increasingly high-strung actress was nervous nevertheless. "Like everybody else in Hollywood, I'd heard the stories and was frankly afraid of him," Wood said. "The longer we waited, the more frightened I became, and as I went through the script I found that he was going to make love to me. After a half hour with everyone watching the door for Dean's arrival, he came in through a large window of the building. All I could think of was, 'He sure knows how to make an entrance!' He was dressed in a dirty sport shirt and had a large safety pin across the front of his pants—jeans, of course. He jumped down on the floor, looked around, picked up a script from the table and sat in a corner. The director said, 'C'mon Jimmy, sit next to Natalie. You're going to have to make love to this girl.' Jimmy didn't even look up. He just grunted."

Wood found Dean attractive but he barely paid attention to her as they rehearsed that morning. As far as Dean was concerned, Wood represented the Hollywood establishment. Then at lunch, he suddenly invited her for a ride on his motorcycle to get something to eat. When he turned on his portable radio, she was surprised that instead of playing jazz or rhythm and blues, the radio was tuned to classical music. They talked a little about the script, when suddenly Dean looked up from his sandwich and said tauntingly, "I know you. You're a child actor." Taken aback, Wood responded, "That's true. But it's better than acting like a child." For a moment, Dean looked as if he didn't understand what she was saying. Then he started to laugh. Wood did not know what to make of Dean, who could be shyly lovable one moment, contemptuous the next.

In many ways, Wood's working relationship with Dean on *I'm a Fool* would prefigure their interaction on *Rebel*. For the first time, she could not get away with mere pretending. She felt she was required actually to delve into herself to find the emotions she needed to display—but she was not always up to the challenge. "Natalie was young and her concentration wasn't the best," recalled director Don Medford. Luckily, Dean compensated. At the end of the teleplay, when her character says good-bye and boards a train, Dean had to take an assertive step. According to Medford, "Just before she boarded her train, Jimmy was relating to her and she turned her head away instead of being eye to eye with him as the moment required. So he grasped her face and turned it toward him!"

Despite her inexperience, Wood found her first encounter with a Method actor thrilling. But if she thought she was finally getting away from her days as a child star, she was soon sadly disappointed. Days after *I'm a Fool* was broadcast, she was sent by her agent to audition for a costume drama called *One Desire*. To get the role, Wood was forced to put her hair in pigtails again and prove that she could look like a twelve-year-old girl. The humiliating ordeal made Wood think that she would never be allowed

33

to grow up. "It was difficult for her because she was physically so teeny," says her friend Mary Ann Marinkovich Brooks, who had known Wood since junior high school. "She always looked like a little girl." And Wood's mother wanted to make sure she stayed a little girl as long as possible because she had always been the family's meal ticket.

Wood was desperate to find something that would prove once and for all that she was more than a child actress—and would help her break away from her mother and gain some control over her life. So when she heard about *Rebel Without a Cause,* she jumped on it.

Unsurprisingly, Wood's mother did not want her to do the movie and risk everything that she had worked so hard to build up. For the first time in her life, Wood decided she was going to run her career, whether her mother liked it or not. She threatened to move out and become an actual juvenile delinquent if her mother did not allow her to audition for the part.

Showing up at a Warners casting call in hopes of getting a test with Nicholas Ray, Wood ran into Nick Adams, an ambitious young actor who would win a small role in *Rebel.* "She thought that the way to impress producers and casting executives with her experience was to dress like a woman of thirty," Adams said. "But the severe black dress, the veiled hat, the sheer hose and opera pumps, in combination with her imp's face, only made her look like a kid dressed up in her mother's clothes." When she finally had her meeting with Ray, she was so nervous that her knees began shaking and her voice cracked. She could tell things were not going well, that she was losing Ray's attention. So she suddenly jumped up and hit Ray's desk, insisting that she was Judy, that Ray could not hire anyone else, and that he simply had to test her.

Ray was not impressed. In fact, Wood's outburst may have simply underscored the fact that she was too young—and, indeed, too Hollywood—for the part. "I wasn't going to cast Natalie Wood in the picture because she's a child actress, and the only child actress who ever made it as far as I'm concerned was Helen Hayes," he said. Ray had already rejected another child actress, Wood's friend Margaret O'Brien, who made the mistake of telling the director that she loved her parents and teachers. Ray was not looking for softhearted kids. But when he saw Wood hanging out in the hallway with a tough-looking boy with a fresh scar on his face, his curiosity was piqued. He turned to the young actress and said, "Let's talk again."

When Wood did not hear from Ray again after their meeting, she realized that she would have to take matters into her own hands. She had learned a thing or two from her mother about aggressively campaigning for a part. She and her friend Jackie Eastes Perry began going to the Warner Brothers commissary regularly in hopes of running into Ray. Perry told Wood to dress the way teenagers did, to put her hair in a ponytail and wear bobby socks, saddle shoes, poodle skirts and little makeup. Their plan worked. They got Ray's attention—but not exactly for the reasons they intended.

One afternoon at the commissary, Ray complimented Wood on her outfit, paid for her lunch, and asked her to stop by his office after she had finished eating. That night, Ray took Wood out to a restaurant in Beverly Hills called Luau and told her he was considering her for the role. Wood was thrilled, but Ray had ulterior motives. Whether it happened that night or shortly afterward, forty-three-year-old Ray and sixteen-year-old Wood became lovers.

Sleeping with the teenage Wood did not cause much of a moral dilemma for Ray. Later in life, Ray would unapologetically write of his "bent towards incest with other people's children and wives, ex-wives and daughters and such." According to Gavin Lambert, Ray readily told him that he took Wood's virginity, though Wood's friends believe that was unlikely. In fact, Wood may have played more than a passive role in engineering their relationship. "I would have done *anything* to get the lead in *Rebel Without a Cause*," Wood told actress Joan Collins. Her friend Mary Ann Brooks agrees: "When she went after this part, she went after it with all the tools that God gave her to accomplish it."

While there might have been a "casting couch" aspect to the affair initially, Wood soon fell for the handsome, roguish director. Ray mentored Wood, giving her books such as Antoine de Saint-Exupéry's *The Little Prince* (a book that Dean also loved) and works by Ernest Hemingway, Edgar Allan Poe, Thomas Wolfe and F. Scott Fitzgerald. He explored her mind—and played to her pride—by soliciting ideas from her about the *Rebel* script. "He opened the door to a whole new world. It was just glorious," Wood would say about Ray many years later.

Amazingly, despite her deepening relationship with Ray, Wood did not achieve her primary goal: the director refused to guarantee her the role of Judy in *Rebel*. The film was too important to Ray and he remained unconvinced that Wood was right for the part. Meanwhile, Dean was pushing for his friend, actress Carroll Baker. Baker, who knew Dean from the Actors Studio, was in town to test for a role in *Giant*, and, on Dean's recommendation, she was staying at the Chateau Marmont, where Ray lived. "The script is crap but the characters are very good," Dean had told her about *Rebel*. "I think if it is cast right we can make a hell of a film. I want you to play the girl's part." Baker met with Ray and he seemed interested in offering her the role. But one day her husband, actor and director Jack Garfein, who had been hearing rumors that Baker was having an affair with Dean, showed up unannounced at the Chateau Marmont in a jealous rage. "Jack was adamant that I turn down *Rebel Without a Cause* and return East with him," Baker said. The role remained uncast, and Wood pressed on with her campaign.

One day, Ray invited Wood and Perry out to lunch at the swank showbiz restaurant Romanoff's. Ray debonairly kissed their hands as they walked in and ordered screwdrivers for his teenage companions. "Natalie was trying so desperately to be sophisticated with the makeup and the hair and he was trying to find out if she could be that person [in *Rebel Without a Cause*]," says Perry. "He made a comment that she wore too much makeup. I kind of covered for her. I said she had just come from a Max Factor shoot so that's why she looks like that." Despite his doubts, Ray gave in. Over lunch, he told her that he had finally scheduled a test for her. Wood was obviously thrilled, but although she might have expected it, Ray did not give her any preferential treatment.

The test took place under the most inauspicious conditions. Ray chose a rainy night because he wanted to see how black-and-white Cinema-Scope—the chosen format for the film—would look in darkness and rain. Meanwhile, Wood was forced to test with several other actresses that very same night. And she did not get to perform with James Dean, who was in New York. Dennis Hopper, a young actor who had already been cast as a gang member, stood in for Dean. "By the time we finished, Natalie and I both felt like wet unhappy animals," said Hopper.

The blond, fresh-faced Hopper, who was born in Dodge City, Kansas, and moved to San Diego when he was a teenager, had just arrived in Hollywood. According to Jim Nelson, an assistant director whose brother Gary would work as an assistant director on *Rebel,* Hopper first came to Ray's attention through producer David Weisbart. Jim Nelson lived next door to Weisbart and was working on an episode of the television show *Medic* called "Boy in the Storm" in which Hopper played the showy role of an epileptic. "I called David and told him I just saw this kid and he was unbelievable," remembers Nelson. Hopper later said he was called by seven studios after *Medic* was broadcast.

The offer from Warner Brothers proved most intriguing to Hopper because it came with the possibility that he would land a role in director George Stevens's prestigious upcoming film *Giant.* If Ray agreed to cast Hopper in *Rebel,* he was told, the studio would put him under contract and he would have a chance to be cast in *Giant.* After meeting Ray, the director agreed to give him a part in *Rebel,* and Hopper signed a seven-year contract with Warners. It was a decision both Ray and Hopper would live to regret.

Hopper was naïve to the ways of Hollywood but incredibly ambitious and eager to please. At first, Ray took Hopper under his wing, introducing him to Wood, who, despite her youth, not only knew the ways of Hollywood but seemed beyond her years in other areas as well. According to Hopper, the day after their screen test together, Wood shocked the young actor by boldly calling him up and asking him out. "She told me she thought I was great looking and really liked me and she wanted to have sex with me—which never happened before or since," said Hopper. "In the fifties to be aggressive like that as a woman was really amazing." Wood told Hopper to pick her up at the Chateau Marmont at 5:00 p.m. just as she was leaving Ray's bungalow. He was stunned when she told him that she had just left the director's bed to meet him. "I thought it was weird," said Hopper. "I was eighteen years old!" Nevertheless, they drove up to Mulholland Drive that night and made love, according to Hopper. After being sheltered for most of her life by her mother, and perhaps emboldened by her relationship with Ray, Wood was suddenly exploring her newfound freedom with unrestrained abandon. Consciously or unconsciously, she was becoming more like Judy, the sexually promiscuous girl she yearned to play in *Rebel.*

• • •

During this time, Wood's emerging sexual adventurism and her desperation to play adult roles in the movies would coincide with one of the most traumatic events of her life. According to Wood's friends, a powerful movie star over twenty years her senior invited Wood to discuss a part he had for her. Her friends' accounts vary on what exactly happened that night. Jackie Perry says that Wood tracked her down at a friend's house at eight the next morning to tell her what occurred. "She was crying," Perry remembers. "She looked like hell. She had dark circles under her eyes." Wood told her that the actor had asked her to come to his hotel room to discuss the part. They sat down and had a drink and "then she said he changed. He got very strange and said that he always wanted to fuck a teenager. She picked up her purse and started to leave and he grabbed her and dragged her into another room and threw her on the bed and proceeded to rip her clothes off. He said, 'If you fight me, it'll hurt you more.'" Wood told Perry that he had raped her without using a condom. "She was afraid she was pregnant," says Perry, who advised Wood that she should tell someone. But Wood did not want to report it. "She said, 'My career would be over,'" says Perry. Two days later, according to Perry, she went to the hospital because she was still bleeding from the incident.

According to Dennis Hopper, Wood showed up at his door later that afternoon and told him about the rape, but said it had happened in a car. "She told me that she had woke up from being unconscious—she thought he'd given her a pill or something—and that she was laying half-in and half-out of the car. And her clothes had been taken off—at least the bottom parts were off, and he was whipping her, very hard, on her thigh. And she woke up screaming, and then he raped her." Her friend Mary Ann Brooks says that Wood told her "a couple of weeks" after it happened and that she also "understood it was in the car." She says that Wood told her the actor had signed his name on the dashboard of the car afterward. Later that year, Wood also told her friend actor Scott Marlowe what happened, according to Wood biographer Suzanne Finstad.

Although Wood confided in her mother about the incident when she had to go to the hospital, she never reported it to the police or discussed it publicly and her mother apparently never pressed her to report it. "In those days, it would have been so shameful and horrible," says her friend Faye

Nuell Mayo. "Girls always felt it was their fault. She would have wanted to hide it. I'm sure her mother told her never to talk about it."

"THEY CALLED ME A JUVENILE DELINQUENT"

Whether or not it was a result of the rape, Wood began to grow increasingly depressed and nervous in the first months of 1955. Adding to her stress, by mid-February she had yet to hear anything definite about *Rebel,* which was scheduled to start shooting merely one month later. In fact, Ray continued to test other actresses for the part of Judy, including blonde bombshell Jayne Mansfield, one of the other women he was dating at the time. "I didn't even put any film in the camera for her screen test," Ray said of Mansfield. "That was just an hallucination of the casting department." However, Hopper, who read with Mansfield, thought it was a serious test. Faye Nuell Mayo believes that Ray wanted Mansfield because he envisioned Judy as a "real trashy girl" at the time, though in later versions of the script the character would evolve into someone softer and more complex, someone closer to Wood.

One night, a frustrated Wood decided to go out and have some fun with Dennis Hopper and her friend Jackie Perry. They began at Googie's, and then proceeded to the Villa Capri, the ritzy hangout of Frank Sinatra and other members of the Rat Pack, where they drank a lot of wine. "They didn't bother asking us for ID," says Perry. "We all were smashed." After they left the Villa Capri, Hopper drove them up to Mulholland Drive in his open convertible to look at the lights, stopping along the way to buy a bottle of scotch before parking on Mulholland where they had a clear view of the city below. While Hopper and Wood drank the scotch, Perry fell asleep. When she woke up, Wood, who at 5 feet 2 inches tall and weighing only ninety-five pounds couldn't hold much liquor, was standing outside the car vomiting. It began to rain so they decided to go back to Googie's to get Wood's car, driving down Laurel Canyon Boulevard, a twisty mountain road, difficult to handle even in the best of conditions. "He really wasn't going that fast," says Perry. "I think he just hit the brake at the wrong time and we slid into oncoming traffic."

They struck another car head-on and all three were thrown out of the automobile. Perry was thrown on top of Wood, who fell unconscious. For a moment, Perry thought that Wood might be dead. In a panic, she called her name repeatedly, and finally Wood came to, groggily asking "Why is my face wet?" The rain continued to fall while some nearby residents supplied blankets and called an ambulance.

All three were rushed to the hospital. Hopper and Perry suffered only cuts and bruises but Wood had a minor concussion. In the hallways of the hospital, Hopper continued to blame himself. "Oh my God, I caused this. It's all my fault," he repeatedly exclaimed. Having just gotten his first big break in Hollywood, Hopper was terrified that he had just thrown it all away by bringing harm to the most famous person he knew at the time.

The doctors wanted to call Wood's parents but she had another idea. "I kept saying, 'Nick Ray. Call Nick Ray. The number is . . . ' I just kept repeating the number of the Chateau Marmont. So that's who they did call."

"I'm sure that the reason she kept wanting to see Nick Ray is because she hadn't gotten the part in the fucking movie! And she wanted him to see her not like a Hollywood type, but really in trouble," said Hopper.

When Ray arrived with his doctor, he was furious. He threw Hopper against the wall, screaming, "How could you do this?"

"I was trying to explain to him," said Hopper, "and I guess he was a little hysterical, and he slapped me very, very hard, pushed me against the wall, and said, 'Shut up, and straighten up.'"

At that point, Ray did not know that Hopper and Wood were having an affair. But he had befriended Hopper and felt betrayed by his carelessness with Wood. "He opened his home, his heart, his life to Dennis and introduced him to us and now he's gotten us in an accident," says Perry. "So you can understand from his viewpoint how he was looking at this." It was the beginning of a rift between Ray and Hopper that would grow wider as the shooting of *Rebel* got under way.

After accosting Hopper, Ray entered Wood's hospital room. And what happened there has become Hollywood legend. In later years, both Wood and Ray would tell a similar story about what occurred when he went into her room to see her. Lying on a hospital bed, Wood grabbed Ray when he came up to her and pulled him down close to her face. Motioning to people who worked at the hospital, she whispered in Ray's ear, "They called me a goddamn juvenile delinquent. *Now* do I get the part?"

Over the years, that exchange between Ray and Wood has become one of the classic *Rebel* tales—an enduring Hollywood fable—but there are some who believe it never happened. Dennis Hopper doubts that anyone in the hospital really called Wood a juvenile delinquent. "Why would they have called her a juvenile delinquent when she was fucking unconscious?" he said. Gavin Lambert says that Ray told him flatly "they made up this story"—which he says was based on an old yarn invented by Warner Brothers publicity—to cover up the fact that she and Ray were having an affair. The real reason Wood called Ray, according to Lambert, was because she "dreaded the scene her parents would make if they learned about the accident."

Whether or not Wood and Ray embellished the story, the fact remained that she had finally achieved the goal she had spent months pursuing. Wood had succeeded in convincing Ray to give her the role that would let her shed her pigtails for good. When Ray left Wood's hospital room, Hopper and Perry heard the director tell the doctors, "Take good care of this young lady. She's the star of my next movie."

CHAPTER FOUR

The Script

With little more than a sketch of an idea, Nicholas Ray had managed to convince the Warners studio executives and the restless, ambitious James Dean to make his movie. "This is all I have, but I know where I'm going," Ray told Dean when he first showed him "The Blind Run," his original seventeen-page treatment. But while Ray may have had a notion about where he was going, there was more than a little bluster in his claim. He had used his gambler's charisma to get Warners and Dean on board, but he knew that before long he would have to show them something more tangible, something that would live up to the grandiose promises he had made—and he was a long way from that goal. Even the partial script that Natalie Wood originally secured—dated January 21, 1955—was far from an acceptable final version.

Ray would have trouble finding a writer who could build on his faith that he was on to something new, who could take his amorphous thoughts and shape them into a workable screenplay. And getting a rising star like Dean on board meant that the clock was ticking. As the buzz around Dean grew deafening, Ray lived with the constant threat that Dean's schedule would suddenly fill up. Ray needed to secure a screenplay that would satisfy him, the studio and Dean—and he needed to do it quickly, before his window of opportunity snapped shut.

Warner Brothers already had a number of *Rebel Without a Cause* screenplays gathering dust in its files, left over from the film based on Robert Lindner's book that producer Jerry Wald tried to make in the 1940s. There was a script by Lindner himself, one by Peter Viertel (who would go on to write *The African Queen*) and even one by Theodor Geisel, the children's author better known as Dr. Seuss. As Ray desperately searched for a writer who could turn his vision into something filmable, he would add a few more rejected *Rebel* screenplays to the studio pile.

Ray approached the idea of finding a writer with some dread. He had an uneasy relationship with writers, as he acknowledged in "Story into Script," a chapter from the book that Ray planned to write about the making of *Rebel Without a Cause.* "There is a traditional writer-director hostility in Hollywood," Ray wrote. "Each resents his dependence on the other. The writer needs the director for his story to be realized; the director needs the writer to give him a story in a form he can realize."

But Ray's resentment of writers was more highly developed than most. He lacked confidence in his own writing talent, yet he could be disdainful of what writers brought to a film. " 'It was all in the script,' a disillusioned writer will tell you. But it was never all in the script. If it were, why make the movie?" Ray wrote.

Ray believed that writing a screenplay required "a difficult kind of abnegation for the writer, who is working in a medium in which the image and not the word has the final impact." But for Ray, directing was something more than the concoction of images; it was a means of imprinting his personal vision on a film, even if it meant subverting, altering or hijacking somebody else's screenplay.

"Nick would change things without telling anybody," said screenwriter Gavin Lambert, who worked with Ray on his films *Bigger Than Life* and *Bitter Victory.* "Studios at that time were very stratified. A script was passed and you shot it. And if you wanted a change, you sent it in to the front office." While making *In a Lonely Place,* Ray locked everyone out of the set except for the actors and cameraman and improvised a new ending, without informing anyone.

Creating a screenplay for *Rebel* would not be easy. Ray's "Blind Run" treatment did not give a writer much to go on, at least in terms of plot. The treatment is strong on character relationships and theme, but the story is largely unstructured. It amounts to a series of violent episodes, some of which would survive in some form—such as the knife fight and a chicken run—but for the most part, "The Blind Run" deviates dramatically from anything ultimately seen in *Rebel:* Jimmy and Eve (later Judy) throw a party that Demo (later Plato) is not allowed to attend. Demo roams the streets instead, and together with two other boys, they "stomp" an innocent man to death. Finally, the largely unstructured treatment sails off into scenes of teenage revolution—"frightening, bizarre almost grotesque crimes," Ray writes, that lead to Demo's arrest and Jimmy's death in a rumble.

Working from Ray's imagination could be especially difficult for a screenwriter because Ray was not always able to convey what he thought. Ray's close friend John Houseman said that the director was often "inarticulate" and that his "mind was filled with original ideas which he found it difficult to express in an understandable form." Ray's occasional lack of eloquence became a joke among some actors he worked with. Walter Matthau would do an impression of Ray answering a question by looking up, thinking, saying nothing and walking away. "He was known in Hollywood for being a guy who, if your phone rang and there was nobody at the other end, it was Nick Ray," said actor Mickey Knox. But his last wife, Susan Ray, thinks this image of Ray is simplistic. "To call him inarticulate is just ridiculous," she says. "He didn't analyze in a linear fashion. He would work with what arose—and dance with it."

Rebel was such a personal project that Ray preferred to hire someone he knew as his authorial dance partner. He turned to playwright Clifford Odets, whom Ray had idolized ever since his days in the Theatre of Action in the 1930s. Odets was the writer of such classic dramas of restive working-class youth as *Awake and Sing!, Waiting for Lefty* and *Golden Boy.* He had been the most famous and successful young playwright in America during the Great Depression, before coming to Hollywood and dissipating his talent through drink and unworthy film projects. When Jack Warner named Odets as a communist to the House Un-American Activities Committee, it looked as though he was through in Hollywood, but when he was called to testify, Odets shocked everyone by naming names himself. Afterward, in one of the many Kafkaesque twists of fate that occurred during the days of the blacklist, Odets continued to be mistrusted by the right, despite having alienated himself from the left. Like Elia Kazan—who would also name names—he would become *persona non grata* among many in Hollywood. Nevertheless—and again like Kazan—Odets retained the support of Nicholas Ray, who, while left-leaning himself, put personal loyalty before politics.

Ultimately, whether the studio saw him as washed up or politically tainted, Warner Brothers refused to let Ray use Odets. But that would not prevent Odets, Ray's neighbor at the Chateau Marmont, from making a few meaningful contributions to the script. Discussing *Rebel*'s hero Jim Stark, Odets suggested that Ray "try to find the keg of dynamite he's sitting on." "That one single concept helped me tremendously in building a character," said Ray. Even more significantly, Odets contributed one of *Rebel*'s crucial lines of dialogue: "I got the bullets!" It's a line that Jim Stark cries during the film's tragic climax, one that James Dean would turn into a resonating adolescent howl, resulting in one of *Rebel*'s most cathartic and heartbreaking moments.

"RAYFIELD"

Instead of Odets, Ray was forced to accept the writer Warners assigned to him. The studio chose Leon Uris, later famous as the author of the epic, best-selling novel *Exodus*. Warners wanted Uris because he had just had a hit that year with his screenplay for *Battle Cry*, based on his autobiographical novel about a battalion of young marines in World War II. (Dean had screen-tested for *Battle Cry* but lost the part to another young rising Warners star, Tab Hunter.) Although Uris was not his first choice, Ray was encouraged by the fact that the writer "was enthusiastic about the subject, seemed to share the point of view." He was also intrigued that Uris had once been distribution supervisor for a San Francisco newspaper where he acted as a "father confessor" for forty boys. Plus, Uris seemed eager to plunge into the kind of firsthand research Ray wanted to do.

When Ray made the film noir *On Dangerous Ground* in 1952, he spent weeks going out on assignments with police to the toughest neighborhoods in Boston. But for *Rebel*, Ray would do more research than he had ever done up to that time. The process of researching juvenile delinquency would become an obsession for Ray, almost as important as making the film itself. "In listening to these adolescents talk about their lives . . . all told similar stories—divorced parents, parents who could not guide or understand, who were indifferent or simply 'criticized,' parents who needed a scapegoat in the family," Ray wrote.

Even before Uris was hired, Ray had begun investigating the subject in depth with producer Weisbart, talking to psychiatrists and social workers, spending time with police and riding around Los Angeles observing young people at drive-in restaurants and movie theaters. Considering Ray's affection for Luis Buñuel's *Los Olvidados,* he may have been inspired by the example of the Spanish director, who also sought out the advice and insight of professionals, and donned threadbare clothes to spend days in the slums of Mexico City before he began his film about wayward youth. (Buñuel himself was inspired by Italian director Vittorio De Sica's work on the neorealist classic *Shoeshine.*)

Enthralled with neorealism, which erupted after World War II, many filmmakers believed that the highest calling of an artist was to inject as much gritty authenticity as possible into their work. Ray was prepared to go to almost any lengths to achieve this goal. Among his most outlandish ideas was to have his nephew Sumner Williams, who appeared in small roles in a number of Ray's films, get himself booked as a juvenile offender. "He's 25, looks 18, ex-G.I., so can handle himself, knows what we're looking for, etc. I think it's a good idea," said Ray in a memo to Weisbart. There is no record as to whether Williams actually went ahead with this plan.

Ray also knew that the research was great public relations. Ray always had a keen eye for publicity and he was very aware of the possibilities of using research both to promote the film and to head off possible criticism. Ray knew that the film might be controversial—especially in light of congressional hearings about violence in the media and its supposed effect on the rise of juvenile delinquency. By talking to experts, Ray could make the claim that everything in the film had a sound scientific foundation. "There is no incident of violence or sexual behavior, or a combination of the two, too shocking to be true," he wrote in a memo to Weisbart. "We need be governed only by considerations of entertainment and good taste—in the majority of cases, the evidence which leads to the inevitability of these acts will be or already has been supplied us by the various experts and specialists whom we have interviewed." In addition, Ray hoped that he could recruit these experts as advocates for the film, if necessary, noting that their cooperation "indicates not only that support and endorsement will be forthcoming on a national scale, should the studio wish to make use of that in its exploitation campaign, but that our approach to the problem is fresh, different and as realistic as the headlines."

Uris eagerly joined Ray in his frenzy of research, spending ten days as an apprentice social worker at Juvenile Hall. He sat in on juvenile hearings and rode with the police. In an October 7 memo to David Weisbart, Ray reported that Uris "is not only gaining insight to the problems and characters, but is already beginning to talk story characters and scenes. In other words, the excitement gathers and I think we will be able to keep it that way."

But Ray's excitement lasted only until Uris put words down on paper. Before beginning to write a treatment, Uris wrote a five-page sketch of an imaginary small town he patronizingly called "Rayfield." "First thing anyone says when he first looks down the main street of Rayfield: 'What a swell place to raise kids,'" begins Uris's unctuous description of the town, which Ray sarcastically described as "one of those quiet 'normal' communities now astonished by the number of juvenile delinquents in their midst." Dated October 13, 1954, Uris's sketch lays the blame for a sudden rise in crime to a "housing project" built during the war to accommodate laborers who migrated to the town to work at a PT boat factory, exactly the kind of "slum area rationalizations" that Ray said he wanted to avoid in his treatment. It was not an auspicious beginning.

On October 18, Ray expressed some frustration with Uris's approach in a memo to Weisbart: "We have provided Lee with incident, contact, theory and practice, characters and situations. He should feel free enough to drop the intellectual approach from this point on and just write the story." Although Ray continued his own research, he pointedly did not invite Uris to a new meeting he had scheduled with a police officer.

Uris's first treatment for the film, consisting of twenty-four pages dated October 20, 1954, was wildly off the mark. The bulk of it is taken up with tedious, clichéd descriptions of adults' petty, quotidian small-town lives. Uris's second attempt, dated November 1, seems to reflect some input from Ray. It is no longer dominated by depictions of family life, and there is much more focus on the kids. But Ray was still not happy with what he read, to say the least. He exclaimed that Uris's work "made me vomit." Uris had utterly failed to get inside the heads of teenagers.

Uris never wrote an actual screenplay for the film. But he did create a tender image that survives into the final film—Jimmy protectively covering his sleeping friend Plato with his jacket. Uris also depicted Amy—who would become Judy, the Natalie Wood role—as starving for her father's affection. Uris wrote that she "tries to replace her mother . . . become the wife of her father." In a daring move, Ray used Uris's idea to underscore the incestuous tensions that might actually exist between a father and daughter, another example of the sexual candor Ray was determined to bring to the film.

"JUVENILE STORY"

Next, Ray turned to Irving Shulman, who coincidentally had also been considered as a possible screenwriter for producer Jerry Wald's *Rebel Without a Cause.* On paper, Shulman looked like the perfect choice. Ray had admired his book, 1947's *The Amboy Dukes,* the first great modern novel about juvenile delinquency, which sold nearly four million copies. It was so shocking and controversial at the time that testimony in 1952 before the Gathings Committee, a House committee that investigated the threat of lurid paperback novels, actually held it partly responsible for an upsurge in juvenile crime. In addition, Shulman had been a schoolteacher, which put him in real-life contact with teenagers. And his interest in sports cars "suggested a promising point of contact with Jimmy Dean," Ray believed.

Unlike Uris, Shulman had no interest in doing any research, but "his talent for inventing or remembering incidents led us quickly forward," according to Ray. Ray's initial discussions with Shulman yielded one of his most important contributions to the story. Shulman remembered reading a newspaper account about a gang of kids holding a "chickie run" in which two teenagers raced their cars to the edge of a cliff to see who would jump out first. From that moment on, the "chickie run" replaced the "blind run" from Ray's original treatment. It would eventually become the turning point of the film.

Shulman and Ray discussed the film's trio of main characters—Jim Stark (the rebel), Judy (the girlfriend) and Plato (the best friend)—who were as yet barely defined. Plato was given a nanny and a neglectful mother, and his only contact with his father comes in the form of a check that says "for support of child." Ray says that Warners particularly objected to this characterization of Plato's father, but for Ray "it had an equally strong reality, as I have two sons in that situation, and it was an idea drawn only too directly from personal experience." Regarding Jim Stark, Ray gave Shulman a note that read: "A boy wants to be a man, quick." And he told Shulman to model Jim's relationship with Judy on *Romeo and Juliet*, which Ray called "the best play ever written about 'juvenile delinquents.'"

Another important element that first appears in Shulman's script is the notion of setting a scene in a planetarium. Ray says that he and Weisbart came up with the idea. While Ray may have suggested the setting to Shulman, Ray biographer Bernard Eisenschitz speculates that there may have been another origin for the idea. A friend of Ray's, Silvia Richards, told Eisenschitz that she gave Ray a copy of a treatment for a film about juvenile delinquency she wrote with architectural critic Esther McCoy called *Main Street, Heaventown*, which Ray tried to sell to a studio. "He lifted from it either consciously or unconsciously," said Richards. "He didn't deny it when I accused him." In addition to a scene set at a planetarium, *Main Street, Heaventown* includes another setting that would figure prominently in *Rebel*—an old, decaying mansion.

Shulman said the theme of his version of *Rebel Without a Cause* was that "juveniles are imprisoned in an adult society which is delinquent, and youth finds itself an unwilling conspirator. If he's lived an 'Eagle Scout' existence during his childhood and wants to behave that way in adult society, he's immediately told he'll be eaten alive if he behaves that way."

Shulman wrote from December 3, 1954, to January 26, 1955, titling his 164-page screenplay *Juvenile Story*. It has much in common with the final film, although it reads like a distorted mirror image. It opens with Jimmy, Judy, Plato and Buzzy (who will become Buzz, the gang leader, in future screenplays) attending a high school lecture at the planetarium, where they plan the chickie run that is to occur that night. At the chickie run, Jim is selected to hold the prize money that will go to the winner. Buzzy and another boy race to the edge of the cliff but the other boy's sleeve gets caught and he goes over the edge.

After some scenes depicting the home lives of Jimmy, Judy and Plato, the action moves to a drive-in restaurant where the gang plans to use Judy to pick up a man so that they can beat and rob him. Judy takes the man to the planetarium but Jimmy stops the attack, letting the man run away, and while Buzzy goes off in pursuit of the man, Jimmy and Judy fall in love. When Plato shows up, they express annoyance and shoo him away. Seething with anger and jealousy he goes off and shoots an innocent woman who has asked him for directions.

The screenplay ends with Judy, Jimmy and Plato trapped inside Plato's house, which has been surrounded by the police. Plato takes Jimmy and Judy hostage, but they manage to escape. Jimmy tries to go back in order to talk Plato out of the house and is shot in the shoulder. When Plato comes out holding a rifle and a grenade, he is shot by the police, falls on the grenade and blows up himself and his house. After this over-the-top, violent finale, the script ends with a plea for understanding.

In Shulman's screenplay, Plato is depicted as a ticking time bomb always on the verge of exploding (until he does so literally). And unlike the caring and sensitive girl Natalie Wood plays in the film, Shulman's Judy is overly possessive toward Jimmy and jealously antagonistic toward Plato.

Shulman's characters are much less sympathetically drawn than the ones in the final film, and the contrasts between them are much more stark—and melodramatic. But Ray said that the real breaking point with Shulman occurred over the ending. Ray wanted Plato to return to the planetarium at the end, "seeking shelter under its great dome and artificial sky," as Ray described it. "It was the kind of unexpected dramatic reference I felt the story should contain; there was for me a suggestion of classical tragedy about it." Shulman disagreed, believing that Plato should seek refuge in his own home. "This was a crucial point for me," wrote Ray, "because it symbolized the more violent statement, the more sweepingly developed conflict that I was searching for and that Shulman seemed unable to accept. It was a gesture of anger and desperation that matched the kind of thing I had heard at Juvenile Hall. The issue made me decide that our points of view were essentially different."

The relationship between Ray and Shulman may have started well. But by the end of the year, it had become strained beyond repair. "I didn't like working with Ray, and the whole project took on a nightmarish quality," said Shulman. The final blow came when, despite Ray's hope that Dean and

Shulman would hit it off due to their similar love for cars, his writer and his star failed to connect. Now Ray had to worry about the possibility of Dean's alienated affections.

THE UNSUNG HERO

In January 1955, without a screenplay in sight, Warners executives began to doubt that Ray would be able to realize the film. "Nick had practically thrown out Shulman's script and was really desperate," said Leonard Rosenman, *Rebel*'s composer. The studio considered abandoning the project altogether and Weisbart and Jack Warner's assistant Steve Trilling found it increasingly difficult to defend their faith in Ray's vision. Rumors floated about the film's imminent demise. "A technician at the studio, someone reported to me, had laid a bet of $250 to that effect," said Ray. Unless Ray could find yet another writer, *Rebel Without a Cause* seemed doomed. Then salvation arrived in the most unlikely form.

Stewart Stern was a shy, earnest thirty-two-year-old writer with only one screenwriting credit, a modest 1951 film starring James Dean's ex-girlfriend Pier Angeli. *Teresa* is about a young GI and his Italian war-bride trying to adjust to newly married life in New York after the war. The self-effacing novice screenwriter would turn out to be the unsung hero in the *Rebel* story.

Stern met Ray for the first time when they were both guests at Gene Kelly and Betsy Blair's star-studded 1954 Christmas party. After a brutally competitive game of volleyball and a round of charades with such glamorous guests as Marilyn Monroe, Ray approached Stern and introduced himself. Ray had seen *Teresa* and was impressed by its sensitivity to young people. "Maybe sometime you want to come out to the studio and talk," said Ray. But while grateful for the compliment, the sometimes timorous screenwriter dismissed the director's vague invitation.

Stern did not have much film experience, but he was no stranger to Hollywood. The man who had brought him to the Kellys' party was his cousin Arthur Loew Jr., whose grandfathers were Adolph Zukor, the founder of Paramount, and Marcus Loew, who founded MGM and Loew's Theaters. Growing up, Stern spent weekends with his cousin at the Loews' forty-bedroom estate in Glen Cove, Long Island, which Stern describes as "a neo-Renaissance Italianate palace with everything from a Tiffany glass-dome breakfast room to a nine-hole golf course, a dairy farm, two private yachts, and a seaplane." Stern passed his summers at Zukor's Mountain View Farms, in New City, New York, a thousand-acre estate where Mary Pickford was a frequent guest. Zukor had married the sister of Stern's mother, who had been a minor actress on Broadway and in silent films. Stern's father, a physician, was a timid man, cowed by the great wealth of his wife's family.

Once they had grown up, Stern and Arthur Loew Jr., did not see each other for many years, until after World War II. Stern had served in one of the frontline infantry units in the Battle of the Bulge, an experience that helped him write the opening scenes of *Teresa*. Loew had been working at MGM as an assistant to Ray's close friend and mentor John Houseman before getting a job as a producer. When they reunited again, Loew hired his cousin to write the screenplay for *Teresa*, Loew's first production.

Serious and bookish, Stern found himself playing straight man to Loew, who was the life of the party, a funny, charming, outgoing bon vivant who could keep comedians, like his friend Milton Berle, in stitches. "His house was the Hollywood salon," Stern says of Loew's home just above Sunset Strip. "Every night from five o'clock the door was never shut. I couldn't believe who was there. On one night, Judy Garland would be singing, Errol Flynn would be passed out at the bar and Oscar Levant would be playing the piano."

In 1954, Loew had invited Stern, who was then living in New York, to spend Christmas with him in Los Angeles. It was there at Loew's home, and just a week before he met Ray, that Stern became acquainted with another—*the* other—key *Rebel* figure. Arriving from the airport just as Loew was leaving for an appointment, Stern was introduced to a young man who happened to be visiting. "That's Jimmy Dean," Loew said, walking out the door and leaving the two to their own devices. *East of Eden* had not yet been released, and Stern was not aware of Dean's mushrooming stature. "I didn't know what to say to this kid; he didn't know what to say," remembers Stern. "We were like two lost souls." They engaged in a few sputtering attempts at conversation, interspersed with long silences. Then Dean began to moo like a cow. Stern found himself mooing back. "Then he became a little alert," says Stern, "and we went through all the animals. I could imitate three pigs eating at the same time and a calf that's been roped in the rodeo. He really was very, very impressed and we began talking."

Dean and Stern struck up an instant friendship. Later that week, the actor invited Stern and Loew to a preview of *East of Eden*. Stern was surprised when the credits flashed on the screen and he saw Dean's name. "I was just demolished," says Stern. "I said, 'If it was hard to talk before, now I won't be able to talk to you at all.'"

Within a week of meeting Dean and Ray, Stern happened to be on the Warner Studios lot and ran into *Rebel* composer Rosenman, whom he knew from New York. Stern confessed that he was looking for a job, and Rosenman immediately directed him toward Ray. "They are looking for a writer and tell him I sent you," said Rosenman. On his friend's recommendation, Stern and his agent set up a meeting with Ray and Weisbart.

A desperate Ray leapt at the chance to try a new screenwriter. He remembered Stern from the Kellys' party, and immediately confided to him that Irving Shulman was not working out. He asked Stern to read Shulman's screenplay, but he never showed Stern either Uris's treatment or his own "Blind Run." Stern found that Shulman's script read like a period story—a tale of Shulman's childhood—rather than an attempt to come to terms with the current situation. And Stern agreed with Ray about the finale. "I was so revolted by the way the story ended," says Stern. "I made the decision that it could not happen in that house. [Plato] had to be a sacrifice on the steps of the temple," referring to the planetarium and suggesting the mythic qualities that Stern would bring to the film. Stern told Ray that he "wanted to start from scratch. I didn't want to be bound to anything that Irving had written. I said, I have to find the ways of linking myself to this material. Otherwise I knew that I could never make it mine." Ray agreed and on January 5, 1955, Warners announced that Stern was "joining" Shulman to write the screenplay for *Rebel Without a Cause*. Unbeknownst to Stern, Shulman continued working on his script for several more weeks. On January 26, Shulman handed in his final version of the script, which was not used, and secured permission from Warners to take his screenplay and turn it into a novel, which he published the following year under the title *Children of the Dark*.

As Ray and Stern began a series of intensive discussions about the

53

project, Stern was finding it just as difficult as his predecessors to figure out what Ray wanted. "Nick was in agony, a kind of private hell, at that time," says Stern. "He had a concept and a vision of what he wanted to say, but he had not found a way to say it through the writers he had had. He was almost inarticulate about what he wanted and why he was not satisfied."

Ray told him he wanted the script to be about middle-class juvenile delinquency and that he wanted it to include the chickie run. "That was virtually the only requirement," says Stern, who quickly learned that the project "had a very special, personal meaning for him, just to find out about young people and their fathers." According to Stern, Ray "thought he was letting Tony down, and that he wasn't spending the time with him, that he couldn't be articulate with him the way he wanted to." Stern told Ray about his own parents, who would become the models for Jim Stark's family—his "sweet" but "passive" father, dominated by his tyrannical mother and a wife "who was not happy in the marriage, because she doesn't like herself, and has to always pick, nothing's ever good." While Ray was blaming himself for being a failure as a father, Stern was blaming his own parents. "So, it was a perfect combination for that project," says Stern.

As they spoke about their fears and frustrations, Stern began to get a sense of what Ray was after. "His bewildered adult talked to my bewildered adult, and out of the horns of our own private dilemmas, I began to get a picture of what we both wanted to say through a story about children," said Stern. But actually getting it down on paper would not be easy.

WRITER'S BLOCK

Stern knew that he would not have much time to write. The studio had scheduled the first day of shooting for late March, giving him only twelve weeks to produce a finished script. "The thought of writing fast has always scared me to death," says Stern, who, throughout his life, would seek therapy to cure his writer's block. "There was a tremendous amount of anxiety. The anxiety, at least initially, was just overwhelming. I couldn't sit still." Stern moved out of Arthur Loew's house into a basement apartment in Laurel Canyon so that he could spend all his time working without distraction.

Stern looked at the research Ray had done with Uris, then proceeded to spend a couple weeks doing research of his own. He went down to Juvenile Hall and posed as a social worker from Wisconsin, talking to kids that were being processed. He took extensive notes, adding character names to the margins when he came across attributes he thought he might incorporate into the screenplay. "She often leaves home and hitchhikes, picks up anyone, has sex relations," he wrote. Next to this passage he wrote "Judy." Next to a description of "a very undersized boy of 14" who is overly polite and nervous he wrote "Plato."

But despite all his research, Stern was having a terrible time getting the script off the ground. "I couldn't figure out what to write," he said. He spent one day just arranging the furniture in his apartment, trying to decide if his desk should face the window or the room. One night as he was staring at a yellow legal pad that was blank except for four words—"Rebel Without a Cause"—Stern got a call from Ray asking how it was going. "I haven't started yet," Stern confessed. After a long silence Ray told him, barely hiding his disappointment, "You'd better start."

One unproductive afternoon, Stern drove down to Hollywood Boulevard to walk around and think. He wandered into a theater that was showing Elia Kazan's *On the Waterfront*—and something clicked. Stern was struck by the film's natural language and lack of artifice. He responded to the tenderness between Marlon Brando's and Eva Marie Saint's characters. And, perhaps, most importantly, he appreciated the way the film seemed to impose a "layer of myth over something so real." Inspired and recharged, Stern rushed home and wrote feverishly. "I felt free, and once I began writing, it felt freer and freer," says Stern. "I found that I could see everything."

Finally, the script was moving ahead. Stern would stop by Ray's office every morning to discuss his progress and trade ideas. One idea that Ray insisted on including in the script (which he also made Shulman put in his version) was a fantasy sequence in which we see the daydreams of the characters on one side of a split screen as the real action takes place on the other side. Once again, Ray may have been inspired by Buñuel, who used fantasy sequences in *Los Olvidados*. But, according to Stern, "I think he was concerned about being able to fill up the CinemaScope screen. Initially, he was a little scared of that." Stern wrote three of these surreal sequences for the first scene in the police station: Judy imagines herself in prison being visited by her father, whom she kisses, and her mother, who wipes off her lipstick; Plato goes fishing with his father in a crayon-colored world in his daydream; and Jim fantasizes that he is at a shooting gallery shooting at balloons bearing the faces of his mother, father and grandmother. When he returns home that night from the police station, Jim also has an extended Freudian dream about a rose tree based on a short story Stern had written. In addition, Ray wanted to have Jim's inner thoughts play on the soundtrack in voice-over.

Stern was not happy with these sequences. "I thought they were so pretentious and intrusive," he says. "The kids themselves seemed so rich and what they acted out in reality seemed so much more revealing than any fantasy that we might project." Stern fought with Ray to cut these scenes, winning Weisbart over to his side, and eventually Ray gave in. Though Stern was allowed to drop the scenes in his next draft, it appears Ray was not completely convinced that they should go. A month later, he told Weisbart that Dr. Douglas Kelley, who had been the chief psychiatrist at the Nuremberg trials, read the screenplay and found the fantasy scenes "not only exciting, but realistic." Nevertheless, they did not make it into the film.

A SINGLE DAY

While Stern gives credit to Ray for some of the ideas in the script, he and Ray would later disagree about who thought up one of the most important aspects of the film—its Aristotelian structure. Stern says that he had been working on an early important scene in the film, when the characters go on a field trip to the planetarium in L.A.'s Griffith Park. As they stand outside the auditorium of the planetarium, after hearing a lecture, Plato plaintively asks Jim, "You think when the end of the world comes it will be at night?" And Jim replies, "No. In the morning." Rereading those lines—lines he had written—Stern had a sudden inspiration. He decided to start the film with the beginning of the day and end at dawn on the next day, to play out the entire story in one twenty-four-hour period, or as Aristotle put it in his description of the ideal structure of classical Greek tragedy in *Poetics*, "a single revolution of the sun."

The "crazy compactness" of the time frame "would be typical of young people who are running away from boredom and who are running away from themselves," said Stern. "Their days are stuffed with such incredible drama, and it's a drama that is going on under the noses of the parents who don't in the least suspect that it is happening, who think that their children are in their beds, when actually they have flown like Peter Pan out the open window."

Stern's revelation would change the entire tone of the film, turning it into an adolescent fever-dream. "We wouldn't be locked into a kind of documentary stridency that would be unreal, but rather to a poetic excess," says Stern. "I knew then that I could do a succession of tremendously powerful scenes with no time to rest between them. And that the momentum could just keep going and going, because that was the nature of their lives." Stern was so excited by his inspiration that he called up Ray in the middle of the night, knowing that he would not be asleep. ("I could never wake him up because he was always prowling," says Stern. "He never slept.") Stern says Ray was equally excited about the idea. "It's perfect because it's operatic," Ray told him, echoing Stern's own feelings. "You know, for teenagers, a whole life is lived in twenty-four hours."

When it came time to award credit for the film, the twenty-four-hour structure would become a sore point between Ray and Stern. Ray would claim that it was his idea. He said he had originally written a note to Irving Shulman telling him "the main action should be compressed into one day." There is no record of this note, and if it existed, Shulman apparently paid no attention to it since his screenplay takes place over several days. Nor does Ray mention the time frame in any surviving memos that he wrote to Shulman regarding his script. Stern's account seems closer to the truth.

Ray would not be the only one who tried to take credit for Stern's work on *Rebel.* Philip Yordan, a screenwriter who became a front for many blacklisted writers, and who worked with Ray on *Johnny Guitar, King of Kings,* and *55 Days at Peking,* claimed that he had written "a couple of scenes for *Rebel,*" including the scene where Jim finds his father wearing his mother's apron. "It's such an antic thing to lay claim to," says Stern. "Why not the chickie run or the knife fight? But the apron scene?!" According to Stern, that scene was directly based on a childhood memory of his own. Screenwriter Lambert agrees that it is unlikely Yordan wrote this scene. "Philip Yordan was quite a rogue," says Lambert. "He didn't write some of the things he got credit for. He had about five young writers in basement cells working away."

But Stern freely acknowledges that there were many aspects of the script that were collaborative. He would go over scenes with Ray and, on occasion, he would also meet with Dean, Wood and Leonard Rosenman. Once the writing began to flow, Stern felt free to visit his cousin Arthur Loew's house at night after work, where Dean was usually hanging out. Slowly and subtly, the actor began to influence Stern's take on Jim Stark's character. "Without meaning to use specific aspects of Jimmy's personality, I became infected by it," said Stern. He even incorporated some specific references to his relationship with Dean, such as the moment in the planetarium where Jim begins to moo, evoking their first meeting in Loew's living room.

Dean seemed to like Stern, sometimes demonstrating his approval by showing up at Stern's house in the morning to take him to the studio on the back of his motorcycle. But although he told Stern, with characteristic terseness, that he liked the script, he apparently had doubts. As late as March 11—two weeks before production was set to begin—an item appeared in the *Los Angeles Mirror-News* reporting that Dean was holed up in his Sunset Plaza apartment trying to decide whether to do *Rebel* at all, claiming "the script wasn't right"—a very public slap in Stern's face.

As Stern neared the end of his work, he would experience another humiliation. Ray sent the writer on a pilgrimage to the home of Elia Kazan in order to get his opinion on the screenplay. Stern had to sit and wait in silence while Kazan read the entire script. Then he sent Stern away without comment. Stern began to sense that Ray's need for approval was deepseated. "I don't know if it was mistrust of the material or mistrust of himself as the director, or mistrust of the audience," says Stern of Ray. "That can certainly be read as lack of confidence. He was probably, at core, a very, very needy, lonely, love-starved man." Before signing on to *Rebel,* Stern recalls that he had been warned about Ray by John Houseman, who told him, "Dear Mr. Stern. Take care. He's an envious man. He has a love-hate relationship with everyone."

Stern turned in his final draft of the screenplay on March 25, 1955, a mere five days before principal shooting began. Comparing this final draft with the film, and with the scripts and treatments written by Uris, Shulman and Ray, it's clear that *Rebel* would never have existed in anything like its present form—and possibly not at all—without Stern. Much of what ended up on-screen is contained in this draft. Although additional lines were improvised by actors or rewritten on the freewheeling set, in the end the great majority of the words and actions that appear in the film *Rebel Without a Cause* came from Stern's imagination.

The years—and the combined mythos of *Rebel*'s director and star—have obscured the importance of Stern's contribution. The credits that appear at the beginning of *Rebel*—"Story by Nicholas Ray, Adaptation by Irving Shulman, Screenplay by Stewart Stern"—do not tell the real tale. The issue of credit—as well as later problems that would explode during the film's production—would leave Stern with some feeling of bitterness. But that does not overshadow his accomplishment. Just as *Rebel* contains a trio of characters who are essential to the plot, another trio was indispensable to the film's success—Nicholas Ray, James Dean and Stewart Stern.

CHAPTER FIVE

Gang Wars

As he struggled with the script during the winter of 1955, Nick Ray continued to assemble his cast and crew for *Rebel*'s late-March starting date—which was coming up fast and would prove to be inflexible. Looming in the background at the Warners studio was another project that would necessitate a drop-dead end date for *Rebel*'s production. The film was *Giant,* a sprawling ode to Texas oilmen, based on the bestseller by the then-queen of doorstop-thick historical novels, Edna Ferber, and starring Elizabeth Taylor and Rock Hudson. The film was slated to be directed by George Stevens, who had far greater clout and a more prestigious reputation than Ray, having just had popular and critical hits with the iconic Western classic *Shane* and one of Hollywood's most glamorous and seductive literary adaptations, *A Place in the Sun,* based on Theodore Dreiser's *An American Tragedy.* On the Warners lot, *Giant* was seen as a *Gone with the Wind* of sorts, an epic American film to which the studio was much more deeply committed—both emotionally and financially—than it was to the fringe teen-market experiment that *Rebel* represented.

With many of its tried-and-true stars aging, and a sea change brewing in the business, Warners was in a new star-building period. As a result, *Giant* would eventually snag three members of *Rebel*'s young cast, including James Dean. As early as Christmas Eve of 1954, four months before *Rebel* began shooting, the press was hinting that Dean was headed for one of *Giant*'s leading roles, that of self-loathing, nouveau-riche oil baron Jett Rink. In fact, if the shooting schedule for *Giant* had not been pushed back two months to accommodate Elizabeth Taylor's pregnancy, Dean might not have been available to make *Rebel* at all.

Dean was officially announced as Jett Rink on March 17, 1955, roughly two weeks before *Rebel*'s first shooting day. *Giant* would begin shooting on May 23, which represented a tight squeeze for Ray. A short thirty-six-day shooting schedule was planned for *Rebel*, despite the fact that the film was slowly mushrooming into an epic to equal or surpass *Giant*, at least in the mind of its director.

Meanwhile, the multitasking Ray continued his seduction of his quixotic star. Although Warner Brothers had officially announced that Dean would appear in *Rebel Without a Cause*, Ray knew that Dean was wildly unpredictable, and he sensed that the actor's commitment was somehow tentative, as it would remain until the very first day he stepped onto the set. When a reporter asked him if he had script approval, Dean said, "Contractually no—emotionally yes. They can always suspend me. Money isn't one of my worries, not that I have any."

As a result, Ray kept Dean close, stoking the natural affinity that existed between them. Over time, their friendship would evolve into another example of what director Mark Rappaport would call the "Gordian knot of unbelievably complicated father-son, older man–younger man relationships" in Ray's life—although, as Rappaport would add, it wasn't always easy to know "who is seducing whom and who is being seduced by whom." Like Ray, Dean was given to twinning, to entering into spiritual marriages with anyone, male or female, according to Dean's close friend Vampira (Maila Nurmi).

Ray kept Dean updated on *Rebel*'s preproduction, giving him script drafts as they came along, and keeping him abreast of casting, although, as late as February, Ray had yet to assemble the supporting cast of gang members, to fill in the world behind his star. And he had not come close to choosing an actor for the pivotal role of Plato, a casting decision that would go right down to the wire. Ray pulled Dean into some of his intensive research on teens and juvenile delinquency, especially once Ray took the next natural step to ensure *Rebel*'s authenticity. He engaged the services of a real gang leader, a true punk.

LEADER OF THE PACK

When pugnacious Frank Mazzola showed up at the Warners lot, looking for a part in *Rebel,* he was stopped dead in his tracks. Although he had worked as a child in such films as *The Hunchback of Notre Dame, Casablanca* and *The Boy with Green Hair,* he was relatively unknown as an actor. But Mazzola had a real-life reputation for wildness that preceded him. Warners casting director Hoyt Bowers refused to allow Mazzola to meet Ray. The young actor was halted at the bottom of the steps to Ray's office and told to get lost, not that he was the type of kid who could be easily deterred. That very day, he would find a way to make it through to Ray's office, and he would go on to play an important role in establishing *Rebel*'s verisimilitude.

Mazzola was well-known as the hotheaded leader of the Athenians, the most infamous gang at Hollywood High. "Basically, the Athenians were a club," said Syd Field, who would grow up to become one of Hollywood's premier gurus of screenwriting, and who was also a member of the Athenians then. "It was a very close-knit group at that time. A typical Saturday night out would be going up to Hollywood Boulevard, walking down the street and trying to pick a fight with somebody, just kind of getting in trouble."

The Athenians were tough guys, boxers and athletes who wore jackets emblazoned with the gang name. With sly understatement, Mazzola describes the Athenians as "guys who could handle themselves." During one high school party that the gang attended, Mazzola punched an interloper from East L.A., sending him flying out a second-story window and breaking his arm. The next week, at a planned boxing match at the Hollywood Boys Club, a boy who resembled Mazzola left the Boys Club and, according to Mazzola, "they grabbed him because they thought it was me. They used a straight-edge razor—144 stitches." The story made the *Hollywood Citizen-News,* which ran with the headline: RAT PACK ATTACKS HOLLYWOOD YOUTH.

The Athenians were also involved in one of the biggest gang mêlées in 1950s L.A. history: the Battle of Big Bear. "What happened became legendary in Hollywood," says Mazzola. His memory of the Big Bear brawl paints a vivid picture of gang warfare at the time.

As Mazzola tells it: "The Athenians went to Big Bear during one Christmas vacation. There was this girl I met up there the year before, a beautiful blonde from Manhattan Beach. All I wanted to do was go up there and make love to her—which is what I planned to do. I'm inside the house and one of the girls comes running in and says there's a bunch of motorcycle guys out front. At that time, all the motorcycle gangs were from San Bernardino. This was the beginning of motorcycle gangs, before the Hells Angels. I walk out and there must have been about fifteen or twenty guys on motorcycles and I'm talking about the real thing, choppers. These guys are looking to beat the shit out of somebody."

"Then this one guy, the leader, starts hassling Syd, just like in a classic corny motorcycle movie. This guy looks at us and says, 'What are you? One of these fucking kikes?' And Syd says, 'What did you say?' And this guy repeats, 'Are you one of these kikes?" All the sudden, Syd punches the guy, and this guy nails him—and the whole fucking thing goes nuts. It was a war. I'm talking broken bottles and tire irons. There was blood all over. Finally, I got this guy and I knocked every tooth out of his head except for his molars. I won't go any further about what else I did to this guy but he was in critical condition. And then the police came so everything had to break up."

Once Mazzola returned to L.A., the motorcycle gang exacted its revenge. On the way to getting his battered teeth checked, Mazzola, his brother Lenny and two other Athenians found themselves suddenly surrounded. "I'm talking this whole street was filled with kids, not kids but teenagers, guys in their twenties," says Mazzola.

Mazzola and his friends tried to find sanctuary by ducking into a drugstore. The owner picked up a double-barreled shotgun and forced the mob to back off, then turned the gun on Mazzola and ordered him to leave through the back door.

"So we go out the back door, which has steps that lead down to a parking lot that's filled with motorcycles, the whole world wanting to chop me up. So that didn't look too good. I thought maybe we'd have a better chance going back out into the street. I remember going over to the counter and picking up these two knives. I figured, 'We'll get as many of them as we can before they get us'—because as soon as I walked out that door, I knew we were dead. I'm driving through the crowd and all of a sudden this highway patrol car comes up. The cops get out and—I'll never forget this—the cop says, 'Fight me.' So the guy threw me on the ground and tried to rough me up. Then they threw us into the squad car and drove out of town." Mazzola was taken straight to San Bernardino jail.

During his rush into the street, Mazzola had stabbed the leader of the motorcycle gang so he was forced to remain in police custody until they were sure of the gang leader's condition. The police told him that they "knew that son of a bitch would meet his Waterloo one day." And, according to Mazzola, all the other kids reacted to him in awe. "It was cool because I got their hero. And I was a clean-cut-looking kid. I stayed there until I knew he was going to live and then my mom came and picked me up. She says, 'I knew you shouldn't have gone on that trip to Big Bear.'

"Anyway, that became like a big deal in Hollywood. Those guys actually came back looking for me again. They thought I lived in North Hollywood and beat the shit out of everyone in North Hollywood."

The Athenians may have been wild street kids but they did not spring from the economic fringes of L.A. "We weren't going around with ducktails," says Mazzola. "We were also student body presidents." According to Syd Field, "Frank's house was upper-middle-class. It was large and it was spacious. It was north of Sunset Boulevard, and had white colonial columns on the outside." Mazzola's background would fit perfectly with Ray's intention to show that columned cushiness could coexist with a wild, rebellious and sometimes violent nature. And while Mazzola may have been vying for the crown of king of the streets, he had another ambition. He wanted to be in the movies.

Many members of Mazzola's family had been in show business for decades, in jobs ranging from producers to grips. His father had been a stunt man and an actor since the days of silent film, having worked with such superstars of the vanished era as cowboy Tom Mix and the Keystone Kops. By the time the *Rebel* cast was being drawn together, young Mazzola was already doing stunt work and extra work on the Warners lot. He had actually landed a very small role in *East of Eden* that was subsequently cut out. But while on the *Eden* set, he had his first experience of James Dean.

"I remember the first time I saw Jimmy. He looked like a wild animal that had just been let out of the cage. It was like: who is this guy? He actually screamed at this girl on the set I knew from Hollywood High School. He was saying, 'What the fuck are you looking at? Don't look at me! Don't get close to me!' She actually made a complaint to the Screen Actors Guild about Jimmy. That was my first impression of him. At that time, I didn't know who the hell James Dean was."

That would change soon enough. In late January 1955, Mazzola heard the news about *Rebel*. And just like every other young actor in Hollywood, he wanted to test for a part. But when the casting director refused to let him meet Ray, Mazzola waited for his opportunity and sneaked up the steps to Ray's office.

"Nick's secretary was very nice, a girl named Fae [Murphy]. She was very politely saying, 'I'm sorry. Nick doesn't see anybody unless you have an appointment.' Then, the door to his office opens up and there's this kid from Hollywood High, a kid named Marc Cavell who was up for the part of Plato. He opens the door and says, 'Hey Nick, this is Frank. He was the guy I was just telling you about.' He was trying to ingratiate himself with Nick by saying he was a part of this gang that I was the leader of. If I had brushed my teeth for ten seconds earlier or missed a stop sign or had an extra piece of toast, it would never have happened."

"I remember walking into Nick's office. There was that famous picture of Jimmy in the trench coat. Nick says, 'This guy here will probably end up being bigger than Brando. He's going to be the biggest actor in the world. Mark my words.'"

Ray and Mazzola spent only a short time together that day, but Ray recognized Mazzola as the real thing. He took a remarkable leap and gave Mazzola a copy of the current *Rebel* screenplay to peruse. Mazzola took it home, read it and called Ray the next day. His reaction could not have been what Ray wanted to hear, although it may have matched his nagging fears. "I was just being honest," remembers Mazzola. "I told him that if this were in the theater, the dialogue of the kids would get catcalls. This isn't how we talk."

Before he knew it, Mazzola found himself wrapped up in *Rebel*, and not just as an actor. He would land the role of Crunch, Buzz the gang leader's right-hand man, but, perhaps more importantly, he would land a role as a consultant, for which he was eventually paid a whopping two hundred dollars (although the notoriously stingy Jack Warner balked at forking over the money until David Weisbart personally stepped in and made sure Mazzola was paid). Mazzola was thrilled with the money and the opportunity. Ray offered him the office next door and told him to vet the script and mark anything he thought was phony. He also wanted Mazzola's input on the cars and the costumes.

Ray felt that screenwriter Stewart Stern should get a close-up view of Mazzola. They were an almost comical pair. Mazzola was unlike anyone else Stern had met in his somewhat coddled life. According to Mazzola, "Stewart always used to tell me: 'I was a little concerned about you, Frank.'" But Ray's instincts bore fruit; Stern and Mazzola proved to be a productive team. Soon, Stern recognized that Mazzola could provide him with a wealth of information about a world to which he related emotionally but which he did not know much about specifically. Together they went to teen hangouts, and Stern listened in on the conversations surrounding him. He even kept track of the slang Mazzola used. Stern eventually presented Mazzola with a list of words he gleaned from their time together. Dated February 7, 1955, with the words "Juvenile Talk" typed at top, the document lists fifty-two slang words and phrases. An entirely new vernacular was emerging, one inspired by the worlds of jazz and drugs, disc jockeys, Negro and military slang, and influential hipster comic Lord Buckley (who was a friend of Dean's). Surprisingly, Stern's list of new phrases contains many words that would persist throughout the 1960s and straight into the present: *wow, too much, twisted, nowhere, cool, grass, fuzz, crazy, flake out, heat, chick, hang loose, dig, flipped, dummy up* and *hothead*.

Stern was not the only person Ray wanted Mazzola to meet and guide. Ray needed Mazzola to meld with Dean, to further bind Dean to the project. "Jimmy was twenty-four at the time and he was kind of hedging his bet," says Mazzola. "I think he was obligated to the film but he didn't really feel comfortable playing a teenager. So Nick says, 'I want you and Jimmy to hang out a lot.'" In March 1955, Dean and Mazzola would interact with some frequency. Together with Ray, they would meet to talk about Mazzola's world, and review issues of manner and dialogue. Mazzola even took Dean shopping to show him how a teenager dressed.

Eventually, Dean would also accompany Mazzola to meetings of the Athenians, although Mazzola did not let his peers know that Dean was an actor who was there to do research. "He used to spar with me a lot," says

Mazzola. "And we'd just hang with the guys. Play basketball. The guys were good athletes. Jimmy was a good basketball player. That was one of his sports."

Former Athenian Syd Field says he did not know who Dean was at the time. But like anyone else who ever came across Dean, he remembers his presence. "My main memory of him is him sitting there with his head down, his hands together on his knees and listening," says Field. "He was very, very quiet, shy and laid-back. I think he was more into an observing mode than he was into a participatory mode. There were a few little razzes. We were trying to have the upper hand. He was coming in as an outsider and it probably helped him in his portrayal. He entered the group and he absorbed whatever it was he absorbed.

"We would regale him with stories about past events, the fight at San Bernardino, what it was like in Juvenile Hall. I think us talking about our parents and what our home life was like was interesting to him. When we were talking about cars, he would tell us about cars. He was really into cars and looking good. He never mentioned anything about where he was from or anything like that."

On February 10, 1955, Mazzola even arranged for Ray to attend a meeting of the Athenians along with Dean. Because of Ray's age, Mazzola was forced to engage in a rather large deception, which he felt guilty about. He introduced Ray as his uncle. But it wasn't enough for Ray simply to sit in Mazzola's living room conversing with the gang. He asked Mazzola to arrange a special event.

According to Ray, "We planned a 'war' and Frank made the rules . . . On the night of the 'war,' about seventy or eighty guys showed up at a pizza joint to wait for a yellow Ford—the signal from the other gang. It was the most bizarre thing I'd ever seen. Two girls outside the pizza joint were having a knife fight."

"Every custom car that went by," says Frank Mazzola, "my guys were out in front, pulling them over, saying, 'Are these the guys, Frank?' That went on for about an hour. Nick and Jimmy were just having a field day sucking this all up. It almost came to blows with some guys."

In line with his penchant for recording everything—a habit he'd had since his early days with folklorist Alan Lomax—Ray was carrying several microphones on his body. "I had a wristwatch for a mike, a tie clasp for a mike, a pocket drop for a mike . . . they'd been developed by Germany during the war for espionage," said Ray. He carried a wire recorder in a holster in his coat pocket. When Mazzola spotted the holster, he thought for a moment that Ray was carrying a gun. "These guys, they were very tough but no guns were allowed, no booze was allowed, no pot was allowed," said Ray. "Only tire chains. No knives."

Ray came away from the experience with what he described as "a very primitive feeling about the whole confrontation. It was a conflict of sex and power." Mazzola had opened an important door for Ray, but he may have also opened Ray up to *Rebel's* deeper possibilities. As Ray continued to think about and research *Rebel*, his sense of where the story could go was continually evolving. Those themes of "sex and power" were crucial to Ray. Throughout the many steps of production, preproduction and postproduction on *Rebel*, he would allow his identification with these kids to alter his method. It even affected something as rote as his auditions for his secondary players. Throughout the next weeks, Ray would turn the audition process into something less actorly than gladiatorial, something less like Hollywood and more like ancient Rome or, at least, a nexus of Rome, boot camp and a high school gym.

KING OF THE MOUNTAIN

Ray needed a large group of young actors—male and female—to play the movie's high school gang of troublemakers. And in keeping with the film's new Hollywood stance, Ray was on the lookout for fresh faces. He spotted Alan Cohen, who would land the crucial role of gangleader Buzz, costarring in a play called *Party Girl* with Beverly Long, who would also earn a small role in *Rebel*. "We played the bad kids," according to Long, which may have been one of the reasons Ray was drawn to them.

After watching Cohen in action, Ray put Hoyt Bowers, Warner Brothers' casting director, on the trail of the fledgling actor's agent. Without any input from Cohen, his agent and the studio decided that, before he could be seriously considered, an alteration in Cohen's persona was called for. They wanted to change his name to the less Jewish-sounding Corey Allen. "Everyone was being transformed," Cohen remembers with some bitterness. "The big thing was to erase the circumcision." Corey Allen was not a name with which he would ever become comfortable, but at the time, he felt powerless to do anything about it.

Corey Allen was the son of gambler and casino manager Carl Cohen, known for his involvement in a particularly infamous showbiz event. "Chairman of the Board" Frank Sinatra—the veritable king of Las Vegas— had been denied credit at the baccarat table at Howard Hughes's Sands Casino, and in a rage, he demanded to see Cohen, then manager of the casino. During their heated discussion, a rampaging Sinatra threw over the table at which he and Cohen were sitting, causing a pot of hot coffee to fly into Cohen's lap. Cohen responded by punching Sinatra right in the face, splitting his lip and knocking out his caps. There are not many people who could claim to have bested the bullying singer in so direct a manner.

Cohen's son did not follow his father's boisterous example. He graduated from UCLA in 1954 with a bachelor's of fine arts in theater and won the department's Best Actor award. Since graduation, he had appeared in approximately twenty plays in the Los Angeles area. Corey Allen took his acting very seriously. He was diligent, and peaceable. "I was not a physical young man at all," Allen said. "I hated violence." So it must have come as a huge surprise when upon arriving for his *Rebel* audition, he was not asked merely to read for a role. Instead, he was required to participate in a series of rough and competitive games.

"There were about 150 boys trying out for several roles," said Allen. "They had us all in the back lot of Warner Brothers, sitting in high school bleachers. Perry Lopez [a young Latino actor who was assisting Ray] blew a whistle and said, 'I want all you guys to go up to the top rows. And when you get up there, turn around and come back down and sit.'"

Understandably perplexed about the point of the game, Allen hit on a unique response to Lopez's instructions. "I was twenty. These guys were all younger. I knew I wouldn't get there before them. So while everybody stampeded, I just started walking, all the time asking myself, 'Is this right?' About three quarters of the way to the top, guys were already coming down, still stampeding. And what I became aware of was: everybody's coming down and I'm going up. So my one figure was visible. I got to the top and I looked around and I looked pretty good. Then I just turned around and walked down. They had to wait for me. And that was the key, I think.

Architect Mies van der Rohe said, 'Less is more.' Well, less was more. And I think that's how I got the role."

If nothing else, Allen certainly caused Ray to focus on him, to notice his confidence, his handsomeness, his air of casual superiority, and the fact that he stood slightly above most of the other actors in size—characteristics that suited Buzz perfectly. But although Allen felt he secured the role that day, his participation in Ray's contests was far from over. Allen recalls that there were about two weeks of these kinds of improvisations. "He ran us through a game we call King of the Mountain, where there's a platform, and you battle to get on the platform and knock everybody else off. All very physical things. Towards the end, the remaining candidates were to bounce a ball. The bad guy—who was Frank Mazzola—came and tried to steal the ball, in order to cause a fight. Then everybody would pile in and try to get the ball."

Of course, if anyone was truly king of the mountain during these games, it was Ray himself. Stewart Stern remembers the way the director would assemble the kids at night, on a huge platform in the middle of the Warner Brothers parking lot. "He would take the kids out there at night and have one light. I don't know if the electric department left a floodlight or something, but it would be the only light in the whole lot that you could see. These kids would be crawling around the superstructure and improvising scenes. He was trying to see how the relationships emerged and how to orchestrate the gang. He'd give them all kinds of exercises. And I think they all idolized him. I don't think there was anything fake about it. Not on his part. I think that he just flourished with that."

Ray had decided that, from top to bottom, *Rebel* should grow directly out of these kids. More than just speaking their language, the movie should align with their natures. Ray may have been reacting in part to his mentor Elia Kazan's use of real dockworkers in *On the Waterfront*, but Ray would go Kazan one better, pushing Kazan's methods even further. Kazan used dockworkers as realistic extras, adding to the texture of his movie, sharpening the edges. But Ray wanted his kids' experiences to bleed directly onto the celluloid, to permeate the movie.

"Nick was getting down to brass tacks," according to Allen, who would go on to become a director and acting teacher. "Not how you say this. But who you are—and what are you going to do about it. It was brilliant.

"It didn't matter whether you hung on to the ball, got to the top of the bleachers or were the king of the mountain; what mattered was the attitude in the effort, the thinking, the psychology," said Allen. "That was a very personal piece of work."

Given the amount of testosterone in the air, there were times when the improvisations got way out of hand. Twenty-four-year-old Jack Grinnage, who passed up a role in *Forbidden Planet* to play gang member Moose, remembers a day when the actors were required to bring their cars to the set. "They wanted it to look like a chicken run," he says. "I don't know how many kids were there. Maybe twenty-five to thirty. They gave us a script, which involved Buzz and five other boys. I asked, 'Which part should I learn?' And they said, 'Oh just learn all of them because Nick hasn't decided yet.' So Nick says 'Action' and we start the scene. Corey starts the scene as Buzz, and no one answered him. So I said the first line of the script. And then Corey said his next line and I said the next line from the script as the second boy. I did the whole scene with Corey. No one else spoke up. Then suddenly as we're standing there, a car came up with Frank Mazzola, Perry Lopez. They jumped out of the car and they grabbed me and said, 'We're supposed to fight.' So there's this big fight. Everybody's fighting. People's cars got dented. People got hurt."

Frank Mazzola recalls one rehearsal in which he and Corey Allen came to blows, kicking off a feud that lasted through the entire production. During the session, they were supposed to play leaders of opposing gangs. "It was all improvisation stuff and we started going too far. Corey is pushing and I started escalating and Corey started escalating. I kind of grabbed Corey and threw him down."

"What the fuck are you doing? You want to prove the casting director right?" yelled Ray, referring to the studio's resistance to hiring the rambunctious Mazzola in the first place.

Mazzola stayed on the payroll. But Mazzola and Allen would not forget that day. By the time he and Mazzola shared their first filmed moment together, the March 23 wardrobe test, there was a visible strain between them. Mazzola sulked in the background: "In my mind, I was thinking 'I don't care about this film. If that fucker says anything . . .'" When Mazzola was called up to stand between Allen and Dean, he refused to look at Allen. Allen, meanwhile, was clearly smoldering. "If Corey did anything, I was probably gonna get off," Mazzola says. "And then Jimmy put his hand over my eyes to try to break the tension. And there was this beautiful look when he smiled." Dean may have tried to diffuse the tension, but it persisted—and it would emerge over and over again throughout the *Rebel* shoot.

THE BLONDE AND THE BRUNETTE

Aside from Natalie Wood, Ray also needed two more girls to play a pair of gang molls named Helen and Mil. Ray did not put his actresses through the physical paces he required of the boys. And yet his approach would remain deeply idiosyncratic. He called them into his office for a little gentle psychoanalysis. "I was standing out in the hall with Natalie at one point. And we were all wondering what was going on inside. I'd never had an audition like that before," said Beverly Long, who would win the part of Helen, the prototypical 1950s ponytailed blonde. "When I was called in, I never had to read anything. Nick just said, 'How did you get along with your mother?' And I said: 'Not really great.' He asked personal questions."

Ray was not only looking for the right attitude, he was looking to cast specific physical types. "Nick Ray wanted contrast," according to Steffi Sidney, who would secure the part of Mil, the brunette gang moll opposite blonde Beverly Long. "He wanted a dark-haired girl. He wanted a blonde. And he got that."

Among the cast, Steffi Sidney was a special case. She was the daughter of the famous and influential Hollywood reporter and columnist Sidney Skolsky, a man who ranked with the famous female trio of Hollywood gossips: Sheilah Graham, Hedda Hopper and Louella Parsons. Skolsky was known for what he termed his "tintypes," mini-profiles of various showbiz characters, and he was one of the first Hollywood columnists to latch on to James Dean. Skolsky began his career as a publicist in New York, but by 1932, he was working out of Hollywood, where he maintained an office at Schwab's drugstore, next door to Googie's, where Dean hung out, and across the street from the Chateau Marmont, where Ray lived. His syndicated columns appeared in newspapers across the country, from the *New York Post* to the *Los Angeles Herald*. The influential Skolsky was one of several people credited with naming the Academy Award "Oscar." According to his daughter, he was also the first to popularize such movie phrases as "preview" and "take." And he was famous for asking celebrities what they wore to bed. Skolsky's trademark question had caused a scandal for Ray's ex-wife Gloria Grahame when she responded, with frankness, that she slept in the nude.

Because of her father, Steffi Sidney had grown up on back lots and been an innocent player on the Hollywood scene. "I learned to play Ping-Pong at Chasen's," she says, referring to the classic Hollywood restaurant. So it's no surprise that there is some disagreement among the *Rebel* survivors as to whether Steffi Sidney got her part because of her father's influence and the light he might shine on the production. Undeniably, that would have been clever of Ray and Warner Brothers. Famed gossip columnist Hedda Hopper's son William would also be cast in the small but psychologically important role of Judy's father, which lends some credence to the nepotism theory. And Sidney had been significantly featured only once before in a film, one her father had produced, *The Eddie Cantor Story*.

The ring of nepotism is also sounded in Sidney's own memory of getting the part. According to Sidney, she did not hear anything for a while after her meeting with Ray. "Then my father came home one night and said, 'Listen, I had dinner with Nick Ray and he says you're going to be in his film.'"

Faye Nuell Mayo, who would serve as Natalie's Wood's double in several *Rebel* scenes, says, "We knew that Steffi was there because of her dad. When she came in for the audition, she did fit in more or less with the group so why not—and it gave them an access to publicity for the film. That's what we kids all thought."

But Sidney was a serious young actress at the time. She was a member of the celebrated Actors Lab in Los Angeles, a breakaway from the Group Theatre in New York. She was a close friend of Susan Strasberg, daughter of Lee and Paula Strasberg, who taught at New York's Actors Studio, where Dean had very briefly studied. In fact, Sidney thinks that it was Paula Strasberg—not her father—who secured her original audition with Ray.

Although she was not particularly stunning by movie actress standards, Sidney possessed an earthy normalcy that Ray might have liked. And she certainly took her small role to heart, prepping studiously for it, creating her own backstory. "My character always carried a brush with her. I was a girl who was very insecure and I wanted to belong to the gang. I was not one that would take chances. I was there mostly because I wanted to please my boyfriend [played by former child actor Tom Bernard, who portrayed Ricky Nelson on the radio version of *Ozzie and Harriet* before the real Ricky joined the cast] and I wanted to be part of a gang because that was the thing to do. But I was not intrepid. Mil was not intrepid. Each of us had to make it up for ourselves to a certain extent—but we had to clear it. I think I cleared it with Nick Ray."

At one point, Ray cut together black-and-white footage of some of the gang members and showed it to them. After it was over he asked, "What's wrong with what we've just seen?" No one had the nerve to say anything, except Sidney. "I don't think we look like we know each other or that we even connect with each other," Sidney remembers saying. "Nick Ray took umbrage at this and he said very sternly, 'I don't want any of this Actors Studio stuff.' I really put my foot in it. From then on, Dennis [Hopper] and I were always singled out like the scapegoats of the film."

Later, Ray apparently had second thoughts about Sidney's criticism and suggested that the gang hang out together off the set. Looking for a bonding experience, the eager-to-please young actors hit Santa Monica beach. They made their way to the abandoned seaside restaurant where twenty years earlier police found the body of actress Thelma Todd. Although her mysterious death was officially ruled a suicide, many believe Todd was murdered by gangsters. The gang broke into the restaurant—which some thought was haunted—and spent much of the night cavorting there.

THE FINAL CUT

By late February, the cast of gang members was cut to size from the original huge casting call. In a March 1 memo to David Weisbart, Ray writes, "On Monday, Tuesday, Wednesday afternoon and night we conducted tests of thirty-two boys and girls for primary and secondary parts in our movie." Actual CinemaScope tests were also conducted with the short-listed cast. After the tests, sixteen gang members would survive, among them Corey Allen, Jack Grinnage, Dennis Hopper, Frank Mazzola, Steffi

Sidney, Beverly Long, Tom Bernard, Clifford Morris, Jerry Olken and Ken Miller.

Actor Nick Adams—who would eventually become something of a poor man's James Dean in a popular Civil War–based TV drama coincidentally titled *The Rebel*—also appeared on the list. Ray would call Nick Adams "the most ambitious actor I've ever known." After hitchhiking to Hollywood from Nanticoke, Pennsylvania, where his father was a coal miner, Adams got his first role when he sneaked onto the set of the navy film *Mister Roberts* in his Coast Guard uniform, falsely claiming he was a signalman in the navy. He managed to impress director John Ford, who not only cast him in the film, but arranged for him to live in the house of John Wayne's ex-wife, though he got kicked out for sneaking girls through his bedroom window. Throughout the filming of *Rebel*, Adams would try hard to ingratiate himself with both Dean and Wood. If the *Rebel* set sometimes felt like high school, Adams was the class clown. He would eventually become a major irritant to the other actors.

According to Ken Miller, who was eventually cut from the film, things on the lot remained loose and surprisingly indefinite even after Ray made his tight cut of players. "They did give us scenes every once in while, just one or two pages and we'd go over them and come back and do improvisations and you would change one part, which was kind of fun. Jimmy loved to do improvisations," says Miller. Sometimes the cast would just hang around and talk. "Nick liked to sit down and say, 'What do you think about what's going on in the world today' and things like that. Nicholas Ray was just the nicest man. He was unlike any other director I ever worked with. He just wanted to talk with everybody. That's how he figured out if people would be right or wrong. He just became one of the gang. This went on for three days. We just would go to the studio and sit around or we'd have lunch. A lot of nothing . . ."

But although Ray's list of supporting players had come together, something about the film was refusing to gel. Time was definitely running out and the studio still had problems with the casting of all three leads. Dean did not participate in the late February tests with the gang. Suddenly, he fled Hollywood for trips back to New York and his hometown of Fairmount, Indiana. During the late February tests, Dennis Hopper played Dean's role. As late as March 2—with the starting date of March 31 coming up fast—a Warner Brothers memo offered other possible backup choices for the part of Jim Stark. Penciled in were the names Robert Wagner, Tab Hunter and John Kerr (who had just played a role Dean passed up, that of a young psychiatric patient in MGM's *The Cobweb*). In fact, on March 11, Warners talent director Solly Baiano urged Ray to look at a twenty-six-year-old New York actor named John Cassavetes, described as "an intense young man tending toward the neurotic."

At least Ray had grown convinced that his current secret girlfriend Wood was perfect for the part of Judy, and he knew that Wood was ready to play the role at the drop of a hat. But even here, there were problems. The studio remained uncertain about Wood's appropriateness for the role. In a March 1 memo, Ray virtually pleaded for Wood: "There is only one girl who has shown the capacity to play Judy, and she is Natalie Wood . . . Although there has been talk of Debbie Reynolds for this part, especially from an exploitation standpoint, I think the studio might develop a star of its own with Natalie Wood. I'd be happy to close with her as I could start work on voice, wardrobe, hair, etc." Despite Ray's persistence, the studio continued to offer up alternatives. A March 2 memo put Wood in second place behind Debbie Reynolds, but above Carroll Baker. Fourteen other names are listed as "girls tested or discussed," including Kathryn Grant (later Mrs. Bing Crosby), Gloria Castillo and Steffi Sidney. "Nick Ray always had Natalie in mind to play Judy but Warner and his henchman Steve Trilling were getting very nervous about it," says Sidney. "So they made up an alternative list. My name was on it—but I know I was never seriously considered for the part of Judy." With preproduction time almost over, the studio had still not settled on Wood.

It's unlikely that the studio felt Wood was too Hollywood—as Dean did—but it certainly felt she was too young. In fact, in a March 1 memo, Warners production manager Eric Stacey points out that "in casting this picture there should be no actors assigned who are under 18 years of age, since minors cannot work at night except under emergency conditions— and then only until 10 p.m.—and this picture is approximately 80% night."

Ray continued to proceed, albeit with uncertainty. As far as he was concerned, Wood and Dean were set in their roles. The gang was solid. But there was still one more important part that had not been settled to anyone's satisfaction, that of Plato, Jim Stark's protégé, the lost-boy character who actually drives the plot. Startlingly, with a mere two weeks to go before filming would begin, the part of Plato had not been cast. No one who auditioned had even seemed close. But fate and luck were about to step in.

CHAPTER SIX

The First Gay Teenager

After Dean's Jim Stark, Plato is *Rebel's*
most distinctive and original character. Unlike Jim, Plato would not leave
an instantaneous craterlike impression on American culture. Instead, he
would have a slow insinuating influence, especially on boys of a certain age
and persuasion. As conceived by Stewart Stern, Plato was a deeply alienated
kid who would find a friend, a soulmate and an idol in Jim. He was a hurting needy teen given to astonishingly naked expressions of hero worship
and devotion. Depending on how Plato was played, his profound bond
with Jim could take on many shades of meaning, some of which might
seem terrifyingly intimate in a 1950s context. So finding the right actor to
play Plato was essential.

   With preproduction time nearly running out, the perfect Plato had yet
to emerge. In his March 1 memo to producer David Weisbart, Nick Ray
stated that he was considering a little-known radio and TV actor named
Jeff Silver, as well as Billy Gray, who would go on to play Bud on the classic
TV program *Father Knows Best*, a sitcom that would present the shiny flip
side of Ray's view of suburban life. In that same memo, Ray even suggested
Dennis Hopper as a potential Plato, but "only after a test with Jimmy
Dean." As it turned out, Hopper would not remain in the director's good
graces for very much longer, especially once the truth emerged about his
relationship with Natalie Wood (which was only one of the revelations that
would rock the *Rebel* set). Frank Mazzola remembers that his high school
friend Marc Cavell, who introduced him to Ray, was set to play Plato. But
although Cavell was mentioned in Ray's memo—with the prototypically

1950s nickname "Butch"—he was short-listed as one of gang members, not as Plato. Mazzola also recalls that his sixteen-year-old brother Anthony was considered for the role. "He was slender. He was a gymnast so he had a perfect body. He was an incredible-looking guy," Mazzola says of his brother, who died in a plane crash in 1974.

Perhaps something about Plato remained unformed in Nick Ray's mind, unfulfilled by any of the actors who attempted to land the juicy part. Ray maintained his drive toward an ever-greater, ever-expanding vision of *Rebel*. By mid-March, there was good reason to believe that—regardless of the time crunch—he was not done with his gestation over Plato.

DEAN'S "STRANGE LITTLE FRIEND"

Plato had been the focus of much wrangling throughout *Rebel*'s development and preproduction. James Dean was pushing for his friend, personal assistant and—according to some—boyfriend, Jack Simmons to play the role. At the time, Dean was living with Simmons, a handsome young actor who patterned much of his look and behavior after Dean. Simmons met Dean at Googie's, the all-night diner where Dean established a beachhead, and introduced him to his friend Vampira. In 1954, right after Dean appeared in the television play *I'm a Fool* with Natalie Wood, Dean used his influence to get Simmons a job co-starring in "The Dark, Dark Hour," an episode of TV's *G.E. Theater* that also starred Ronald Reagan. Dean and Simmons played juvenile delinquents who hold a man and his wife prisoner in their home. At one point, Dean uses a gun to force the future president of the United States to medically treat Simmons's character, who has been wounded. Dean and Simmons enjoyed working together, although director Don Medford later commented, "I'm afraid we did Jack a terrible disservice by casting him, because after that he thought he was an actor!"

In a *Photoplay* article entitled "Demon Dean," columnist Sidney Skolsky wrote insinuatingly about the dynamics of the relationship between Dean and Simmons: "Jack is always around the house and set. He gets Jimmy coffee or a sandwich or whatever Jimmy wants. Jack also runs interference for Dean when there are people Jimmy doesn't want to see. There are many people trying to contact a nobody who has just become a star. Dean has a loyalty to old friends, but he also enjoys the attention or service they give him."

"I think Jack was in love with him," says actor Jack Larson, who played Jimmy Olsen on the *Superman* TV series. He would often see Dean and Simmons at Googie's. "Neither of them were very physically clean. This was the time of the beatniks. They were very good friends."

The ubiquitous Simmons can be seen in a series of famous pictures taken by Hollywood photographer Phil Stern at Googie's. (Stern met Dean when the actor's motorcycle nearly plowed into his car at the intersection of Crescent Heights and Sunset Boulevard, close to Googie's. "He screeched on his brakes and I screeched on mine and I came within inches of killing James Dean. I wish I did. That would have been great for my career," says the photographer sardonically.) In Stern's series of shots, Simmons is sitting next to Dean, very much his right-hand man, and very much his mirror in matching eyeglasses. Simmons also appears in a series of publicity stills taken on the Warners lot where he cavorts almost effeminately in a striped sailor suit. Outrageous or courageous as Simmons was, he did not fit squarely with the other kids on the set. Beverly Long referred to him as Dean's "strange little friend."

"Jimmy used to bring him to the set," she said. "I remember that they would show up, a lot of times, together. He would bring him and take him home. I don't know *how* he knew him. Nobody ever explained it to me. He was like a little bird, flitting about. Most of us didn't have too much to do with Jack Simmons. We would all kind of look at each other and say, 'Who is this guy?'"

Dean insisted that Simmons be tested for the part of Plato, which caused some consternation among those who cared about the film. "I was very worried when Jack Simmons was supposed to play Plato," says screenwriter Stewart Stern. "Jack was gay, and he was very androgynous, and you would have thought he was like a little girl. He was feminine—and pert and puckish and adoring. I talked to Jimmy about Jack playing Plato, and I said that I thought it would put a different coloration on the relationship that might not be healthy." Although Stern had clearly written a character who, in his near consecration of Jim Stark was, at the very least, sexually ambiguous, he was not prepared to see Plato's repressed characteristics so ostentatiously displayed. "I wanted the role to have homosexual over-tones—but he was too much," said Stern.

Dean liked to stay close to members of his small entourage. Having Simmons by his side throughout the film would make for a certain comfort level. "The loyalty was built in, the adoration was built in, and he was help-ing a friend," says Stern.

Ultimately, Ray agreed to test Simmons. Dean and Simmons would tackle one of Plato and Jim's most difficult and multilayered scenes. It takes place soon after the chickie run, following Buzz's fatal drive off a cliff. Early versions of this scene—which would be revised again and again because of the studio's fears of both its emotional and homoerotic content—feature Jim and Plato laughing together after Buzz's tragic death in a car crash. Their laughter was loaded; it was supposed to serve as an ironic outlet for their shock and despair.

Stewart Stern was on hand that day and remembers, "It was the longest preparation for two actors to come on to a set because Jimmy was trying to get Jack to relax." Dean knew what to do. He was a master at drawing peo-ple out and he loved to use the set as a playground.

The test was shot on the still-standing set of the staircase in front of Stanley Kowalski's New Orleans apartment from *A Streetcar Named Desire*, where several *Rebel* screen tests were done. Simmons did not think he would be able to laugh on cue, so Dean started cutting up. From the top of the staircase, he began shouting, "Stella-a-a-a!" imitating Marlon Brando's most famous line from *Streetcar*. Clearly, he was unable to pass up the chance to play Brando on the very set on which his idol stood. Then Dean ran down the stairs and disappeared with Simmons behind a wall.

"All of a sudden," Stewart Stern said, "these two streams of pee came over the wall. They decided to have a peeing contest, to see who could pee highest. That was Jimmy trying to relax Jack."

Although Stern was dead set against Simmons, he had to admit that the two actors were completely comfortable with each other in front of the camera. But Stern remained unconvinced—as did Ray, whose test of Sim-mons may never have been more than an attempt to indulge Dean's whims. Simmons did not get the role, although he would land the smaller part of gang member Cookie. The issue of Plato remained unresolved, with pre-production nearly over. Billy Gray continued to be the actor most mentioned for the role, although it's questionable whether the likable Gray possessed the complexity and raw nerve needed to bring Plato to life.

Then came Sal Mineo.

THE CASKET MAKER'S SON

The doe-eyed Sal Mineo was only fifteen years old the day he arrived on the Warners lot. He would become the youngest actor cast in a major role in *Rebel*. And like Dean and Ray, he was a walking contradiction—dark and light, sensitive and tough, shy yet determined, naïve yet surprisingly mature.

Raised in Throgs Neck in the Bronx, New York, Mineo had suddenly found himself all alone in Hollywood, far from his large extended Italian-American family, living by himself in a hotel. Mineo had been shipped to Hollywood to do some dubbing on his first movie, *Six Bridges to Cross*, in which he played Tony Curtis's character as a boy. After dubbing, Mineo was supposed to return home to his family on the East Coast but he stayed on to pursue his career.

Mineo was the youngest child in his immediate family, which also included two older brothers, Michael and Victor, and a sister, Sarina. Mineo's father, Salvatore, was a coffin maker who ran his own business, the Universal Casket Company. His mother, Josephine, was the prototypical protective Italian-American matriarch. It was she who started Mineo on his showbiz career, sensing a certain delicacy in her youngest son. She signed him up for dance lessons in order to keep him off the mean streets of the Bronx.

Mineo described his younger self as "always in all kinds of trouble . . . always trying to prove myself—through competition with my older brothers. At age eleven it had reached the point that meant either being sent to a home, because my parents couldn't deal with me, or agreeing on some kind of thing to keep me out of the streets. One of the social workers suggested a school down in Manhattan that takes kids at a very early age and teaches them singing, dancing, acting lessons, and all that, for very little money."

His mother signed him up and, before they knew it, a star—at least a neighborhood star—was born. He had not been taking classes for very long when eleven-year-old Mineo was spotted by the famed theatrical producer Cheryl Crawford, who gave him a walk-on role in Tennessee Williams's Italian-themed comedy-drama *The Rose Tattoo*. Mineo had one line: "The goat is in the yard." He would say it well—and for more than a year.

In August 1952, his *Rose Tattoo* experience led to his landing a part in the original Yul Brynner production of *The King and I*. Eventually, he would take over the important role of the Crown Prince of Siam. Right from the start, producers were drawn to Mineo's exoticness—his dark skin, large limpid eyes and full lips. Mineo appeared as the prince almost nine hundred times.

"At thirteen, my brother was as serious about his career as a veteran trouper," according to his sister Sarina. " 'Gotta be on time for rehearsal,' he'd say. Or, 'What if I have got a cold? The show must go on. I can't miss a performance.' He never did."

Taking the subway from the Bronx to Broadway night after night was an intimidating prospect for a thirteen-year-old. Mineo began carrying a pistol filled with blanks. One evening on the subway, when an older man tried to pick him up, Mineo drew his gun, forced the man to his knees and fired. "Jesus, the sound was so loud it scared the shit out of the guy," said Mineo. "He thought he was dead."

After *The King and I* closed, Mineo would land the occasional TV job. And eventually he got his big movie break, in the Boston-based production of *Six Bridges to Cross*. When additional looping was needed, Mineo was shipped to Hollywood—an adventure the fourteen-year-old took on all by himself. Mineo was supposed to return to the Bronx right after looping was completed. But he landed a second small role in a Universal picture titled *The Private War of Major Benson* starring Charlton Heston. It was during his time on the Universal lot that he heard what all young actors were hearing: the buzz about *Rebel*.

Mineo showed up at the Warners lot answering a casting call for two minor gang-member roles that had yet to be cast. He did not have the aura of a young thug, and stood out from the crowd. "I had this baby face," he said, "that made me look like a wheat-flour dumpling or something."

"I saw this kid in the back who looked like my son except he was prettier," Ray said, an admission with startling Freudian connotations. Throughout the development of the script, Ray thought of his son Tony as "a Plato of sorts." Gavin Lambert says, "When Nick saw Sal Mineo, he just had that click: that's what Plato should look like. Nick was very instinctive in casting. He would look at somebody in the eye and say, I think he can give me what I want. He was good that way."

"I called him over and asked him what he'd done," said Ray. "I asked Sal to take off his jacket and start sizing up those big guys. I called Corey Allen over, and because of the improvisation they did, I decided Sal would be great for the part of Plato."

Ray must have been relieved finally to have found a potential Plato. But he wondered if Dean and Mineo would have the necessary chemistry. So Ray asked Mineo if he would come to his bungalow at the Chateau Marmont that Sunday afternoon and read with Dean.

"I was almost sick, I wanted the part so badly," said Mineo. "I thought I was dressed pretty sharp for those days—pegged pants, skinny tie, jacket— until Jimmy walked in with his tee shirt and blue jeans."

Ray did not like to give his actors too much information beforehand. So when Mineo arrived that Sunday afternoon at the Chateau Marmont, he was in the dark.

"I'd just like to go over a couple of scenes," Ray said, without telling Mineo which role he was supposed to be playing.

They sat on the floor, and Ray asked them to read the same scene he used for Jack Simmons's screen test. No longer able to hide his embarrassment, Mineo spoke up. "I don't know which role you want me to read."

"Which role would you like to read?" asked Ray.

"Definitely you want a Plato," Mineo answered.

Dean and Ray were both surprised to hear Mineo's response, especially since the character of Jim Stark had many more lines.

"Well, I just think it's a better role," Mineo said.

Mineo and Dean began reading the scene but before they got very far, Ray told them to drop the script and begin improvising. "I had no idea what he was talking about," said Mineo, "but I wanted that role very badly. I picked it up from Jimmy, realized that he was doing the scene but making up his own dialogue, and that that's what improvisations are. So we 'improvised' the sequence.

Wood, Dean and Mineo rehearse the gazebo scene during Mineo's screen test on the yet-to-be-struck set of Elia Kazan's film version of *A Streetcar Named Desire*.

(Photofest)

Nicholas Ray and then-wife
Gloria Grahame on the set of
Ray's film *In a Lonely Place*.
(Photofest)

Portrait of Stewart Stern taken by
his friend actor Paul Newman
around the time of *Rebel*.

*(Photograph by Paul Newman;
collection of Stewart Stern)*

he first read-through of the *Rebel* script, photographed by Ray's secretary Fae
Murphy in the director's bungalow at the Chateau Marmont. Clockwise from cen-
r: Natalie Wood, Nick Adams, Mitzi McCall (whose small role as a carhop was
t), Leonard Rosenman (knee only), Frank Mazzola, unidentified player, Dennis
ock (manning the tape recorder), Nicholas Ray, Stewart Stern, Steffi Sidney (feet
ly), James Dean, Dean's friend Jack Simmons (reading the part of Plato) and
n Backus.

ollection of Stewart Stern)

High above L.A. at the Griffith Observatory, Ray joins a pensive Dean (in eyeglasses). Although Dean wore glasses in the film's abandoned black-and-white sequences, Ray convinced his star to remove them once *Rebel* switched to color.

(Photograph by Dennis Stock, Magnum Photos)

Natalie Wood shows off a ring to Ray during an intimate moment on the *Rebel* set.

(Collection of Susan Ray)

Sixteen-year-old Sal Mineo in the suit and tie that mark Plato as an outsider at Dawson High.

(Photofest)

Buzz's gang in the driveway at the Griffith Observatory. Clockwise from center foreground: Corey Allen (with knife), Frank Mazzola, Dennis Hopper, Clifford Morris, Steffi Sidney, Tom Bernard, Nick Adams, Jack Simmons, Jack Grinnage, Beverly Long and Natalie Wood.

(Photograph by Dennis Stock, Magnum Photos)

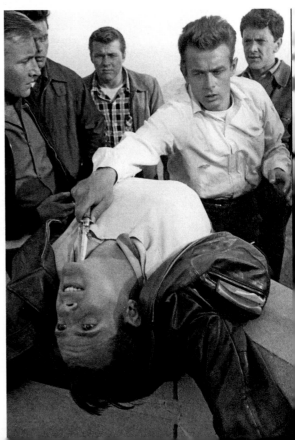

Preparing for the knife fight, Dean holds a switchblade to Corey Allen's throat, closely watched by members of Buzz's gang (Nick Adams, Clifford Morris, Tom Bernard and Jack Simmons).

(Photograph by Dennis Stock, Magnum Photos)

The intricately constructed police station set featuring (left to right) Louise Lane (as a policewoman), Natalie Wood, Sal Mineo, Marietta Canty and James Dean.

(Photofest)

Wood and Dean relax during an exhausting day spent shooting and reshooting at the Griffith Park location.

(Photofest)

"You're tearing me apart!"
Dean erupts for the first time
in the police station sequence.

(Collection of Susan Ray)

Dean slumps in a chair on the set
of Jim Stark's bedroom.

(Collection of Susan Ray)

Ray and Dean collaborate on the blocking of a pivotal scene between Jim Stark and his parents, played by Ann Doran and Jim Backus.

(Collection of Susan Ray)

Dean shocks actor Jim Backus when he throws him across the room during a traumatic confrontation between father and son.

(Photofest)

Judy's father (William Hopper) guiltily recoils when his daughter attempts to kiss him. This scene was so controversial, studio censors showed up on set during the day of the filming.

(Photograph by Dennis Stock, Magnum Photos)

James Dean makes eye contact with Sal Mineo while throwing his arms around both his co-stars at the Getty mansion. Mineo's candelabra is lit by a wire that runs through his coat.

(Photofest)

A world of their own: Mineo, Dean and Wood meld into a surrogate family during this pivotal scene set at the Getty mansion.

(Collection of the authors)

A defiant Sal Mineo faces his attackers (Jack Grinnage and Frank Mazzola) at the bottom of the Getty mansion pool, which was originally built for the film *Sunset Boulevard.*

(Collection of Jack Grinnage)

Downtime during the week at the Getty mansion. Left to right: Nicholas Ray, James Dean, Dennis Stock, Sal Mineo and Natalie Wood.

(Collection of Susan Ray)

Rebel's original opening sequence: the gang confronts a man (played by Harold Bostwick) returning home with Easter gifts. This scene, shot at Wattles Garden Park in Hollywood, was subsequently cut, leaving behind the mystery of the toy monkey.

(Collection of Jack Grinnage)

Dean puts his feet up as Wood places her chin on his forehead as it evocatively appears in their big love scene. The scene climaxes in what is often cited as the former child star's first on-screen kiss, although Wood actually kissed Dean once before, in the TV drama *I'm a Fool*.

(Photograph by Dennis Stock, Magnum Photos)

Dean improvises the opening scene of the film, after working almost twenty-four hours straight. The Huntington Hartford estate looms in the background.
(Photograph by Dennis Stock, Magnum Photos)

The camera crew shoots close-ups of Natalie Wood during a long cold night at the chickie run. The image of Wood signaling the race's start would become iconic, although in the long shot, Wood was replaced by her double, Faye Nuell Mayo.

(Photographs by Dennis Stock, Magnum Photos)

After the chickie run: Wood and Dean pretend to be looking over the side of a cliff, but it's actually a platform erected on the Warners back lot.

(Collection of Susan Ray)

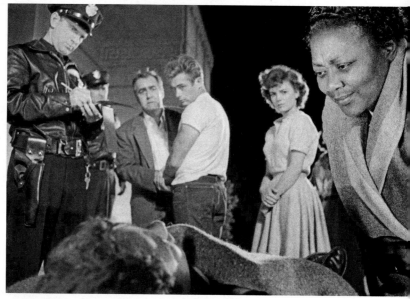

The last sequence in the film prominently features actress Marietta Canty (who played the small but important role of Plato's nanny) mourning over the body of Sal Mineo. Backus, Dean, Wood and two policemen look on.

(Photograph by Dennis Stock, Magnum Photos)

Producer David Weisbart comforts Ray during one of the agonizing final days of shooting at the Griffith Observatory.

(Photograph by Dennis Stock, Magnum Photos)

Nicholas Ray (right) and Dennis Hopper reunite at the Broome County Airport, Binghamton, New York, during the actor's visit to Harpur College in the fall of 1971.

(Photograph by Mark Goldstein)

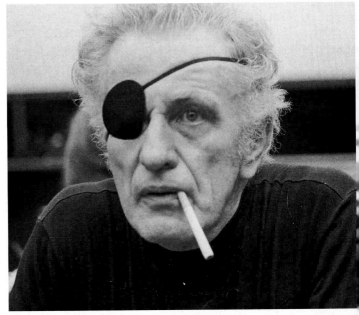

While teaching at Harpur College, a sixty-year-old Ray poses for a portrait taken by one of his students.

(Photograph by Mark Goldstein)

"We went through a scene and nothing happened between us. Nick finally walked over and suggested we sit and talk for a while. When Jimmy found out I was from the Bronx, we started gabbing about New York and then progressed to cars, and before we knew it we were buddies. Then we went back to the script, and this time it went off like clockwork. When we reached a part where we were supposed to laugh hysterically, Jimmy gave out with that special giggle of his, and I couldn't help but follow along. Pretty soon we just couldn't stop laughing."

For Mineo, meeting Dean was a case of adoration at first sight. "I realize now, twenty years later, that from the moment I met Jimmy my whole life took on a completely different meaning," he said in 1976. "It was only years later that I understood I was incredibly in love with him."

Mineo may have been too young to comprehend what he was feeling at the time. But his reactions were clear to Dean and Ray. They had finally found an actor who might give them what they were looking for.

"It became quite clear that Sal Mineo was very attracted to Jimmy Dean," says Gavin Lambert. "And as Nick knew that Dean was bisexual, he told Dean to encourage that." At one point, Ray asked Mineo what he wanted most in the world. And when Sal replied, "My driver's license," Nick Ray said, "Fine. Look at Jimmy as if he is your driver's license." Going even further, Dean asked Ray to "tell Sal Mineo to look at me the way Natalie looks at me."

The mansion sequence—a romantic idyll featuring Jim, Judy and Plato—was chosen to be the ultimate test of Mineo. Once again, on March 16, the *Streetcar Named Desire* set was used. (Given Ray's obsession with Elia Kazan, Ray may have viewed the *Streetcar* set as somehow lucky.) Surprisingly, Mineo was not the only actor tested that day. Although Ray was leaning toward Mineo, he also auditioned seventeen-year-old Richard Beymer, who was suggested by a Warners executive. Beymer, who would later co-star with Natalie Wood in *West Side Story*, remembered Ray as being "gruffly unhelpful because he didn't want me." He called the test a disastrous experience, made even more uncomfortable because the other actors had already begun to become cliquish. "Dean kept changing his moves," Beymer said. "Suddenly I couldn't find him—he'd gone halfway up the staircase. And Natalie gave me no help either. Dennis Hopper was around, although not in the scene, and the four of them were always whispering together, schmoozing, whatever. I was the outsider." It was clear that Ray was seeing Beymer only to satisfy the Warners brass. Mineo's test went much better.

On March 23, just a week before production began, Ray filmed a final rehearsal of the mansion scene, in CinemaScope and black and white. For its body language alone, the scene is incredibly revealing. It begins with a shot of Mineo, who, unlike Jack Simmons, has no trouble laughing. Almost immediately, he captures both the sense of freedom in Plato's laughter and the pain behind it. Dean, who always liked to make a physical on-action entrance, comes racing down the steps. He leaps off the balcony and engages Mineo in some playful wrangling, light wrestling that ends with the two actors arm in arm, staring into each other's faces, nearly mouth to mouth. Mineo moves his arms up and around Dean's neck. Dean draws away but then, at the last minute, he displays the kind of push-and-pull that was a key to his personality—and popularity. He grabs Mineo around the waist and leads him toward the floor. There, Dean continues to deflect Mineo's advances with horseplay but Mineo ends up in close proximity to Dean. Eventually, together with Natalie Wood (who is mostly mute and watchful throughout the scene), all three lie on the floor, bodies overlapping, with Dean of course at the center. Mineo smokes—which he does not do in the movie—and relates a lie about his parents. All along, he is resting with his head against Dean while Wood stakes her own claim by rubbing Dean's forehead and running her finger down the bridge of his nose—a move that is startling for its intimacy. This filmed sequence is the first to capture the psychosexual complexities that would keep *Rebel* emotionally potent for generations. Ray must have been pleased.

Stewart Stern always felt that this dress rehearsal was better than the scene that made it into the film. "The other one is far more staged and much more rigid," he says. But while the scene in *Rebel* is more reticent—perhaps because of mounting concern on the part of the studio about Plato—it's just as powerful for that reticence.

Still, it cannot be denied that this first run-through eloquently demonstrated what Ray had in mind for *Rebel* as a whole and for Plato in particular. Mineo himself was not entirely aware of what he was being asked to register. Later in life, he often discussed his naïveté in this regard, both on-screen and off. "I couldn't understand, couldn't comprehend what was happening. *Something* was happening to me," he said. And certainly the moral climate of the 1950s forced people to hide any gayness that might peek out from the slats in their personality. Nevertheless, Mineo had the courage, determination and ambition to do what was asked of him. And he had a sheer talent for surrendering to reverie. Whether he knew it consciously at the time or not, later he would proudly claim that Plato was "the first gay teenager in films."

CHAPTER SEVEN

Chateau Interlude

Nick Ray loved living at the Chateau Marmont.
And as the first days of filming drew closer, the classic Hollywood hotel increasingly became *Rebel*'s headquarters, its base of inspiration. Ray's loyalty to the Chateau says a lot about his relationship to the studio town. It was the perfect place for him: hip, impermanent (by its very nature as a hotel) and discreet. As Harry Cohn, head of Columbia Pictures, once said: "If you must get into trouble, do it at the Marmont." Discretion was essential to the rule-bending Ray, for while the Chateau was a locus of much creativity, it was also the site of psychological and sexual intrigue. Over the months of preparation for the *Rebel* shoot, the hotel would become a second home for the film's key players, the place where Ray seduced, groomed and subsumed them. "He enthroned himself as guru at the Chateau Marmont," screenwriter Stewart Stern said, "where he seemed to possess the souls of both James Dean and Natalie Wood."

Staying at the Chateau also put Ray in touch with the best of Hollywood: not its grinding daily realities so much as its spectral past. A look at the history of the hotel—before and after Ray—scans like a set of showbiz flashcards. Since it had opened in 1929, the Chateau Marmont became a retreat for countless legends from Errol Flynn to Dorothy Parker, Boris Karloff, Greta Garbo, Orson Welles, William Holden and Paul Newman. Jean Harlow trysted with Clark Gable there—while she was on her honeymoon with another man. Montgomery Clift recuperated there after his disfiguring auto accident. In the 1950s, the hotel became the West Coast headquarters of alumni from New York's Actors Studio. In the 1960s, when the hotel began to take on a funkier cachet, members of Led Zeppelin rode Harleys through the lobby and Jim Morrison injured himself trying to swing from the roof into his window. The history of the hotel also has its darker side. More recently, in 2004, photographer Helmut Newton died while pulling out of the driveway and crashing his Cadillac into a wall across the street. And most notoriously, John Belushi died there of a drug overdose, in a bungalow like the one Ray occupied for so many years.

The Chateau Marmont rises above the relatively flat lines of Sunset Boulevard west of Crescent Heights Boulevard. Spired and turreted, the sprawling structure was originally meant to function as an apartment complex. Architect Arnold Weitzman styled the building after the massive Royal Chateau at Amboise in the Loire Valley, built in the 11th century and home to many French kings as well as the place where Leonardo da Vinci lived out his last years. Appropriately, for a place that would become the temporary residence of so many actors, the hotel was indirectly named after a silent-screen star, Percy Marmont. Marmont had nothing to do with the hotel per se. Its driveway happens to open up on Marmont Lane, a side street off Sunset Boulevard named after the actor. Although little remembered today, Percy Marmont experienced a meteoric rise to stardom in Hollywood during the 1920s, racking up fifty film credits. In 1928, Marmont left Hollywood and returned to his native London, where he appeared in three films by Alfred Hitchcock (*Rich and Strange, Secret Agent, Young and Innocent*). He continued to act throughout his life, and passed away in 1977, but his greatest contribution to the history of Hollywood was the lending of his name to an infamous hotel.

The Chateau has become a more rarefied and luxurious environment in recent years, but things were decidedly different back in the 1950s. "It was more like living in your aunt's run-down mansion than in a sterile, impersonal hotel," according to actress Carroll Baker, who was staying there at the time. On her way to and from the hotel, Baker would see such notables as Clifford Odets, Carol Channing, Gore Vidal—and Nicholas Ray.

Ray lived in Bungalow 2, one of the hotel's small, shingled houses— freestanding units that lie at the feet of the main hotel. As Ray doubtlessly appreciated, Bungalow 2 sits in a commanding position, one that provided him with a unique combination of privacy and access. It is set deep in the shadows of tall pine and eucalyptus trees but lies just inside the gate of the

Chateau, right by the main entrance and driveway. Along its backside runs the Chateau's oval pool ("a navel filled with sweat," as Gore Vidal called it), where Ray could throw pool parties that made it seem as if he commanded the entire space, giving him the cachet of inhabiting a grand Hollywood home without his having to actually own one. The Chateau was situated at a nexus of Hollywood activity: across the street from Googie's and Schwab's drug store. Ray's bungalow sat on a rise, behind a wall, above the noise and furor of Sunset Boulevard, although never out of earshot. It was a great place for a king, and a Hollywood dreamer like Ray.

DANGEROUS LIAISONS

Actress Shelley Winters remembered that Ray's bungalow was "surrounded by night-blooming jasmine"—an appropriately sensual detail, given the fact that Ray's bungalow was the site of many carnal adventures. Among the women who reportedly made nocturnal visits to Ray in Bungalow 2—including some he dated while he was involved with Natalie Wood—were Winters, Jayne Mansfield, Marilyn Monroe and Judy Holliday. As if dating a sixteen-year-old girl wasn't a risky enough career move, he was also involved with Edie Wasserman, the wife of the man who was not only Ray's agent but also one of the greatest power brokers in Hollywood, Lew Wasserman. It was rumored that Wasserman almost left her husband for Ray.

In his memoir, *Palimpsest,* Gore Vidal claims that one of Ray's affairs at the hotel was even more transgressive: "Nick Ray lived in one [bungalow], preparing *Rebel Without a Cause,* and rather openly having an affair with the adolescent Sal Mineo, while the sallow Jimmy Dean skulked in and out, unrecognizable behind thick glasses that distorted myopic eyes." No one has ever corroborated Vidal's assertion of a tryst between fifteen-year-old Mineo and forty-three-year-old Ray, and given Mineo's later claims of being deeply in the closet at this point, an affair between them seems unlikely. Gavin Lambert doubts that Vidal is correct. "I think Gore made it up, quite frankly," he says. "Nick was very much the father figure. He liked playing the father both to Dean and to Sal." Then again, Ray was not above occasionally crossing the line between patriarch and lover. The porous boundaries he established led to many wild and unsubstantiated rumors.

Certainly, Ray continued to rendezvous surreptitiously with his next youngest star, Natalie Wood. Throughout the making of *Rebel,* Wood and Ray used the Chateau as their meeting place, which they most often occupied in the afternoons. It was important for them to hide their affair. Certainly, the studio would not have approved of Ray's illegal liaison with an underage star. Meanwhile, Ray and Wood did not want to cause any unnecessary tensions on the set—although that would prove impossible to avoid. Even during their most discreet days, Wood and Ray could occasionally be reckless. Adele Essman, then wife of *Rebel* composer Leonard Rosenman, recalled coming upon Wood and Ray taking a shower together in a poolside cabana at the Chateau. Wood's friend Mary Ann Brooks remembered how Wood and Ray would disappear into Bungalow 2's upstairs bedroom from time to time. "Natalie was so enthralled with him because he was like a god to all these kids. When he would pay so much attention to her, she interpreted it as more than work. 'See. He really cares about me.' And I'd sit back and say, 'Yeah right, honey. You and everyone else.' I didn't buy all that crap."

During this period, Ray and Wood were also engaged in a different kind of collaboration: the *Vertigo*-like transformation of the young actress. This would not be the first time Ray would attempt the makeover of an actress with whom he both worked and slept. Wood's friend Jackie Perry remembered Ray's stories about his ex-wife Gloria Grahame. "In order to give her a sexy look, he padded her lip with cotton," she recalls. "It was like he created her." In fact, it was in Grahame's first film with Ray, *A Woman's Secret,* that the press began to notice Grahame's "incredible repertoire of mouths," as *Screen Facts* magazine put it. The same magazine also went on to note how Grahame "enlarged her upper lip to mammoth proportions and also began an endless assortment of hair styles." Now Ray concocted a similar makeover plan for Wood.

Right up to the first days of shooting, the studio continued to doubt that Wood could pull off the part of Judy. Ray needed help in convincing Warner Brothers once and for all. He summoned costume designer Moss Mabry, a handsome, fast-rising Florida native who had only been at the studio for two years, to the Chateau Marmont and enlisted his covert aid in the transformation of Natalie Wood.

Ray told Mabry that he needed to make Wood look a little older and more voluptuous. Mabry could see the problem. The actress, Mabry says, was "built like a choirboy." Working with his team, Mabry decided to re-sculpt her body from top to bottom. He padded her hips and rear end—changes that would not sit well with Wood's demanding mother. But most decisively—and significantly, as far as the history of Hollywood undergarments is concerned—he developed a special push-up bra that would lend her cleavage. "To this day it's still known as the Natalie Wood bra," says Mabry, who refuses to divulge the secret of its design, although he would note that "it was comfortable." To add to the effect of newfound sophistication, Wood's makeup was toned down, and her hair was altered: darkened and cut below her ears in waves. Mabry said that Wood and Ray were ecstatic about what he had done. "Ray just hugged me and said, 'Oh my gosh, this is a miracle.'"

A new look was not all that Wood required. According to Jackie Perry, Ray hired a walking coach "so she could learn how to swing her hips . . . It was like *Pygmalion.* He was trying to re-create her." There was the persistent problem of Wood's voice, which could run thin and high, even after she had matured. In a memo on March 31, 1955—after production on *Rebel* had already begun—producer David Weisbart wrote to Jack Warner's right-hand man Steve Trilling about her voice, stating it was Warner himself who suggested sending Wood to a vocal coach after looking at some of her tests in the company of Ray. Ray recommended Nina Moise, a vocal coach suggested to him by actor Robert Ryan, with whom Ray had worked on *On Dangerous Ground.* Moise had an intriguing résumé. She had been a director, mounting productions of the early plays of her friend Eugene O'Neill. And she had also been a vocal coach to seductive Hollywood bombshell Rita Hayworth. Moise would be hired to handle Wood's intonation and modulation, at the rate of fifteen dollars an hour.

In the end, Ray managed to convince Jack Warner that Wood was right for the part—but there was still the matter of her contract. The deal was clinched when the frugal studio chieftain realized he could get her cheaply. According to Wood, "When they offered a certain amount of money, my agent said, 'Natalie won't do it for that.' He brought me into the room and asked me if I'd be willing to work for so little money. I wanted the part so badly I blurted out, 'I'll do it for nothing.' Jack Warner said, 'In that case, she's under a seven-year contract deal.'" Although Wood was happy to get the part at the time, she would later regret the control the studio had over her post-*Rebel* career.

SURROGATE SON

Ray did not exhaust his star-making energies on Wood. Throughout the winter and spring of 1955, Dean could also be found lounging around Bungalow 2. Ray continued to hold Dean close, no matter how troublesome and demanding he became. Occasionally, Ray would use the Chateau to stage a royal audience of sorts. When Andrew Solt, screenwriter of Ray's *In a Lonely Place*, was summoned to the Chateau specifically to meet Dean, he remembered Ray as glowing with pride. "There sat in the corner a little boy, emaciated, the whole thing could have been 125 pounds, a little effeminate, dark, the only thing that made him a little interesting was that he had a cat on his shoulder. Then Nick came out, positive and beaming, and he said, 'Bundy, hi, I want you to meet my new star, Jimmy Dean.' We talked, I forget what about, and he said, 'What do you think of him?' I couldn't lie. I said, 'This, a star?' He said, 'He'll be the biggest star.' I said, 'Well, I wish you lots of luck,' but I couldn't see it. And of course he saw exactly what this boy would look and act like on the screen."

With his horn-rimmed glasses, tousled hair and a cigarette dangling from his lips, Dean was a constant presence at the Chateau. He could often be found at Ray's Sunday parties, beating the bongos. Roger Donoghue, a young boxer and all-purpose assistant to Ray, would swim with Dean in the Chateau pool, when he wasn't giving him fighting lessons. "I was teaching him to box—left jab, hook off a jab, right upper cut, and all the combinations," said Donoghue. The Chateau would also become the site of some reckless behavior on Dean's part, all of which was conspicuously indulged by Ray.

Shelley Winters remembered heading down Sunset Boulevard to the Chateau one night in a car with Marilyn Monroe. Dean came roaring down the street on his motorcycle and began circling them, "playing chicken with us" according to Winters. By the time they all pulled into the Chateau's underground garage, Winters was livid. Monroe was paralyzed with fear. But Dean was sanguine. "He stood there grinning like a little boy who had been playing a practical joke. His face was so childlike," Winters said. They all proceeded to settle in at Ray's bungalow, where Dean continued to act out. "Jimmy was sardonic and made fun of everything, especially things about Hollywood that pained or embarrassed him," said Winters. After a few piña coladas, mixed by Ray, Winters told Ray how enraged she was at Dean. But Dean was unfazed, switching on the TV to watch his pal Vampira, although he turned the sound down as Winters continued to complain about him. Winters sensed that Ray and Dean had developed a father-and-son-like relationship and, in effect, she was entreating Ray to act like Dean's parent. But Ray was not about to reprimand his wayward son. Dean was prince of this particular house.

If part of Ray's intentions for *Rebel* had been to create a common ground between himself and his estranged son Tony, Tony seemed to have been rapidly superseded by Dean, at least in terms of time and energy. During this period, Tony was occasionally seen around the bungalow but seldom as more than a hovering presence. "One day we were going to lunch and Tony answered the door," remembers Jackie Perry. "Nick came to the door and said, 'This is my son Tony' and Tony was just leaving and appeared to be a little upset—and that was it. I think whenever Tony saw him it was financial. I don't think there was much love between them." Stewart Stern also remembered seeing Tony at Ray's parties during this period: "I remember Tony as being very, very quiet, very self-effacing, watchful, happy if you caught his eye and smiling. Nick might say, 'Get so-and-so a drink.' But I never saw anything that was not fatherly—or anything that was especially fatherly."

Tony could not hope to compete with Dean, who was doing more than merely hanging out at the Chateau. Following the principles of Ray, leisure evolved into work, and vice versa. Throughout their time together at the Chateau, Dean and Ray were intensely involved in the development of *Rebel*. Ray continued to allow his actor a level of input on the script that was unprecedented during the days of studio contracts. Stretching all the way back to January 1955, when Irving Shulman was still toiling on the screenplay, Dean and Ray were continually reworking pages. They would work late nights together at the Chateau, feeling out the dialogue, blocking out scenes and improvising. Creatively, they fed on each other. And often it was their experimentation that brought the scenes to life.

The most important of these improvisatory sessions occurred in reaction to what Stern had concocted for a critical sequence that takes place at the movie's midpoint. It was the scene in which Dean's character, Jim Stark, returns to his parents' home after the tragedy of the chickie run. As written by Stern, the scene took place in his mother's bedroom. But Ray did not like what he was reading at all. "It was beginning to get on my nerves," said Ray in a 1977 interview. "It was too claustrophobic . . . So I said to Jimmy, 'Come on over to the house tonight, will you? I want to try something. I want to do something about that scene.' And this we would often do . . . We'd do a lot of work at the house and away from the studio." Together that night, Dean and Ray would devise the famous milk bottle sequence.

"I said, 'Jim, here are the conditions: You come to your home and you have one action. You want to get upstairs without being seen, without being heard, without a confrontation. But yet you've got to spill your guts out to someone. You have to talk to somebody. Now I'm going to play your father. And I want you to go out and come through the back door as if you've just come from the garage. And I'm going to be sitting here as your father.

"I went over to the TV set and turned it on to a dead channel so it would have more of the feeling of being late at night. And I sleep. And I kept one eye open to catch what he's doing. And Jimmy comes in, comes past me . . . he tiptoes past me, he can't quite decide whether to go up, keep on going, and he goes up to the couch and then I see the milk bottle cooling his head."

Dean's improvisation took Ray by surprise. The actor had gone over to the refrigerator in Ray's kitchen, gulped down some milk straight out of the bottle, then rubbed the bottle on his forehead. It was a startling yet entirely natural move. It possessed an electric charge that carried directly into the film, where it would read as completely true to the sensibility of the milk-fed American teen, caught between maturity and childhood. "He was always drinking milk because he needed nourishment," says Stern. "He needed a mother." (Ray may also have been experiencing the shock of recognition. According to Susan Ray, the milk bottle scene was an example of Dean aping Ray's behavior.)

That was not the only memorable idea Ray and Dean would hatch together that evening. Ray and Dean would also conceive a 180-degree turn of the camera—a complete movement from upside down to right side up—that would become the boldest camera move in *Rebel*.

Dean and Ray continued these sessions throughout preproduction on *Rebel*. Occasionally, Natalie Wood, Sal Mineo and even composer Leonard Rosenman would join them. "Nick and Stewart Stern would tell us what they had planned for a scene and then we'd react," said Rosenman. "Natalie might say, 'Well, I don't think I should say that.' Or someone would say, 'Why can't Jimmy just go into the precinct . . .' It was a pretty free-flowing discussion. We wrote and rejected and retained. But what really happened was, we got to know each other as people and recognized ourselves as a pretty good team."

Ray would record the actors' efforts on tape, and then play it back for them. "That was the first time I'd been exposed to that kind of work," said Wood, "because I had worked for many years as a child, and most directors never asked me my opinion, my thoughts. The less they heard from me, the better. And suddenly Nick Ray began saying, 'What do you think?' He would encourage me, and get annoyed if I didn't bring in lots of notes or ideas, or even changes of dialogue, or I didn't challenge certain scenes."

Wood said that when they rehearsed at the Chateau, the result was pretty much the same as if they were rehearsing on the set. In fact, so many rehearsals were done there, Ray had his bungalow copied for the set of the Starks' living room in *Rebel*. "I called the art director in, and the set that we used in *Rebel* was designed on the basis of the living room where we did the improvisation," said the director. Ray had done this type of thing before, copying the design of his living quarters into 1950's *In a Lonely Place*. It was one of the ways he gratified his urge toward autobiography—and it underscored another aspect of his particular genius. As critic David Thomson would write, "Few other directors had a sense of the effect of locations and interiors on people's lives . . . his characters contract or expand according to the emotional tone of the place in which they find themselves."

With the script almost completely locked in—or as locked in as Ray would allow—the improv sessions evolved into readings. Eventually, Ray staged an official read-through of the entire script, which was captured in a series of iconic photographs by Ray's secretary, Fae Murphy. The photographs show most of the cast sitting in a circle in Ray's living room at the Chateau.

Sal Mineo was not there since he had not yet been cast, so Jack Simmons read the part of Plato, while Gene Evans played the kindly policeman Ray Framek, although he would later be replaced by Edward Platt. Prominent in the pictures is Ray's "big Mad Man Muntz black-and-white TV set," as Shelley Winters described it, and on top of the set, a mysterious box that intrigued the observant Winters. "What I didn't know," she wrote in her autobiography, "was that the long, thick wire leading from the TV to the dial changer was rigged with a microphone leading to this mysterious box, which was one of those newfangled tape recorders." In Murphy's photographs, Ray's omnipresent reel-to-reel recorder has pride of place, sitting on the floor at his right foot. Young photographer Dennis Stock, who had been hired by Ray as *Rebel*'s dialogue coach, manned the tape recorder, although it may not have picked up much that was useful. Nearly everyone in the cast, under the thrall of Dean's mumbling approach and the internalizing influence of the Method, was inaudible. "It all sounded pretty monotone to me," says Mitzi McCall, who read the part of a carhop that was then given to Jayne Mansfield, before being completely cut from the film.

Mazzola remembers that during the reading the tensions between Ray and Dennis Hopper were already starting to simmer. Hopper was reading the part of Crunch, the most important gang member after Buzz. It was a role Mazzola wanted. "I thought, there's no chance I'm going to get Crunch," says Mazzola. "He was very kind of out there and I was very laid-back. Then Nick said to me 'I want you to do Crunch' and after I read it he turned to Dennis and said, 'Now I want you to read Crunch the way Frank read Crunch.'"

The reading was an important event for the *Rebel* crew. It represented the first real coming together of cast, director and script. Despite any technical problems or subterranean tensions, it was a session that most of the *Rebel* survivors recall warmly, as a special night. They also recall the night's most dramatic event: the arrival of actress Marsha Hunt.

Just before the reading started, with everyone assembled and ready to begin, Marsha Hunt, who had been cast as James Dean's mother, came through the door of Bungalow 2. Hunt was perhaps the best known of the actors who had been hired. Throughout the 1940s, she achieved a level of stardom as an MGM contract player. She was never a huge star but often received special praise for her intelligent performances in films such as *Pride and Prejudice, The Human Comedy* and *Smash-Up: The Story of a Woman.* "She walked in and I was starstruck," says Corey Allen. But when the veteran actress greeted the cast, she made a comment that would startle them. "Hello, everybody," she said. "I'm what's left of Marsha Hunt."

Many of the *Rebel* survivors remember the instant chill that spread through the room. Allen interpreted Hunt's attitude as a put-down of *Rebel,* which must have been a shock given the level of eager anticipation the rest of the cast were experiencing. "She meant her career was over," said Allen. "And she was glad to get this role. She was doing the best she could." But Hunt herself denies this, saying it would have been very unprofessional to cast aspersions on the project at hand. Beverly Long may have come closer to the truth. "Her whole attitude was like she had been through the mill," Long says. "It must have been the blacklist. It had to be."

Marsha Hunt was only one of many performers whose careers would be severely damaged—if not utterly destroyed—by the House Un-American Activities Committee (HUAC), which was created in 1938 to investigate alleged subversive activities throughout the United States. "My experience was so unusual," said Hunt. "I was never subpoenaed, I was never named or listed or held up to any kind of question mark to the general public. I had no interest in communism." However, she was involved in *Hollywood Fights Back,* a 1947 radio show co-written by her husband, screenwriter Robert Presnell Jr., which protested HUAC and featured many of the biggest stars in Hollywood. And in 1950, her name appeared in *Red Channels,* an infamously well-circulated pamphlet that printed the names of possible communist sympathizers in the industry. The periodical went so far as to list all the leftist petitions she had supposedly signed ("Some I'd never heard about," said Hunt). After the appearance of *Red Channels,* Hunt's phone stopped ringing.

When Marsha Hunt arrived at Bungalow 2, she had not appeared in a film since 1952. And her proposed part in *Rebel* would not change that fact. She would never get to play the role of Jim Stark's mother. Hunt would be replaced by actress Ann Doran.

The official reason given was a scheduling conflict that could not be resolved. Hunt had promised to appear in the play *Anniversary Waltz* at

L.A.'s Carthay Circle Theater. But Warner Brothers was aware of Hunt's previous commitment, and at least at first, everyone felt the timing could be worked out. "It was a fragmentary role," said Hunt of her part in *Rebel.* "The mother only worked now and then, and was not that much in the film. So it was felt that it could be managed if everyone was cooperative about scheduling. Warners promised to release me in time." But as the film's actual start date grew nearer, the studio's attitude mysteriously began to change. "I do remember," said Hunt, "being surprised that all that cooperation that had been promised began to tighten. I thought that it was just that they were faced with the reality of scheduling and how much it would cost to film on a given set on a given day, things that didn't concern me but that would certainly affect what they were able to do." But all these years later, Hunt still cannot deny that the blacklist may have played a role.

In hiring or, at the very least, approving Hunt for the role of Jim Stark's mother, Ray may have been trying to lend the actress a helping hand. His sympathies—and his politics—were certainly similar to those who had been blacklisted, graylisted or classified as guilty bystanders. Ray was one of the signers of an advertisement supporting *Hollywood Fights Back,* which operated out of his agent Lew Wasserman's offices, and Ray maintained relationships with many friends who were blacklisted. At the same time, Ray also remained friendly with those who had "named names" in front of the committee, such as playwright Clifford Odets, whom Ray initially wanted to write the *Rebel* screenplay; Budd Schulberg, who later produced and wrote the screenplay for Ray's film *Wind Across the Everglades;* and director Elia Kazan. "He could be friends with everybody," said actor Perry Bruskin, who worked with Ray in the Theatre of Action. "He could be friends with his old radical friends, because he hadn't done anything to hurt them. He could be friends with the Howard Hugheses and . . . anybody!" While Elia Kazan's cooperation with the committee shadowed him throughout his life—severely damaging his relationship with previously loyal friends such as Marlon Brando—Ray never turned his back on his mentor. According to Ray's old New York friend actor Norman Lloyd, "Nick's feeling was, 'I don't want to know about those other things. This man gave me my career. I have a life because of Kazan. Therefore I remain loyal no matter what he did.'"

Ray always seemed to hover above the fray when it came to the blacklist—which, given his history and affiliations, seems miraculous. It's no surprise that his luck has always been a subject of conjecture. "There are secrets still out there. About who did what," says Lloyd, although he is quick to add, "Nick would have disagreed with giving names."

THE FILE ON RAY

Having worked with so many left-leaning groups, beginning with the Theatre of Action in the 1930s, and possessing a well-known sympathy for their cause, Ray had plenty of reasons to worry about his career with the rise of HUAC. He had to be careful. Ray came to the attention of the FBI as early as 1942 when a box he left at a friend's apartment was reported to the agency as containing communist literature. Agents interviewed neighbors, landlords and past employers, looked at his bank records and even confiscated an innocuous postcard written to his first wife, Jean Evans.

Among the bits of incendiary innuendo investigators collected was the slyly racist insinuation that "subject has had numerous, well dressed colored visitors who come with bundles of leaflets" and a statement by an unidentified informant that Ray "spends most of the night in his room typewriting" what the informant "believed to be Communist propaganda." Although the investigation did not turn up any specific evidence that Ray was a subversive, he was nevertheless given a "dangerousness classification" of B-2, and a card was placed on file with his name, address and the notation "Communist," which was personally signed off on by J. Edgar Hoover. Ray was one of a number of American citizens, including journalists and even members of Congress, placed on this "custodial detention list," a secret file of potential subversives who could be rounded up in times of national emergency.

The FBI kept an especially close watch on Ray's behavior during his time as a contract director for RKO. "There were certain traps that every studio had," Ray pointed out, "and the one at RKO was a film called *I Married a Communist*. It was so ludicrous—like a 1917 Hearst editorial, with the bomb-throwing Communist—I thought we might make a comedy out of it. I got calls from my friends on the left: 'Nick, what the hell are you doing? Are you out of your mind?' I'd say, 'Shut up!' and hang up the phone."

Eventually, Ray managed to charm his way out of making *I Married a Communist* in a face-to-face meeting with Howard Hughes, then chief of RKO. He flattered Hughes, discussing the millionaire's career as an aviator. Then Ray equated the film with an airplane that simply won't fly, using a metaphor he felt Hughes would understand. According to Ray, Hughes was so impressed with his spunk and aero-metaphors, he released the director from the project and, more importantly, said Ray, "A year later he asked me to run the studio for him."

Ray would never run RKO Pictures. It's highly probable that Hughes never suggested he should. The entire story may be an example of Ray's mythmaking panache. But it is true that Hughes came to depend on Ray as an all-around fix-it man at RKO. He reshot parts of several troubled films such as *The Racket* (1951) and *Macao* (1952). He also made contributions to *Roseanna McCoy* (1949) and *Androcles and the Lion* (1953), shooting a racy "Vestal Virgin Bath" sequence that was subsequently cut from the film.

Perhaps it was because of Ray's work for RKO that Hughes decided to protect him from the blacklist. Although no documents have been uncovered to prove Hughes helped him, Ray publicly claimed it was a fact. "It was in his stable of anecdotes," according to Susan Ray. It is the story told by most of his old friends, including Gavin Lambert. "Hughes certainly had the power to say, 'Lay off Nick Ray,'" Lambert says, emphasizing "the sinister link in this country between big business and the government."

During his lifetime, Ray also offered another reason why he escaped from the claws of HUAC, claiming the Office of Strategic Services, the forerunner of the CIA, had already "thoroughly investigated" him when he worked for the Office of War Information during World War II. "They knew every goddamned thing about me," Ray claimed, including details of his sex life. "On the night of so and so, such and such a young lady was seen to enter your apartment at 8:30 at night, and not leave until eight the next morning. What do you have to say to that?" Ray said they asked him. "Finally, I said, 'Gentlemen, when I volunteered to serve the United States in this war, I was not asked to take a vow of celibacy.'"

Some doubted Ray's explanations for why HUAC left him alone. Ray's first wife, Jean Evans, suggested that Ray might have arranged to meet the committee in a closed session, where he could speak in private. "I think that's what Nick did," she told Ray biographer Bernard Eisenschitz. But it's unlikely that Ray met in secret with the committee. According to Bill Davis, researcher at the Center for Legislative Archives, there is no record of Nicholas Ray's testifying either in executive or open session before the House Un-American Activities Committee or its predecessor, the Dies Committee. Davis says the HUAC files contain only three references to Ray, one citing him as the director of the WPA Theater Project's 1936 production of *The Living Newspaper* and two references to him as one of the signers of a 1947 statement by the Committee for the First Amendment attacking HUAC.

Still, the influence of HUAC persisted in Ray's life. He would sound a coded protest in the two Westerns about mob hysteria he directed immediately before *Rebel:* the baroque and melodramatic *Johnny Guitar* and the novelistic Western *Run for Cover.* The experience of the blacklist would certainly contribute to Ray's often expressed feeling that his was a generation of "betrayers." "I don't particularly care for my generation," he would say. "I like the promise, I like the hope [of youth]."

Undoubtedly, the crisis in Hollywood played a major role in instigating Ray's desire for more freedom from studio dominance. It stirred up his already distrustful nature, and led to his sudden insistence on freelancing in 1953 just after Hughes left RKO. The HUAC period left a cloud over Hollywood, and it seemed to have left Ray eternally looking for escape routes in an increasingly hostile environment. He developed a deeper-than-ever need for independence, a trait for which his rented bungalow at the Chateau Marmont was a persistent symbol. Ray was beginning to envision a future for himself as an autonomous filmmaker, and he knew any independent production company he might create needed a powerful actor at its center—which is why, as far as *Rebel Without a Cause* was concerned, the stakes could not be higher.

CHAPTER EIGHT

The Red Jacket

Rebel's official starting date finally arrived— Friday, March 25, 1955. Stewart Stern handed in his final draft of the script, and Nicholas Ray quietly began shooting the film's initial footage. None of the principal cast was actually involved that Friday, as Ray directed a few routine preproduction shots of students walking in and out of Santa Monica High School. By that first day, it had begun to look as if *Rebel* had a real chance for success. Kazan's *East of Eden* had opened in Los Angeles a week earlier and garnered great reviews for Dean, proving once and for all that he was the real thing. Meanwhile, tremendous buzz surrounded MGM's *Blackboard Jungle*—another foray into the world of juvenile delinquency— which coincidentally opened on March 25, paving the way for *Rebel*. As far as the history of Hollywood demographics is concerned, *Blackboard Jungle* was the film that declared the shift toward youth. It began with a burst of rock and roll—Bill Haley and His Comets' "Rock Around the Clock"— which reportedly caused riots in movie theaters across the country as teens slashed their seats and danced in the aisles. But although the film captured some of the violent, edgy energy of the new teen, the story was told from the point of view of adults, and *Blackboard Jungle* continued to portray adolescent rebellion as little more than a social problem. Nicholas Ray knew he was about to go much further. As a result, his inaugural day of shooting should have been deeply satisfying, brimming with excitement and possibility. But Ray had a problem, a monumental problem: his star had vanished.

DEAN'S DISAPPEARING ACT

At first, there was no cause for hysteria. Dean was not slated to appear on set until five days later. Certainly, he had exhibited capricious, even childish, behavior before—without reneging on his commitments in any significant way. Just forty-eight hours earlier, Dean took part in a wardrobe test and gave no sign that anything was wrong. But it was disconcerting that neither his agent nor his friends knew where he had gone. And as his disappearance dragged on through the weekend, panic set in. "Warners was frantic," said screenwriter Stewart Stern. The studio contemplated suspending Dean and suing him for breach of contract.

Dean's vanishing act had begun innocently enough, with a relatively minor infraction. He had entered his first major auto race in Palm Springs, even though the studio made it clear that he was forbidden from racing and potentially endangering its investment in him. Driving the Porsche Speedster he had just bought with his earnings from *East of Eden*, Dean placed first in the Palm Springs Road Race competition for novices, taking the lead early and never giving it up by gunning his car to its maximum speed of 100 miles per hour. The following day, he placed second in the finals (after being bumped up from third on a technicality). It was an amazing feat for a beginning driver. He won the respect of the other drivers, who had dismissed him as a Hollywood poseur out for publicity. But Dean did not head back to Hollywood after his success. Instead, he flew home to New York, where he silently hunkered down while the studio scrambled.

A few days after Dean's disappearance, at four o'clock in the morning, Stewart Stern's telephone rang. When he answered it, he heard a loud "mooooo" coming from the other end. Immediately, Stern knew who it was; he and Dean had played this mooing game when they first met. So Stern mooed in return. Then Dean blurted out, "I'm not sure I should do this movie, because I'm not sure I can trust Nick."

According to Stern, Dean's rave reviews in *East of Eden* had made him doubt whether he had made the right career choice in choosing the black-and-white *Rebel Without a Cause* for his next project and Ray as his next director. In looking back on *East of Eden*, Dean knew he had been with a master. Even though their relationship had been incredibly contentious,

Dean felt confident turning himself over to Kazan. Now, Dean was closer to Ray than he had ever been to Kazan. They had become partners in the *Rebel* project. But perhaps for that very reason, Dean's confidence in Ray's ability to take control was shaken.

"I could understand Jimmy's doubts, because I'd had my own problems with Nick," said Stern, who was already beginning to mistrust Ray for the way he would praise a scene Stern had written and then change his mind without explanation. But at the time, Stern kept his misgivings to himself. He acted diplomatically.

"Do you want me to come back and do this movie?" Dean asked Stern.

"I can't tell you that," said Stern. "If you're experiencing this kind of mistrust, I can't reassure you. But I know that Nick adores you and that he's passionate about this movie—partially because he feels so guilty about what he's going through with his own son right now.

"I can't say I don't want you to come back," continued Stern, who also had much to lose if the *Rebel* project collapsed. "But I'm not going to tell you to because the most important thing is your comfort with the director."

"If I come back, it'll be because of you," Dean finally told him. But Stern refused to take that responsibility.

"If you did it and were miserable in it or if the picture turned out badly, then it would be on my head."

"Well, I'm not coming back," Dean answered. "Talk to ya."

And he hung up.

That was the last reported contact anyone in Hollywood had with Dean in New York. Then suddenly, a couple of days later, Dean showed up in Stern's office, acting as if nothing was wrong, as if he had never disappeared. He did not even say hello to Stern. Instead, he simply said, "I love the way your office is decorated." Staring at a blank wall, he pretended to be admiring a Picasso painting. "I think he was looking at Picasso's *Guernica*," remembered Stern. "He asked me if it was real or a reproduction, and I said, 'Oh, God, it's real of course!' And he said, 'Well, you writers . . . and just because you're a nephew of Arthur Loew . . .' But he never talked about where he'd been or why he'd come back. I don't know what scared him, but I know he was scared."

Dean would pull a similar stunt on his next film, *Giant*, fleeing for an entire day to protest his treatment at the hands of director George Stevens.

It's possible that his sudden retreats were a bid for power, an attempt to underscore the fact that these films could not be made without him. Ray may have been thinking that he and Dean were moving toward some kind of long-term professional partnership, but Dean's loyalty and cooperation would prove much harder to harness than Ray expected.

THE GRIFFITH OBSERVATORY

Despite his lack of faith, Dean seemed to be in good spirits the night before *Rebel* was scheduled to start principal shooting. Hanging out at Arthur Loew Jr.'s house, he began sparring with Stern. "It was open-handed, just wrestling around the living room," remembers Stern. "All of a sudden I punched and smashed his glasses." Horrified, Stern told Dean not to open his eyes while he plucked splinters of glass from his eyelashes. Luckily, Dean was unhurt. But he had difficulty seeing without his glasses. They had to call the studio to get an emergency prescription so that he could study his lines for the next day. Nearly blinding the star had ensured his "banishment for life," Stern joked, but in reality he had already made a crucial decision. Stern decided to return to New York and not spend any time on the set. "I knew it would be disaster for me to be on the set because I would be bound to take sides in one situation or another, and I knew that would be destructive to the picture," said Stern. Ray promised to call Stern in New York if he decided to change anything in the script. It was a promise that Ray would break many times over.

With new glasses, Dean actually showed up as scheduled for his call on the morning of March 30, 1955, the first of thirty-six planned days of black-and-white shooting. The setting was Los Angeles's Griffith Observatory. There, the cast of kids would film some of the movie's most important establishing scenes, including the first major confrontation between Jim Stark and Buzz Gunderson, which would result in an unexpectedly bloody knife fight.

Dean had worked at the observatory before, filming a commercial for Pepsi in 1950 with future *Rebel* cast members Beverly Long and Nick Adams. Griffith Observatory was a popular movie location. It had served as Jor-El's Krypton castle in the *Superman* television pilot and the palace of

Emperor Ming the Merciless in the *Flash Gordon* movie serials. But it will always be best remembered for its appearance in *Rebel Without a Cause.* The scenes that Nicholas Ray filmed there would become so legendary that a bronze bust of Dean, designed by Kenneth Kendall, was placed on the observatory's lawn.

Built in 1935, the white concrete art deco temple to science and technology topped by three copper domes was designed by architects John C. Austin (who was also one of the architects of Los Angeles City Hall) and Frederick M. Ashley. Located on the south slope of Mount Hollywood with a view of the Los Angeles basin, the observatory was named after wealthy mining tycoon Colonel Griffith J. Griffith, who donated the land that became Griffith Park. Infamously, Griffith once served time in jail for shooting his wife in an alcoholic haze, convinced that she was conspiring with the pope to murder him, though luckily she managed to jump out a window after he shot her, and survived. The observatory was one of the projects Griffith initiated to rehabilitate his reputation.

From the first, Dean dominated the observatory set. His status—and his ego—seemed to be growing by the day. Dean-mania was in its initial stages. Suddenly the press had an unstoppable interest in him, although he hated dealing with them. And fascinated reviews of his work in *East of Eden* kept pouring in. In 1955, critic Pauline Kael would describe Dean as the embodiment of "the young boy as beautiful, disturbed animal, so full of love he's defenseless. Maybe his father doesn't love him but the camera does, and we're supposed to; we're thrust into upsetting angles, caught in infatuated close-ups, and prodded, 'Look at all that beautiful desperation.' The film is overpowering." In the wake of such lavish praise, Dean was justifiably reeling, and there were signs that success was going to his head. "After *East of Eden,* he sometimes used his success to be cruel," Ray would say, although some might view Dean's behavior as merely bratty or self-involved.

On set, Dean would indulge in all sorts of mind games with his fellow actors. His behavior was so erratic, in fact, that no one was ever sure where he or she stood in his estimation. "In the mornings you never knew whether he was going to speak to you," said cast member Beverly Long. "That made you extremely wary, because one morning you would say, 'Good morning, Jim,' and he would look through you as though you didn't exist. On another morning you would not say hello, and he would say, 'Well, good morning,' like his feelings were hurt, and then he would give out with that mischievous grin and giggle. You never could win."

Dean would sometimes race his Porsche around the streets of Griffith Park during breaks. At one time or another, he offered rides to almost all the cast members, who were often wary of taking him up on his offer. In one of many foreshadowing tales that loom in friends' memories of Dean, Beverly Long recalls telling him, "I'm not going to ride with you Jimmy. You drive too fast." Dean replied dramatically, "I have to. I'm not going to be around very long."

Dean was also prone to raunchy schoolboy humor. Once while waiting for the crew to set up for the scene where Buzz slits a tire on Jim Stark's car, Dean handed Beverly Long the tire iron he was carrying. "Ever feel anything so hard in your life?" he asked lasciviously. Long immediately dropped the tire iron and everyone started laughing. "I was mortified," says Long.

Another time on the Griffith Observatory set, he came up to her with a manila envelope and said, "Do you want to see some pictures?" Long thought he was going to show her "dirty pictures," but they turned out to be photographs of him racing his car in Palm Springs.

While waiting endlessly for camera setups, Dean and the always assertive Nick Adams—who said he was one of Dean's best friends although many of the gang members deny his claim—would sometimes entertain the cast with their impressions of Elia Kazan and Marlon Brando. Dean would play Kazan, who was known as "Gadg," and Adams would be Brando, whose nickname was "Bud."

Poking fun at "the Method," Dean would say, "Down on your knees, Bud."

And Adams would fall to his knees and stammer, "Y-y-y-es, Gadg."

"I wantcha to tear that grass—tear it out—out by the roots!" Dean would yell. "You hate that grass, Bud! Tear it up!"

And Adams would tear up the grass like a lunatic. Dean and Adams claimed they were going to turn this routine into a nightclub act and take it to Las Vegas.

Whether jocular or coercive, Dean made sure that his presence on the set was a strong one. And his long shadow also extended to his effect as an actor on his co-stars. Corey Allen says that Dean "was kind of like the black hole, with magnetism so great that nothing can go in the other direction." Ray was worried that Dean's acting would overly influence Allen's performance. He warned Allen: "Don't get caught up in Jimmy's rhythms." Throughout the production, there would be countless sound problems as the cast followed Dean's mumbling method.

As far as Sal Mineo and Natalie Wood were concerned, by the time the movie actually began shooting, Dean's dominance was a given. During rehearsals at the Chateau Marmont, they had both fallen under the spell of Dean, who could not only be sexy and charismatic, but had also come to represent the future of their chosen profession. In Ray's original "Blind Run" treatment, he described the Plato and Judy characters as Jimmy's "two new worshippers." Dean managed to inspire the same level of intense devotion offscreen.

"We all tended to idolize him," said Mineo. "If he didn't say good morning to me I'd be a wreck the whole day. If he put his arm around me, that was fabulous, because I knew he meant it."

At the time, Mineo found Wood's feelings for Dean to be nearly obsessive. "He was all she could talk about," Mineo said. "Every night for weeks in a row, she went to see *East of Eden*—she must have seen it over fifty times. She even taught me to play the theme song from the picture on the piano." Wood and Mineo's on-set tutor, Tom Hennesy, remembers that Wood "was very flirtatious" with Dean, trying to hang around him as much as she could.

The passionate feelings that surrounded Dean gave him tremendous power and confidence on set. His brashness stood out in comparison with what was viewed, early on, as Ray's indecisiveness. It was clear from the first day that Ray still had some details to work out, that despite all his planning and preparation, he still did not have a completely clear vision of what he wanted. His uncertainty would stoke Dean's doubts as shooting proceeded, leading him to complain to an on-set friend in a fit of pique, "This man does not know what he's doing; Kazan did."

Ray had decided to let Dean wear his glasses for these early scenes, for example, though a few days later he would change his mind. He also had second thoughts about the way Wood looked when she appeared on set that day. Following Ray's instructions, costume designer Moss Mabry padded her hips and rear end in an effort to make her look older. But when Ray saw Wood in costume for the first time, he knew they had gone too far. "What do you have on?" he said, grimacing at the absurdly overstuffed Wood. Before filming any footage of her, Ray ordered the wardrobe department to reduce the padding. Cast member Jack Grinnage says that when Ray revealed his knowledge of the true contours of Wood's body, many in the cast realized that something was going on between them. But that wasn't the only clue to their affair that surfaced on the first day of shooting. Ray had sent Wood a dozen roses that day, which infuriated Dennis Hopper, who had become even more deeply infatuated with her since their accident. When the jealous actor found out about the flowers, he "completely freaked out, started calling her all kinds of nasty names," according to Frank Mazzola. Anyone who did not already know about the relationship between Ray and Wood knew what was going on after Hopper's tirade. "He was crazy about Natalie, and he felt it was horrible for the director to be fooling around with an underage girl," said Long. "Everybody agreed with him, but it wasn't any of our business." Hopper told Steffi Sidney that he had become so agitated about Ray's affair with Wood that one night he even went over to the Chateau Marmont with a gun, looking for the director, who, luckily, was not home.

Ray also had problems with the unwieldy CinemaScope process. While all films involve downtime for the actors, *Rebel* racked up more time than most because the crew was not familiar with this relatively new widescreen process. Invented just two years earlier and first used on 1953's *The Robe*, the rectangular CinemaScope frame was two and a half times larger than the standard squarish frame. It was meant to offer a gargantuan alternative to television. Originally, Ray had wanted to hire cinematographer Franz Planer, who had already worked on a CinemaScope film, *20,000 Leagues Under the Sea*, and who had also shot *High Green Wall*, the television drama Ray directed right before *Rebel*. But Planer had signed a contract with Twentieth Century Fox and was not available. So the studio suggested veteran cinematographer Ernest Haller. Haller had shot almost one hundred and fifty films by that point, getting his start in the silent era, and was nominated for seven Oscars during his career, winning one for *Gone With the Wind*. Haller was also responsible for the memorably noirish light and shadows in *Mildred Pierce*, but he was probably best known as

Bette Davis's favorite cinematographer, shooting fourteen films with the actress, one of Warner Brothers' biggest box-office stars. "Haller was a brilliant cinematographer," said *Rebel* second assistant director Ray Gosnell Jr. "He was very energetic, very into the picture and always involved." But Haller had no experience with CinemaScope.

Ray used Haller to shoot some of the screen tests he did with the actors, as a way of familiarizing him with CinemaScope, but was not happy with the result, telling producer David Weisbart in a memo, "The maximum was not achieved." By the time shooting began, Haller was still struggling with the process. Because the frame was so much wider, crews were unaccustomed with where to put lighting setups so that they would be out of the frame. Trailers and equipment had to be hidden far from view so that they would not get into the shot by mistake. The frame was also higher, which meant shots were often ruined by the microphone boom dipping into the frame. What made the process especially unwieldy, however, was that the camera operator had to look through an anamorphic lens, which squeezed and distorted the image like a funhouse mirror. The cinematographer didn't know what the image looked like until it was unsqueezed with another lens and projected on a screen. The edges of the frame were particularly difficult to see. "Nobody knew exactly what was going to get into lens," says Steffi Sidney. "So we were always called to be in the shot just in case. We stood on our feet for a long time."

Although Ray would eventually become known as one of Hollywood's masters of the widescreen image, these initial struggles with the CinemaScope format could not help but provoke further misgivings in Dean, who watched Ray closely. (According to a studio publicity memo, Dean was keeping a "director's notebook," hoping to become a director himself in the future.) These early tensions between Ray and Dean would reach a very public climax during one of the most important scenes filmed at the observatory: the knife fight.

FIRST BLOOD

The knife fight marks the first major confrontation in *Rebel,* and it represents one of the key shifts in the movie's tone. It takes place thirty minutes into the movie but was initially approached during those first three days on set. Up until that point in the plot, newcomer Jim Stark (Dean) has been floating at the edges of the movie's unnamed "gang," led by Buzz (Corey Allen). He has been trying to ingratiate himself with Buzz's clique and particularly with Buzz's girlfriend, Judy (Wood). During a school field trip to the observatory, after they have listened to a foreboding lecture that would be filmed later, Buzz attempts to draw him into a knife fight. His glances and languorous movements almost suggest a seduction, while Wood shows clear signs of sexual arousal at the thought of ensuing violence. But Jim resists, relying on verbal thrusts instead.

"You know something," Dean says: "You read too many comic books." (This is a divergence from the script, which reads: "You watch too much television." The improvisation may have been a response to Senator Estes Kefauver's committee on the effect of comic books on juvenile delinquency; the committee had just released its final report.)

"He's real abstract," Buzz responds. "He's different."

"That's right," Dean says, "and I'm cute too."

But despite his efforts to defuse the situation, Jim is eventually backed into a corner. He picks up a knife, supplied by Frank Mazzola's character, Crunch, and the battle begins.

It is a significant sequence in the film, one that ratchets up the movie's sense of danger and violence. The scene would be considered so brutal that in 1962 it was selected by scientists to test the theory that media violence increases aggression. (The experimenters concluded that those who watched the knife fight were more likely to administer electric shocks to someone who incorrectly answered questions on a quiz.) Ray was determined to display the psychological forces at work—the "conflict of sex and power" he had observed during his gang experiences with Frank Mazzola. It could not be just another Hollywood fight scene.

The stark setting already lent the scene a desolate tone. The knife scene was shot against the concrete walls of Griffith Observatory overlooking a panoramic view of Los Angeles. Director and critic Eric Rohmer would write that "the harshness and the beauty of the landscape . . . make us forget that it is only a children's game." The fight choreography was also crucial—and Ray had a definite vision of how it should look. Just as the film would find a perfect balance of the concrete and the abstract, the realistic and the hyperrealist, Ray wanted the scene to work as both a true fight and a ballet. "Jimmy knew how to move," said Ray. "He was really in tune with his body and understood how to use it as a carefully tuned instrument. He learned more studying dance with [choreographer] Katherine Dunham than he ever did from the Actors Studio. He knew what I wanted—the precision of the dance."

For help with the scene, Ray solicited advice from Frank Mazzola. The day before they shot it, Ray asked Mazzola to help choreograph the fight by showing Dean and Allen what happened in a real battle he had experienced. "The first guy I ever directed in my life was James Dean!" Mazzola says.

Dean's stand-in on *Rebel*, Mushy Callahan, a former world junior-welterweight boxing champion who had coached Dean on the fight scenes in *East of Eden*, also helped choreograph the fight. Callahan was one of several boxers frequently found on the *Rebel* set, along with Roger Donoghue. Donoghue quit boxing shortly after his 1951 bout with George Flores at Madison Square Garden led to his opponent's death. He went on to coach Marlon Brando in *On the Waterfront*. Dean was thinking about accepting the role of world middleweight champion Rocky Graziano in the biopic *Somebody Up There Likes Me*, so he spent time between takes on the *Rebel* set sparring with Callahan and Donoghue.

As he crafted the knife fight, Ray remained open to the input of the younger actors on set, taking tips when they seemed appropriate. Some of the gang members pointed out that the staging of the scenes preceding the knife fight was not realistic. "Nick had all these kids running down the alley, shouting and carrying on," said Beverly Long. "We told him it just wasn't done like that. When gangs rumbled, they didn't invite twelve hundred people. They did it kind of surreptitiously and quietly, otherwise the authorities would come." So Ray cut back on the amount of extras.

At one point, there had been reason to fear the knife fight sequence might not make it into the film at all because of interference from the Hays Office, the industry association that held sway over the moral content of films. A censor from the Hays Office with the sleuthlike name of Geoffrey Shurlock saw early drafts of the *Rebel* script and wanted the scene cut out entirely. But he agreed to let it stay in the film after Ray made some concessions. "If this knife-duel is to be approved it will have to be treated without too much emphasis, and not shown in too much detail," Shurlock wrote in a memo to Jack Warner. A shot of Buzz kicking Plato on the ground was cut from the script as too brutal; the line "No killing" was changed to "No sticking," to avoid the implication "that these high school kids do occasionally fight to the death with knives"; and the idea that Jim suddenly becomes aggressive and "pricks Buzz again and again" was cut from the screenplay's directions.

But whatever graphic qualities were lost from the screenplay, Ray hoped to reestablish in the actual shooting of the scene. He was determined to show that violence lay close to the heart of the new teen identity, however uncomfortable that information might be for the censors—and other adults. He and Dean agreed on that mission. Instead of rubber blades, Dean wanted to use real switchblades with the edges dulled but the points intact for many of the shots. And despite the studio's nervousness, Ray backed Dean up.

"We all argued against [Dean's] decision to use a real knife," Nick Adams remembered. But Dean quickly silenced them. "All we had to do was catch the look in his eyes as he stared in protest to us, to let us know that a prop was too dull, let alone unrealistic, as far as he was concerned. So he might get cut. So what?"

A Warners publicity memo claims that the studio could not buy its own switchblades because they were illegal. Instead, the prop department borrowed, from Los Angeles Juvenile Hall, thirty knives that police had confiscated "from young hoodlums who had been picked up on various charges ranging from narcotics possession to larceny." Corey Allen and Dean both wore metal chest protectors under their shirts but the rest of their bodies was unprotected, which meant that there was a very real possibility that the actors could get hurt.

Allen, who describes himself as a "book nerd," found himself dreading the scene. Increasing the potential for danger was the fact that both actors were inexperienced at fighting and had little time to rehearse. "I was new so I didn't know I could have a double," says Allen. Ray's direction was simple: "When he comes at you, don't let him hurt you."

Two cameras were set up for what would be a tense two days of shooting. The first few takes, however, went badly. "The boys circled each other gracefully and menacingly, but neither one wanted to close the distance enough to make the fight look real: Each was fearful of hurting the other," wrote Joe Hyams, one of several reporters invited to the set that day to generate buzz about the film.

"I was so fucking nervous," said Allen. "We did take after take and it was just *awful.* Finally Nick told us to take a break. Everybody went for a soda, but I just stayed on the set." Allen had been drinking the night before and he felt bleary-eyed. According to makeup man Henry Vilardo, Allen would sometimes take a nip from a thermos he carried around. ("It wasn't coffee," jokes Vilardo. "It was a *special* mix.")

When they began shooting again, Dean and Allen were a lot more aggressive. As they began to get into the spirit of the battle, tension mounted among the cast and crew and the gaggle of reporters that Ray had invited to witness the moment. There was a palpable sense of peril as both actors became more and more frenzied. Suddenly, Ray shouted in a frightened voice, "Cut! Get a first aid man to Jimmy on the double." Allen had nicked Dean on the ear and a trickle of blood had begun to run down Dean's neck.

"I committed a cardinal sin," Corey Allen said. "I hurt the other actor on the set." But despite the blood, Dean was not concerned at all about his injury. Instead, he was incensed at Ray. In a fury, he turned to the director and shouted, "Goddamn it, Nick! What the fuck are you doing? Can't you see this is a real moment? Don't you ever cut a scene while I'm having a real moment! That's what I'm here for!"

No one had ever heard an actor talk to a director like that before. It was an embarrassing moment for Ray. It exposed, for all to see, the struggle for power on set. Moments like this led some to wonder who was really directing the film.

While a first-aid man was summoned, Dean rested in a chair, wiping his brow, which was soaked with sweat. According to Nick Adams, Dean was delighted to have been cut, "a feeling based not only on the fact that he had lived his role more than he had pretended it, but that there was a kick to this way of acting."

One of the invited journalists, Neil Rau of the *Los Angeles Examiner,* went up to Dean and asked him, "Isn't this pushing realism a bit?" Dean replied, "In motion pictures, you can't fool the camera. If we were doing this on stage, we'd probably be able to gimmick it up—but not in a picture.

Film fans are too critical these days." Rau's story, "The Fight Was for Blood—and They Got It" provided the kind of publicity—and street credibility—that Ray would gladly have paid for. Despite the hype, the only lasting result of Dean's injury was the razzing he had to put up with from the cast, who told him he should not be allowed to shave because he might cut himself.

Dean changed his white shirt, which had gotten stained with drops of blood, and the scene was finally finished, though Dean's stuntman, Rod Amateau, stood in for Dean in a few shots. No matter how much Dean insisted on doing it himself, Ray was not going to risk the entire film on another accident. When they finally wrapped the knife fight scene without another incident, the crew spontaneously burst into applause.

IN LIVING COLOR

Corey Allen was relieved that the difficult knife scene was behind him. Alone, he went to the Hamburger Hamlet—a restaurant that, like Googie's, had established the kind of low prices and long hours that attracted young actors. He was relaxing over dinner when Ray walked in and asked if he could sit down. "He look pained," remembers Allen, who thought, "God, what have I done?" When Ray said, "I've got something to tell you," Allen really began to get worried. "This may shake you, but we have to do the knife fight again," Ray told him. Allen was mortified. "What went wrong?" he asked. "It was filmed so well." Ray reassured him, telling him that, on the contrary, Warner executives loved the footage and had decided the film should be shot in color. Everything they had filmed in black and white that week would have to be done again.

The exact reason Jack Warner took the drastic step of switching to color once production had already begun has always been something of a mystery. Cast member Steffi Sidney says she was told by studio insiders that, after seeing footage of the knife fight, Warner and his assistant Steve Trilling thought the film looked too much like *Blackboard Jungle*, which was growing into a sizable hit, and they were afraid that *Rebel* might suffer by the comparison. A few days later, the *New York Times* ran a story claiming that Warners was forced to change *Rebel* to color by Twentieth Century

Fox, which owned the CinemaScope trademark and whose approval was required for any studio using the process. "Warners had reported on Saturday after five [sic] days shooting on 'Rebel' that a switch to color photography was being made but gave no reason for the decision," according to the *Times* article. "The fact of the matter, it was verified today, was that the studio had overlooked the stipulation in the contract," which required that CinemaScope pictures must be made in color.

It seems odd that the studio could have overlooked such an important condition in the contract or that Twentieth Century Fox would not have known that *Rebel* was being made in black and white beforehand since Bausch & Lomb, which made the lenses, would have seen the black-and-white tests. And despite telling Corey Allen at the time that Warner ordered the switch to color after being pleased with the dailies, Ray would further muddy the waters by telling a competing story about the studio's attitude. He claimed that Warners had actually almost shut down production completely. "They didn't know what I was doing and didn't want me to finish the picture," said Ray. "I said, fine, take me off salary and sell me all the rights to the film. The executives hesitated and said, 'We'll call you back.' Then Steve Trilling went to the projectionist and asked him what he thought of the rushes. 'Mr. Trilling,' he said, 'frankly, I think it's the only picture worth something on the lot.' So they called me back and said, 'Okay, Nick, finish it.'"

In a memo to *Rebel* producer David Weisbart, dated Saturday, April 2, 1955, Jack Warner seems unequivocal about the film, writing in capital letters, "THIS IS A VERY IMPORTANT PICTURE." That memo indicates that the success of *Blackboard Jungle* and *East of Eden* might have figured into Warner's thinking when he okayed the shift to color. "We started out making a routine program picture in black and white," recalled Jim Backus, who was cast as Jim's father. "It was going to be a picture about teenage kids that I thought was going to be a sort of *Ozzie and Harriet* with venom. Then the reports started coming in on *East of Eden,* and they knew they had a star on their hands."

Whatever the reason for Warner's decision, the switch to color would provide the movie with the last element it needed to secure its classic status. Shaking off the old-fashioned—albeit classical—effect of black and white, Ray now had a movie with a look that matched his themes. Cinema-

Scope had already given him the opportunity to cast his characters' alone-ness against a giant pitiless backdrop—"with enough open territory to soak up any amount of adolescent sorrow," according to critic Geoffrey O'Brien. But with color added, the film took on the look of a brand-new world. "It was a modern world," wrote O'Brien, recalling his adolescent re-action to the film, "and it was going to be ours." With the saturated colors and its CinemaScope size, *Rebel* presented a visual universe that, in many ways, harkened back to Ray's days with Frank Lloyd Wright. It was a place of horizontality that not only defined a new frontier but also, specifically, California. From its very first image of a sprawling, twinkling L.A. night landscape, *Rebel* could be seen as a film about the West Coast—still a metaphor for new beginnings and eternal promise—although the place it-self is never mentioned.

Immediately after Warners issued its new orders, Ray called in a color consultant, John Hambleton, whom he had known as a stage designer with the Group Theatre and who had also worked as a color consultant on Kazan's *East of Eden*. Together, they paged through *Life* magazine looking for ideas. *Rebel* costume designer Moss Mabry remembers that Ray also showed him an image from *Life*. "It was a college picture with all these stu-dents going somewhere," says Mabry. "I remember thinking, 'That's what he wants?' That's what he got." Although Mabry calls the costumes in *Rebel* "plain, simple, everyday clothes," many of the costumes had surprisingly glamorous Hollywood histories behind them. After Mabry let the cast loose in the Warners wardrobe department, Steffi Sidney ended up with a cos-tume that was worn by Dorothy Malone in *Young at Heart*. Tom Bernard's leather jacket was the one Alan Ladd wore in *Shane*. The fur collar on Wood's red dress had once draped the neck of Bette Davis. "Bette Davis was such a big star," explains Mabry. "I thought it might bring me luck—or bring Natalie luck—if I put it on her."

Together with Mabry, Hambleton and production designer Malcolm Bert, Ray went on to develop a vivid, primary-colored landscape for *Rebel*. "The use of primary color in film is as significant as the use of close-up," Ray said. Ray preferred working in color. He was fascinated by its optical impact and symbolism. In fact, in later life Ray would become enamored of *The Lüscher Color Test,* a book by Dr. Max Lüscher. According to the book jacket, "The principle of the Lüscher Color Test is that accurate psychological information can be gained about a person through his choices and rejections of colors."

"It was something he was exploring," says Susan Ray. "He was always into the psychology of color. He would test a lot of people with it and play with it." In *Rebel*, Ray used color coding both to define and to evoke the emotional life of his main characters, pointing out "the emergence of Natalie from the gauche red of the lipstick and coat she wore as a 15-year-old tramp on the streets into the soft fluffy pink—sentimental, but a graduation, and important in the development of the personality of the girl. Then the yellow-orange of Corey Allen. All were significant." Plato would wear a somber black jacket and blue sweater that suggested his personality. But the most inspired color breakthrough of all—producing one of the most iconic pieces of clothing ever worn by a Hollywood star—was James Dean's flame-red jacket.

Everyone has a story about the origin of the red jacket, with Ray often claiming that he was the one who found it. According to Ray, after he was told about the switch to color, "the first thing I did was pull a red jacket off the Red Cross man, dip it in black paint to take off the sheen and give it to Jimmy." Others say that the jacket was actually purchased from Mattson's, a now-defunct clothing store on Hollywood Boulevard. Frank Mazzola accompanied Dean on a shopping trip to Mattson's—where, as Jack Grinnage remembers, the cast was taken to buy some of the wardrobe they wore in the black-and-white footage. "The red jacket was really an Athenian jacket that we bought cheaply at Mattson's," says Mazzola. "They were blue, so the guy at Warner Brothers dyed it red." After *Rebel* was released, Warners referred fans who wanted the jacket to Mattson's, which sold red jackets for $22.95.

Moss Mabry tells a completely different story about the origins of the red jacket. Mabry says that he, in his role as costume designer, fashioned the red jacket, three of them in fact. According to Mabry, Ray had originally told him the jacket should be khaki. So Mabry cut some khaki-colored swatches from fabric he had found in the Warners wardrobe department. He went to get Ray's approval but, while waiting outside the director's office, Mabry says, "This guy walked in with a red jacket just trying to get a part. And I was fascinated. How good he looked in that red jacket. So I went back to the wardrobe department and cut off a swatch of red." Ray approved. So Mabry began to develop a pattern for the jacket using a bolt of red nylon. "Even though the jacket looked simple," Mabry says, "it wasn't. The pockets were in just the right place; the collar was just the right size." Mabry worked through the details, and James Dean's legendary look was born.

In the film itself, the introduction of Dean's red jacket signals a surge in dramatic intensity. Jim Stark would begin the film wearing a more neutral brown sports coat, but just before the pivotal chickie run, Dean grabs the red jacket out of his bedroom drawer. He flings it down the stairs, toward the camera. It's almost as if Ray foresaw the cultural impact the appearance of the jacket would have. It nearly pops off the screen, especially after Jim slips it over his bright white T-shirt. Stewart Stern's screenplay already had Jim changing into a jacket at that point in the plot, although its color was not specified. And, although Stern says he didn't realize it until it was pointed out to him by a student years later, he had subconsciously assigned the jacket symbolic meaning. "My whole use of the jacket in *Rebel* was an echo of the use of Terry Malone's jacket in *On the Waterfront*," says Stern, "which was given to one worker and then another worker, and finally Terry got it, and that's the armor that he wore when he went to make his final confrontation." But now, with the addition of color, the jacket would become so much more. "When you first see Jimmy in his red jacket against his black Merc, it's not just a pose," said Ray. "It's a warning. It's a sign." And certainly, the cadmium-red jacket evokes plenty of passionate associations: the anger of adolescence, the audacity of rebellion, the threat of blood and violence, as well as a definite sexual bravado. And during a time of hysteria about the dangers of the Red Menace, it was a color tinged with subversiveness.

Almost immediately upon *Rebel*'s appearance, the jacket was embraced by teens. "After the movie came out," says Steffi Sidney, "I'd go past my old high school, Fairfax High. It had a huge lawn in front where kids used to eat lunch. And if you'd go past it in 1955, all of the boys would be wearing the red jacket." Bob Dylan, who saw *Rebel Without a Cause* at least four times as a teenager in Hibbing, Minnesota, also bought a red jacket just like Dean's.

Almost thirty years later, when Moss Mabry was working in Colorado on the film *Continental Divide* with John Belushi, the actor demanded a red jacket of his own. Mabry flew to Los Angeles and revisited the wardrobe department at Warner Brothers. He explained why he had come, and the man in charge took him to the fabric room. He unrolled a familiar bolt of red nylon, and sitting inside the roll was the pattern Mabry originally used to make the red jacket. "That was very exciting," says Mabry. He made three more jackets—one for Belushi and two for his bodyguards.

Other than the red jacket, the most important costume change Ray made after the switch to color was to eliminate Dean's glasses, making him less bookish and guaranteeing his status as a future icon of cool. The white T-shirt and blue jeans Dean puts on when he dons the red jacket would also have a seismic impact on fashion. Dean's attire would become the uniform of rebellious youth around the world. In 1957 the *New York Times* reported that groups of teenage James Dean fans in Indonesia had shocked locals when they doffed their traditional sarongs and "strolled through the streets in 'blue jeans and red jackets.'" And in 2003 a poll of Irish movie theatergoers would declare *Rebel Without a Cause* "the most stylish movie ever."

The coming of the red jacket—and color in general—would designate a new day for *Rebel.* It would mark the movie as something grander, more ambitious, something finally capable of the amplitude Ray wanted for it. On the Warners lot and throughout Hollywood, it increased everyone's sense of the film's importance. It changed the movie—and the making of the movie. And ultimately, it may have even given Ray the momentum he needed to readjust the power play on set.

CHAPTER NINE

Starting Over

Despite the switch to color, *Rebel* continued to move at a breakneck pace. Shooting went on as scheduled without the slightest pause. That Saturday, April 2, right after spending the first three days at Griffith Observatory, the production jumped to Santa Monica High School, renamed Dawson High School in the film. ("Dawson" was picked from a list of approved fictitious names for Los Angeles high schools provided by the Warner research department. The other possibilities were Davison, Johnson and Markham.) Nevertheless, the change to color did cause some unexpected delays behind the scenes. As the cast was on its way to the high school that morning, someone on the crew realized that there was a problem with their costumes. Ray had been forced to use the studio's own color process, called WarnerColor, which would be discontinued a few years later because of its unpredictable quality. Certain blues tended to bleed in WarnerColor, which meant that none of the scenes with the gang members could be shot until their blue jeans were re-dyed a more acceptable shade. "Until they got that done and handed them out again it took until twelve noon. That pushed us all back," remembers Steffi Sidney. Ray spent the entire morning shooting scenes with Sal Mineo, whose character was not wearing jeans, while he waited for the rest of the cast.

Meanwhile, Ray was scrambling to make other changes. New script pages were drafted without Stern being informed, despite Ray's promise to him. The film's time period, which had been Christmas, was changed to Easter, most likely because "it was in California and it would have been difficult to make it look like Christmas," Stewart Stern believes. Starting over also meant that the rest of the production would always be over budget and eventually fall behind schedule, putting mounting pressure on cast and crew right up to the last day of shooting, especially since Dean was scheduled to leave for Texas to begin filming the epic *Giant* in a mere two months. If *Rebel* wasn't finished by then, there was no question which film would take priority, no matter how important *Rebel* suddenly might have become.

Beginning again would also have an impact on the actors who played the gang members. Despite Corey Allen's misgivings about revisiting the knife fight, the rest of the cast members were generally excited about the thought of reshoots. "More money!" as Steffi Sidney succinctly put it. But the movie's heightened profile led to a slew of new considerations regarding the gang, and despite all the time and commitment they had put into rehearsals, the actors who played gang members would find their parts growing smaller.

Actor Ken Miller, who was not called back after the film switched to color, believes that Ray decided there were too many characters getting in the way of Dean. Tom Bernard, who remained in the film, went from thirty lines to one. Bernard's line, "I bet he fights cows," which he says at the planetarium after Jim moos, is actually heard offscreen.

In the final script, Beverly Long's character, Helen, speaks all her lines in French, exclaiming during the knife fight, for example, "Les jeux de courage!" (games of courage!). "She was supposed to be taking French in school and showing off," explains Stern. "I don't know where that came from. A desperate attempt to characterize somebody." Ray obviously shared Stern's lack of affection for these lines. Every one of them was cut. "Forever after, Corey Allen would call me on the phone and say my lines in French on my machine," says Long.

For the most part, the gang would become less important as individuals and more important as a whole, as a convincingly integrated entity. Yet somehow the ever-cocky Nick Adams managed to gain a line of dialogue or two. Adams saw what some of the other cast members had done in the first black-and-white go-round. So when it came time to reshoot the observatory scenes, he proceeded to steal their bits. "All the things that Nick Adams was doing—like 'Heil Hitler!'—that was mine," says Sidney, referring to the moment when Adams grabs the cap from the security guard and gives him a Nazi salute. "I did that in an improv in the black-and-white sequence. Mr. Adams stuck his nose right in front of me in the color sequence and took stuff away from me. He did that to everybody. I had a lot of footage in the black and white I don't have in the color thanks to Mr. Adams." The gang members began to dislike Adams for the way he constantly angled to get into a shot or stand next to Dean, stepping in front of other actors or pushing them aside, and Dean apparently began to find him obnoxious as well.

Once, while Adams was trying to entertain the cast during a game of charades, Dean snuck up behind him and began to mock everything he did. Then Dean broke a donut in two and stuck the halves in his ears. "Nick thought we were laughing at him, so it just egged him on more," remembers Long. When Dean, now imitating Chaplin, fell into a trash can, Adams turned around and realized that everyone was laughing at Dean, not him. "That wasn't funny," Adams pouted as he stormed away. "Jimmy thought Nick Adams was just a buffoon, trying so desperately to be a star," says Long.

As the shooting moved toward its second week, the relationships between the film's lead actors began to gel. Because they were underage and required by law to spend three hours of every day in school with a tutor, Natalie Wood and Sal Mineo continued to bond. Their tutor was sometime actor and stuntman Tom Hennesy, a towering, 6-foot, 5-inch former college football player, police officer and game warden, who that year had played the creature in the sequel to *Creature from the Black Lagoon,* and would go on to be John Wayne's stuntman in a number of films. The gruff, no-nonsense Hennesy also doubled as Wood and Mineo's on-set guardian, and he made it clear early on that he had the final say on their well-being. Hennesy attempted to shield the young actors as much as possible from the influence of the other cast members and crew. "I did have to control the profanity that was on the set from actors and other personnel," he says. "I'd just go up and tell them to knock it off, watch their language."

Hennesy found that keeping Wood in line was a full-time job. "Natalie was a little bit difficult to keep supervised," he recalls. "She was more advanced for her age because of the years she'd spent in the industry. A lot of these young guys—at that time there was a lot of dope and so forth around—some of them I didn't have a very high regard for. Every chance she'd get she'd take off to be with these kids." Though Wood—unlike

Mineo—was a good student, she often bristled under Hennesy's control, resenting the fact that although she may have been playing her first adult role, she was still treated as a child. Sometimes she would steal away from Hennesy's watchful eye to smoke a cigarette or sneak off set with Dennis Hopper and Nick Adams to have lunch in Hollywood—until Hennesy found out and put a stop to it. At one point he became so concerned about the gang's influence on her, he complained to Ray and producer Weisbart. "We just howled, because she smoked more than we did—and swore!" said Sidney.

Mineo had more trouble fitting in with the rest of the gang. "He tried to hang out with the kids on-set but was left on the wayside," says Hennesy. The young actors who played the gang members were "harassing him," according to Hennesy, "inferring he was gay," ironically treating him just the way their characters treated Plato. "He was withdrawn and did not socialize that much because of that," says Hennesy. "He was very sensitive. If you made a joke about something that he felt was connected to him, he brooded over it for days." Beverly Long agrees that most of the actors playing gang members "never paid any attention" to Mineo. "He was just young—and weird," she says. "He was a raging homosexual even in those days. He was very precious—no fun at all." Now, however, she admits, "We could have been nicer."

The other cast members may have been somewhat jealous of the attention that Dean paid to Mineo. "If anyone was a bit closer to Dean it was Sal Mineo," says Gary Nelson, who worked as a second assistant director on *Rebel*. "If he talked to anyone, it was Sal."

Unlike Wood, who sometimes brought friends to the set, no one who worked on the film can recall Mineo's ever being with anyone, and his life outside the film was a mystery to them. His makeup man Henry Vilardo recalls that one morning Mineo looked at his open mouth in the mirror and asked, "Do you ever get syphilis of the mouth?" Vilardo began to suspect that Mineo was not as innocent as he seemed. "I think he had a wild night," Vilardo says, though Mineo never elaborated on what prompted his query.

As the shooting progressed and the film's prestige at Warners grew, there was also a marked change in Dean's behavior toward Ray. Although Dean would continue to be trouble, he and Ray seemed to reestablish the delicate balance they had during preproduction—or perhaps those observing began to better understand the nature of their working partnership.

"Nick wouldn't go until Jimmy said so," says Corey Allen. "He and Nick had an understanding that Jimmy had latitude to do his work the way he saw fit. That meant taking as much prep time as he needed, even if we had to sit and wait."

"I think Jimmy interpreted his own part," says Tom Bernard. "But I think Nick Ray gave him that freedom to do his part." But not everyone agreed. "Jimmy ran that film. There's no question about it. Because Nick wanted to accommodate him and succeed," says *Rebel* dialogue coach Dennis Stock, whom Ray hired partly because of his natural rapport with Dean. "It was a pissing contest with Kazan. I think Nick wanted to show that he could do something equally good. They really modeled that whole film around whatever Jimmy wanted."

"In my opinion James Dean directed *Rebel Without a Cause*," said Dennis Hopper, "from blocking all the scenes, setting the camera, starting the scene and saying 'cut.' Nicholas Ray intelligently allowed him to do this."

Gavin Lambert once asked Wood whether she thought Dean directed *Rebel*. She said, "No. You might think so because very often he would kind of take over and almost say fuck off to Nick Ray." But, according to Lambert, "Nick saw so much of himself as a young person in Jimmy Dean that he gave him this leeway to get what he wanted."

Dean was not the only actor Ray indulged and protected. Before every scene he was in, Corey Allen followed a strange ritual. Just after the assistant director would tell the actors to take their places, Allen would let out an enormous roar, yelling at the top of his lungs. "I've always hated my voice," says Allen. "I always felt it was childish. That was my way of giving myself the franchise to do what I wanted." Nick Adams, who loved to do impressions, began imitating Allen's roar. Soon everyone in the cast was mocking Allen, even Dean. Allen admits that, while the teasing was not intentionally mean-spirited, "it bothered me." Sensing Allen's discomfort, Ray called an on-set meeting of all the actors. "Everybody here has his own way of preparing," Ray said. "If I feel any one of us is doing anything to make it difficult for another to prepare, he's off the picture." Allen was touched by Ray's gesture. "It was harmless but he stepped in before harm could come of it."

"He was very fatherly," says gang member Jack Grinnage of Ray. "He didn't yell or scream. He was very quiet about direction. He gave you a lot of support in what you were doing, unlike other directors who would really cut you down a lot and make you feel inferior." Many directors at the time ran autocratic sets, barked orders at cast and crew, wore formal attire and were seldom addressed by their first names. But Ray was something completely different. "Nick was way before his time, wearing Levi's and walking around in bare feet," says Long. "They just didn't do that in 1955. Everybody at the studio was in a suit and tie."

Instead of talking to actors in front of the entire cast and crew, Ray would take them aside and speak to them alone. Actor Jack Larson, who once worked with Ray when he was auditioning actors for *Jet Pilot* (which was eventually directed by Josef von Sternberg), remembers being surprised by Ray's directorial style. "He'd come to you and say, 'Let's take a little walk, Jack,' and he put his arm around me and walked me around the soundstage. I had never seen it before or since." Larson says he felt there was something sensual in the way Ray dealt with him. "It never occurred to me it was homosexual, but I felt definitely I was being loved. I felt I was being romanced in a way as an actor with a director."

But while Ray's low-key style endeared him to the young actors, some on the crew continued to interpret his gentleness as weakness. Because Warners operated on a strict seniority system, virtually everyone in the crew was older and far more experienced than most of the actors. "Crews were in their forties and fifties," says second assistant director Gary Nelson. "I was always amazed everyone was so old. The film business was a society to keep young people out." The generation gap depicted in the film was paralleled in real life on the set. No one in the crew had ever worked on a film where teens and twentysomethings were given so much leeway. Makeup man Vilardo thought Ray was weak. "Nick didn't direct that much," says Vilardo. "I would say he was a mediocre director." Nelson, who worked on *The Searchers* with John Ford right after *Rebel*, found Ford to be much stronger. But he does give Ray some credit. "With so many young people in the cast it would be difficult to pull this all together," he says. "Everybody's trying to make a mark, to be different. It must have been a horrendous juggling job."

Of course, Ray had help keeping the restless young cast in line. The man in charge of keeping an eye on the actors and making sure they were available when needed was assistant director Don Page, who despite his difficult job was one of the best-liked men on the crew. "We refused to come unless Don Page called us by the name of 'principals,'" remembers Steffi Sidney. "We used to tease him. There was always a big mystery about him." Page, whose real name was José Paige, had once been known as Don Alvarado when he was an actor during the silent era, a romantic Latin star in the mode of Rudolph Valentino. But he had difficulty making the transition to sound pictures because of his heavily accented English and then suffered another blow when his wife, Ann Boyar, left him to marry Jack Warner. She later joked that the reason she left him was "the talkies, of course." Perhaps in compensation for stealing his wife, Warner offered him work behind the scenes. According to Jack Grinnage, "Don Page had a permanent job at Warners for the rest of his life."

Ten days after the film switched to color, on Monday, April 11, the cast and crew returned to the Griffith Observatory location to begin reshooting what had been done in black and white. They began with scenes that take place inside Griffith Observatory, because it was the Monday after Easter and the planetarium was closed to the public. For the first time, the call sheets listed the film as being "behind schedule." But that did not stop Ray from letting the cast improvise. "We wrote some of the scenes ourselves," says Long. "We would rewrite the script every day." When Sidney sneezes during the lecture in the planetarium and Wood responds "Gesundheit!" it was actually an accident. Ray opted to keep it in. The moment after the lecture when Dean examines the lighting board in the planetarium was not in the script either. And Ray spent most of one afternoon letting the gang members improvise an entire scene around the Foucault pendulum that hangs in Griffith Observatory's lobby. As Ray once described it, "This big circular thing was swinging around like the rhythm of the earth, and Corey Allen takes out his comb and starts beating a rhythm on the ledge, and then someone takes out a set of keys, then a steel comb, a tube of lipstick and so on until they're going around and around beating this rhythm . . . boom . . . baboom . . . boom . . . baboom. . . ." At one point Ray told Mazzola to grab Wood and dance with her. "It seems like he was always throwing stuff in and giving you an action," Mazzola says. Despite all the work that went into this scene, however, it was ultimately cut from the film.

Beverly Long remembers that she, Steffi Sidney and Jack Grinnage sneaked up to one of the planetarium's domes, which were off limits. "Jack hit some buttons and the dome started turning and we ran like crazy." Afterward, Ray and the head of the planetarium summoned them for a dressing down. "We sat there sheepishly. We could have cost them a huge amount of money," she says.

Wood's friend Mary Ann Brooks, who visited the set, also remembers the cast acting up: "We had a lot of fun in there making funny noises and carrying on and they'd get angry. When they'd all be real serious, all of a sudden you'd hear a funny noise." But while the gang may have been hard to control at times, they were acting exactly as their characters did in the film. Ray did not come down too hard on any of them, with one clear and obvious exception.

When the crew set up another shot inside the planetarium, Don Page told the gang members they could step outside for a cigarette. Dennis Hopper was hungry and wanted to get a hot dog. Beverly Long tried to stop him from leaving, warning him that "they're going to start shooting in a minute." But Hopper took off anyway. When Page came out and hollered, "Places, everybody," Hopper was still missing.

"School buses started arriving from the city school system," says Long, "and they threw us out. And they had to leave their huge cranes behind and they never got their shots. Dennis cost them, I don't know, fifty thousand dollars. He cost them a lot of money."

Dennis's disappearance may have given Ray the opening he was looking for. By that time, Ray knew that Hopper was having an affair with Wood. And when Hopper finally returned to the set, Ray fired him, right in front of the other cast members, on the steps of the observatory. But Hopper would not be that easy to get rid of. According to Long, "Steve Trilling, a Warner Brothers henchman, came up with his big cigar and informed Nick, 'We can't fire him. He's under contract here.' So Nick said, 'Well, I'm not going to direct him anymore' and he gave all of his lines to Jack Grinnage. So from the planetarium on, you'll notice Dennis has nothing to say."

Although the call sheets for that day say, "Corey Allen and Dennis Hopper left set. Could not find in time to complete shot," no one remembers Ray's being angry with Allen, only Hopper. And cutting his lines was not the only way Ray undermined the young actor. Soon afterward, Ray went to Wood's mother and told her about Hopper's affair with her daughter. Wood's mother complained to the studio and according to a Warners publicity memo, Wood's tutor Hennesy "ordered" her mother to the set to help curtail her daughter's relationship with Hopper. At the time, no one mentioned that Ray was also having an affair with Wood. Certainly Hopper did not have enough power to do so. But he continued to fume. "Nick snitched on me! I was furious with him: the studio came down on me, and he came out of it as pure as snow," Hopper recalled. "I resented this, and showed it." Despite any ban that Ray, the studio or Wood's mother hoped to impose, Hopper kept dating Wood anyway. And Ray would continue to find ways to abuse him throughout the shoot.

"WHAT DOES HE KNOW ABOUT MAN ALONE?"

Aside from the knife fight, the cast had another important set piece to complete at the Griffith Observatory: the lecture at the planetarium. The scene would not only state some of the film's most important themes, it would set the groundwork for the film's remarkable expansion from the sociological to the psychological to the metaphysical. "The infinite doom, the divine hand of God, is announced right from the beginning," Ray said.

If the students had attended an actual Griffith Observatory show at the time, they would have seen an optimistic, forward-looking presentation called "A Trip to the Moon." The possibility of space travel was a passion of the observatory's influential director, Dr. Dinsmore Alter, who had a lunar crater named after him.

The lecture in the film is not as hopeful as the future portrayed in "A Trip to the Moon," although the scene begins playfully with Ray's visuals wickedly chiming with the words of the planetarium's lecturer (played by Ian Wolfe). The students are listening to the lecture in a darkened auditorium, which clearly reflects the experience of sitting in a movie theater. At the moment when Wolfe says, "For many days before the end of our earth, people will look into the night sky and notice a star, increasingly bright and increasingly near," Dean enters the planetarium. Wolfe seems to have been talking about him. Wolfe pauses, then continues, "As this star approaches us, the weather will change."

A few minutes later, when the lecturer mentions "Gemini the Twins," the words momentarily overlap with a two-shot of Jim and Plato. It's at this moment that Jim and Plato speak to each other for the first time in the film. "I was just thinking that once you been up there, you know you been some place!" Jim says to him. According to Stewart Stern, this line was inspired by his interview with the troubled son of a prominent tough-guy actor whose identity he promised not to reveal.

Next in the film, the lecturer points out the constellations in the planetarium's faux sky, and the students begin to joke among themselves. When he mentions the constellation Cancer, Buzz (Corey Allen) says, "I'm a crab," imitating pinchers with his fingers, which scuttle across Wood and grab Hopper's nose. To ingratiate himself with the gang, Jim moos as the lecturer points out the constellation Taurus the Bull. It's a joke that falls flat, causing the gang members to taunt him and refer to him derisively as "Moo."

The scene takes a dramatic turn away from high school highjinks at the climax of the lecture. A mock destruction of the universe is staged. Sound effects, flashing blue lights and dissonant strings (supplied by composer Rosenman) simulate a world destroyed "in a burst of gas and fire," awakening even the most bored student. With subtle foreshadowing, the awestruck, uncomprehending face of Buzz is contrasted with Plato's frightened and vulnerable reaction. Both of them will die violently before the night is over.

The cataclysm is followed by the lecturer's last words: "Through the infinite reaches of space," Wolfe says, "the problems of Man seem trivial and naïve indeed. And Man, existing alone, seems himself an episode of little consequence." Given how seriously the film's teens take themselves—and how seriously the movie takes them—Wolfe's closing lines have tremendous resonance, rocketing us onto a higher plane, startling us with their sudden switch to an Olympian viewpoint.

As the students get up to leave, Jim Stark notices that Plato is still hiding, crouched behind his seat. Dean reaches over to touch him. (According to cast member Jack Grinnage, "Jimmy left. He'd been excused. The hand on Sal's head—that's me.") Jim quips, "Hey. It's all over. The world ended."

And latching on to Jim's gaze, Plato delivers one of his most memorable lines of dialogue, a line rife with teenage angst, alienation and attitude. Referring to the lecturer, Plato says, "What does he know about Man alone?"

The planetarium scene is important for being the first in which Plato and Jim truly connect. And it also sets up the temporal structure of *Rebel*, the way time is distorted and telescoped. Having the students looking up at the night sky in the middle of the afternoon, watching the entire universe destroyed in a matter of seconds, is a chilling augury of what is to come, when Jim, Judy and Plato return there just a few hours later, to have their own worlds shattered.

Stewart Stern says that when he read Irving Shulman's original screenplay, he felt the planetarium scene lacked "dramatic purpose." Stern decided he wanted to use the scene to reflect the characters' "thoughts, their whole emotional being, their sense of disaster and nothingness and coldness," an idea that would be so beautifully captured in Plato's haunting line. What had been a pedestrian scene of students listening to a boring lecture was transformed by Stern into existential poetry for the incipient space age. Just two years later, the Russians would launch the Sputnik satellite, kicking off the space race. It would not be the last time *Rebel* supplied a signature statement for the world to come.

CHAPTER TEN

Meet the Parents

As Ray was dealing with one star's expanding reputation and ego, he had to contend with another star's insecurity and timorousness. Ray had laid himself on the line for Natalie Wood, working overtime to convince the studio that she could handle the demanding part of Judy. While her first scenes at the Griffith Observatory required her only to function as a believable member of the ensemble, Wood had a make-it-or-break-it moment coming up, a major scene that would lay the entire emotional groundwork for Judy's character—and focus on her alone. Wood's big, anxiety-producing scene was scheduled for the first day of filming the ambitious police station sequence, as the cast and crew moved from shooting on location to the soundstages of Warner Studios.

The police station scene was initially approached from April 5 to 9 between the black-and-white and color reshoots of the observatory sequence. In the finished picture, it would serve as the opening set piece—directly following the credits. Right from the movie's start, Ray wanted the audience to know that *Rebel* was no ordinary film. The seventeen-minute sequence is a declaration of his ambitions. It would paint crisscrossing, highly charged psychological portraits of his three protagonists—all of whom have been picked up by the police—and it would do so in a particularly intricate and cinematic way.

Falling back on his early experience in architecture and his keen sense of how interior space affects action, Ray had art director Malcolm Bert build a mazelike set for the police station. Its construction allowed all three of the film's principal cast members to be glimpsed through glass partitions simultaneously, though they sat in different cubicles, visually linking Jim, Judy and Plato—who, at the beginning of the film, are strangers to each other—while at the same time emphasizing their isolation. Like much of the film, the set itself was an example of Ray's particular brand of heightened realism. Ray had conceived of this design during the film's intensive research period, when he and Stewart Stern visited Los Angeles Juvenile Hall. "I remember, in Juvenile Hall, there was a large room with a corridor that went down the center and these glass offices along both sides," says Stern. "From the beginning, Nick wanted to take advantage of that." The set even contained a roof, which both added to the realism and allowed Ray to get around some of the difficulties the unwieldy CinemaScope format presented.

The police station sequence represents the first in a series of successful experiments that grew out of Ray's and cinematographer Ernest Haller's inexperience and frustration with CinemaScope. They refused to shoot the film in long, straight-on master shots, as many directors did when using CinemaScope, as if the audience were passively watching a play from a theater seat. They decided to employ sharp angles, quick cuts and close-ups—breaking all the rules put forward in a 1955 pamphlet entitled *Photographic Techniques of CinemaScope Pictures,* published by Twentieth Century Fox. Close-ups, it was believed, would be too frightening for audiences when magnified to wide-screen proportions. The pamphlet recommended dispensing with close-ups altogether, ludicrously calling them "a relic of the silent era . . . necessary in those days to show facial expression, because the screen was small and there was no dialogue to convey what the scene was about." The pamphlet also recommended a "minimum of cuts" because the "vast screen area . . . requires new adjustment of the eyes each time the scene is changed." Ray and Haller ignored all of this advice—which did not make shooting any easier. Ray had mapped out a series of complex camera moves that required precise positioning of the actors as the cameraman swept through the police station. But Haller was still not sure how to keep all the actors in focus and in frame. And the police station set was difficult to navigate. It was a lot smaller than it looks in the film. "They used a deep-focus lens to make it look bigger," says Steffi Sidney, who watched from the sidelines. Even though CinemaScope was new to him, and despite all the technical and spatial limitations, Haller managed to film a brilliantly fluid sequence.

The dialogue evolved from Ray's and Stern's observations of police interviews. The audience learns about the protagonists' dysfunctional home lives in quick, incisive dramatic flourishes. We meet Jim—who has been picked up for drunkenness—and his family: his ineffectual father (Jim Backus), his harshly critical mother (Ann Doran), and his condescending grandmother (Virginia Brissac). We meet Plato, who has been arrested for shooting a litter of puppies, accompanied by his black housekeeper/nanny (Marietta Canty) instead of his parents, who, in effect, have abandoned him. And we meet Judy, who has been picked up for wandering the streets late at night, seeking the affection withheld from her by her father (William Hopper).

On the day Natalie Wood's crucial scene was shot, she spent the morning nervously preparing herself. In the scene, Judy experiences an emotional breakdown while being interviewed by Ray Framek, a paternal policeman played by Ed Platt, who would later gain fame as the Chief on the 1960s sitcom *Get Smart*. (According to Stern, it is just a coincidence that Ray Framek, one the few sympathetic adults in the film, shares a name with the director, although Nicholas Ray apparently didn't object.) Wood's interview with Framek was scheduled to be filmed right after the opening shot of the precinct scene, when a drunken Jim Stark is dragged into the station by police officers. Watching Dean act compounded Wood's jitters about her upcoming scene. His ability to transform even a routine scene into something astonishing—such as the moment he is frisked by a police officer and improvises a ticklish giggle—made her wonder if she was really up to the task ahead. "She was scared to death, because she felt that James Dean could act circles around her," said her friend Jackie Perry.

But what was making Wood particularly agitated was the fact that her scene required her to cry. Crying scenes had been especially traumatic for her since her earliest days as a child actor, when her mother would resort to cruel methods to get her tears flowing on cue. To produce Natalie's tears in the screen test for her first major film, *Tomorrow Is Forever,* her mother ripped the wings off a live butterfly in front of her. Directors were astounded by the little girl's amazing ability to cry on cue, not realizing what she suffered to accomplish this feat. "Whenever I did a movie, I always counted the crying scenes," Wood said years later. According to director Henry Jaglom, who became a close friend of Wood's in the 1960s, "Ever since she was a seven-year-old actor in *Tomorrow Is Forever,* she'd been begging for love. She was constantly asked to cry, praised and admired when she did, realized that if she could cry authentically, everyone adored her, and she soon established a connection between love and pain." This time, the connection would be even more acute. She had to manufacture tears on her own, without her mother's prodding, and for a man who was both her director and lover.

As Wood's anxiety about her scene grew, Ray's ambitious plans for the morning were already causing difficulties and delays. Ray wanted to introduce Jim with an extremely complicated camera maneuver consisting of a dolly and a pan that would also show off the set, but it took all morning to shoot it. "Natalie had just gotten herself geared up for the crying scene, and then they broke for lunch," remembers Jackie Perry, who was on the set that day. "She wanted to continue and Nick said, 'Let's not.'" When the crew broke for lunch, Wood became hysterical, throwing a tantrum that was so terrible her tutor, Tom Hennesy, had to pick her up and carry her kicking and screaming to her dressing room.

By the time the crew had eaten lunch and Ray had shot another angle of Dean being brought into the police station, it was already four in the afternoon. Because of child labor laws, which regulated how many hours Wood could work each day, she had only an hour and a half to get the scene right. But Wood had worked herself up into such a frenzy by that point she wasn't sure she could do the scene at all. Beverly Long found her huddling in the bathroom. "I can't do it! I can't do it! I know Nick wants me to do it but I can't do it," Wood cried. "Natalie, you're doing it now," Long said. "Don't waste it. Just walk in there and let go."

When we first see Judy in this scene, she makes a bold visual impression. The actress is literally up to her neck in red—dressed in a scarlet dress and coat that seem too large for her, with a crimson bow tied to her throat, and her mouth garishly outlined in thickly applied red lipstick. Judy has fashioned herself as a teenage Jezebel, in an outfit far too old for her age.

Police inspector Framek questions Judy about why she was "wandering around at one o'clock in the morning." (In an early draft of the script, Judy was supposed to have been talking to a sailor when police picked her up, but censors nixed the implication she was arrested for soliciting.) When Framek asks about her father, Judy says he called her "a dirty tramp!" and then bursts into tears. To make sure those tears flowed, Wood employed a trick. She wore a little ring made with a cup on it that she filled with Vicks. Surreptitiously, she rubbed a little on her eyes, irritating them until they began to water.

But after shooting the scene a few times, Ray grew dissatisfied. He didn't just want tears. He wanted Wood to feel Judy's pain. Desperate to finish the scene before time ran out, he finally resorted to manipulative tactics that were uncharacteristic for him. The usually soft-spoken director began berating her. According to Frank Mazzola, Ray accused her of being a bad actress and asked himself out loud, "How did I ever hire her?" Ray "just ripped her apart and she started crying. And then he said, 'OK, let's go.'"

After seven takes, Wood finally rose to the occasion. But it was not a major breakthrough. Her acting is melodramatic, forced. She does not look confident on camera. She seems to be crashing against the limits of her own abilities. Yet, in many ways, that works for her character. Wood seems sincerely shaken, and combined with her sad, inappropriate costume, she elicits tremendous sympathy, a protective impulse, tilting toward pity. She did not take a monumental leap as an actress—that would come later in the production. Still, she binds us to Judy. And the Warners publicity department would later crow that Wood matched an on-screen record: her prolonged five minutes of crying "equaled the mark set by Bette Davis in 1948 in Warners' *Winter Meeting*."

MR. AND MRS. STARK

Up to this point, Ray's focus had been on getting his young cast to cohere as a family, with Ray as the generally permissive parent. But as week two of the shoot began, the insular world that Ray created with the kids would be complicated by the arrival of actors playing the film's adults. These actors had spent little time with Ray and although they all possessed long Hollywood résumés, none of them had ever experienced anything like the atmosphere of improvisation and borderline anarchy that reigned on the *Rebel* set. As with so many other aspects of *Rebel*, the generational clash depicted on-screen was paralleled offscreen.

Actress Ann Doran was perhaps the least prepared of all of the major adult actors for what was to come. A seasoned Hollywood professional who made her debut in the 1922 silent version of *Robin Hood* when she was four, Doran was called literally at the last moment to play James Dean's mother after Marsha Hunt's sudden departure. At six in the morning of the first day of shooting the police precinct scenes, she was suddenly awakened by a telephone call from her agent, who told her to report immediately to Warner Studios. She had no idea what part she was to play or what the film was about. All she knew was that she was to appear in a film directed by Nicholas Ray and starring James Dean. Doran didn't know who Ray was, but she had heard of Dean. Her mother, Rose Allen, who was also an actress, had a bit part in *East of Eden*. She "raved" about Dean, telling Doran, "He's a funny little kid, but by God, he can act!"

Although Doran had never met Ray or Dean, there were some familiar faces in the cast. Jim Backus, who had the role of her husband, also had played her spouse in several previous films, including *The Rose Bowl Story*—in which Natalie Wood portrayed their daughter. Shortly after Doran arrived on set, Backus dropped by her dressing room to welcome her to the cast. "I haven't met this boy who's playing my son," she said to him. "Whoo! Wait'll you meet him!" he told her.

Intrigued, she decided to sneak over to the police station set with Backus to take a look at Dean. "We crept up to the set, and sat way, way behind the camera to watch him in a scene," remembered Doran. "All of a sudden everything got quiet and he got down in this fetal position. We waited and waited. Finally, he stood up, and they said, 'Action!' Jim [Backus] and I practically fell on the floor laughing. We had never seen such a bunch of crap in our lives. We snuck out, because we broke up the scene by our laughing."

Neither Backus nor Doran had any experience with improvising or Method acting. Backus, in fact, had never even played a dramatic role. He was known primarily for such comic characters as the snobbish Hubert Updike III on *The Alan Young Show* on the radio (a character that was the prototype for his Thurston Howell III on TV's *Gilligan's Island*) and as the voice of cartoon character Mr. Magoo. Corey Allen, for one, was puzzled by Ray's decision to cast him in the role. "Ray was so into achieving truth and Jim Backus was so into mocking the truth. It was a different style," says Allen.

Ray may have been uncertain himself about how the older actor was going to work out. He made sure Backus got together with Dean before shooting started to see how they meshed. "We spent a lot of time discussing the relationship between the father and son and analyzed the motivation of each scene, rather than simply going over the dialogue," said Backus, who was unaccustomed to such detailed preparation. Backus had actually met Dean once before, spending the previous Thanksgiving with him at actor Keenan Wynn's home, but Dean seemed so unlike the other actors there, and talked so much about cars and motorcycles, that Backus thought he was a garage mechanic.

Doran and Backus were joined by an actress who presented an even more problematic casting decision: Virginia Brissac, who played Jim's grandmother. Brissac was a veteran stage actress who usually portrayed stern teachers and society matrons. According to the screenplay, she was supposed to play a "chic, domineering woman" but Brissac was far too regal for the role. "How in the world did they ever cast that woman?" says Stern. "She could never have been either of their parents. It was totally wrong casting to bring the Duchess into that." Brissac, in fact, would disappear from the film after her initial scenes, her image appearing only once more, in an oil portrait that Dean kicks as he storms out of the Stark abode. It's difficult to figure out why Ray took so much care in casting his younger actors, yet made such seemingly lax and counterintuitive choices for some of the actors who played the adults.

Ray would later confess he had some difficulty working with these actors. He deliberately avoided using the word "improvise" with them, fearing they would dismiss the term as "artsy." And they would have problems relating to the young cast members. "We got a lot of flack about Method acting from the older actors," said Corey Allen. "I'm sure most of us young actors wondered how this was going to work."

The contrast between the styles of the older actors and Dean is indeed jarring. They seem shrill and cartoonish in comparison with Dean's raw emotion. But the difference also makes Dean stand out. When Jim Stark tries to stop his parents' squabbling during the police station sequence by screaming, "You're tearing me apart!" his cry of pain cuts through the near-comic tone of the scene and immediately spins the film onto another emotional plane. Dean forces the audience, as Jim forces his parents, to pay attention. He seems to be channeling a generation's worth of frustration and emotional claustrophobia.

Behind the scenes, the relationship between Dean and the older actors was just as tense. Before going on set the first day, Backus had warned Ann Doran about Dean. "He's not easy to work with. He's opinionated, and he'll also tell you how to act," Backus told her. "That, he'd better not do," she replied icily. But in their first scene together at the police station—in which a drunken Jim is sprawled out like a wayward prince on a thronelike shoeshine stand—Dean did just that, attempting to direct the actress, who was twenty years his senior. Doran was not about to let Dean intimidate her. "Look, junior," she said to him. "I've been around a long time, and you're new. Don't tell me how to do it. Let me make my own mistakes." At one point, in a take that did not make it into the final film, Dean suddenly turned the gooseneck lamp sitting on Framek's desk up into Doran's face. "She was totally stunned by that," says Beverly Long. And Doran was also annoyed by a habit she says Dean sometimes indulged in on set, which would become a source of great friction between parents and their kids in years to come. "I couldn't stand his marijuana smoking," she said. "I absolutely refused to let him come into my room if he'd been smoking."

House Peters Jr., who played the policeman who tells Dean, "Hey! That's enough static out of you," says that Doran was so upset by the way Dean was behaving that she issued an ultimatum. "This young chap would use such foul language, she finally went to the producer and director and said out loud on the set, 'If you don't tell this guy to calm down and quit using this bad language, I'm going to leave. You can get somebody else to play his mother,'" says Peters. Peters, the son and namesake of a prominent silent film star and later the original Mr. Clean in television commercials, was also appalled by what he saw as Dean's rude behavior and had no patience for the eccentricities of Method acting. It violated his sense of protocol when Dean "would cut himself in the middle of a scene and say, 'No, I want to try something else.'"

Dean's intensity was often startling to some of the older actors on the set. Marietta Canty, who played Plato's nanny, remembered a day when Ray was unhappy with Dean's performance. He kept shooting a scene again and again. "Finally, Jimmy walked away from the set and over to a wall where he began to hit it with his fists as well as his head," recalled Canty. "I went up to him and told him that if he kept it up he would soon have a concussion. So, he turned to me and said, 'Who cares?' I said, 'Well, for one, I care.'

140

Then he said, 'Well, God doesn't care. Just look at the dirty trick he played on me with my mother and father.'" Canty, who knew nothing about the early death of Dean's mother or his estrangement from his father, did not understand this remark, but she was struck by his sensitivity. "When he felt the director wasn't pleased with him that really hurt him, right in his heart," she said. "He would stand there and cry like a baby."

Ray continued to go to great lengths to coddle Dean and make sure that he wasn't distracted. He let Dean bar the cameraman from saying "Speed" or "Roll 'em," making him use a silent cue instead, "the way they do it with animals," Backus pointed out with bemusement. James Baird, who played Judy's little brother Beau—and already a Hollywood veteran at nine—remembers that "everyone on the set would have to be quiet for a good two minutes" while Dean meditated to prepare for a scene, and then Ray would silently signal the cameras to roll when Dean lifted his head. "I had never seen anything like that," he says.

Doran believed that Ray was letting Dean get away with too much. By the time Dean shot the scene where Jim punches a desk in Ray Framek's office, two weeks after the rest of the police station sequence, Backus was starting to agree with her. Dean kept everyone waiting while he prepared for the scene in his dressing room, drinking cheap red wine, banging on his bongo drums and listening to Wagner's *Ride of the Valkyries,* which he can be heard humming earlier in the scene. "They were trying to get him on the set, but he wouldn't come out until he was ready," said Backus. As the production department began to fret about how much money Dean was costing the studio, Backus overheard one older crewmember say, "What the hell does he think he's doing? Even Garbo never got away with that."

Finally, after being holed up for an hour in his dressing room, Dean emerged to shoot the scene. The script called for Dean to let out his frustrations by smashing his fist against the desk, "letting loose for a moment." But no one was prepared for the fury that Dean unleashed. "We rehearsed that scene so Jimmy would be able to hit without hurting his knuckles," recalled Ray, "but when we began to shoot, it was clear that in the intensity of the scene he was hurting himself. I resisted the temptation to cut, and he continued to play the scene." He nailed the scene in one take, "so brilliantly that even the hard-boiled crew cheered and applauded," according to Backus, but Dean had seriously injured himself. After wrapping the scene, he was taken to the hospital to have his hand X-rayed. Although it was not broken, his hand was so badly bruised he had to wear an elastic bandage on it for a week. It began to seem there was no limit to how far Dean might go.

MOMISM

Working with Dean was not Doran's only difficulty on the film. She was also unhappy with the way her role was written. She lobbied Ray throughout the shoot to make her character more sympathetic. "Look, all you do is show the bad side of me," she said to him. "You never show any of the softness in me." Doran thought that the film at least could have presented her side. "She had a mother-in-law who was a horror, and a husband who was an ineffective jerk," says Doran. "How else could she be?"

The film's relatively broad portrait of Jim Stark's parents—domineering mother, weak father—is often considered the movie's major fault. According to both Stern and Ray, their intention was that the audience should see the parents not as they are but as they appeared through Jim's eyes. But the film does not always make this idea explicit. In general, Stern's—and Ray's—treatment of the parents seems to reflect the great weight that Hollywood gave at the time to Freudian psychological theories.

Back when Warners first tried to make a film based on Robert Lindner's book, the popularity of psychoanalysis was considered one of its major selling points. (In a memo to Warners about a potential *Rebel* project, producer Jerry Wald tried to persuade the studio by claiming the book "contains all the Freudian theories.") Freudianism became shorthand for screenwriters searching out character motivation, and Method actors used analysis to help them bring psychological depth to their acting. In his script, Stewart Stern not only incorporated psychological theories that were then in vogue, he also patterned Jim's parents after his own. "I was blaming my parents for everything because I had just started analysis," says Stern.

As Stern describes his own family, his physician father was a "sweet man of morality and ethics" who "because of his own mother—my dad's mother was a tyrant—was very passive in many ways and covered up the passivity with throat-clearing authority." Stern's mother, a minor actress on Broadway and in silent films, was a "determined woman who was not happy in the marriage and has to always pick, nothing's ever good." The weak father, henpecking mother and tyrannical grandmother were clearly models for Jim's family, just as Stern's family was the inspiration for the parents in his previous film, *Teresa*.

In fact, the *Rebel* scene that most strikingly illustrates the weakness of the father came directly from Stern's own experience. In the film, Jim comes home from the knife fight seeking his father's advice as to whether he should go to the chickie run that night. Finding his father dressed in his mother's apron on his hands and knees cleaning up a dinner tray he dropped, Jim mistakes him for his mother. Stern's own father would don his mother's apron and take dinner to her on a tray when she was ill. He still remembers "the way I felt when he sat down for dinner with the apron on, snapping the evening paper. I remember watching this apparition and thinking: Oh dad, poor dad, mama's hung you in the closet and I'm feeling so sad." The sight of Jim Backus in an apron became a prototypical image of the emasculated 1950s man.

In an interview with a reporter visiting the set, Ray cavalierly claimed that he could sum up the theme of the entire film in one sentence. Mr. Stark, he said, "fails to provide the adequate father image, either in strength or authority." With this simplistic analysis Ray was pandering to the idea, widely accepted at the time, that adolescent rebellion was chiefly the fault of weak, effeminate fathers and smothering, domineering mothers. In a best-selling book of the time, *Generation of Vipers,* writer Philip Wylie coined the word *momism* to describe women he believed had turned their sons and husbands into dysfunctional weaklings, claiming outlandishly that the ills of American society—from "hoodlumism" to "moral degeneration" and "chaos and war"—could be blamed on the growing power of women at the expense of men. Some of this male panic at the changing role of women would unfortunately seep into *Rebel* in ways that seem unnervingly misogynist by today's standards. "If he had guts to knock Mom cold once, then maybe she'd be happy," Jim says of his father after pounding the desk in Ray Framek's office. It's a line that may induce winces from modern audiences, more sensitive to the problems of spousal abuse, but it is also an accurate expression of Jim's rage.

Like the scene of Jim's parents bickering in the police station, the apron scene could easily have devolved into caricature, but once again

Dean's reaction brings an authenticity to the moment that keeps it from skirting over the edge into comedy. "When I first put the apron on, the crew laughed," said Backus. But Dean anticipates this reaction in the way he plays the scene, seeming amused himself at first, letting out his characteristic high-pitched laugh. But his amusement transforms into embarrassment, scorn and rage. He takes the audience with him through these emotions. The way he speaks his lines seems so realistically inarticulate that the viewer feels like a voyeur. Other actors always know the next line they are going to say because it is written in the script. Yet Dean gives the impression that he genuinely has no idea what he is about to say next. As good as Dean is, however, Backus also deserves credit. Backus may not have had much depth as an actor, but nevertheless he brings more sympathy to the role than was present in the writing and is comically touching in his apron, ineffectually suggesting that they make a list of the pros and cons of going to the chickie run. It is his best scene in the film.

"We knew we were walking a very thin line, so we'd do it, watch it, do it over, watch it again," said Backus. "We did it so many times that the lines were no longer cued. It became a real moment between Jim Stark and his father." But at that point, Backus was unaware of the far more real—and violent—confrontation that was in the offing, one in which Dean deliberately crossed the line between reality and fiction.

"DEAN TERRORIZES FILM SET"

The tension between Jim Stark and his father would reach its very threatening apex in a sequence that occurs just after the chickie run. It's a scene Dean and Ray had improvised at the Chateau Marmont long before film production started. After witnessing the death of Buzz, Jim returns to his home to find his father asleep in front of the television. Jim takes a bottle of milk out of the refrigerator and uses it to cool his forehead. He goes over to the couch and lies down; his red jacket against the red couch emphasizes the film's doubled sense of danger. (Red-on-red would be an attention-getting color move that Ray employed throughout his career.)

As Jim lies with his head upside down over the edge of the couch, the film suddenly cuts to *Rebel*'s boldest camera move. As his mother comes downstairs, we see her upside down, and then the camera turns 180 degrees to right itself. Ray and cinematographer Ernest Haller achieved this complex shot in three takes, also filming one version without the 180-degree effect just in case. The shot risks accusations of grandstanding, but it plays an integral part in the film. "The shot came to express my feeling toward the entire scene," said Ray. "Here was a house in danger of tipping from side to side. It was organic to the scene."

In fact, the 180-degree effect represents the only time that we clearly feel what Ray and Stern intended in their portrait of the parents: that we are seeing them through Jim's eyes. And it is both literally and metaphorically the pivot of the film. In *Rebel*'s topsy-turvy moral universe, it is Jim's parents who advise their son not to go to the police, to shirk responsibility, to forget what happened at the chickie run, while it is Jim who wants to do the right thing. At a time when fears of juvenile delinquency, of a generation that had gone morally astray, were reaching hysterical heights, *Rebel* proposed the radical idea that it was actually the adults who had lost their moral compass.

As a now-upright Jim argues with his parents at the foot of the stairs about whether he should go to the police, their skewed morality is signaled by off-kilter, almost comic-book camera tilts. "A boy—a kid—was killed tonight!" Jim cries. "I don't see how I can get out of that by pretending it didn't happen!" When his mother persists in arguing that he not go to the police, warning "a foolish decision now could wreck your whole life," Jim says to his father, "Dad, stand up for me." At this point the screenplay's directions say, "He leaps at his father, dragging him to his feet, hands at the man's throat." But Dean had something far more provocative in mind.

Only Ray knew what Dean planned to do at the end of this scene. "Nick wanted the shock value of it," says Jackie Perry, who was on the set that day. "I don't think that Jim Backus really knew what was going to happen." The *Los Angeles Herald-Examiner*'s Harrison Carroll, one of several reporters on the set that week, described what happened in an article headlined: DEAN TERRORIZES FILM SET.

Instead of simply pulling Backus to his feet, as the script called for, Dean leapt at him like a wild animal let out of his cage, grabbed the two-hundred-pound actor's lapels, dragged him down the stairs and across the living room and threw him over a chair, which tumbled over backward. Then he wrapped his hands around Backus's throat and began to choke him. When Doran cries out, "You're killing him! Do you want to kill your own father?" her fear is real. "Backus was really shocked by what happened," says Perry. "And I think Ann Doran was just as shocked."

To Doran, Dean was totally out of control. But things were not exactly how they seemed. "I thought I was a goner," Backus told Harrison Carroll. "I might have been, but this boy is as strong as a bull. Even while he was flinging me around, he held onto me so that I wouldn't fall." When Carroll went up to Dean and said, "You had Backus jittery," Dean seemed amused for a moment, then replied defensively, "Yes, I know, but I have never hurt another actor in my life."

Although the Oedipal implications of this scene would shock audiences, for Stern it was a crucial moment in the film. It demonstrated a key turning point in Jim's passage into adulthood, which had come out of Stern's own feelings toward his father, feelings of "wanting my father obliterated and, at the same time, saved."

Backus took it all less seriously. "Welcome to the Elia Kazan Hour," he joked.

THE "NEGRO WOMAN"

Jim Stark's broadly written mother and father are not the only parental figures in *Rebel* that might cause a little unease for a contemporary audience. Plato's nanny, played by Marietta Canty, is the only guardian he is supplied in the film, but her character did not even have a name. In the script, she is dismissively referred to as "Negro Woman." To this day Stewart Stern regrets this oversight.

Asked why he did not give her a name, he plainly admits, "I have writhed with that question." Stern says that he is particularly pained because, like Plato, he was "raised by the help" and also had a black nanny, named Ethel, whom he adored. When he was three years old, she was fired because he and his nanny began spending time at the estate of his uncle, Adolph Zukor, and the other nannies complained about having to eat at the table with a black woman.

By the time Marietta Canty was cast in *Rebel,* she was a veteran of over fifty films, including *Sea of Grass, The Bad and the Beautiful,* and *Father of the Bride.* She had gotten her first big break as an actress in 1936 when Ray's friend John Houseman saw her perform in a series of three one-act plays in Harlem. She starred in a number of plays on Broadway and on tours throughout the country, breaking the color barrier in Miami by becoming the first black actress to appear onstage with a white cast in that segregated Southern city. In 1942 she went to Hollywood, and Marlene Dietrich was so impressed with her performance in that year's *The Lady Is Willing* that she had a role especially written for Canty in her next film, *The Spoilers.* But Canty, a deeply religious woman who did not drink or smoke, and had never before lived outside of Hartford, Connecticut, felt out of place in Hollywood. "The first time I went to California, it was December," she remembered. "I wanted to get a Christmas tree—it was 98 degrees. I went out and couldn't find a green tree anywhere. They had been sprayed pink, blue, all different colors except green. I was in tears."

In virtually all of Canty's films, she was cast as a maid. "She was rather upset with those roles," her sister Emily Anderson said, "but it wasn't the time for blacks to be in anything but those insignificant roles." Homesick and frustrated with the parts she was getting, she returned to Hartford in 1952 to care for her dying mother. After her mother passed away, she returned to Hollywood to take a part in *A Man Called Peter,* a religious film about a Scottish minister who becomes chaplain of the U.S. Senate. But her next film, *Rebel Without a Cause,* would be her last. She was offered the role of the maid in *The Danny Thomas Show,* but turned it down and went back to Hartford to take care of her father, who was himself now ailing. Canty never went back to Hollywood. She became a nurse and justice of the peace, and was very active in her church and community, even making two pioneering but unsuccessful runs for city council as a Republican.

The fact that Canty's character has no name is just one example of *Rebel*'s silence on the issue of race. (Ray shot a scene that included Mexican children in the police precinct but it was cut from the final film; the children can be glimpsed in the background as Dean is being checked in.) *Rebel*'s silence is surprising considering that Ray was determined to break so much ground concerning American hypocrisy and was so responsive to the issues of the day. The year 1955 was a critical time for the civil rights movement. Less than a year before, the Supreme Court had issued its land-mark decision in *Brown v. Board of Education* banning segregation in schools. In April 1955, while *Rebel* was being shot, the Supreme Court heard arguments concerning remedies for carrying out its order in *Brown,* issuing its famous decision a month later ordering the desegregation of schools "with all deliberate speed." Before the year was over, fourteen-year-old Emmett Till would be murdered in Mississippi, and Rosa Parks would refuse to give up her seat on a bus, setting off the Montgomery bus boy-cott, events that catalyzed the modern civil rights movement.

Of course, Ray had no special responsibility for dealing with issues of race. And *Rebel* does reflect the demographics at the time of Los Ange-les, a largely segregated city still suffering from the effects of race riots that had erupted during World War II. Yet *Rebel* seems to be in denial on issues of race, especially when compared with its rival teen film, *Blackboard Jungle.*

Blackboard Jungle may have been several significant steps behind *Rebel* in its treatment of juvenile delinquency, but when it came to race, it was much more forward-thinking. The diverse classroom in *Blackboard Jungle* featured Sidney Poitier, the first African-American actor to win an Acad-emy Award, in his breakout role. At one point, Richard Dadier, the teacher played by Glenn Ford, gives an impassioned speech about the harm done by racial epithets, spewing the words *spic, mick* and *nigger* with a rawness that is as shocking today as it was in 1955. After he is falsely accused of racial bigotry for saying these words, the school's principal tells him, "I don't care if a boy's skin is black, yellow or purple. He gets the same teach-ing, the same breaks as any white boy. There's enough immorality in the world without your adding to it."

There is nothing so groundbreaking in *Rebel*'s considerations of race. In general, Canty's character is conceived within the boundaries for black maids and nannies onscreen. "How many times have we seen her!" James Baldwin once complained of the stereotype. "She is Dilsey, she is Mammy, in *Gone With the Wind,* and in *Imitation of Life,* and *The Member of the Wedding*—mother of sorrows, whore and saint." This stock Hollywood character was often embraced as part of the family, as Canty is here, but Baldwin reminds us that "she would appear to have no family of her own." Nevertheless, Canty—and Ray—deserve some credit for enhancing the script at key moments to provide the "Negro Woman" with a measure of character and heft.

Wherever possible throughout *Rebel*, Canty and Ray attempt to expand the sense of the nanny's importance as a surrogate mother in Plato's life. As played by Canty, Plato's nanny becomes the only truly sympathetic adult, aside from Officer Ray Framek. Canty is the only one of the film's caretakers who really seems to care. And her outsider status gives her a position that is unique in the film. She offers compassion to the teenagers and a rebuke to the white adults in the film. She loves Plato unconditionally and, despite his problems, she does her best to protect him.

When we first meet Canty, in the police station sequence, she is watching carefully and protectively as Jim offers Plato his jacket and Plato refuses, a motif that will be echoed at the end of the film. When Plato is called into a policeman's office for an interrogation about why he shot the puppies, Stern's screenplay calls for Canty merely to follow Plato. But in the film, she holds him, supports him and walks him into the room, signaling a profound difference in their relationship. Canty's character explains to the policeman (played by Robert Foulk) that she is there because Plato's parents are divorced and his mother, as often seems to be the case, is out of town. (The script originally offered the absence of Plato's mother as the explanation for why he shot the puppies—"They were nursing on their mother and I did it"—a line inspired by a jealous boy Stewart Stern interviewed who killed some ducklings for the same reason.)

Late in the film, when three of Buzz's henchmen descend on Plato's house, the script calls for the housekeeper to open the door while Plato runs past her inside. But onscreen, Canty takes a muscular and fearlessly maternal step, pulling Mineo into the house and pushing the gang members away. It's a small moment yet an important one. And in the movie's finale, Ray would give Canty so many close-ups it would raise the nanny's stature immensely.

Though she never made another film, Canty never expressed bitterness about her time in Hollywood and looked back fondly on *Rebel*. "It was probably the most outstanding film of my life," she told an interviewer in 1982. One might think that with the passing years Warner Brothers would finally come around to recognizing her achievement. Yet in a 1990 book sanctioned by the studio and co-written by Warner archivist Leith Adams,

James Dean: Behind the Scene, a picture of Canty from *Rebel Without a Cause* misidentifies her as another black actress, Louise Beavers. Nobody, apparently, bothered to check.

DADDY'S GIRL

While we are introduced to Plato's nanny and Jim's parents in the police precinct sequence, we do not meet Judy's family until much later in the film, during a dinner scene at Judy's home, which was actually shot right after the color reshoots at the planetarium. Judy's mother—played by Rochelle Hudson, a onetime ingénue who had worked in films only sporadically after leaving Hollywood during World War II to work for Naval Intelligence—is something of a cardboard cutout of the typical 1950s mom, imported directly from an early sitcom. Judy's father was portrayed by William Hopper, who played small roles in more than a hundred films, and eventually landed the part of investigator Paul Drake on *Perry Mason.* But he was perhaps best known as the son of powerful Hollywood gossip columnist Hedda Hopper. Judy's relationship with her father would set off another battle with the censors.

During the dinner scene in which Hopper is introduced, Judy repeatedly tries to kiss her dad, who rebuffs her attempts at affection. "You're getting too old for that kind of stuff, kiddo," he tells her. But Judy won't let the matter drop, making her father angrier. Given the situation, his reaction seems suspect. And finally, when Judy jumps up and innocently kisses him, he viciously slaps her and she storms out of the house.

This scene is redolent with sexual implications. And according to Stewart Stern, the erotic subtext was intentional. It was suggested as far back as Leon Uris's original *Rebel* treatment. Stern says that the relationship was supposed to reflect "that whole terrible confusion in a man when his daughter reaches that age. All of the feelings you're not supposed to have as a father come out. This child you held on your lap—without an erotic arousal—is still a child inside. She needs all the same affection. So you can do nothing except reject her, punish her for your feelings."

It was unusual and daring for a Hollywood film to explore such a taboo subject as the attraction between a father and daughter. But it was in line with Ray's determination to address the messy truth about sexuality and family, to instinctively pursue certain themes that haunted him at least since he discovered his ex-wife in bed with his son. However, ever-watchful censor Geoffrey Shurlock was having none of it.

In a memo to Jack Warner, Shurlock wrote: "This scene between Judy and her father should be handled without any objectionable flavor of an incestuous reaction. As now written the father's reaction of being shocked by Judy kissing him, and later slapping her, seems to point up this objectionable inference." He offered a suggestion on one way the scene might be played. "In order to avoid any questionable flavor to this scene," he suggested, "we urge that Judy do not actually kiss her father on the lips, but only move towards him with this in mind, which will bring about his reaction. This will omit the actual kiss."

Warner Brothers' Code representative Finlay McDermid was able to convince Shurlock that he was reading too much into the scene and to wait and see how it played on film. McDermid was apparently unable to grasp what was really happening in the scene. "I don't quite understand what Shurlock's point is here," he told Steve Trilling in a memo. Ironically, Shurlock's ability to perceive sexual taboos lurking in seemingly innocent scenes was often more sophisticated than that of studio executives or even many critics. Although it was his job to sniff out and snuff out any possible innuendo, it's remarkable how insightful he was at a time when even the most erudite film reviewers failed to notice the subtle—and not so subtle—references in *Rebel* to such off-limits topics as incest and homosexuality.

But when it came time to shoot the scene, the studio was still clearly worried. "The day I kissed my father on the mouth and he slapped me, four executives with briefcases showed up on the set," Wood remembered. As it turns out, Judy does not kiss her father on the mouth; she merely pecks him on his cheek, allaying the censor's concerns. It is also possible that Ray may have been trying to further mollify Shurlock by casting an older, less sexually attractive actor like Hopper to play her father, though Stern's screenplay described the father as "boyish, attractive and debonair." The father's guilt remains provocative, and Hopper's coldness results in a portrayal that is deeply unsympathetic. He comes off as another sharp-lined caricature in *Rebel*'s gallery of poisoned parents.

Looking back on the film, Stewart Stern agrees with many critics who found his depiction of the parents too harsh. But he also feels that Ray "failed to correct it in performance. I think he compounded my error. I think that was the great fault in the writing, whatever it was that prompted both Nick and myself to really be tough on all parents." Clearly, Ray was dealing with his own issues concerning his alcoholic father—and authority in general. He overidentified with Jim Stark's point of view, failing to perceive how an audience might react to the parents. But Ray also seems to be channeling all the guilt he had about his own failures as a parent to his two sons, who were growing up with his ex-wives, estranged from their father.

Ray dumped all of his messy, contradictory feelings into *Rebel*, spilling an amazing amount of raw anguish and unresolved emotion onto the screen. And while critics may be correct in finding fault with the portrayal of the parents, the film does seem to absorb all of the ambivalence, confusion, self-righteousness—and wrongheadedness—of adolescence. *Rebel* does more than merely present an adolescent's conflicted feelings toward his or her parents. It embodies them. Its flawed portrait of the parents is a manifestation of the film's total identification with youth, which contributes to its status as *the* teen movie of all time.

CHAPTER ELEVEN

A World of Their Own

During the fourth week of production, with the film three days behind schedule, Ray and his crew established camp at *Rebel*'s most hauntingly atmospheric location: the abandoned Getty estate. The time had come to shoot the mansion sequence—the emotional heart of the movie—which would mark an important shift in the relationships between the movie's stars. Ray knew there was a lot riding on the effectiveness of the mansion sequence. In a film full of fragile moments, these scenes required a special delicacy. If the yet-to-be-shot "chickie run" sequence would prove to be *Rebel*'s most spectacular and action-packed, the mansion scenes are its most quietly profound and romantic.

The key scenes at the mansion had a hushed, hothouse quality. And it's during this sequence that *Rebel* taps into its most important new idea: the sense that teenagers had the power to form a world of their own. Ray gave wing to the poignant, latent wish of many newly empowered kids to see adolescence as a beautiful, dignified, stand-alone state, not just as a holding pattern in which they waited aimlessly for adulthood to arrive. In many ways, Ray anticipated the birth of the notion of "teen culture." The scenes he crafted at the mansion still have the power to rouse the dormant teen in the oldest moviegoer.

In the finished film, this lengthy mansion sequence takes place after the chickie run—the movie's fulcrum—where Jim and Buzz race to the edge of a cliff and Buzz plunges to a watery death. From the chickie run forward, *Rebel*'s mood darkens. After Buzz is killed, the characters disperse to their homes—but they find little solace there. Later that very same night,

Jim, Judy and Plato reunite at a deserted mansion. As the sequence begins, three members of Buzz's gang—Crunch (Frank Mazzola), Goon (Dennis Hopper) and Moose (Jack Grinnage)—are searching for Dean to exact revenge for Buzz's death. Eventually, they track him to the deserted mansion, where a chase and fight ensue. But before that happens, Dean, Mineo and Wood share a suspended moment of happiness, exploring the deserted estate, playing in its empty pool. It is during this crucial interlude that the three stars meld into a surrogate family. Eventually, Plato falls asleep at Jim's feet, and Jim and Judy share what would be Natalie Wood's first movie kiss.

The primary mansion scenes had been rehearsed and rehearsed. But getting things right would not be easy. For the film to resonate, this sequence had to be everything it could be. Certain barriers between Ray's stars—particularly Dean and Wood—would need to be finessed. Some emotional maneuvers would be required. And Ray hoped that the sprawling mansion would serve as a stimulus to creativity, a liberating environment for his actors.

THE PHANTOM HOUSE

Although the mansion would become one of the film's most indelible settings, the idea for the sequence grew out of a plainly logistical problem with the script. Screenwriter Stern was having trouble figuring out how to bring his three main characters together again after they had dispersed to their homes following the shock of Buzz's death. He needed to put them in a place where they would have time to develop their three-way relationship, which in turn would lay the groundwork for the movie's tragic climax. In a typical movie, these scenes could easily have taken place the next day, but that notion violated Stern's sense of *Rebel*'s structure, his sense of the film as a night journey.

Stern confessed his problem to Ray at the director's studio office. Together they discussed where and how the trio could come together. They brainstormed for only fifteen minutes before they hit on a perfect solution. "We began to talk about what kind of place it would be," remembered Stern. "And one of us mentioned *Sunset Boulevard*. That mansion.

Nick knew that it was still up and we thought that that would be terrific as a set." The mansion's stateliness—its Mediterranean-style porticos, pillars, balustrades, gardens, pool and fountains—instantly appealed to Stern and Ray, as did the house's air of dreamy dilapidation. The house had been used as the home of Norma Desmond, the megalomaniacal silent screen star in director Billy Wilder's classic film. It became a metaphor for that character's deteriorating state of mind and her declining position in Hollywood. Obviously, the house served well as the cinematic symbol of a dying world. Ironically—and somewhat devilishly—Ray also envisioned the sad old villa as a giant playhouse for his kids. "He had a notion that they would play games there and that there could be a wonderful kind of crazy Walpurgis Night celebration, that maybe Jimmy would pretend that he was a real estate man. So that seemed very exciting to me," said Stern.

After their brief discussion, Ray went off to lunch with David Weisbart, but Stern stayed behind to work. He felt a rush of creativity as he sat in Weisbart's outer office with a yellow legal pad on his knee. The mansion provided the ideal inspiration for Stern. He was able to draw on his own background of privilege, his memories of the sprawling Long Island estate of his uncle Arthur Loew Sr. "It took me less time to write that sequence than any other sequence," says Stern. "It just wrote itself." But securing the use of the mansion would not come as easily.

Built in 1924, the grand estate originally belonged to sugar magnate and United States Consul to Mexico William O. Jenkins. He spent the then-astronomical cost of a quarter of a million dollars on its construction. But Jenkins and his family resided in the palatial fourteen-bedroom estate for only a year before abandoning it and returning to Mexico. In 1936, the deserted mansion was purchased by oil millionaire J. Paul Getty—who never lived in it. Dubbed "the Phantom House" because it stood empty for so many years, its status as a defining set in two classic films can be traced to the wife of *Sunset Boulevard*'s set designer, John Meehan. She recommended it for use in Billy Wilder's film, and her husband would go on to share an art direction and set design Oscar largely based on the mansion's effectiveness. The fact that the house—which sat at the intersection of Wilshire and Crenshaw boulevards—was unoccupied should have been good news for Ray and Warner Brothers. But nothing would ever be that simple for the *Rebel* production team. As it turned out, the mansion was slated to be destroyed.

Starting in mid-February, the Warners location staff—led by W. F. FitzGerald—tried to delay the house's destruction, but had trouble immediately contacting Getty, who was away in Europe. Meanwhile, they searched frantically for a replacement mansion. As a backup, the studio considered the mansion from another film about Hollywood, Vincente Minnelli's luxuriously melodramatic *The Bad and the Beautiful*. But on contacting MGM, FitzGerald and his staff discovered that, even though they were studio pros, they had fallen for a classic Hollywood illusion. *The Bad and the Beautiful* house was almost entirely fabricated. As a Warners in-house memo explained in detail, "The entrance gate to this was the Lewis Estate Gates. The exterior of the house was a Newcomb [matte] shot made on their back lot. The interiors were shot on the stage set."

On February 21, Warner Brothers finally heard from Getty through his secretary. He agreed to let the studio use the house at a cost of $250 a day. By April 7, agreements were signed. The destruction of the house would be postponed, and the shooting dates were locked into place. "In order to secure this location," wrote FitzGerald, "we have to confirm with the dates as follows: April 16th, 18th, 20th and to finish on April 21, 1955. Any change with these dates from their attitude will not be accepted by them." Getty had recently won a lawsuit against residents who tried to stop the mansion's demolition, so he wanted to knock it down as soon as possible and replace it with the headquarters of Getty Oil before they put any more roadblocks in his way.

But before filming could begin, *Rebel* art director Malcolm Bert and set decorator William Wallace made certain changes at the mansion, to emphasize its look of abandonment and to give Ray a variety of settings in which to stage his "Walpurgis Night." Actor Jack Grinnage remembers that "the whole gazebo and all that stuff behind the swimming pool was built for *Rebel*." The Getty swimming pool—which would figure prominently in the mansion scenes—had been built by Paramount specifically for *Sunset Boulevard*. The studio had promised to remove the pool after the Wilder movie had wrapped. Luckily, Paramount did not follow through. The pool—which lacked a drain since it was never intended to be used as a real pool—now stood empty, creating a sunken stage that would be a perfect setting for the kids' nocturnal reverie.

THE NICK RAY 50-HOUR CLUB

From the beginning, things went wrong at the mansion. The studio was putting the squeeze on Ray to speed up the pace of shooting, especially on location. But although time was tight and inflexible, Ray was not about to rein in his vision or ambitions. On the first day of shooting at the estate, Saturday, April 16, he planned to use a fifty-foot crane to create a grand master shot of the fight between Mineo and the gang in the empty pool. But the crane was an hour late in arriving. Ray had time only to do one quick rehearsal of the boom shot, which involved some complicated fight choreography that the kids themselves were improvising. He had to complete the boom shot and several closer shots before Mineo's time was up. Like Wood, the other minor on the set, Mineo could not work past eleven that evening. But in the middle of the boom shot, Mineo collapsed. As Ray wrote in a memo to David Weisbart, Mineo "folded on me. I had to keep rolling while he revived in order to save the time absorbed by resetting and all the other mish-mash that goes on after a cut." Ray had only ten minutes to complete the shot.

This couldn't have happened at a worse time. Weisbart had been putting pressure on Ray about his use of exceptionally long takes, which Weisbart felt were a waste of footage. Ray was forced to defend this long boom shot in his memo to Weisbart. Trying to appease the producer, Ray added, "I just don't want you to think I am unmindful of our discussions about long takes and excess footage. There's always a reason—I'll try to make sure they're good reasons." To further mollify the studio, Ray asked cinematographer Ernest Haller to work with him the next day—Sunday, their usual day off—to preplan for any further lighting problems at the mansion, as well as at two night locations that were left to shoot: those for the chickie run and the finale at the planetarium. Ray was clearly feeling the pressure from the studio. Then again, Ray derived great amounts of creative energy by working against authority. And by his own admission, he was a man who liked to work on his projects all day, every day. Later in life, he would jokingly refer to one of his movie sets as the "Nick Ray 50-Hour Club."

The fifty-eight-year-old Haller—whom most *Rebel* survivors remember as a kind soul, often willing to share his many Hollywood stories—was not always amenable to Ray's driven and impetuous ways. Haller was more of a classicist, having toiled for the studios since the days of silent film. According to Frank Mazzola, "Nick was hassling with Ernie Haller a lot because of the time it took to do things. Nick did a lot of unique shots. They were very instinctive. He'd suddenly say, 'Put the camera here.' He'd say, 'Let's move the camera and get this one shot before the evening.'"

Ray knew he would not be able to return to the mansion at a later date, so he insisted on the widest possible variety of shots and angles. It was always Ray's style—and an essential aspect of the cinematic energy of his films—to shoot from multiple points of view, to strive for dynamism. Ray wanted to break away from old shooting formulas that carefully moved from long shot to medium shot to close-up. He found this studio-bred style to be "tepid." He favored Billy Wilder's approach. "With Billy, you're there, and it's WOW! Over to the right, WOW! Over to the left, BANG! To the center." Ray also liked the kind of cutting he found in comic strips. "Some of the strips take you from close-ups to extreme long shot, but there will always be some key object in the center that leads you out." He wasn't afraid of images that "violently oppose" each other. And he liked to make his cuts in mid-action, which added to the kinetic quality of his films.

On the following Monday, April 18, all the principals met at the mansion for the first time. Wood was on hand and, once again, her core insecurity was showing. She was nervous about the challenging intimate moments that were coming up, especially the kiss. Dean had just returned from four days off. Sal Mineo, Jack Grinnage, Dennis Hopper and Frank Mazzola were back. Although she does not appear in the mansion sequences, Beverly Long was also present. And adding to the haunted-house atmosphere of the set, Vampira dropped by to visit Dean, along with Jack Simmons. Ray had crafted the schedule to ease his major players into a comfort level with the mansion. Dean and Wood would not have to shoot their all-important love scene until the very last day at the estate. For the first two days that week, the cast and crew shot more of the gang's fight with Plato at the bottom of the empty pool, including a scene where Goon (Hopper) jumps into the bottom of the cement pool from its ten-foot-high diving board. Ray shot the scene three times, pushing the scapegoated Hopper so hard that he ended up with sore and swollen feet.

The beginning of the week also gave Frank Mazzola a chance to show off. After the gang battles Plato in the empty pool, his character Crunch was set to be shot by Plato and fall down a flight of stairs. Mazzola made the most of his big moment. Throughout the film, the young actors who made up the gang were grateful for any extra cash that came their way. And Mazzola was wily enough to create his own moneymaking opportunities. He had already secured one extra paycheck by acting as gang advisor for Dean and Ray during preproduction. Now he talked assistant director Don Page into allowing him to do his own stunt.

"I negotiated with Don Page," said Mazzola. "He asked, 'How many times do you think it's going to take?' And I said, 'It's not up to me. It's up to the director.' So I said, 'For every stunt I do, we negotiate a price.' I think I got $125 for each time I went down the steps." All in all, Mazzola fell four times, adding up to a solid bonus of $500. According to Beverly Long, "Every time he fell down the stairs, he would do something wrong so he would have to do it again."

Ray also shot a scene in which Jim runs over to Crunch to make sure he is all right, letting the audience know that Crunch survives the shooting. This scene, however, was cut from the final film and the fate of Crunch has always remained a mystery to *Rebel* viewers. "I can understand as an editor why it's not there," says Mazzola, who went on to a career as a film editor. "It slows the action down."

On that same day, when attention turned back to the fight in the empty pool, Mazzola created another problem for Ray. Crunch was supposed to take a fall when Plato hits him with a rubber hose. But the combative former Athenian did not like the idea of being taken down so easily. It ruffled the machismo of the real-life gang member. "It felt weird," Mazzola said. "Believe me; a hose isn't going to stop me from going after a guy." Ray demonstrated his quiet power over his kids by gently taking Mazzola aside and assuring him that everything would be fine. According to Mazzola, "Nick would say, 'Just trust me.' You'd put yourself in his hands. He would take you there."

"DROWN THEM LIKE PUPPIES!"

Although Ray and company were weeks into *Rebel*'s production, discomfort continued to exist between James Dean and Natalie Wood. There were some reports that Wood was actually angry with Dean during the mansion week. According to her friend Jackie Perry, Wood complained because Dean would come to the set but refuse to speak to her. "When they weren't in front of the camera, he had nothing to do with her. She had never experienced this before," says Perry.

In a magazine article that was written by Wood (or, at the very least, carried her byline), she professed a certain level of understanding regarding Dean's silences, which were sometimes interpreted as an element of his process. "Boy, is he intent," Wood wrote. Dean "made it plain he wanted no conversation. He was kind of working himself into the role. Flailing his arms about, going through a bicycle type movement with his legs. 'I'm concentrating' was all he said." Wood was drawn to Dean's approach to acting—in theory—but the young Hollywood-bred child star remained uneasy with him. "She was not happy with the way Jimmy would do this kind of—attention getting—let's put it that way," said Wood's friend and Dean's *East of Eden* co-star Dick Davalos.

Dean could be cruel and contemptuous of Wood on set. During her close-ups, he would taunt her from behind the camera, climbing a ladder and whistling loudly at her as if he were a train. According to Ray, "When he was off-camera he'd always try to break her up, and she'd go into tears. I had to play the scenes with her."

Actress Carroll Baker recalls hanging out with Dean and Mineo on the Warners lot when Dean spotted Wood, who was dressed in a peasant blouse and gypsy skirt. Dean motioned her over "like an animal trainer calling a dog to heel" and proceeded to embarrass her. He shook his head disapprovingly and called Wood's outfit corny. Then he turned to Baker and said, "Carroll, why don't you teach Natalie how to dress?"

Wood felt humiliated, and so did Mineo. "Little Sal Mineo," said Baker, "not knowing where else to look or what else to do, had by this time dug the toe of his shoe into a crack in the pavement and was having difficulty dislodging it. That instant Jimmy must have tired of his sadistic game. He grabbed me by the hand and pulled me onto the motor bike."

Although Mineo could obviously be cowed by Dean, he was much more comfortable than Wood with Dean's behavior on set and off. From the very first, he could handle Dean's constant improvisations, simply responding with creative solutions of his own. In fact, throughout the shooting of *Rebel*, Mineo continued to deepen his bond with both his co-stars. Mineo and Wood had developed an antic and supportive sibling-like alliance. "Every time we'd get together, or talk by phone," said Wood, "we'd assume different accents—English, Mexican, Swedish, German, anything you could think of." Mineo "enjoyed horseplay with Natalie," said their on-set tutor Tom Hennesy. "Sometimes if I'd go to the head and be gone for five minutes, I'd come back and they'd be doing things like getting on the couch and pretending they were necking—which was way out of reality." According to Ann Doran, Mineo had been advising Wood on how to deal with Dean. "Honey, it's his way of doing things," he would tell her. "Just get with him." In the mansion sequence's pivotal garden and gazebo scenes, Mineo could be counted on to provide the link between Dean and Wood. He completed the circuit.

The garden scene occurs at the beginning of the mansion sequence. In the film itself, the mansion is introduced in a highly stylized, horror-movie master shot, a perfect example of Ray's bent toward heightened visual effects. It is a cloudy, blue-gray night. The dark, abandoned mansion looms in the foreground, with its shutters half torn off. The celestial lights of the nearby planetarium are matted into the background. The sound of shattering glass is heard as Jim and Judy break in. Almost immediately, Plato also arrives at the mansion on his scooter to warn Jim that members of Buzz's gang are looking for him. Director Francis Ford Coppola remembers being especially affected by this scene when he first saw the film as a teenager. "I was very haunted by the story of Sal Mineo," says the director, who particularly identified with Plato. "The most moving thing to me was when Natalie Wood and James Dean go into the [mansion] and their friend Plato is knocking on the door, excluded as he always was."

When Dean finally lets Plato in, he discovers Judy is also there, perched on the grand black walnut staircase. (A Warners publicity memo states that a microphone was disguised as part of the staircase.) Together, the three of them play out a fantasy. Plato pretends to be a real estate broker showing a young couple around the house. This was the beginning of what Mineo would call his favorite stretch of the movie. Full of darkness and deep shadows, it captures the essence of an enchanted "night journey," just as Stewart Stern had hoped. Plato leads Judy and Jim through the mansion holding a candelabra, which, in contrast to the romantic tone of the scene, was connected to a gas jet that went through Mineo's arm and down his leg. The wire and its shadow can actually be spotted onscreen.

As they make their way out into the garden, the trio shares some sweet, poignant dialogue written by Stewart Stern to reflect their naïve but wounded view of their parents' attitudes. Jim and Judy pretend to be interested in buying the house, which Plato describes, with a child's disregard for money, as costing "only three million dollars a month."

Judy adds, "Oh, there's just one thing. What about . . ."

> PLATO: *Children? See, we really don't encourage them. They're so noisy and troublesome, don't you agree?*
> JUDY: *And so terribly annoying when they cry. I just don't know what to do when they cry, do you dear?*

Suddenly, at that point, Dean erupts in a strange unscripted sound—a comical "Arrrrh." Then he growls his line: "Drown them like puppies." Although it is not indicated in the screenplay, Dean is actually—and outrageously—imitating Mr. Magoo, the nearsighted cartoon character voiced by Jim Backus, the actor playing Dean's father. Dean had been known to imitate Mr. Magoo before, notably when he once spotted Backus and his wife stumbling around in a dark movie theater, looking for their seats, which, according to Stewart Stern, gave Dean the idea to use the imitation in *Rebel*. It's a funny joke, one that underscores the playfulness of the garden scene. And it was a daring move on Dean's part, concocting an inside joke that might actually have upset the fictional dream Ray and company were striving to maintain. Nevertheless, the moment works; Dean's self-referential joke brings a zing of postmodernism to the film.

The improvisation also caught the attention of the studio brass, but they felt there was room for improvement. They were not pleased that Dean had referenced a character from another studio. They suggested he substitute Mr. Magoo with Warners' Bugs Bunny. According to Jim Backus, "Jimmy's reaction was: 'Get your ass out of here!'" Ironically, Dean's evocation of Mr. Magoo was entirely true to the spirit of Warners' cartoon characters, who often broke the fourth wall to wink at the audience.

It was not the only quick-witted improvisation Dean would concoct that day. Dean was inspired by the mood of the mansion. It had worked its magic, just as Ray and Stern had hoped. Dean tossed in many funny asides that were not in the script, reacting open-heartedly to the environment. ("Hey, you forgot to wind your sundial!" "Your house is a mess.") His work was deeply responsive—and, in the finished film, his reactions play beautifully, adding to the scene's sense of emotional freedom.

But the garden scene was merely a prelude to the sequence shot on Wednesday, one of the most moving scenes in the film. The trio concludes its journey through the garden by walking across the bottom of the empty pool (an ineffably magical moment that Ray captures in a stunning crane shot). Then, all three retire to a gazebo. Dean lies down in Judy's lap; Plato sits on the floor at their feet. Suddenly, Ray's camera moves slightly above his characters for a close shot of all three faces, and a limpid sadness comes to the fore.

Plato talks about his estranged parents, and the mood of playfulness changes into something much more naked and tender. A magic circle is formed. Mineo lies about his father—saying he was dead and a "hero in the China Sea"—but Jim reminds him that previously he said his father was alive and a "big wheel" in New York. Plato shrugs as if he can barely remember the truth. It's as if they are slowly forgetting the world outside.

Although the shiver-inducing, hypnotic strength of the mansion sequence would be the result of great work on everyone's part, the emotional core of the scene can be attributed directly to screenwriter Stewart Stern. From childhood, Stern was entranced by Peter Pan. "It's the lost boys of Never Land and it's Wendy and Peter," says Stern. "He would teach me to fly."

Stern saw the safe space the teenagers create as "a magic world built on the armature of Jim's unfulfilled wishes about his parents." According to Stern, Jim "created an idealized family in which he was the father, Judy the mother and Plato the child. He could act out all those things he wished his father could have been able to do—defend him against his own rage, disarm his anger with understanding, risk his life for him."

But more than family relationships are evoked. A three-way current of desire runs beneath the surface of this scene, and it would make itself known in a striking—indeed groundbreaking—moment of intimacy.

The gazebo sequence is the one that secured Mineo's role in *Rebel* when they rehearsed it in front of a camera several weeks earlier. Throughout that rehearsal, he and Dean maintained nearly constant physical contact. But in the final film, their interplay is more restrained, which only makes its subversive highlight all the more startling. Plato's pliant position on the floor is already psychologically loaded, as is the look in his eyes. And throughout, Dean seems to be as deeply responsive to Mineo as he is to Wood. But then suddenly, in an entirely natural movement, Plato lays his head affectionately on Jim's arm. The scene has been so chaste up to this point that the moment leaps off the screen. It rattles one's sense of what was allowed between two men, especially two young men, in the mid-1950s. But just as quickly, like a mirage, the image disappears. The film cuts to a close-up of Mineo and his head no longer lies on Dean's arm. Ray had pushed the envelope and then pulled back. Still, a boundary had been crossed.

The ancient Greeks had four words for love—*philia* (friendship), *storge* (familial love), *eros* (sexual love) and *agape* (unconditional or sacrificial love)—and what is remarkable about the relationship between Jim, Judy and Plato, what ultimately makes their love so powerful, is that it does not fall neatly into just one of these categories, but encompasses all four. They are friends; they create a surrogate family; they have an erotic connection. Then, in the film's climax, the bonds they form at the mansion lead Jim and Judy to risk their lives trying to save Plato, a boy they had met just that morning.

Looking back, Stewart Stern views this sequence as the beginning of something new in American culture. "The whole movement toward getting in touch with your feelings, that whole flower child movement, it all happened in the wake of *Rebel*. I don't mean *Rebel* started it, but it was an early rendition of *permission*, that whole thing of reaching out in love and greeting. The kids in those famous photographs putting flowers into the muzzles of the rifles. I think *Rebel* is all part of that."

• • •

The gazebo scene may be weighted with meaning, but it ends on a lightly poignant note, the result of a mistake made by Mineo. Plato falls asleep on the ground as Judy pats his head while humming a lullaby. Jim and Judy decide to leave Plato and explore the house. Protectively, they cover his body with his coat, alluding to the moment at the beginning of the film when Jim offers Plato his jacket and anticipating a similar scene at the film's emotional climax. Then, just as they are about to steal away, they discover that Plato is wearing red and blue mismatching socks. It's a detail that releases the tension of the scene while underscoring the protectiveness Jim and Judy feel.

"Must have been a nervous day," Jim says.

"He must have started out nervous," Judy responds.

But this moment does not appear in the script. "It was an accident," says costume designer Moss Mabry. Apparently, Mineo was having a nervous day himself. He simply put on the wrong socks and Mabry hadn't noticed. Many weeks later, on May 14, Ray shot a close-up of the red and blue socks for insertion into the final film.

SCENE 252

With the gazebo sequence completed, there was only one more emotionally rigorous set piece to shoot: scene number 252. It was Dean and Wood's big love scene, one that is often thought to mirror a sexual current running between the actors. But the current seemed to run only one way. "Natalie was mad for James Dean," according to Mabry. "Everyone was. We used to talk about him in her dressing room." Wood herself was quoted as saying, "I found myself constantly hoping to grow up to him so that we might start dating." According to her friend Jackie Perry, Wood had become so obsessed with Dean that she stole his personal scrapbook while visiting his home. "We went through it page by page," Perry says. "I remember there was this one article he had that was [about] ways for a boy to get a dog. It was pictures, poems, things that touched his heart. It had nothing to do with his life or his career. It was an odd thing for someone like him to collect. I found it to be sensitive and sweet." However, according to Perry,

Wood was also aware that Dean did not reciprocate her feelings about him. "She had a crush on him and he wasn't interested in her at all."

Like many of Dean's other pals, Lew Bracker agrees that "he had no interest in Natalie. No interest at all." But Bracker also believes that Dean did sleep with her on one occasion. "We were having this big debate as to whether it was possible to screw a girl in a Porsche," Bracker says. "One night, Jimmy came by with his Porsche and with Natalie. I wasn't there. When I talked to Jimmy the next day, I said, 'Who was with you when you came by?' He said, 'Natalie. I came by to tell you it can be done.' I knew exactly what he was talking about. I absolutely believe it. But it was a one-time thing." (Bracker adds, for the record, "I don't think he did it on the seat because that's impossible. He might have done it on the hood.")

But Wood's confidants understood their relationship to be nonsexual, and according to Gavin Lambert, who would become a good friend of Wood's, "There was never any hint of any affair. She was too busy. She had Nick Ray going and Dennis Hopper going. I mean give the girl a break." Lambert believes that Wood knew Dean was bisexual. "It was kind of an open secret at the time. Natalie knew it, too, at the time. She had extraordinary radar—for all kinds of things. But particularly anything sexual."

Nevertheless, Dean appears to have made some effort to get closer to Wood in the days preceding their love scene. Dean and Wood suddenly began appearing in public together. On Monday and Wednesday of that week, Dean and Wood were seen out together at the Hamburger Hamlet— "fueling rumors," according to a Warners publicity memo. Dean liked to extend the dynamic of the day's shooting to his behavior off the set— which is how many of the surviving gang members justify his haughtiness toward them. Now that the plot of *Rebel* had driven Jim and Judy closer, Dean may have felt the need to warm up to Wood.

Getting scene 252 right would not be a mere matter of star chemistry. Ray knew that the scene needed to convey tenderness, heartbreak, the sense of two lost souls finding each other in an emotional wilderness. It was another crucial scene—the third that week. It required much writing and rewriting, and it had been the subject of exasperating interference from the censors, who, it seemed, were attempting to crush the very life out of it.

Censor Geoffrey Shurlock was concerned that the characters were too young to be having sex. He ordered the scene to be rewritten to keep the clinches down to only one kiss. And Shurlock insisted that there should not be the merest hint that sex followed the fade-out after their kiss. Shurlock instructed that in the moment following the love scene "there be nothing about her appearance or actions that suggests that there has been a previous sex affair between her and Jim. The same, of course, applies to Jim's appearance."

Stewart Stern had written two lines that suggested Jim and Judy were virgins, simple naïve lines, and suitably vague.

> JIM: *There's something I should tell you, Judy.*
> JUDY: *I know already.*

"I really wanted them both to be virgins," says Stern. "I wanted as big a contrast as possible to their behavior. Everyone was always boasting about who they laid in high school and no one was laying anybody." But surprisingly, this allusion to virginity did not please the censors either. It, too, was cut.

Late on Thursday of that week, Wood and Dean began shooting the love scene in the claustrophobic ten-foot-square library of the mansion, which had been constructed like a bank vault with thick concrete-and-steel walls. For the scene, Dean and Wood positioned themselves with their heads close, her chin touching his brow. "That was specifically copied from a [1952] photograph of mine," says unofficial set photographer Dennis Stock. "It was part of a story I did for *Ladies' Home Journal* called 'Love Story.' Jimmy was impressed and he just imitated it. That indicates the influence that he had. There's a uniqueness to the physicality of it. It's very classic in the sense that, at one point, they have two profiles looking in different directions." A short dolly shot of the two stars was finished at the very end of the day, just before Wood had to go home at midnight.

Then, in a puzzling piece of scheduling, the entire cast and crew abandoned the mansion for the full day on Friday, returning to the studio to shoot more of the police station sequence, including the scene during which Dean pounded a desk so hard that he accidentally hurt his hand. (No sign of that injury is noticeable in the love scene shot the next day.) According to the April 7 agreement between Warners and Getty, Thursday was the last day Ray was allowed to shoot at the mansion. Ray may have needed to secure permission to return to the mansion for one more day.

On Saturday, the cast and crew reassembled for their last day at the Getty Mansion. And with just one day to get the difficult love scene right, there was little margin for error, which magnified the pressure Wood was already feeling. Just as she had been a bundle of nerves before her big crying scene at the police station, she was once again unsure if she would be able to conjure what was needed.

"Natalie was so nervous before the scene in the mansion," says Beverly Long. "She wanted to get it right. She was very inexperienced in kissing—in the movies, at least." Ironically, although this would be Wood's first movie kiss, it was not the first on-camera kiss she shared with Dean. She had previously kissed him in *I'm a Fool*, the television drama in which they co-starred four months earlier. That fact did not make her any less anxious or insecure. According to Corey Allen, "She didn't seem to me to be familiar, or particularly comfortable, with exploring the things which are awkward for any adolescent . . . and not only sexually." Ray would need everything Wood had to give that day. He wanted to see her heartbreak and loneliness and, despite the censors, he wanted to see her desire.

They began shooting the scene at 12:30 that afternoon. "They closed the set when Natalie and Jimmy did their love scene," said Jack Grinnage. "They made us all go away and be quiet." Any directions from Ray were handled very quietly, more so than usual, during what Ray liked to refer to as his "terribly intimate exchanges with actors." "When Nick had something to say he'd come up very close and whisper," said Beverly Long. "He didn't shout it from back by the camera: 'Really grab her and kiss her now!' He talked to them very quietly."

Dean knew that Wood was jumpy. He tried to get her to relax—albeit in his own teasing way. "You look green," he said, while they waited to begin the love scene. "And you know how green photographs in color." But his jab did not break through. "I managed a grin, I think," Wood said. In his narcissism, Dean may have felt that Wood was nervous about him. But Wood was not actually thinking of him at the moment, which may have been the problem. Instead, her mind was on her technical performance, the mechanics of the kiss. "I felt like a fighter before a match—let's go in and get it over with. Jimmy was saying something, but all I could think of was:

Is this the way—should I do it the way I rehearsed? Maybe that was too smooth. Maybe I should fumble a little."

The big moment came for the kiss. Their lips met and Ray called cut, but Dean continued to press his lips against hers, and Wood (ever the pro) could tell that the camera was still rolling. "I didn't exactly know what to do," Wood said, "but I had no choice. Jimmy held and held and held. 'Might as well enjoy it,' he kidded me afterwards as I turned from green to red." This time, Dean's audacity worked. According to Wood, "the nervous spell was broken."

In the completed film, Wood seems to have experienced a breakthrough with Dean. She did not merely rise to the occasion as she had in her big police station scene. Back at the police station, she had channeled her nervousness. At the mansion, she transcended it. The love scene represents her best work in *Rebel*, and maybe the best work of her career. Even her readings of the simplest lines—"I love you. I really do"—are suffused with yearning, vulnerability and a hint of masochism. It is as if she, like her character, was discovering love—with all its dire resonance—for the first time. At that moment, she became a different kind of actress, far less studio-tooled, more daring and more mature. No wonder Wood referred to her *Rebel* year as "1955 A.D.—after adolescence."

Wood must have been thrilled to have pleased Ray, whose presence also contributed to her nervous condition. And, according to Ray, Wood had arrived at the point where she finally delivered what he termed an "involuntary performance." That was an extremely high compliment from Ray. "After an involuntary performance," he once explained, "the actor is kind of stunned and bewildered, he doesn't know what just happened to him. He is in shock at having caught sight of his own evasions, tricks, and clichés . . . At such moments the director knows he has found something, released something which nobody in the world could have told the actor was there."

In the future, Ray would say that it was Mineo who delivered an involuntary performance throughout *Rebel*. He would mention Dean's work, especially in the milk bottle sequence. But he would cite Wood only with regard to this love scene.

On that last day at the mansion, it had taken more than six hours and seven takes to get the love scene right. Then, after the dinner break, more connective shots were filmed, fleeting moments plainly described in the daily camera reports as: Plato runs out; Jim falls; Judy looks at Crunch. Shooting concluded at 2 a.m., at which point the crew packed up and turned out the lights. They left the Phantom House to its future demolition, which, despite the sense of urgency that had been communicated to Ray, would be delayed for two more years. Though filming at the mansion had not begun very well, Getty's old dark house eventually cast its spell.

Yet *Rebel* remained behind schedule, prompting the studio to issue a dictum at the end of the mansion week. It was a memo that would cause the movie's shooting to become even more frantic. The studio was wary of the amount of night footage yet to shoot—and the accumulated cost in lighting equipment and overtime pay. In a memo to Ray's assistant director Don Page, production manager Eric Stacey wrote: "The pattern to be followed is not to shoot any close shots on night exterior locations that can be done successfully in the studio." With one fell swoop, the studio managed to shoot down Ray's plan to stay away from the studio as much as possible. Warners had gained increased control over the movie's cost—and Ray. He could not have been pleased.

CHAPTER TWELVE

Jim Kisses Plato?

"Jim kisses Plato?"

These incredible and incredulous words actually appear in a four-page scrawl of handwritten notes buried in the Warner Brothers *Rebel Without a Cause* archives. The question is scribbled on a yellow legal pad with the name "Trilling" capped and underlined at the top. The words jump off the bottom of page two.

Most of these four pages of criticism from Warners head of production Steve Trilling are typical for a studio executive. They regard the sharpening of certain narrative points to avoid ambiguity, make the hero more sympathetic and head off potential censorship problems—elements viewed as threats to commercial success. But the idea of Jim kissing Plato posed a new kind of problem, a different kind of threat. The serious consideration of homosexuality had barely reared its head in film at that time. With a desire for new and adult themes on the part of the studios, that situation would soon change to some degree. But in early 1955, the thought of two boys kissing represented a nerve-wracking leap for any studio.

There is no reference to a kiss in any surviving version of Stewart Stern's script. And Stern says he never wrote such a direction. But all of Trilling's notes, on this particular yellow pad, are pegged to precise moments in the screenplay, so it is possible that his question—"Jim kisses Plato?"—is a response to something Trilling saw in, or inferred from, some version of the script. Perhaps Trilling was responding to notes that may have been added to his particular copy of the screenplay. Ray was always adding and subtracting to the script, keeping the process fluid and looking for opportunities to push the envelope. A kiss between Jim and Plato would have been the most audacious step yet taken by the iconoclastic director.

Referring directly to the film's homosexual subject matter in a 1977 interview, Ray says that he felt confident that he would get away with it. He relied on his feeling that "Warners didn't know what the hell I was doing." But hawkeyed censor Geoffrey Shurlock continued to display his frustrating perspicacity. On March 22 he shot off a memo to Jack Warner stating, "It is of course vital that there be no inference of a questionable or homosexual relationship between Plato and Jim." After that, the studio was on alert. In his four-page memo, Trilling proposed that the kiss be replaced by a shot of Dean stroking Mineo's head—which, in and of itself, would have been a daring move, a studio concession to the boundaries through which *Rebel* was smashing.

Trilling's notes place the kiss sometime between the chickie run and the mansion scene. The only scene that Dean and Mineo share at that point in the film takes place in the alley beside Plato's house—a scene that was actually shot after the mansion idyll. Dramatically, it would have been the perfect place for a kiss. In the alley scene, Jim drops Plato off after the trauma of watching Buzz plunge to his death over the edge of a cliff. Before they go their separate ways, a shaken Jim and Plato share their most tender colloquy.

This scene was filmed on May 10, a date the surviving cast members refer to as "the 24-Hour Day." It was a time when the entire production schedule finally went haywire, as it had been threatening to do for weeks. In a strenuous effort to play catch-up, myriad scenes were shot that day at different locations—but a kiss was never filmed, as far as any *Rebel* survivors know or remember. Yet the simple reference to a kiss in Trilling's memo spotlights one of *Rebel*'s most forward-thinking facets.

Trilling's resistance and Shurlock's canniness did not prevent Ray—and his co-conspirator Dean—from mining the gay possibilities in Stern's *Rebel* screenplay. Even without an action so explicit as a kiss, they would fill *Rebel* with visual clues, subtle suggestions and actorly allusions to homosexuality. "Nick would always enjoy that kind of thing," says his friend Gavin Lambert. "He loved intrigue of any kind. It was subverting the studio and it was also the theater of life for him." And, of course, he and Dean employed the invaluable aid of a naïve but not completely clueless Sal Mineo.

Right from the start of *Rebel,* Plato's desire is palpable. In the scene at Dawson High, Plato is standing in front of his locker combing his hair in a mirror tacked up inside the door. He glimpses Jim's reflection in the mirror, and we can see the sudden intensification of Plato's gaze. He angles his mirror to get a better view, then turns his head to follow Jim's movement, all with a distinct look of recognition on his face. It is a provocative moment, but perhaps even more suggestive is what's pinned up under Plato's mirror: a black-and-white glossy of handsome Hollywood leading man Alan Ladd.

A reference to an actor's photograph does appear in Stern's screenplay, although the script specifies a picture of Burt Lancaster. "I thought Lancaster was who Plato would idolize. He was an athlete, he was strong, he was a trapeze artist, and he looked great. Alan Ladd, he was a joke because everybody was guessing how high the platform was," says Stern, referring to the fact that directors often had to place the 5-foot 6-inch Ladd on a box so he would seem taller than his leading lady. The studio may have asked for the change to Ladd because he was making films for Warner Brothers, while Lancaster had set up an independent production company that was competing with the studio.

But why would Plato have a picture of any male star in his locker? In response to this question, Stern recalls his own boyhood. "I don't know why I had pictures of Johnny Weissmuller on my wall," he says. "Because he was my savior." Hero worship may have been Stern's intention, but that is not the only way the image reads, especially once we get to know Plato better.

Even though Stewart Stern has admitted that "Plato was the one who would've been tagged as the faggot character," the screenwriter intended for the relationship between Jim and Plato to be much more ambiguous, much less specifically homosexual. "The gay community just wanted to own that movie," he says, with some resentment. Indeed, the signs of Plato's desire lie less in Stern's script than in Mineo's performance and elements of the staging. Stern had nothing to do with another sly, telling detail that adds to the suggestiveness of the locker scene. Before Plato spots him in the mirror,

Jim accidentally walks into the girls' bathroom. This subtly gender-bending moment does not appear in any version of the script and must have been improvised by Ray and Dean on the set.

Throughout the film, Mineo continues to drop plenty of clues about Plato's desire: the way he rests his head on Jim's arm in the mansion scene, the way he softly touches Dean's shoulder in the planetarium scene and sweeps his eyes across Dean's face and hair, the way he physically surges toward Jim when he arrives at the chickie run.

"I heard [Dean] explaining things to Sal," said Ray. " 'You know how I am with Nat. Well, why don't you pretend I'm her and you're me . . . Pretend you want to touch my hair, but you're shy.' Then Jimmy says, 'I'm not shy like you. I love you. I'll touch your hair.' I took one look at the kid's face . . . he was transcendent, the feeling coming out of him."

The boldest expression of Plato's desire in the film occurs in the troublesome alley scene. As Stern originally conceived it, Jim and Plato are alone in front of Jim's garage when they begin to laugh hysterically in reaction to Buzz's death. According to the directions written by Stern, "They fall onto each other. Silence. After a moment Jim breaks away. He is crying." (Could Trilling have interpreted this moment of falling together as a kiss?) At this point, Plato says, "Come home with me."

"This was an important scene from many points of view," Stern says. "It showed a reaction to tragedy which is not only bare and honest, but a reaction which, though probably the truest, has not been seen on the screen before, at least to my knowledge. It was a scene with which everyone who has come close to tragedy and felt the guilty impulse to laugh in celebration of their own relief of being alive may fully identify. Beyond that, it's only because of the hysteria gripping him that Plato gets the nerve to invite Jim to his house, and to express his real need for companionship. Plato was a shy and timid boy and would never permit himself fear and rejection as acutely as he does, to stick his neck out quite so far, unless he were fully involved about something else, which would let him pretend to minimize the importance of what he is really asking."

Oddly enough, Plato's proposition was not as much a problem for the studio as the boys' laughing fit. Their laughter would not remain in the film, although, amazingly, Plato's proposition did. "Why don't you come home with me?" Plato says in the film. "I mean nobody's home at my house—and I'm not tired, are you? I don't have many—people I can talk to." Then, Plato says a line that is not in Stern's script: "Gee . . . if you could only have been my father."

When word of these cuts and changes reached Stern—who was in New York—he was particularly incensed. He fired off a letter to Steve Trilling about what was being done to his script. "I think that under no credible circumstances would he, even in hysteria, refer to Jim as his father here," he wrote. "It seems totally out of key and character and achieves with its boldness nothing that is not inherent in the story as it stands." Stern had reached an understandable level of writer's panic. He feared that the studio and Ray were in danger of destroying the film. As he wrote, "The thing I feared most and expected least seems to be happening now, with a harrowing and bewildering thoroughness, a bit-by-bit emasculation of an original treatment in an effort to make it conform."

Surely, Stern's laughing scene would have resulted in another great moment in the film, especially given the contagious nature of Dean's unguarded and childlike giggle. But Stern did not have to worry about Plato's reference to Dean as a potential father figure. It seems entirely in keeping with Plato's persona. The line can easily be read as the closeted Plato's own ersatz rationalization for wanting Jim to spend the night. It does little to erase the psychosexual undertones of the scene. And it gave Ray an opportunity to, once again, blur the line between father and lover. It is a strong and daring moment, with the power of Plato's desire cutting through any of the scene's emotional clutter.

Once the scene was shot, Ray was pleased. Even without the kiss or the laughter, he knew he had gotten away with something. Proudly, he went up to Dean and said, "Geez. I like that scene. You know, I think they're going to like it in Paris."

Rebel's prodding of the status quo seems even more astonishing when you consider that in the 1950s homosexuality was considered an illness by the vast majority of Americans. At that time, homosexuals were often characterized as members of a secret cabal working to weaken American society from within. And in Hollywood, gays were hunted by scandal sheets such as *Confidential,* edited by Howard Rushmore, a red-baiting journalist. Rushmore went after homosexuals with the same zeal he displayed in his pursuit of suspected communists, even driving Rock Hudson to marry his agent's secretary when the magazine threatened to out him in 1955.

But although Ray and Dean showed an amazing amount of courage and audacity in taking on gay themes, they did not do so in a vacuum. While the Production Code prevented movies from dealing with the subject of "sexual perversion," openly gay artists such as Allen Ginsberg, Gore Vidal, James Baldwin and Tennessee Williams were beginning to emerge in literature and theater. Perhaps most importantly, in 1948 Alfred Kinsey published his report *Sexual Behavior in the Human Male,* concluding that 37 percent of males had at least some homosexual experience, which began to sow doubt in the minds of some psychiatrists who had judged homosexuality to be an illness. Judd Marmor, an analyst who had a large gay clientele during the 1950s, would become a leading advocate for removing homosexuality from the American Psychiatric Association's list of mental disorders. Coincidentally or not, James Dean was seeing Marmor while he was shooting *Rebel.*

Dean's and Ray's interest in addressing the shadowy existence of homosexuality certainly highlights questions about the exact nature of their own sexuality. These questions have persisted for years. And for any assertion in one direction, there's a ready—indeed anxious—counterassertion. Like so much gay history, the facts must be mined from half-clues, rumors and contradictions.

In Ray's case, there is support for the notion that he was bisexual. Rumors of his orientation go all the way back to his salad days in the 1930s, when he was dismissed from a Taliesin Fellowship, Frank Lloyd Wright's architectural apprenticeship program. Ray biographer Bernard Eisenschitz reports Ray's perplexing explanation for his dismissal: he and Wright had an argument over the use of the word *organize.* But years later, Ray's first wife, Jean Evans, described to Eisenschitz a meeting with Wright in which she found him "very moralistic and vindictive, and he said that Nick was homosexual."

Author Gavin Lambert had an intense affair with Ray in the years following *Rebel,* from 1956 to 1957, often sharing the director's home at the Chateau Marmont and co-hosting Ray's parties. Lambert remembers that, although Ray's many affairs with women were notorious, very few people knew about his gay proclivities. "One or two people did make cracks about it," says Lambert.

"He didn't have anything obviously gay or bisexual about him," says Lambert. "And anyway, that side of him was much less than the straight side. And since he had slept with a lot of women, and presumably enjoyed it, that was his main reputation. He was known to be great in the sack, which surprised me given how much he drank, but nevertheless he could do both. And of course that made it more important to be very discreet about the other side. He warned me. And I understood, really. In movies then, you had to be discreet. You still have to be."

In his autobiography *Front and Center*, producer John Houseman, one of Ray's first mentors, attempted his own thumbnail explanation of Ray's sexuality. He wrote that Ray was "a potential homosexual with a deep, passionate and constant need for female love in his life. This made him attractive to women, for whom the chance to save him from his own self-destructive habits proved an irresistible attraction of which Nick took full advantage and for which he rarely forgave them." Houseman also claimed that Ray was fired from the Office of War Information after he told the draft board of "his homosexual experiences as a young man." But Ray's fourth and last wife, Susan, feels that Houseman had his own agenda: "I love John. I knew him well—and I know he was in love with Nick."

According to Susan Ray, her husband "was curious and he probably experimented once or twice or three times. When I knew him, I knew about his affairs and they were all with women. But I never saw a charge between him and a man. I wouldn't say, 'No, he was never with a man.' But he was so open about this stuff. He would have told me about it. It just wasn't something that he was ashamed of. He was very open about his exploits."

In a 1977 television interview, Ray was bluntly asked about the bisexuality in *Rebel*, and it is the only time during the interview when he noticeably drops his cool, languorous manner and becomes slightly apoplectic and incoherent: "I'm not sure whether you mean the bisexuality of Jim, or the bisexuality of Sal, or the bisexuality of myself . . . I am not bisexual but anyone who denies having had a fantasy or a daydream denies having eaten a bowl of mashed potatoes. It has the same reality."

Later in life, Ray began an autobiography that he did not live to complete. In it, he described his student days at the University of Chicago. "I didn't know whether I wanted to be a homosexual or not," Ray wrote. "Homosexual was not in my vocabulary. Did I love and revere men more than women? I think I did." He goes on to tell the story of a well-respected, older professor who took him parking one night at the edge of Lake Michigan. Ray said, "I knew the approach of a man who liked other men was about to happen . . . He caressed me. I wanted to please him. God knows I wanted to say thank you, somehow I wanted to say thank you. I said thank you. He unbuttoned my trousers. I wanted to come if he wanted me to come. I stroked his grey-white hair. I couldn't come. We drove back to campus."

Whether or not one feels Ray was officially "bisexual" depends on one's definition of the term. Ray seems to have viewed his own homosexual encounters and affairs in a manner closer to Susan Ray's than Gavin Lambert's. But even toward the end of his life, as he took those few trenchant stabs at autobiography, it is apparent that he could not let the subject rest.

In many ways, James Dean's sexuality is a trickier matter. He did not live very long, yet mountains of contradictory stories have amassed regarding his sexual activities. And in the decades since his death, the facts of his life have become hard to distinguish from his stature as a legend—and a major gay icon.

When Dean was younger, he formed close relationships with two older men who later came forward to say that these relationships had been sexual. The Reverend James DeWeerd, who befriended Dean while he was in high school, later described to reporter Joe Hyams how he and Dean became intimate during long drives in the country in his convertible. "Jimmy never mentioned our relationship nor did I," DeWeerd told Hyams. "It would not have helped either of us." And while working in the parking lot of CBS when he was twenty years old, Dean met Rogers Brackett, an elegant thirty-five-year-old radio director with an advertising agency, and moved into Brackett's fashionable apartment above Sunset Strip. Brackett helped Dean get bit acting parts, and according to Brackett, they also had an affair. "My primary interest in Jimmy was as an actor—his talent was so obvious," said Brackett. "Secondarily, I loved him, and Jimmy loved me. If it was a father-son relationship, it was also somewhat incestuous."

Some Dean biographers have tried to explain away his affairs, claiming he slept with men only to further his career, that he was not homosexual but merely hungry to succeed. Apparently, some of these Dean historians believe it is better to be seen as cravenly ambitious than gay. Others saw his gay liaisons as an example of his experimental, all-encompassing nature. Regarding his sexuality, Dean was famously quoted as saying, "Well, I'm certainly not going through life with one hand tied behind my back."

As the decades passed, and homosexuality became more accepted, more of Dean's friends and bedmates began to open up about their sexual experiences with him. In a 1980 slice of memoir with the tabloidlike title "Author Reveals—'I Had Sex with James Dean!'" screenwriter John Gilmore discussed their relationship. "Jimmy liked to cuddle in bed," he wrote. "He liked to be held and he liked to be kissed." Later, in his 1997 biography of Dean, *Live Fast—Die Young: My Life with James Dean,* Gilmore would go into much more explicit detail about their sexual exploits. William Bast, who met Dean at UCLA and later followed him to New York, wrote the first biography of Dean in 1956, which he adapted into a television movie in 1976. While the TV movie implied that their friendship was at the very least homoerotic, he refused to label Dean as gay. "Gay, as a descriptive term, would categorize Jimmy in such a limited manner," he said. "He tried a lot of things and he was always open to new experiences, but I can't give an answer only because it would restrict rather than expand his personality. He was so many things and responded so easily to just about any stimulus." Many of Dean's peers tend toward this image of him as nearly godlike in his expansiveness.

While Dean was making *Rebel,* there were persistent rumors that he was having an affair with his roommate and fellow cast member Jack Simmons, but Simmons never spoke publicly about their relationship. According to actor Jack Larson, years after Dean's death when someone casually mentioned Dean's name in conversation, Simmons was "reduced to absolute tears and had to leave." Larson once had an unusual encounter with Dean and Simmons that suggests they were more than just good friends: "One night when I left Googie's, I had to go into a market at Sunset and Fairfax. Much to my surprise, Jack Simmons and Jimmy Dean had also left Googie's and come down. Jack Simmons was in the market and wanted to talk to me. There was a pad in Laurel Canyon and they wanted me to go with them. It may have been Jack Simmons's pad. I don't know whose it was, but it was obviously going to be the two of them and me. It was very clear. Jimmy was out waiting in the car. I just didn't want to." When Larson told his friend, poet Frank O'Hara, who worshipped Dean and eventually wrote several elegiac poems in his memory, that he had refused Simmons's and Dean's offer, O'Hara "was shocked and it almost ruined our friendship."

Besides the torrent of private memories, hearsay, gossip and rumors about his homosexual liaisons, Dean was also linked to a number of women. On the *Rebel* set, Dean had a dalliance with an unnamed female extra, according to Beverly Long, who came upon them during a sudden blackout that occurred while shooting scenes at the Getty mansion. "So I know he wasn't totally homosexual because they were having a great time," she says. A number of women have spoken publicly about their affairs with Dean, including Dizzy Sheridan, best known as the actress who played Jerry Seinfeld's mother on *Seinfeld,* who lived with Dean in New York, and Swedish actress Lili Kardell, who met Dean at one of Arthur Loew Jr.'s parties in February 1955.

Actress Betsy Palmer, who appeared with Dean in two television plays, also dated him during his first years in New York. "I have to laugh about it now," says Palmer. "He wanted me to talk dirty and I didn't know how.

"Neither of us had any money and he would come over to my little apartment and I would cook for him. We talked about acting. We would play music and make love." Their nine-month affair ended the day Palmer came home to find Dean rifling through her dresser and uncovering her diaphragm.

"I thought you were a virgin," he said.

"What does that have to do with not wanting to get pregnant?" she retorted. "And what are you doing going through my drawers anyway?!"

According to Palmer, she "finished the whole thing right there."

Then there is the well-known Hollywood tale of Dean's star-crossed affair with Pier Angeli, a young Italian actress, discovered by *Rebel* screenwriter Stewart Stern, who was the eponymous star of his first film, *Teresa* (and who committed suicide in 1971). According to Dennis Hopper, "James Dean was not gay. The two great loves of his life in Hollywood were Pier Angeli and Ursula Andress. Pier Angeli married Vic Damone. Jimmy sat in the rain on his motorcycle outside the church. She'd asked Jimmy to marry her. He'd asked her to wait until he saw how his career was going. Ursula Andress married John Derek and proceeded to parade him on the set of *Giant* after Jimmy refused to marry her for the same reason."

Dean's good friend during that period, Lew Bracker, doubts that Dean was serious about the voluptuous Swiss bombshell Andress, and apparently Andress was not that serious about Dean. Andress, who because of her pouty lips had been dubbed "the female Brando" by the press, was also seeing Ray's former boss Howard Hughes while she dated Dean.

But Bracker does believe that Dean "was heartbroken" when Angeli left him to marry Damone. Bracker also remembers one night at the Villa Capri when Dean claimed he, not singer Vic Damone, was actually the father of Angeli's son, Perry Damone.

Director Elia Kazan thought the Dean-Angeli relationship was serious, though tempestuous. He wrote in his autobiography that he could hear them "boffing but more often arguing through the walls," when Dean lived next to him in his dressing room on the Warners lot.

Gavin Lambert says, however, that Ray told him that the legendary relationship between Dean and Pier Angeli was a studio concoction—"a fabricated affair." According to Lambert, Dean's bisexuality was an open secret at the time. "There was a lot of publicity done by the studio to make him straight, and he went along with it."

Ray himself might have been trying to put the question to rest when he stated, "Some—most—will say he was heterosexual, and there's some proof for that, apart from the usual dating of actresses his age. Others will say no, he was gay, and there's some proof for that too, keeping in mind that it's always tougher to get that kind of proof. But Jimmy himself said more than once that he swung both ways, so why all the mystery or confusion?"

With so much conflicting, unverifiable, utterly personal testimony, there is no way of knowing with complete certainty whether Dean was actually bisexual or moving toward a total embrace of being gay. Perhaps he died too early for anyone—even himself—to know where he would have ended up on the spectrum of sexuality. In an odd and touching anecdote, *Rebel* screenwriter Stewart Stern reveals that Dean was startlingly unformed and ambivalent right up to the end of his life.

The last time Stern ever saw Dean was at a party at the house of Arthur Loew Jr., after Dean got back from filming *Giant*. "I was sitting on a stool at a bar, talking to some lady," he remembers. "I felt these two hands over my eyes and I could smell the saddle soap and leather jacket. I kind of knew it was Jimmy but I hadn't seen him since he got back. I looked at him. Then he laughed, and then he asked me to go outside, and we took a walk around the garden. He was very, very open, very available. Out of nowhere, he said, 'It's a good thing my mother died when she did, or I would have been queer.' He was holding my arm, and I didn't know, I couldn't make sense of it. And then we just went back into the party."

Despite what we know and can't know about Dean's sexuality off-screen, he certainly altered the image of maleness onscreen. Whatever ambivalence he may have felt, he refused to be locked into the four-square 1950s Hollywood view of manly behavior. He was not afraid to show fragility that might be characterized by some at the time as feminine. He was not afraid to cry on screen. And his desire to seduce anyone who locked into his gaze knew no gender boundary.

Dean was not the only actor attempting to reshape Hollywood's conception of maleness at the time. "We were all spoon-fed on strong-jawed heroism and supermen," said Corey Allen. "And then along came three guys who were saying, 'Hey, it's OK to be scared. It's OK to be vulnerable.' I think most of us remember that they were Clift, Brando, and Dean. These days, we talk about vulnerability very easily partially because of people like Dean who were willing to put it on the line."

Dean took the fragility and naturalism of Montgomery Clift and the rebelliousness and emotionally unbridled sexuality of Marlon Brando and created his own enlarged space for male behavior on the screen. According to Dennis Hopper, "He said he had Clift in his lowered left hand saying, 'Please forgive me,' and Brando in his raised right hand saying, 'Go fuck yourself.'" Critic Parker Tyler went so far as to describe Dean as "a homosexual parody of Marlon Brando."

In 1957, writer Jack Kerouac described Dean as an example of a new kind of man "of exceptional masculine beauty and compassion and sadness," a "new American hero" free of "the barriers of ancient antiwomanism." As Jim Stark, Dean represented a fresh truth, and his honesty and expansiveness clearly elicited a passionate response.

Explaining his original conception of the Jim Stark character, Stewart Stern said, "It was an attempt to define masculinity in a different way at a time when it seemed all to be leather and boots. The kids caught that. They caught the undercurrent of sweetness in Jim Stark and in the actor who portrayed him and the longing for a lost, loving world, where people could drop their bravado and treat each other gently."

Stern's own conceptions of masculinity were formed by his exposure to male camaraderie in World War II. "The army was built on the buddy system, very consciously," says Stern, who was a staff sergeant in the infantry and fought in the Battle of the Bulge. "In order to stay out of the rain, you tended to be as close together as you could. And that also reinforced that bonding, which was unbelievably sentimental, and very romantic, and not sexual per se." Stern believes that when men returned from the war, the bonds they formed had a profound effect on them. "I think a kind of love was born that skipped sexual definition," he says. "It had nothing to do with that. It had to do with something so deep and so particular, but it awakened, I think, in men a kind of permission to be tender. No men hugged other men in those days. Now, I think, Democrats do.

"That whole experience has informed so much of my writing," says Stern, whose screenplays—from *Teresa* to *The Rack* to the immensely underrated *The Ugly American*—offer a panoply of remarkably sensitive men and are often built around male relationships that sometimes tip toward the homoerotic. And his ideas about masculinity certainly found a sympathetic hearing from Nicholas Ray.

Ray had been quietly expanding Hollywood's notion of gender since he introduced a skinny, vulnerable Farley Granger in his first film, *They Live By Night*. Many gay characters—or those tilting toward gay prototypes—leaked into Ray's films throughout his career. Author Richard Barrios points to several gay supporting characters: Mel Ferrer's effete portrait painter in *Born to Be Bad*, the lesbian masseuse in *In a Lonely Place*, the sexually ambiguous female rodeo rider in *The Lusty Men*. Famously, two extremely tough women—Joan Crawford and Mercedes McCambridge—ignite his febrile Western *Johnny Guitar*. Ray suggested the possibility of homoerotic attraction in many of his films, especially in macho genres such as the war movie (*Bitter Victory*) and the Western (*The Lusty Men, Johnny Guitar*). And he was drawn to vulnerable young leading men whose prettiness reads as distinctly homoerotic: the young Robert Wagner in *The True Story of Jesse James*, John Derek in *Knock on Any Door* and again in *Run for Cover*, and Jeffrey Hunter as a beautiful blue-eyed Jesus in his 1961 religious epic *King of Kings*.

In *Rebel*, during Dean and Natalie Wood's love scene at the mansion, Ray added a few lines that tenderly reflect his attitude. Before they kiss, Judy tells Jim what kind of man a girl really wants: "a man who can be gentle and sweet. Like you are . . . And someone who doesn't run away when you want them. Like being Plato's friend when nobody else liked him. That's being strong." This dialogue does not appear in the final script by Stern, who concurs that it "must have been one of Nick's gifts."

Ray's tendency toward diffusing machismo is a major source of his enduring relevance. As Ray himself wrote: "I believe that I have been or would be successful in exposing the feminine in the roughest male symbol the public could accept. I always suspect the warmth or tenderness or color range of a person who publicly disports himself in either too strict a feminine or too strict a masculine role."

Ray might have become determined to push these notions even further once he was goaded by Dean's implicit challenge. Tilting against Hollywood's homophobia represented another in their series of instinctual leaps into the unknown, and it profoundly affected many who have watched the film over the decades. After *Rebel*, Hollywood would begin to deal more openly with the subject of homosexuality in such films as *Tea and Sympathy* (1956), *Cat on a Hot Tin Roof* (1958), *Suddenly, Last Summer* (1959), *The Children's Hour* (1961) and *Advise and Consent* (1962). Together, Ray and Dean helped push Hollywood's closet door open just a crack.

THE 24-HOUR DAY

The controversial alley scene between Jim and Plato was the first scene tackled on May 10, the exhausting "24-Hour Day." The sequence was filmed at 2 p.m., although the cast and crew had left the studio for the sub-urban Baldwin Hills location more than six hours earlier. On-site re-hearsals over the worrisome alley scene probably caused some of this delay, as did a thick morning fog that would not lift. Even nature seemed to be conspiring to make May 10 as troublesome as possible. Eventually, wind machines had to be sent down from the studio. Placed in a semicircle, they dispersed the fog and shooting could begin.

Delicate and complicated as it was, the alley scene itself took less than an hour to actually shoot. But there would be much more to get in the can before the cast and crew would be able to call it quits. The remainder of the 24-Hour Day was a marathon, the result of an awful bungle in scheduling, a sure sign that *Rebel* was continuing to spin out of control.

After the alley scene was finished, Ray and his crew continued to film more of the Baldwin Hills scenes, which they had initially worked on the day before. These scenes involved a friendly Jim and an icy Judy's first con-versation on their way to school. It's a well-written scene of cat and mouse that includes this choice exchange courtesy of Stewart Stern:

> JIM: *You live around here?*
> JUDY: *(shrugging) Who lives?*

Jim asks Judy if she wants a ride to school but she responds, "I go with the kids," and on cue they arrive, eight members of the gang—Corey Allen, Dennis Hopper, Nick Adams, Jack Simmons, Frank Mazzola, Tom Bernard, and the molls Steffi Sidney and Beverly Long—swooping into frame via Buzz's crowded convertible. It's at this moment that we can hear the kids yelling "Stella-a-a-a," a reference to Marlon Brando in *A Streetcar Named Desire,* and another of *Rebel's* cannily self-conscious movie references, in-dicative of how teens were rapidly moving to stake their claim on the pop-culture landscape.

In this scene, which was originally supposed to take place at a gas sta-tion, Ray's attempt to get his gaggle of young actors to come together as a gang truly pays off. The overactive interplay between them, while packed into Buzz's car, is convincing and contagiously kinetic. At one point, while sitting in the driver's seat, Corey Allen turns around to crack Nick Adams on the top of the head. In turn, Adams—who wouldn't dare strike at the serious Allen—shoves the edge of a rolled-up piece of paper into the face of Jack Simmons, who is seated next to him. Simmons seems sincerely shocked—and possibly hurt, dropping his actor's guard for a moment but quickly recovering.

In the midst of the scene's crisscrossing dialogue, Judy delivers one of her most pungent and prophetic lines, given Dean's infectious influence over every generation to follow. "What's that?" Buzz asks her, referring to Jim Stark. "That's a new disease," she answers.

The 24-Hour Day was interminably long and boring for the kids in the gang, who found ways to entertain themselves. "We had hours and hours between takes," remembers former child actor Tom Bernard, who played one of the gang members. "We were all standing around, and one of the guys had found one of these sticks you use to pick up trash, with a point at the end of it. He hauled back and threw it and the thing hit my foot. It actually penetrated my left foot so I ended up having to go to the infirmary at Warner Brothers." Bernard's foot swelled up and he had difficulty walking for several days.

At 5:40 p.m., the cast and crew finally wrapped the scenes in Baldwin Hills. On a normal day, it would have been quitting time. But on that day—and in a move that was technically "against the law in those days," according to Beverly Long—a second crew was called in. The cast made its way up into the Hollywood Hills, to a dead-end street near Wattles Garden Park and the Huntington Hartford estate, where they would film until 4:30 the next morning.

The plan was to film the very first scene of the script, a pre-credit sequence. But most of the scene did not make it into the finished film. The final cut of *Rebel Without a Cause* opens with a mysterious low-angle close-up of Dean lying flat on an empty street, playing with a toy monkey. It is a powerful scene—bolstered by composer Leonard Rosenman's heraldic main theme and the film's slashing red title credits—but the presence of the decidedly surreal monkey is never explained.

The monkey is actually left over from the unused scene shot that night. Dressed in Easter clothes, the gang comes across a man returning to his family with an armful of presents. According to the script, "Buzz ignites a match and holds it near the man's face for a second, searching it. Then he ignites the whole box under his nose. The man shrieks, and his packages fall. Buzz slaps him sharply, his smile gone. The camera pans away as the figures enclose him, and holds on a small mechanical monkey which has dropped from its wrappings. It begins to dance madly on the pavement, then runs down." The gang proceeds to stomp the innocent man, and then they run off. At that moment, a drunken Jim Stark turns the corner, falls into the street and finds the monkey. That is where the actual film begins.

By the time the actors began shooting the stomping scene, their nerves were already frayed. "We shot way into dawn on Sunday," says Steffi Sidney, "but when it got past eighteen hours, I was drooping. I said to the rest of the gang, 'We've got to say something. This is absolutely against union rules.' But they wouldn't speak up." According to Jack Grinnage, "They wouldn't do it today but they had a whole trailer full of any kind of liquor you wanted. That's how they kept people working in those days."

At one point, the old irrational tension between Frank Mazzola and Corey Allen reasserted itself. "We almost got into a fight. The assistant director had to pull me off the set," says Mazzola. "I had to walk around the block a couple times just to settle down." It did not help that members of Mazzola's gang of Athenians were around the set that evening, although—in what might have been an attempt to offer distraction and lighten the mood—Dean took a camera from photographer Dennis Stock and began shooting pictures of the Athenians.

But for all their efforts at endurance, the stomping scene would never see the light of day, although a few casual references to the scene remain in the movie. (Amid the overlapping chatter of the previously shot scene in Buzz's car, you can hear Judy tell Buzz that he's lucky the guy lived. "They always live," Buzz responds.) As it was, the whole idea for this violent scene was a leftover from Ray's pulpier, more lurid approach to the subject way back in his "Blind Run" treatment. The mood and texture of the picture had changed by then. Buzz would take on a mantle of existential heroism. Stomping a guy nearly to death would have cast the gang in far too menacing a light.

Ray may also have been reacting to a memo from the literal-minded Steve Trilling: "You're opening a keg of peas with Jim being picked up at scene of the crime of the stomp gang. He would automatically be held for questioning in connection with that crime, unless there is an explanation . . . that he had no connection with it."

Dead on their feet as they all were, Dean pulled off something of a miracle that night. As written, Dean's first scene required him to fall drunkenly into the street, pick up the mechanical monkey, wind it up and watch it dance. But Dean told Ray that he had an idea in mind and he wanted Ray to keep the cameras rolling while he worked it out. Ray did not know what Dean had planned, but he agreed.

"We were all sitting there, on a curb, freezing to death," says Beverly Long. "Ernie Haller, who was the cinematographer, was lying on his tummy with the camera and they were shooting up at Jimmy as he came around the corner."

Dean stumbles to the ground, where he sees the monkey, but he does much more than merely rewind it. Lying flat on his stomach, in his crumpled Easter suit, the drunken Jim Stark gently prods at the toy, trying to get its attention. Then he reaches for it and stares directly into its eyes, smiling wryly before rewinding it. Finally, in a totally unexpected move, Dean lays the monkey on its side and covers it with the crinkled gift wrap that is lying by its side. He puts a gold ribbon on its head, like a crown, and then, strikingly, he cuddles up beside it in a fetal position. It's a startling scene, vintage Dean. As Stewart Stern says, "It summarized the themes of the film," simultaneously evoking all the roles that Dean would assume in *Rebel*—parent, child and lover. According to author David Dalton, Dean was attempting to evoke Manet's famous painting *Dead Toreador,* which was one of the actor's favorite works of art. It was a moment that inspired awe in the usually cool and blasé players who made up the gang.

"Jimmy did his opening scene many times," says Steffi Sidney. "He didn't go into the fetal position to begin with. He just looked at the monkey. It evolved. Ray and he would go off to the right. Nick had a lot of conferences with Ernie Haller. We all watched and were absolutely fascinated with the fact that it was all improvised."

"I was no further than a few feet away from him," says Beverly Long. "And I was stunned at his ability to create this whole aura for himself. It was worth everything we went through that day. We all sat there with tears in our eyes. It was so beautiful."

"Where did that come from?" asked an admiring Dennis Hopper. "It came from genius, that's where it came from. And that was all him. Nobody directed him to do that. James Dean directed James Dean." Over the years, Hopper—who, of course, had his problems with Ray—always remained the most well-known and vocal champion of the notion that Dean directed *Rebel*. And on the 24-Hour Day, when Ray seemed to have lost control of the schedule, Dean's accomplishment does stand out in contrast. But as Nick Ray himself once admitted, "I don't know any other way to do it but to let it happen, and when it happens, grab it."

Dean's achievement certainly put a happy ending to the strenuous and seemingly never-ending day. Although one unnamed player sued Warners over the long hours, the suit was settled. "Somebody reported it to their agent who reported it to SAG," says Sidney. "Not me. I didn't want to be a squealer." And most of the players were pleased when they opened their salary envelopes. "It was a great day," Bernard says, "because we all made a bunch of money on overtime." According to Long, "We'd only get around $350 a week. In 1955, that was great. But the day we shot the twenty-four hours—they gave us a whole extra paycheck for that. We got an extra $350 for that one night because they were trying to be hush-hush. They didn't want anybody to know."

Steffi Sidney came away with something even more valuable than a paycheck. "They had extra monkeys. They always had doubles of everything. Just in case a monkey didn't work properly." So Sidney decided to grab one. "I don't know if it's actually the one that's in the film. But it's definitely one that was used. I auctioned it at Sotheby's about fifteen years ago," she says, revealing a decidedly different aspect of the *Rebel* legacy. Despite the foul-ups that happened on the 24-Hour Day, *Rebel*'s potential impact was becoming clear. "There was no doubt in my mind that the movie was going to be something special," Sidney says. "That's why I took the monkey."

CHAPTER THIRTEEN

Chickie Run

As *Rebel* was about to enter its last month of shooting on April 30, 1955, Dean was given a day off to prepare for *Giant,* which would begin production in less than four weeks. *Giant* director George Stevens had scheduled a wardrobe test for Dean that day, but Dean did not show up. Claiming he had laryngitis, he headed instead to Bakersfield, California, to register for his second auto race, taking place the next day. Dean knew Warners would be horrified to discover that its newly valuable star was continuing to engage in his hazardous hobby—especially since he was jeopardizing not one but *two* major productions.

In his own defense, Dean was quoted as saying, "If I thought I was risking my life, I wouldn't participate. I love life too much. There are too many things I have to do." But even the official program of the Bakersfield event highlighted the potential risks. Over a spectacular picture of a car flipping over in midair, a headline blared: "Road Racing is *Dangerous!*"—which, as it turned out, was not an idle warning.

Four thousand fans came out to watch the race on that day. It was windy and rainy, which made the track at Minter Field, just north of Bakersfield, muddy and treacherous. Dean was scheduled to compete in two races that day. He did well in his first race, coming in third behind veteran drivers Marion "Joe" Playan and John Kunstle, and first in his class. But in the very next race, in which Dean did not compete, disaster struck. Jack Drummond, a thirty-two-year-old driver who had been racing only four months, hit a bale of hay and flipped over. Suffering from head and chest injuries and a broken neck, he was rushed to the hospital but pronounced dead on arrival.

Despite Drummond's fatal accident, the day's events went on as scheduled. When it was time for Dean's second race, the track had become so wet and slippery, the competition had to be shortened. Inexperienced with driving in such conditions, Dean finished a disappointing ninth. The race was won by Johnnie Von Neumann, driving a Porsche 550 Spyder. Von Neumann, the owner of Competition Motors, the American importer of Porsches, had owned the first Porsche Spyder in California, which he totaled in a crash that nearly killed him. Dean realized that day that his Speedster was no match for the superior speed and power of the Spyder. If he wanted to win his first race, Dean knew he had to have that car. It was a conclusion that would lead to tragic consequences.

As Dean continued to come into his own in Hollywood, his passion for cars and racing grew unstoppable. Early on, during *East of Eden,* Elia Kazan had banned Dean from racing. But Nicholas Ray never lifted a finger to stop him. "I encouraged his racing," he said. "I felt it was good for Jimmy to do something on his own with clarity and precision." Dean's fervor for cars reflected an obsession of an entire generation—an obsession that *Rebel* popularized even further. Just as Dean flirted with death via automobile, so would his *Rebel* character, in what would become one of the movie's most imitated and influential sequences—the chickie run.

The chickie run is *Rebel*'s dramatic turning point, and the most technically ambitious scene in the film. It was the one scene that Ray insisted Stewart Stern retain, in some form, from Ray's own original "Blind Run" proposal. In the final film, Buzz (Corey Allen) challenges Jim (Dean) to participate in a chickie run after the knife fight. From that moment, the film progresses inexorably toward this test of honor. As night falls, the young cast—including Mineo, Wood and the gang members—assembles on a high bluff overlooking the ocean. To measure their courage, Buzz and Jim agree to race toward the edge of the cliff to see who will jump out first and get branded a "chicken." Jim bails out in time, but Buzz's sleeve gets caught on a door handle. He falls to his death—and *Rebel* takes on a far bleaker tone. In their reckless attempt to give some form to their existences, these kids are shaken to their very foundations as they come face to face with mortality. The chickie run would change everything in *Rebel.* Ray was determined to make it a defining moment and to make sure the ritual of the race—and the vehicles involved—were absolutely authentic.

THE '49 MERC

In many ways, it was the automobile that made teenage rebellion possible. Because of the booming postwar economy, teenagers were able to own cars for the first time, which gave them a freedom and mobility they never had before—and it offered them new ways to get in trouble. Cars brought together greater numbers of teenagers from greater distances, empowering them to create a culture of their own, away from the watchful eyes of parents. In their cars, teens could blast music, drink alcohol and smoke marijuana. And perhaps most importantly, the backseat finally provided a place where teens could have sex outside the home. The car might have been as important as the birth control pill in setting off the sexual revolution of the 1960s.

For one branch of the teen car culture—hot-rodders—automobiles themselves became a fetish, offering new ways to skirt danger, and new opportunities for self-expression. "The war was over and a lot of guys came back and they needed something interesting to keep them going," says Joe Playan, the driver who beat Dean in the race at Bakersfield. Hot-rod culture had its own art, its own lingo and its own lifestyle, all invented by teenagers. In 1947 *Hot Rod* magazine began publishing, and in 1951 the National Hot Rod Association was founded, building makeshift racetracks that gave hot-rodders places to compete other than the streets. It was at these events that Dean would often race.

Ray knew that if *Rebel* was going to feel real to teen audiences, he had to use the right type of automobiles. When Ray showed an early version of the script to gang member Frank Mazzola, he immediately zeroed in on this aspect of the story. "They had cars in the script that were like a model the Dead End Kids would drive," says Mazzola. "They weren't custom cars like we had." To keep *Rebel* credible, Ray hired George Barris, a man who was already a legend among L.A. hot-rodders. Barris handled the look of all the cars in the film. He was not only one of the most famous car customizers in Los Angeles, he helped invent the art. Years later, he would be immortalized in Tom Wolfe's famous essay "The Kandy-Kolored Tangerine-Flake Streamline Baby," which compared him to Picasso. Barris restyled factory models in any number of imaginative ways, including lowering the body, smoothing over the seams to streamline them, adding or removing chrome and giving cars fancy paint jobs to make them flashier, sleeker, cooler. He later customized cars for such stars as Elvis Presley and Frank Sinatra and designed such famous movie cars as the Batmobile, Herbie the Love Bug and the Munster Koach.

Like many customizers, Barris not only wanted his cars to look better but also to go faster. Hot rods were streamlined to make them more aerodynamic, and amateur designers and engineers tested their creations in illegal drag races. "Hot-rodders were militants," says Barris. "We were young engineers and designers that wanted to enjoy our craft. We didn't have a place to do it other than in the streets. The cops never could catch us because we were too fast. I would wake up in the morning and find bullet holes in my trunk." Eventually, what Barris and other customizers were doing caught the attention of auto companies. In 1958 *Motor Trend* magazine pointed out that Detroit designers were actually copying Barris's designs. It was just one of the ways in which teen culture was beginning to have a real impact on corporate America.

There is some controversy over who chose the 1949 Mercury to be the car Dean's character drove that night and throughout *Rebel*. According to a March 28, 1955, memo, Mazzola advised Ray "on makes of cars to purchase, and other technicalities of drag races." Mazzola says that every car in the film was also owned by members of his gang. He drove a 1949 Mercury and chose that car for Jim. But the car was also a favorite of George Barris. Barris's first customized version of a Mercury became one of his most popular creations and helped establish his reputation. "We all made suggestions about cars," says Barris. "The Merc was my suggestion because I was the king of Mercs at the time."

There is no doubt, however, that the Mercury was a popular car among hot-rodders, and its association with Dean and *Rebel* would turn it into a staple of Hollywood's teen iconography. In fact, *Rebel* would help transform how automobiles were depicted in the movies. "We were able to show that cars also could become stars," says Barris. Dean's Mercury would become the first of these celebrity cars. In his song "Cadillac Ranch," Bruce

Springsteen mentions some of the automobiles that inspired him from the movies, beginning with "James Dean in that Mercury '49."

According to Barris, the car was so admired at the time because "it had good proportions—the body design had contours and curves and some basic aerodynamics" while other cars of that period "were like a square box." For the Mercury that Jim drives in *Rebel,* Barris made only slight adjustments. He nosed the car (removed the emblem from the hood) and decked it (lowered the chassis) and added flared fender skirts (the panels that cover the tops of rear wheels), which came from a 1951 Mercury. The 1946 Ford that Jim drives in the chickie run was also nosed and decked. Although few people in the audience would have recognized these subtle changes, having the characters in *Rebel* drive customized cars signaled to savvy teenagers that this was no typical Hollywood film about their lives.

Dean already knew about Barris's reputation when he met him on the set of *Rebel.* "He approached me and said, 'I know you're the guy who does a lot of these customs and I like what you did to the Merc.' To me he was not only an actor, he lived the part," says Barris, who saw Dean as a kindred spirit, "a militant, a person who didn't go along with the establishment." Dean would later ask Barris to customize his Porsche Spyder and Barris would see him off the day Dean began his final, fateful drive to Salinas.

"YOU GOT TO DO SOMETHING"

While *Rebel Without a Cause* may have been the first Hollywood film to depict a chicken race, Nicholas Ray did not invent it. With the rise of hot-rod culture and juvenile delinquency after the war, teenagers' playing chicken was seen as a growing menace. A 1949 *Life* magazine article on hot-rodders linked the subculture with chicken in the public's mind. "In Los Angeles and Dallas, where 'hot-rodding' is at its peak, hundreds of youngsters spend their spare time in suicidal games on wheels," reported the piece, which was illustrated with grisly photos of car accidents and reenactments of chicken games.

Across the country in the early 1950s, alarming reports of youths playing chicken terrified parents and public officials. A teenager and a baby were killed in Elyria, Ohio, in 1950 in what a report called "one of the newer juvenile death-thrill road games." A Fort Pierce, Florida, man was killed playing chicken in 1952. That same year the Traverse City, Michigan, police chief warned that his department was on the lookout for juveniles playing chicken and that anyone caught would lose his driver's license. And in 1953 the *Los Angeles Times* reported that six Murrieta, California, teenagers were injured when their cars smashed into each other head on at 50 mph in a "contest called a 'chicken' game in the teen-ager vernacular."

Frank Mazzola says that he had participated in chickie runs, although they were somewhat different from the one depicted in *Rebel*. "When we played 'chickie,' we just drove our own cars down the street at each other and whoever swerved lost. The guy who beat you won your car," he says.

Ray's original conception for a race in "The Blind Run" was closer to how Mazzola remembered them: two cars barreled toward each other in the Sepulveda Tunnel. But, according to Ray, "Irving Shulman made a more dramatic suggestion for this key scene after reading a newspaper item about a chickie run at night on Pacific Palisades." *Rebel*'s chicken run off the edge of a cliff was modeled after that newspaper account.

The shooting of the chickie run took place on the Warner Ranch, a 2,800-acre plateau in Calabasas, California, about twenty miles from Warner Studios, on two cold Friday and Saturday nights, May 13 and 14, 1955. It would prove to be the film's most complicated sequence, a logistical nightmare. "It took a lot of time to prepare," says second assistant director Ray Gosnell Jr., who points out that they had to dig tracks for the cars to race along toward the cliff edge, in order to keep them exactly in frame. "They were concerned about the track showing on the big screen," says Gosnell. "The CinemaScope screen was so big you couldn't hide anything."

Lighting was another big problem. "You needed to have lights close enough to the actors to be able to light their eyes," says Gosnell. But with the CinemaScope screen, lights could not be set up so close to the action. The crew had to figure out how to illuminate the scenes while keeping the lights far enough away to be out of frame. Two and sometimes three cameras were used to shoot the scenes from different angles, meaning that lights had to be set up so that they were out of frame for each camera. "At that time, lights weren't as powerful as they are now," says Gosnell. Huge arc lamps were used, and simply moving them was a big job. "Arcs are monsters," says Gosnell. "Two men had to pick them up." The carbon filaments in these lamps, which had no bulbs, would constantly burn away and had to be changed again and again.

While the crew painstakingly set up shots, the cast spent hours shivering in the cold, damp air. "None of us had dressed warmly enough," said Corey Allen, who was shooting his last scenes in the film. At one point during the night, Allen went looking for a blanket to keep warm. He climbed up onto the back of the prop truck and found himself looking down at the mannequins of six dead bodies. "They were all me!" he recalled. "And they were in my wardrobe. Calm down, I told myself, they're only dummies. But they had my likeness and their eyes were all open."

With the production now nine days behind schedule—and after the debacle of the 24-Hour Day—Ray became more worried than ever about time. The night before, at the Baldwin Hills location, he had been forced to stop shooting at 2 a.m. because neighbors complained about noise from the generators. The next morning, he fired off an anxious, angry memo to David Weisbart demanding "to have it very clearly stated as to what my limitations in working hours are to be." But as the hours ticked away while the crew set up the complicated shots, Ray was butting up against a time restraint he could not fight. Since it was a night scene, shooting was to begin at twilight and end at dawn. Meanwhile, Daylight Savings Time had shaved another precious hour off the schedule. After arriving at the ranch at six the first night, the crew did not begin filming the first shot—of Jim driving up to the area where the chickie race would take place in his 1949 Mercury—until 10:20 that evening.

One of the most important shots scheduled that night was the moment when Judy signals for the race to begin. Ray planned a long shot of Wood with her arms thrust high in the air, brilliantly illuminated by two parallel rows of headlights stretching behind her to the cliff's edge. But by 11 p.m., the crew had still not finished setting up the complex array of camera angles Ray needed for that scene—and, once again in a production that always seemed to be backed into a corner because of its employment of minors, Wood's allotted time was running out. Ray was specifically concerned about getting the wide shot of Wood before she had to go. As it was planned, the shot would encompass the entire bluff, so there was no chance

Ray could fake it later on a studio soundstage and edit it in. He needed another solution, and he needed it fast.

At eleven o'clock, assistant director Don Page approached Faye Nuell Mayo, one of the extras hired for that day, and told her that Ray wanted to see her. "I thought, 'What did I do?'" remembers Mayo. "So I go into the trailer where Nick is with wardrobe and a dozen other people. About that time, my hair was very similar to Natalie's. Before I knew it, I was in her wardrobe." At midnight, Wood's tutor Tom Hennesy strode onto the set and told Ray that Wood had to go. And Mayo stepped in as her double, in one of the most iconic shots of Wood's career.

Mayo had been working primarily as a dancer at the time and took the extra work in *Rebel* to make a little money on the side. She had no idea that she was about to be immortalized, albeit without credit. After Wood yells, "Hit your lights," the scene cuts to the wide master shot. "And that's me," says Mayo. "Nick could have asked me to do the scene mechanically. But he explained to me what the scene was about, which was very generous of him." That long shot of an illuminated Judy with arms ritualistically upheld is one of the great images in widescreen cinema, and would help mark Ray as a master of CinemaScope.

Mayo ended up shooting many of the long shots of Wood in the chickie run sequence and remained throughout the rest of the shoot, stepping in whenever filming went beyond Wood's allotted time. Initially, Wood was not thrilled with the arrangement. "She was a little wary of me at first," says Mayo. "Who is this person coming over to be me?" But Mayo immediately caught the eye of someone who would make her feel accepted—James Dean. She became close to Dean, causing jealousies to flare, but with Dean on her side no one dared express them out loud. Dean invited her to spend hours with him in his trailer. "He was playing bongos or the flute," says Mayo. "I was not starstruck. I think he was comfortable with me." Some suspected that there was more than bongo playing going on, but Mayo denies that they were anything more than friends. Dean spent so much time in his trailer with Mayo the night of the chickie run, it delayed the shoot even further. "One of the reasons we ran so long on the night of the chicken race was that he was busy in his dressing room . . . enjoying life," is how cast member Tom Bernard euphemistically puts it. Dean got along so well with Mayo that Ray had her read off-camera lines to him. "Nick asked me to pick up a script and do some stuff with Jimmy," says Mayo. "They did close-ups of him over my shoulder."

While Wood may have been nervous about Mayo initially, Wood eventually accepted her—largely because of her association with Dean, says Mayo. Eventually, the two women formed a close friendship that lasted well after the picture ended. But it must have seemed ironic to Wood that while Dean did not share her strong feelings for him, he had suddenly taken up with her double.

Then again, Wood's life on set was complicated enough. She already had two men vying for her affections. And the tensions created by the awkward ménage à trois between Wood, Ray and Dennis Hopper would reach the breaking point that stressful night at the Warners ranch.

Mr. and Mrs. Gurdin—Wood's parents—paid an unannounced visit to the set because they were worried that the chickie run might be dangerous. Ever since Ray told Mrs. Gurdin about the Hopper-Wood relationship and got the young actor in trouble with his new studio, the hostility between Ray and Hopper had been building. When Hopper questioned Ray about a direction he had given, Ray exploded. "Nick suddenly started yelling at me and sent me to my trailer, in front of her parents," remembered Hopper. "I realized that the reason I was getting into this kind of a problem with Nick was because of Nick Ray's relationship with Natalie and my relationship with Natalie. I realized that I could be expendable in Nick Ray's world. And he could blame me and get off. I wasn't gonna let it happen."

Hopper decided to confront Ray. "Nick, I know that you've been fucking Natalie," he said. "You're now using that against me. I know that you've now told the studio that I'm having an affair with her. This has gotta stop . . . [or] I'm gonna beat the shit out of you right now." Hopper put up his fists and challenged Ray to have it out with him right then and there. But Ray was unfazed. Instead of trying to justify his own risky behavior—which easily could have put the film, and his career, in jeopardy—Ray suddenly transformed from jealous lover to stern patriarch. "See, that's your problem," he coolly said to Hopper. "You have to use your fists. You can't use your brain. Someday you're gonna have to start using your brains." Before walking away, Ray told Hopper he would have to change if he wanted to be "a serious actor" and ordered him to get off the set. "At that point, I lost my aggressiveness," said Hopper.

Deeply stung by Ray's words, Hopper went off in pursuit of Dean, whom he knew was Ray's ideal of the "serious actor." Hopper had barely spoken with Dean since the shoot began, and what Hopper did next must have caught Dean by surprise. "I grabbed Jimmy and threw him into one of the cars that was lined up with its headlights on to light up the run," said Hopper. "I told him I thought I was the best young actor in the world, but I didn't even understand what he was doing, that I was flabbergasted by his spontaneity, his ability to do scene after scene different each time without changing the words." Dean then asked Hopper a strange question: "Do you hate your family?" Hopper said that he did and Dean replied, "Yes, me too. That's our drive to act." He told Hopper that once he went to his mother's grave and cried out, "Mother, why did you leave me?" and that those feelings transformed into "Mother, I hate you. I'll show you. I'll be somebody." Suddenly, Hopper realized that "our drive was the same in the beginning, misguided anger and hate; and wanting to communicate through playacting and creating." From that point on, Hopper joined the roster of people who felt a special kinship with Dean—who became Hopper's personal acting coach.

The battle between Ray and Hopper was not the only long-simmering feud that flared up that night. Frank Mazzola and Corey Allen, who had been combative since the first auditions, almost came to blows. Allen always thought that Mazzola was jealous of his gang-leader role in the film. After all, as Allen says, "After hours, Frank was Buzz. He was the kid with a gang at Hollywood High." As they were rehearsing the scene where Buzz and Crunch are inspecting the cars that will be used in the chickie run, Allen and Mazzola suddenly caught each other's eyes. The two had succeeded in avoiding trouble until now, but the cold night and late hours had made their nerves raw. "You have two Buzzes with nothing to do and it's cold and we were just looking at each other," says Allen, likening it to "one of those stupid things where you're on a bus and you catch some guy's eyes and you ain't gonna look away and he ain't gonna look away." For a brief moment, the two young actors were on the verge of pummeling each other on the set, for no specific reason at all. Then just as suddenly, as if waking from a dream, the moment passed and they went back to work.

Years later, with their youthful antagonism long behind them, Mazzola would remember going to Allen's house in the Hollywood Hills and talking about those days. They shared drinks and Allen said, "I have to tell you, Frank, you were an asshole."

"You were a bigger asshole," said Mazzola.

The pointlessness of Allen's and Mazzola's adolescent hostility toward each other would be echoed in one of the most affecting moments in the chickie-run scene. Just before the actual race, Jim and Buzz stand at the edge of the precipice and share a cigarette together. Suddenly, their macho swaggering slips away and we are able to glimpse briefly the potential bond that exists between these young men. It's a surprising moment that challenges our expectations. Essentially, the chickie run was a test of machismo, a way of proving who was really a man and who was a "sissy" or "chicken." But Stern subversively chose this moment to once again expand on the notion of masculinity, to let us glimpse their vulnerability.

"One of the things I wanted to show in *Rebel* is that underneath all the bullshit macho defense, there was that pure drive for affection, and it didn't matter who the recipient might be," Stern said of this scene. "There was a longer time in those days for young men to be in the warrior phase, where a lot of romantic attachments were formed before heterosexual encounters. My favorite moment in the film is not between Jim and Plato but between Jim and Buzz, who dies in the 'chicken' race. It was tender and loving, and the killing of that boy, whom Jim had known for all of twelve minutes, motivated the entire last half of the film."

In the film, Buzz grabs the lighted cigarette from between Jim's lips, takes a drag from it, and hands it back to him. It's a warm gesture of commiseration, reminiscent of two buddies in a war movie, which was one of the few acceptable contexts at the time in which men were allowed to express affection for each other.

"I like you, you know?" Buzz suddenly says.

"What are we doing this for?" Jim asks.

And Buzz replies—in one of the film's most famous lines—"You got to do *something*."

With this simple exchange, Jim and Buzz get to the heart of the existential question that the aimless post–World War II generation had been asking themselves. Corey Allen knew it was a key line in the film. "It was the best line in the picture," says Allen. "It was one of the first times in my acting career that I had a chance to do something that truthful."

To Allen, this exchange captured the feelings of several generations of American kids, much like the mansion scenes had done. "It was the sociological gift this picture made to the hippies," Allen says. "It's the underlying question of each generation. Here we are; what do we do? The answer may have been different but the question was always there. Kids in the '50s didn't have any cause. What are we going to do?"

The centerpiece of the chickie-run sequence was, of course, the actual race itself. Hours of preparation went into setting up the cars so that they would perform as needed, staying in frame, on track, in a suspenseful headlong rush to the edge. But despite the crew's planning, the first attempt at shooting the cars forward was a disaster. The cars, without drivers, had been set up on inclined wooden platforms. At the right moment, someone was supposed to release the brakes so that they would roll down the platform and onto the tracks, which led to a ravine with a thirty-foot drop. But before the cast and crew were completely ready to shoot, one of the cars broke loose. As it careered toward the cliff, both Nick Adams and Steffi Sidney sprung into action, attempting to run after the speeding car. In an almost suicidal gesture, Adams leaped in front of the car and managed to grab hold of it, but it was going too fast and got away. Ray yelled for everyone to run toward the pit anyway and look over the edge, as if the car had gone off the cliff, to at least salvage the end of the shot. A duplicate car was brought in, but that car's wheelbase did not fit the tracks, so they were unable to repeat that particular shot. Ray would be forced to rework it on a later date back on the Warners lot.

Other angles of the chickie race were filmed using stunt drivers. Dean had wanted to do his own stunts and argued with Ray about it. Although Ray was willing to let Dean put his life in jeopardy on the racetrack, letting Dean drive the car in the chickie run was a risk he wasn't prepared to take. Instead, Ray assembled a crack crew of stuntmen to handle the cars in the film, choosing them with as much care as he chose the cast. Dean became quite close to some of these men, who were among the most knowledgeable car experts in Hollywood, pumping them for information and hanging out with them off set to pick up driving tips.

Two legendary stunt drivers coordinated some of the stunts on the chickie run: Bill Hickman and Carey Loftin. They would later both work on the two most famous car-chase sequences in Hollywood history, the race through the twisty streets of San Francisco in *Bullitt* and the 90-mph pursuit of a New York subway train in *The French Connection*. After the film, Hickman and Loftin became Dean's racing gurus.

Doubling for Dean as the driver of the 1946 Ford that Jim drives in the race was Rodney Amateau. Amateau was an old friend of Ray's, a jack-of-all-trades who had worked on scripts and assisted Ray on such films as *In a Lonely Place, Born to Be Bad,* and *Flying Leathernecks.* Before going on to become a director himself, he did stunt work in a number of films. Among his many uncredited jobs, he played the old lady in the wheelchair whom Richard Widmark pushes down the stairs in *Kiss of Death.* After Amateau finished his scenes, Dean rushed up to him and barraged him with questions. "He was interested in anything and everything that had to do with cars and driving," said Amateau. "Until then I thought he was pretty stand-offish."

Dean asked Amateau to show him how to jump out of a car for the camera, and when it came time to shoot the scene where Jim Stark escapes from the car before it goes over the cliff, Ray reluctantly agreed to let Dean try this stunt himself. A prop man put down a mattress to break his fall, but Dean made him take it away, telling him, "People will say Dean can't even do his own stunts—he has to have a mattress." The prop man complied, although not before pointing out that the mattress had once been used by Errol Flynn. Dean proved to be a good student. Shot with two cameras, with the film slowed down to speed up the action, the scene was wrapped without a hitch in two takes.

A second unit shot the footage of the cars plummeting onto the rocks below the cliff a few days after shooting at the Warner Ranch, on a bluff in Palos Verdes along the Pacific Coast Highway. Even though Dean was not required for the shot, he was so fascinated with this aspect of the film that he showed up anyway just to watch, according to George Barris, who was also there. To shoot the scene, the studio first had to get permission from the Air Pollution Control Board, which would allow only three minutes of burning per hour. All fabric and upholstery had to be removed from the cars, and Shellane liquefied petroleum gas was used to create the flame effect. Photographed from miles away in the afternoon but treated in a lab to make it look like a night sky, this shot of the austere cliff with the ocean's waves lapping against the rocks below momentarily steps back from the action to evoke a more detached, omniscient point of view. Suddenly, we are back in the universe depicted in the planetarium, where, according to the lecturer, "the problems of Man seem trivial and naïve indeed." After Judy's "hit the lights" moment, this is the most potent and memorable Cinema-Scope image in the chickie-run sequence.

The chickie run is *Rebel*'s keynote action sequence. And Ray wanted plenty of shots to give the scene a vibrantly kinetic feel. After all their work on the Warner Ranch, many chickie-run insertions remained, including close-ups that would have to be shot at the studio. As a time- and money-saving move, the studio had ordered Ray not to shoot close-ups on location. But because of mishaps like the runaway car, even some of the longer shots of the cars had to be readdressed on a soundstage.

The sequence also includes a number of process shots that had to be done in the studio, including the close-ups of Jim and Buzz driving in the chickie run and eyeing each other nervously to see who will jump first, and the shot of Buzz's face as he plunges over the cliff to his death.

The first time they shot this scene, Allen opened his mouth to scream and nothing came out. For him, not being able to scream was his "truthful" reaction. But Ray wasn't happy. "I'd like to do it again, this time with the voice," Ray told him. Allen protested, "I want to do what you want but it's not the truth." They shot the scene once more. But once again, when it came time for Allen to cry out, all he could manage was a silent scream. Ray said, "Cut. Print it," and they moved on to another scene. Allen believed that he had persuaded Ray he was right. "I was very big on just having discovered the truth," he says. Then in postproduction, Ray dubbed in another actor's voice screaming. The incident taught Allen a lesson that would later prove useful when he became a director himself. "You don't argue with the actor if you don't have to," Allen says. "You can do it behind his back."

For other studio shots, the plateau was re-created on Warner's legendary Stage 7 (now Stage 16), which at the time was the biggest soundstage in Hollywood. Stage 7 owes its massive dimensions to the man who would be the model for Charles Foster Kane in *Citizen Kane:* newspaper ty-coon William Randolph Hearst. In a last-ditch power move to resuscitate her fading career, Hearst's mistress Marion Davies insisted that the stage be raised from its original height to a towering ninety-eight feet to shoot musical scenes for her next-to-last film, 1936's *Cain and Mabel.* Jack Warner agreed—as long as Hearst would pay for it. The stage is still used today, more recently for such films as *Titanic* and *The Perfect Storm.*

The scenes of the cast looking down into the ravine at the wreckage of Buzz's car were filmed on Stage 7 throughout the last week of production. But Dean had difficulty getting into character for this scene since he was actually looking over a fake ravine at a black velvet cloth covering the floor of the soundstage instead of Buzz's remains. "He couldn't relate to the blank cloth," said Corey Allen, "so he took an apple core, covered it with ketchup, threw it down on the floor and pretended it was me."

Ray and his cast worked on scenes from the chickie run right up until the final day of shooting. The sequence required plenty of postproduction. In fact, the chickie-run scenes were so troublesome that a second unit had to come in and shoot even more footage in the studio a month after production wrapped. In the end, Ray, editor William Ziegler and producer Weisbart were able to assemble all of this disparate footage together to create a sequence whose impact on the culture was even greater than Ray himself could have imagined.

THE ATOMIC AGE

With the chickie run, Ray had hit upon an image that crystallized all the recklessness and angst of adolescence. Other filmmakers seized on it. In the wake of *Rebel,* a host of films about juvenile delinquents would also mount chicken races, including *Dragstrip Girl* (1957), *The Wild Ride* (1960), *Faster, Pussycat! Kill! Kill!* (1965), *Footloose* (1984) and *The Heavenly Kid* (1985). But the chickie run would not only become a metaphor for adolescence, it would become a metaphor for the Cold War. In his history of game theory, *Prisoner's Dilemma,* William Poundstone traces the connection between chicken and the Cold War, citing *Rebel* as the film that brought "the game of chicken . . . to public attention." Philosopher Bertrand Russell first made the analogy when he compared chicken and "brinksmanship," a policy that claimed the United States could guarantee peace only by showing it was prepared to go to the brink of nuclear war with the Soviet Union. In the 1960s, the chicken race would be studied by mathematicians and political scientists, becoming one of the best-known models in game theory. Game theorists at the RAND Corporation, such as John Nash (the subject of *A Beautiful Mind*) and Herman Kahn, analyzed games like chicken to advise the U.S. government on Cold War strategy. "It seemed for a while that game theory might be able to solve realistic problems. This was an exciting prospect: Swap 'Jimbo' and 'Buzz' for America and the Soviet Union, and you could see parallels with the Cuban missile crisis of 1962, or with the Cold War more generally," writes science journalist Robert Matthews. Kahn, who believed the best strategy for winning a game of chicken was to convince your opponent you are suicidally insane, actually proposed that the U.S. build a "Doomsday Machine" that would destroy the world if the Soviet Union attacked (which is where Stanley Kubrick got the idea for the end of *Dr. Strangelove*).

By having Jim and Buzz race toward the abyss, "Nicholas Ray gave his version of chicken a Cold War twist," according to linguist Geoffrey Nunberg, who credits *Rebel Without a Cause* with popularizing the phrase "playing chicken." But while it is doubtful that Ray was consciously creating a Cold War analogy when he first described the chicken race, the sense that adolescents were imitating a world gone mad was certainly behind his choice of this potent concept. A 1954 study on the rise of juvenile delinquency actually cited Cold War tensions as one factor in the increase in youth crime, and *Rebel Without a Cause* was made during a particularly tense period of the Cold War. On the day shooting of the chickie run began, in fact, the Warsaw Pact was ratified, ensuring the Soviet Union's domination of Eastern Europe. Meanwhile, Communist China and the United States were engaged in a global game of chicken: President Eisenhower threatened to use nuclear weapons if China invaded Taiwan.

Tensions were so high during this period that, on May 5, 1955, a week before the chickie-run scenes were shot, the entire West Coast was put on alert that a nuclear attack was imminent. In Los Angeles, air raid sirens began wailing at 10:40 a.m. and radio stations went off the air as confusion and panic gripped the city. It took nearly a half hour for authorities to realize it was a false alarm and sound the all clear. The next day embarrassed officials called it a "horrible mistake."

That same day, the U.S. government conducted one of a series of controversial atomic tests called Operation Teapot, designed to examine whether nuclear weapons could be used routinely in the battlefield. In the specific test conducted that day, mannequins of typical American families—like the middle-class families depicted in *Rebel*—were set up in various suburban-style dwellings, equipped with appliances and cupboards stacked with food. The mannequins were placed in normal-looking poses: a family having dinner, a child asleep in a nursery. Almost all the houses—and the mannequin families inside—were obliterated. A headline in the *Los Angeles Times* the next day summed up the disappointing results: ATOM CITY SHOWS FEW COULD HAVE SURVIVED FURY OF THE BLAST.

But despite the headlines, most of *Rebel*'s cast members were not paying attention. "People may have known about atomic testing at the time but we weren't interested," says Beverly Long.

Stewart Stern would work an ironic reference to the times into the screenplay. In the dinner scene at Judy's house, her mother explains her daughter's behavior by saying, "She'll outgrow it, dear. It's just the age."

Abruptly, her little brother Beau fires his toy ray gun into the air and gleefully yells, "The atomic age!"

Looking back on the movie, James Baird, who played nine-year-old Beau, says laughing, "I had no idea what it meant, but I said it anyway. That's the great actor I was."

Rebel's young cast may have been blissfully ignorant of the world around them, but just as they were about to shoot the last shots of the chickie run at the Warner Ranch, they would witness a terrifying sight that would bring the world situation a little closer to home. At five in the morning on May 15, the cast and crew of *Rebel* were racing to finish shooting the last scenes before the sun rose. All that were left to film were the scenes in which the gang members watch the cars go off the edge of the cliff, then run to their own cars and drive away. Three cameras would record these final shots, which took two hours to set up. But just as Ray was about to say "Action!" the night sky suddenly lit up as if the sun had risen in an instant and exploded.

"Everybody was bewildered," says Long. "It lit up everything like daylight. I thought it was a big meteorite." Sidney remembers seeing the flash and thinking, "What the devil is that? It looks like an atomic bomb." She would later find out she was right. What they witnessed was the final atomic test of Operation Teapot at the Nevada Test Site in the Yucca Flats more than two hundred miles away. "It was so flat out in the valley in those days," says Sidney. "Nothing was built up, so you could see for miles." Code-named "Zucchini," the test involved dropping a twenty-eight-kiloton thermonuclear bomb from a five-hundred-foot tower. The explosion was so powerful that night was transfigured into day for miles around. It was like a real-life version of the scene earlier in *Rebel* when the cast watched the world explode in a flash of light while sitting in a darkened planetarium in the middle of the afternoon. "You think the end of the world will come at nighttime?" Plato asks Jim at the end of *Rebel*. "No, at dawn," he replies. For a brief moment, it seemed as if these words had come true.

CHAPTER FOURTEEN

Last Good-bye

With *Rebel* ten days over schedule and the entire ending and numerous scenes from other sections of the film yet to be shot, pressure on Ray had never been so intense. He had only two weeks to finish the film. "We were running way over, budgetwise and timewise," remembers Faye Nuell Mayo. "Jack Warner was screaming that he was going to take the camera away: it was very chaotic. Every time the word would come down, Nick would become upset. There was a period of a couple of weeks toward the end where things were getting very hairy." Meanwhile, George Stevens—who had much more studio clout than Ray—was lobbying to get at Dean as soon as possible to prepare for *Giant*. "I believe every effort should be made on *Rebel Without a Cause* to finish with Dean as early as possible as we need every day that we can obtain for preparation of our picture," Stevens had written back in April. With a June 3 starting date for Dean and with *Rebel* still not finished, Stevens was getting anxious.

But with Warner and Stevens breathing down his neck, Ray continued to remain focused on the fine points of the film, refining and redefining *Rebel*'s bravura finale. He would work and rework this finale as long as he possibly could, almost as if something inside of him refused to let go of the project.

According to the script, the finale called for the police, the parents, Jim and Judy to descend on the Griffith Observatory, where Plato is holed up. Jim runs into the planetarium building and tries to calm a distraught Plato, who has a gun and has gone over an emotional edge since being attacked by several gang members at the mansion. Jim convinces Plato to surrender to the police. But Plato suddenly balks and runs up to the dome of the planetarium, where he is shot by police and plummets to his death.

Ray wanted to add one final image to Stern's conception of the scene. It would be shot from inside the dome as its slot closes, like stage curtains. That final shot was filmed, but the rest of the roof sequence proved too complicated and expensive. "It is neither possible or practical for a man to climb on the real dome," according to a memo from Warners production manager Eric Stacey, who pointed out that creating an alternate dome on a soundstage would cost five thousand dollars. And it would take a week to build—a week they did not have. Ray was urged to rethink his final scene.

Producer David Weisbart wanted the picture to wrap up more quickly anyway; he felt the ending was going slack. He proposed cutting an important scene between Jim and Plato inside the planetarium before Plato is shot, but Ray objected: "To lose the momentary isolation of Jim and Plato is, I believe, wrong," he wrote to Weisbart in a memo. In the scene, Jim speaks tenderly to Plato, gently trying to persuade him to leave the planetarium and turn himself in. He gives Plato his jacket and surreptitiously removes the bullets from the gun, before giving it back to him. Without this scene, which humanizes Plato and reaffirms his friendship with Jim, the last images of Plato would be those of a raving, gun-toting psychotic who has already shot one boy (Frank Mazzola's Crunch) and is shooting at the police. The emotional impact of his death would not be nearly as poignant and tragic. What's more, losing this scene would compromise the twenty-four-hour structure of the story, which Ray felt was crucial. Ray wanted Plato to get shot just as the sun is coming up on a new day, but if the transitional scene between Jim and Plato was lost, the abrupt shift from the dead of night to the break of dawn would be too jarring. If the scenes inside the planetarium were deleted, Plato would have to die at night. "It is terribly important for us to end the picture with the beginning of a new day," Ray wrote to Weisbart. "I really believe our story is in jeopardy if we play it as a night sequence."

Despite the time crunch, Ray decided to shoot the finale his way. The crew returned to Griffith Observatory on May 16 and spent five days crafting the film's original ending, with Plato dying on the roof of the planetarium, though they did not film many critical shots, including Plato falling from the dome. Everyone was exhausted and strains were beginning to show. Wood tripped and fell while they were shooting the scene of her running up the steps of the planetarium and she had to be treated for cuts and bruises. Dean blamed weariness from all the hours he spent shooting *Rebel* that week for his late arrival at a May 18 press luncheon to publicize *Giant.* When Dean finally showed up unshaven and sloppily dressed, he refused to remove his sunglasses for photographers because he said he had bags under his eyes. He spent the lunch slouching in his chair with his elbows on the table looking bored. Stevens was furious at his behavior and Dean was forced to apologize.

On May 23, with only three more shooting days left in the schedule, Ray asked Weisbart and editor William Ziegler to assemble the finale footage he had already shot, which he admitted was incomplete. "I warned you about the sequence on the top of the roof, that I would shoot it only to get a partial location of the people in case we wanted to complete it on stage," he wrote to Weisbart. It is possible that he hoped once they saw the scene cut together in the studio, they would give him the time and money he needed to finish the film his way.

While Weisbart and Ziegler assembled the footage of the final sequence, Ray spent the day shooting scenes that could be accomplished at the studio. One scene was shot on a still-standing Warners set known as the Court House, which was used in *O Brother Where Art Thou* and as the library in the original 1962 version of *The Music Man.* It was a relatively minor scene—Crunch, believing Jim is going to rat them out to the police, briefly confronts him on the steps of the police station—but it proved to be difficult. Dean seemed irked and distracted. At one point, he loudly spat on the ground. "Everybody stopped and Nick Ray just stood there and it was absolute quiet and this poor little guy came in with a sweeper pan and swept it up and walked out," remembers Beverly Long. "I think Nick would get very disgusted at him doing things like that." Finally, Ray approached Frank Mazzola and asked him to find out what was wrong with his star. Dean's problem, as it turned out, was Mazzola himself.

"You know, Frank, I've got the whole movie," Dean told him. "This is an important sequence for you. You've got to pay attention where you are."

"I disappeared in a lot of shots because I have my back to the camera because I didn't want to look at Corey," says Mazzola, referring to his ongoing feud with Corey Allen. Dean proceeded to give Mazzola a lesson in playing for the camera. "I'm walking down the steps and you're moving this way so the camera is going to be seeing your ear and seeing my face," Dean told him. "At least swing yourself so we get a profile."

"At that moment, if you look at the film, my performance goes up a notch," says Mazzola. "It's like he sprinkled some dust on me."

Ray also filmed the process shot of Jim's parents driving to the planetarium with Ray Framek that day. Ann Doran had been nagging Ray about including something that would soften her character throughout the shoot. "I fought like crazy!" said Doran. "I found this speech in the paper, and said, 'Here's something that shows what kind of a woman she is. Can't you put this in someplace?' Every time I'd see him, I'd say 'What about that speech? Surely, you can use that speech.'" Finally, Ray relented. In the scene, Doran looks directly in the camera and, in *Rebel*'s most hackneyed moment, she portentously states, "I don't understand. You pray for your children. You read about things like this happening to other families, but you never dream it could happen to yours." Stewart Stern found these lines patronizing and "incredibly offensive."

Stern would also be disturbed to discover that a crucial confrontation between Jim and his father had been cut out of the finale. In the scene, as Stern wrote it, Jim's father tries to stop his son before he goes into the planetarium, fearing he will be shot by police. But after Jim explains that Plato needs his help, Mr. Stark reluctantly lets him go and even restrains police officer Framek when he tries to block Jim from running into the planetarium. Stern says that this scene was meant to show "the growth of the father. You saw his conflict. Here he is sacrificing his son, knowing that the son needs this moment to actualize everything the father has always preached but has been afraid to do himself." Without this scene, the sudden transformation of the father at the end of the film does seem contrived, a half-hearted attempt at closure, but it is easily passed over as our emotions stay with the tragedy of Plato.

Meanwhile, Weisbart and Ziegler had quickly assembled the footage Ray shot of Plato's death, and it was clear that the finale was not going to work as Ray conceived it. So the next day, May 24, he was forced to go back to Griffith Observatory to reshoot the scene, filming at night—and without Plato climbing on the dome. Ray had to accept the fact that Plato would be shot on the steps of the observatory.

"I GOT THE BULLETS!"

Returning to the Griffith Observatory once again, James Dean was unfocused and combative. He was facing an overwhelming flood of contradictory emotions. He was on his last location for a film that was very close to his heart. The following week he would start shooting *Giant,* which he thought would be the most important film of his career so far, and he had virtually no time for preparation. He also had to deal with the distraction of his rocketing celebrity status. During the making of *Rebel,* Dean's fan mail had increased from 400 letters a week to 1,200 letters a week. So many fans had shown up at the Griffith Observatory set that night, barricades had to be set up to keep them back. At one point, Dean went over to the crowd and signed autographs for twenty minutes.

Dean enjoyed the first flush of success after the opening of *East of Eden,* but over time the pressure had begun to get to him. He was growing increasingly hostile to the press, which would begin hitting back in articles with such bluntly provocative titles as "Genius or Jerk?"

"Maybe publicity is important," Dean said. "But I can't make it, can't get with it. I've been told by a lot of guys the way it works. The newspapers give you a big build-up. Something happens, they tear you down. Who needs it? What counts to the artist is performance not publicity. Guys who don't know me, already they've typed me as an oddball." As one journalist would remark, Dean was either "very shrewd or very honest."

Nick Adams remembered an incident with Dean at the Warners commissary. "He saw his picture on the wall with all the studio's stars; he tore it down, muttering, 'What do they want to do? Kill everyone's appetite.'"

During the last weeks on the film, an increasingly distressed Dean asked Ray for the name of his psychiatrist. But although Ray was usually happy to keep Dean bound to him—especially since the two of them had begun to seriously discuss forming an independent production company—he refused to give Dean his analyst's name, at least not directly. "I'll give you the names of four or five of the most reputable in Southern California and you choose your own," Ray said. Following his own instincts, Dean picked the same analyst as Ray.

The mounting demands on Dean were making it difficult for him to concentrate on his work at the planetarium. "Today my emotional apparatus is, I don't know, is plugged up or something," Dean told Shirley Thomas, a radio reporter who was on the set while they were shooting the final scenes. "I'm kvetching and pushing and passion-pumping. It's not coming easy for me." He was already worried about falling "back on the securities that made you famous or successful" and actor's "tricks," he told her. The more Dean questioned himself, however, the more frustrated Ray was becoming with him.

Dean's most important line in the film's finale occurs just after Plato is shot. At a peak of despair, Jim Stark screams, "I got the bullets," indicating that he had removed the bullets from Plato's gun and that the police did not need to shoot him down. Dean's friend Lew Bracker, who was visiting the set, remembers that Dean had trouble with that line of dialogue, which had originally been suggested by Clifford Odets. "Jimmy couldn't get it quite the way he wanted it," Bracker remembers, "and I think he was in conflict with the director." Dean and Ray privately discussed the scene as they had done so many times before. Then, Dean went off by himself. "I think Nick wanted more emotion and Jimmy was going for more anguish and futility," explains Bracker.

Chuck Hicks, who played the ambulance driver sent to remove Plato's body, remembers that Dean tried the line any number of ways, stopping and asking to do it again. "Sometimes he'd come out real panicky and other times he'd stand there and say, 'No, no, no, no,'" Hicks remembers. Eventually, Dean nailed it, and the line became *Rebel*'s last great outburst—a *cri de coeur* launched against authority and the prevailing social order.

During the scenes Dean played over Plato's body, he demonstrated his deepest empathy and most naked instincts. With Plato's body stretched out on the cold, hard cement, Dean drags himself around like a wounded animal, pulling himself with his arms as if his legs are paralyzed, as if he has been shot himself. He straightens out Plato's right leg and looks down at the red and blue socks and starts laughing, and then he collapses in tears. "I wanted to do that scene over and over again," Sal Mineo remembered, "and each time we did it, he'd position me in the kind of repose that would work best for him to get the emotion going," Mineo remembered. "It was very moving for me, because *he* was very moved."

Dean became so caught up in the anguish of the moment that—once again—it spilled over into real life. He began to act as if Mineo himself was the one about to die. "He was very protective," Mineo said, "and for the whole day he'd never let me out of his sight. He was always there."

"In Plato's death scene I understood what being loved meant," said Mineo. "Here was the chance for me to feel what it would be like for someone close, someone that I idolized, to be grieving for me. It was an opportunity to experience what kind of grief that would be—what would he be like, what he would sound like, what would he be thinking?"

Mineo would later come to believe that it was these very feelings of love that condemned Plato to death. "[Jim] had the hots for Natalie *and* me. Ergo, I had to be bumped off, out of the way," Mineo said. In his landmark book *The Celluloid Closet,* author Vito Russo agreed with Mineo. "The explosion of bottled-up feelings over this kind of emotional attachment kills Plato and Buzz, though Jim is left safely in the arms of Natalie Wood," Russo wrote. "Homosexuality is considered 'normal' until the end of adolescence; after that it is arrested development."

But while there may be some validity to this analysis, it falters in the face of *Rebel*'s emotional power. Filmmaker Eric Rohmer wrote that while the film may give a psychoanalyst plenty to scrutinize, "he certainly won't be able to appreciate how much we, the audience, *feel* . . ." Plato's death gives the film the emotional catharsis that its structure requires. It is played entirely as tragedy, with no lingering sense of moral comeuppance. If any blame exists, it falls on the authoritarian structure that surrounds these kids. In fact, the studio was actually hesitant about having Plato die at all. Ray was instructed by Weisbart to shoot an alternate version of the ending in which Plato lives. In his notes to Ray about the script, Steve Trilling seemed less concerned with killing off the gay character, as critics like Russo believed, than with setting up Jim as a hero. "Jim has to do something to resolve the story," he wrote. Comparing Jim to Marlon Brando's character in *On the Waterfront,* Trilling continued, "Brando took a stand." Trilling also proposed that Jim be wounded by the police (which occurred in the conclusion of Shulman's version of the script).

Surprisingly, Stewart Stern says that originally he wanted both Jim and Plato to die. "The father goes to Jim and says, 'I really wanted to talk.' And Jim says, 'We're busy,' while reaching out to Plato, 'we're busy . . . very busy dying.' The studio said they thought that would be a little depressing."

While it may be true that both Buzz and Plato die after showing affection for Jim, the fact that Jim returns their affection contradicts the notion that the film is trying to impose some sense of "normal" on the story. As Ray would note years later, "They shot the wrong guy. Dean's the dangerous one."

Dean continued to be more restless and reckless than usual those last nights at Griffith Observatory. After he finished shooting the night scenes at the planetarium, according to actress Marietta Canty, "Jimmy would jump in his sports car, put his foot down on the pedal right to the floor and just zoom down the hill. Everyone would just stand there with their mouths open; I mean, we thought the kid was going to kill himself right then and there."

Canty, who played Plato's nanny, was on hand to shoot her last scenes in the film. Brief though they were, Canty would give a deeply moving performance. Ray gave Canty as much screen time as the story would allow at this climactic point in the film. Chuck Hicks says Ray took away his one line as the ambulance driver in order to place more emphasis on Canty. Throughout the scene, Ray cuts to more close-ups of Canty than another director might have, considering the size of her part.

According to the script, Canty's character—Plato's housekeeper, nanny and surrogate mother—also makes her way to the observatory that night. When Plato is shot, it is Canty's anguished look and heartbreaking scream of "John!" (Plato's real name) that punctuates the moment and reminds us of the important role she played in his life. When the stars of the film gather around Plato's body, Canty crouches at the left hand of Dean as she takes off a medallion she is wearing and puts it around Plato's neck, saying, "This poor baby got nobody. Just nobody." Finally, at the end of the planetarium sequence, as everyone is leaving, she gets the very last close-up in the film—its penultimate shot—her tear-streaked face choking back emotion as the ambulance's siren wails in the background. It's an impassioned moment, confirming the nanny's status as outsider, and closing the movie with a powerful look of despair. Sadly, these are the last shots of Canty that would ever be filmed in Hollywood.

Canty may have been the focus of the film's penultimate shot, but Ray was saving the final shot for no less a participant in *Rebel* than himself. Even before shooting had begun, Ray had expressed the urge to appear in his own film, but not in the manner of that most famous of cameo-prone directors, Alfred Hitchcock. Hitchcock popped into his films as a winking gesture to the audience. But Ray's appearance in the film was not meant to be an inside joke. It was tantamount to an artist's signature, scratched directly onto the celluloid.

When Ray told Stewart Stern what he was planning to do, Stern was appalled. "I thought it was completely tasteless," he says. Ray first divulged his idea back when the two of them visited the planetarium to block out the scenes set there. "I can't really say that I blame him because it had all been his dream," Stern says. "He was really proud of what he had done, rightfully. He wanted a curtain call." But Stern also felt that appearing in the film was Ray's way of grabbing total credit. "I wish he hadn't," Stern says. "I think it had something to do with ownership. It's like it's a Nick Ray production without crediting anybody and I felt he was staking his claim to the entire operation. It was unforgivable hungry ego."

Stern's mixed feelings are especially understandable considering what was happening between them during the time Ray was shooting these final scenes. Just a few days before, Stern discovered that Ray wanted to take sole credit for *Rebel*'s story, even though Stern had invented much of the plot. He wanted to give Irving Shulman credit for adapting the story and Stern credit only for writing the screenplay. Ray claimed that he deserved sole story credit because the plot was based on his treatment, which Stern would not actually see until decades later. When Stern confronted Ray, asking him what aspects of the story were in his treatment, Stern says that Ray told him that he originally had the idea of setting all the action in one day and ending at the planetarium, which is, in fact, not in Ray's original treatment, though Stern didn't know it at the time. Stern says that he asked Ray "why he was so shocked and surprised and pleased" when Stern came up with that idea of the twenty-four-hour structure and Ray told him, "I was glad that you realized what I finally had on my mind." Stern felt hurt, betrayed and angry by Ray's rush for credit, and it caused a breach in their relationship that would never heal. The two of them would never work together again after *Rebel*.

Even with the story credit, Ray felt the need to put his imprimatur right on-screen, via his physical presence. After shooting all night—and so alarming local residents with arc lights that emergency switchboards were jammed with callers believing that Griffith Park had caught fire—Ray filmed what would be the closing shot of the movie. It was 6:55 on the morning of May 25. Although Ray had lost the battle with Warners regarding Plato's death at dawn, the last shot of the film does take place as the sun is rising, giving the film the Aristotelian sense of closure the director had sought. As the camera boom pulls up and back from the grounds of the planetarium, the Stark family drives away in a police car. A man in a long gray overcoat carrying a briefcase walks by, idly looking at the cars as they move off. Unaware of the tragic drama that has just unfolded, he is a visual metaphor for the universe's indifference. A solitary figure, the man ascends the steps of the planetarium, signaling the start of a new day. That man is actually Ray himself—"awaiting," as filmmaker Mark Rappaport would write, "the next busload of new teenagers."

THE FINAL DAYS

The night at the observatory was followed by two drop-dead final days of shooting back on the studio lot. Ray was nearly out of time. Yet a tremendous amount of loose ends and connecting shots were left to film. Ray and his cast scrambled to get everything done. It is as if they were replaying the entire movie in two frantic days. The crew had assembled thirty partial sets on Stages 5 and 7. And the cast ran quickly from setup to setup. They would switch from Stage 5 for a close-up of the mansion love scene to gigantic Stage 7 for more pickups of the chickie run. They filmed process shots of Jim and Buzz inside their cars, and on a mockup of the planetarium steps they even shot eight more takes of the troublesome scene where Dean shouts, "I got the bullets!"

As the film began to wind down, Lew Bracker, who visited Dean on the set that week, detected a sense of desperation among some of the cast members, and not just because of all the work they were racing through. "There was some interesting interaction among the young actors," he says. "Everybody knew Jimmy was going to be a superstar. There was terrific competition to be Jimmy's friend among that young group, vying for first position. You could cut the jealousy with a knife."

But there was also a sense of loss that this experience was coming to an end. "Everyone was kind of sad because it was all over," said Ray's assistant, Roger Donoghue. For a few months, since the film's unorthodox auditions, Ray and his cast had become incredibly close, almost tribal in their connectedness. None of them would ever have an experience quite like *Rebel* again.

By the time the film ended, even the actors who played the parents had fallen under the movie's—and Dean's—spell. Jim Backus came to appreciate Dean's acting abilities, and the two formed a bond with their dueling Mr. Magoos. And while Dean and Ann Doran had "squared off," as she put it, their relationship grew surprisingly close toward the end of production. Dean would visit her home at odd hours to go over scenes. "He liked to rehearse at any time—one, two, or three o'clock in the morning," said Doran. "He would drink gallons of coffee and even smoked marijuana until I told him it was making me sick. Though I'm a great talker, I did a lot of listening. He widened my life." One night, he even showed up at her house shouting, "Mom! It's your son!"

Ray spent a large portion of the last production day shooting an important scene of Judy and Jim talking in an alley after the chickie run. But during these last frenetic moments, even Ray's camera equipment seemed to be exhausted. A bad camera magazine ruined some footage and the sound ran out in the middle of another take. Then after racing to shoot more inserts for the chickie run and planetarium scenes, Ray realized that he still needed a close-up of Jim and Judy's love scene from the mansion. But it was already 10 p.m. and Wood had to leave. Wood's mother stepped in and paid off the person who was watching over her daughter's schedule that evening. She handed the watchdog an envelope filled with cash and said, "Natalie has got her schooling now, hasn't she?" Ray got his close-up, and after reshooting some of the alley scenes that had been ruined earlier, he was finally done. *Rebel* wrapped at 2:45 a.m. on the morning of May 27, eleven days over schedule.

Suddenly, it was all over and no one knew exactly what to do. No one wanted to go home. On other shoots, Wood established a tradition of getting fellow cast members to sign her suede jacket. But during these last moments on the set, Dean spontaneously took one of his red jackets and draped it over her shoulders. Then, he autographed it. It was as if he had finally made her a member of his club.

"We didn't really want to admit it was all over," said Ray. "I said, 'Let's go. We've nothing more to do here.'" As exhausting as the last two weeks had been for him—battling with Weisbart and Warners over the various endings, racing to finish the last shots before time ran out—even Ray wanted to prolong this moment of departure. He suggested that they all head over to Dean's favorite hangout, Googie's.

Ray, Wood, Dennis Hopper and Ray's assistants, Perry Lopez and Roger Donoghue, all piled into Ray's Cadillac, and Dean jumped on his motorcycle. They headed up over the Cahuenga Pass to Sunset Boulevard. When they were a few blocks from Googie's, Ray marveled as Dean threw his legs back over the rear of his motorcycle and stretched out his arms "like a flying angel."

"That should be the end of the film!" Ray exclaimed.

CHAPTER FIFTEEN

Crash

Immediately after _Rebel_ wrapped, Ray and his three stars all had big projects scheduled. James Dean and Sal Mineo headed out to Marfa, Texas, to begin shooting _Giant,_ along with Dennis Hopper. Natalie Wood had been cast in a small but crucial role in another film destined to be a classic, John Ford's Western _The Searchers._ And while Ray continued postproduction work on _Rebel,_ he would direct a film about Gypsies (_Hot Blood_) that he had spent years trying to get off the ground. Ray was also feverishly anticipating the next phase in his moviemaking career. Dean agreed to join him in an independent production company. With a star as powerful as Dean in tow, Ray imagined that he would finally be able to call his own shots, while Dean himself had been promised the opportunity to direct. That summer looked bright for all concerned. But unbeknownst to the _Rebel_ cast and crew, they were careering toward a crushing dose of reality—which would come that autumn on September 30, 1955.

On May 27, 1955, the day after _Rebel_ closed down production, postproduction work immediately went into full swing. The studio was intent on releasing the film quickly, making the most of the heat under Dean. Mineo, Wood and Dean were all called back to dub dialogue before moving to their new film locations. An unusually large amount of looping was required. Mineo had to redo some dialogue to eliminate his Bronx accent (although it is still prominent in lines such as "You mean a head shrinkah?!"). Other lines had to be dubbed because of technical problems such as noise from the planetarium machinery that drowned out dialogue. But the biggest sound problem was the cast's continual mumbling. "Dean was a mumbler. Brando was a mumbler. That was part of the whole scene being a Method actor," explains cast member Tom Bernard. "You were supposed to mumble."

Ray had been warned about these vocal problems in the very first week of production. In an April 1 memo to Ray, producer David Weisbart wrote that "the boys, Buzz and perhaps Jim, too, are not projecting enough" and a month later he reiterated his concerns, writing "I have been getting notes from the sound department indicating quite a bit of post-syncing (looping) that is going to have to be done on this picture. Unfortunately some of our key scenes are involved. I have been told that if the actors would project a little more, this condition wouldn't exist in so many places. Will you keep an ear on this Nick? Looping is never as good as getting the performances on the set." But apparently Ray had not taken Weisbart's warnings seriously enough and now he had to pay the price in long redubbing sessions.

Weisbart was especially concerned about Dean's looping, writing in a memo to the sound department that sounds amazingly portentous in retrospect: "Will you please make sure that all the loops for post-syncing are prepared and kept up to date so that we can start cleaning up some of this, especially those involving Jimmy Dean as he goes into another picture immediately—and we may never see him again."

Sound was not Ray's only postproduction challenge. There were hours of footage to be sliced through and arranged, and Jack Warner was breathing down Ray's neck, insisting on viewing a rough cut as soon as possible. Warner wanted to see *Rebel* before he was grilled by the Kefauver Committee in mid-June. The committee, which had been investigating popular culture's effect on juvenile delinquency for two years, was now zeroing in on Hollywood. Sight unseen, *Rebel* had already been placed on the committee's list of excessively violent films.

On June 7, Ray sent a letter to Warner informing him of the status of the film. The letter's tone—both defiant and obsequious—perfectly captures his attitude toward the studio system. "Dear Jack," he wrote: "My name is Nick Ray and I just finished making a picture for you called *Rebel Without a Cause*. I thought maybe you'd forgotten my name because the last time we met any closer than bowing distance was in your office late at night and you wished you'd never met me and I thought you should have felt just the opposite." Ray went on to ask for more time to complete the rough cut, telling Warner that he knew "every important frame of it as if it had been printed on my skin." Ray assured Warner that "we have a wonderful show, and I would like your first viewing of it to contain as much of its true value as we can get in even a limited but not unreasonable amount of time."

Work on *Hot Blood* fell by the wayside as Ray concentrated on *Rebel,* spending hours making notes for editor William Ziegler and producer Weisbart, who had once been an editor himself. Although most directors in the 1950s were not as involved in postproduction as they are today, Ray took a more hands-on approach. After all the personal trauma he channeled into this production, he was not about to let *Rebel* slip away from him. On July 12, with the starting date on *Hot Blood* less than a week away, Ray sent Weisbart a meticulously detailed six-page memo of cutting notes. He warned Weisbart of the "danger of over-explaining" the characters, but also cautioned him: "We must not cut the content of this show, for sake of time and smoothness."

Sometime during this period, Ray's relationship with Natalie Wood ended, which, given the fact that *Rebel* had wrapped, might have been predicted. It was a difficult time for Ray with postproduction on *Rebel* and preproduction on *Hot Blood* straining his abilities to keep up. He began drinking more heavily to cope with the pressure. In the midst of all this studio pressure and alcohol intake, Ray had to deal with the possibility that Wood was pregnant, after she missed her period. Wood made an appointment with her doctor, and before joining Ray in bed that evening at the Chateau Marmont, she placed a urine sample in the refrigerator to take to the doctor the next morning. Sometime during the night, Ray went down to the kitchen looking for something to quench his thirst and, in a twisted variation on the milk-drinking scene from *Rebel,* which had first been improvised in that very same room, Ray, drunk and half asleep, gulped down the urine sample. "That was pretty much the end," says Gavin Lambert. "She wasn't amused by that." When the pregnancy test came out negative, Wood took the opportunity to break off the relationship. One night, while Ray was out, she used her key to enter Bungalow 2. On Ray's table, she left the key and some books that he had lent her, ending their affair with a romantic flourish, and without confrontation.

• • •

Meanwhile, Ray, Weisbart and Ziegler continued to tweak *Rebel*. On June 30, the moment of truth arrived, the first major test of *Rebel*'s cohesiveness and power. Jack Warner was finally shown a rough cut and, to Ray's great relief, he was pleased with what he saw. "The picture itself is excellent. Dean is beyond comprehension," Warner wrote, although he added, "There are places to make it move about which all of us are aware." Warner viewed the film without its musical soundtrack, which Dean's close friend Leonard Rosenman was busy composing. "It is one of the most important factors in the picture," Warner's memo continued. "Do not let them go arty on us."

THE COMPOSER

Warner's warning may have sprung from rumors he heard about the challenging music Rosenman had just completed for Vincente Minnelli's melodrama *The Cobweb,* the first twelve-tone score ever composed for a Hollywood feature film (and perfectly suited to the film's hyperneurotic version of life in a mental institution). At a time when most film scores were heavily influenced by 19th-century Romantic European composers, Rosenman brought modern 20th-century music styles into film composing, weaving the serialism of Arnold Schoenberg and Alban Berg, the rhythms and dissonances of Béla Bartók and Igor Stravinsky, the American romanticism of Aaron Copland and the jazz of Stan Kenton into his diverse style. Rosenman, who had studied under such avant-garde composers as Schoenberg and Roger Sessions, saw himself as destined for a career as a serious classical composer—until, that is, he encountered James Dean. Dean took director Elia Kazan to see a concert of Rosenman's work after he was cast in *East of Eden,* and when the concert was over, Kazan offered Rosenman the job of writing *East of Eden*'s score. Rosenman liked to say that he was offended by Kazan's offer. "Are you telling me that my music sounds like movie music?" he responded. But his ex-wife, Adele Essman, doubts he was as offended as he seemed. "He had mixed feelings," she says. "He was very excited and scared and he had actively sought a connection with Kazan."

Rosenman ultimately took the assignment on one condition: he

223

wanted to be on location, composing the score as the movie was being shot, the way Russian composers sometimes worked. Kazan consented and Rosenman was often on the *East of Eden* set, playing the piano as the actors performed.

After *Eden*, Dean introduced Rosenman to Ray, who was open to any of Dean's suggestions and welcomed Kazan's collaborators. Ray gave Rosenman the job of writing the score for *Rebel*. But because he was also hired to compose the score for *The Cobweb*, he could not be present on the *Rebel* set. Rosenman was forced to compose *Rebel*'s music in the usual way, after the film was completed. Rosenman wrote much of his music for *Rebel* at the piano in his apartment across from the studio—and Jack Warner's office—during the hot summer of 1955. One day, he received an angry telephone call from Jack Warner himself, who barked, "Would you please stop making that music or close your windows!"

Although more accessible than the score of *The Cobweb*, *Rebel*'s music is still groundbreaking. More than Rosenman's first two scores, *Rebel*'s score shows the breadth of his influences, from the lyricism of the "Love Theme" (which was turned into a song called "Secret Doorway," which Sal Mineo covered when the studio attempted to turn him into a pop star) to the cacophonous rhythms of the knife-fight music, to the eerie cosmic dissonances of the planetarium sequence. According to Rosenman, the *Rebel* score employed "a lot of jazz in it but it was like a twelve-tone type of jazz." Perhaps the most innovative element of the score, however, is not the music Rosenman composed but rather the music he left out. At a time when most Hollywood films were scored from start to finish, Rosenman experimented with long passages of silence. "In many cases, I tell filmmakers that they do not need music—or that they do not need so much of it," Rosenman once said. "Sometimes silence is the most wonderful sound they can have."

Rosenman was flexible enough, however, to alter his original intentions when it suited the film. Ray Heindorf, the head of the Warner music department and who conducted Rosenman's score, helped the composer understand how a score could transform a scene. Originally, Rosenman had not composed any music for the police station sequence. But when preview audiences saw Dean hit Ray Framek's desk in outsize fury, it made them snicker. "Ray [Heindorf] says to me, 'You have to write just a small piece of music just when he bangs his hand on the desk because that will keep them from laughing,'" Rosenman recalled. Though skeptical, he wrote a short explosive cue to follow Dean's eruption, the only piece of music in that scene. "It was extraordinary," Rosenman said, "because we went to see the film afterwards and as he banged his hand they started laughing but then the music came and they stopped."

Oddly, unlike *Blackboard Jungle*, and many of the teen films that followed *Rebel*, the film does not include any rock music or rhythm and blues, either in its score or on its soundtrack. This omission may add to *Rebel*'s timelessness, but it seems an oversight, given Ray's desire for teen credibility and the fact that the decade's first bright bursts of rock had been fervently embraced by adolescents. Even the song that, at one point, Buzz's gang mockingly dedicates to Jim Stark on the radio is not contemporary. It's the World War II–era tune "Five O'Clock Whistle."

The lack of rock music may have had something to do with Rosenman's unfamiliarity with pop genres. Ray had wanted Rosenman to compose a piece of music for the "jitterbugging" scene he shot at the planetarium, where all the gang members begin banging out a rhythm with combs and keys and lipstick. "This begins a beat that was to begin a suite that would continue through the fight scene," explained Ray. "But Leonard Rosenman couldn't write the suite that I wanted, so without music the scene was cut. It was one of my favorites."

Nevertheless, Rosenman's music brought a new level of sophistication to Hollywood film scoring. His music was so complex, it required an unusual amount of intensive rehearsal. The studio orchestra needed to record it in three separate sessions, three weeks apart. Once completed, the score would help usher in a variety of musical ideas—polytonalities, fractured rhythms, the fusion of jazz and classical motifs—that would become commonplace in the next few years, and not just in Hollywood. Rosenman's *Rebel* score would also be a great influence on Leonard Bernstein's celebrated juvenile delinquency musical *West Side Story*, which opened on Broadway two years later and was turned into a film starring Natalie Wood as another young girl caught in a storm of adolescent passions.

A LONG HOT SUMMER

While Rosenman was composing the music, *Rebel*'s major players went off to the other projects they had scheduled for the summer. Dean had been excited to work with George Stevens, calling him "the greatest director of them all," but almost as soon as he arrived on the set he began to butt heads with the domineering filmmaker. Unlike Ray or Kazan, Stevens was not an actor's director. Actors were just one component in his vast production machine. He did not understand Method acting and he exasperated Dean by shooting the same scene over and over again from every possible angle, piling up hundreds of feet of footage. Like a surgeon with all his implements laid out before him, Stevens liked to have every member of the cast ready at all times just in case he wanted to use someone.

During the first week on the set, Dean complained to Hedda Hopper, "I sat there for three days, made up and ready to work at nine o'clock every morning. By six o'clock I hadn't had a scene or a rehearsal. I sat there like a bump on a log watching that big, lumpy Rock Hudson making love to Liz Taylor. I knew what Stevens was trying to do to me. I'm not going to take it anymore." He told Stevens that if he were made to wait around again, he wouldn't show up for a day. When it happened again after they returned to the Warners lot to film the interiors, Dean disappeared. Warner sent studio detectives to search for him, but they came up empty-handed. When Dean showed up on set the following day, Stevens dragged him up to Jack Warner's office to chew him out. But Dean was not intimidated. "I am not a machine . . . I came in ready to work and you kept me sitting around all day. Do you realize I'm doing emotional memories?" he angrily railed at Stevens in front of Warner. "It was really depressing to see the suffering that boy was going through," lamented Nicholas Ray. "*Giant* was really draining him and I hated watching it happen."

Giant would also be difficult for Mineo and Dennis Hopper. Virtually all the footage Mineo shot would be cut out of the final film, reducing him to little more than a walk-on. Hopper, meanwhile, had trouble getting into character and received little help from Stevens. He was especially anxious about shooting a scene where he angrily smashes a mirror when a Texas beauty salon refuses service to his Mexican wife. Ironically, the actor, who would be so terrifying in *Blue Velvet* and *Speed,* was worried that he wouldn't be able to summon up the violence and anger necessary to play the scene. He asked Steffi Sidney for advice and she told him, "Just pretend the mirror is Nick Ray." That did the trick.

Meanwhile, Natalie Wood was also having a miserable time with director John Ford on the Monument Valley, Utah, set of *The Searchers.* Unlike Nicholas Ray, Ford despised improvisation and expected his instructions to be followed to the letter. He had even developed a punishment for actors who strayed from the script: they were dunked in a barrel of cold water. One day, Wood was suffering from sunstroke so severe that she spent the afternoon bandaged up and lying in bed. She refused Ford's summons to rehearse. When Ford told an assistant to tell her "to go shit in her hat," Wood exploded. "I don't want to be talked to that way, and screw him, and just put me on a plane and send me home," she cried. "I hate it here. I hate my part. I don't want to be put in a barrel."

Nicholas Ray was also growing unhappy with *Hot Blood.* He had spent years trying to make the film, but now he found himself losing interest. "I only want to make pictures with kids, young people," he told his friend Roger Donoghue. Ray had planned to do the kind of research into Gypsy life that he did on the subject of juvenile delinquency, but he ended up sending out a surrogate and also left work on the troubled script to others. He tried to re-create some of the experience he had making *Rebel* by holding rehearsals at the Chateau Marmont with the film's stars, Jane Russell and Cornel Wilde. The actors, however, were baffled by this approach. "[Ray's] speech was somewhat broken and slurred," recalled Wilde. "I know Nick drank some but I think he was on something else, too. His expressions were so vague that frequently I didn't know what he was getting at." After one disastrous rehearsal, Ray abandoned the idea of improvising with Wilde and Russell. *Hot Blood* would not live up to Ray's original expectations and it was a failure at the box office, although the film's embrace of artifice and musical energy make it more appealing now. "The tragedy and the flaws in the film," Ray would later explain, "can be attributed to my overestimation of my own capacities and my underestimation of my involvement in *Rebel Without a Cause.*"

THE FIRST PREVIEW

With the film edited and the music completed, *Rebel* was finally ready for its first preview, held on September 1, 1955, in Huntington Park, California. Much of the cast attended, including Dean, with his temples shaved to make him look older for his role in *Giant*. The Huntington Park sneak preview went even better than expected. "Audience reaction on sight of his name and appearance proved conclusively James Dean strong important star up there with Marlon Brando," Steve Trilling reported enthusiastically in a telegram. "Story, performances, entire picture received excellently."

While the audience's reaction was encouraging, screenwriter Stewart Stern was upset to see that many of his favorite scenes had been cut or altered. He also remembers the film as being a little slow. Stern felt that Ray had become too enamored of Dean, leaving too much of him in the film, including moments where Dean was actually only preparing for a scene. "I was very noisy about my objections," he says. Jack Warner, who was at the screening, agreed. "I think 45 minutes has to come out of this picture," he said hyperbolically.

Editing notes dated September 18, 1955, support Stern's impression in outlining thirteen cuts to be made in the film, virtually all of them to speed up the action. In some cases, continuity was sacrificed. In the scene where Jim meets Judy before school, the tie he had been wearing suddenly disappears. And at the chickie run, Sal can be seen eating a hamburger that was once in Judy's hands. Still, these editing elisions add to the film's sense of compressed time, as if the story were being narrated by a breathless teenager.

After the preview, much of the cast headed over to Villa Capri to celebrate. The Villa had become Dean's new hangout. It was more upscale than Googie's, better suited to Dean's rising position in Hollywood. It was also a favorite haunt for Humphrey Bogart and Frank Sinatra and other members of the Rat Pack, who sometimes kidded Dean by sending milk and crackers to his table and telling him to groom his hair with a comb instead of a wet rag.

At the Villa Capri, Dean and his friend Lew Bracker ran into Natalie Wood, Dennis Hopper and Nick Adams, who sat in the booth next to them. Dean noticed that Wood was crying. The actress was upset because her favorite scene had been cut, a brief moment in the alley between Jim and Judy's house where Judy suggests she has been around but never been in love. Dean comforted Wood, telling her that she should take pride in the work she had done, that she should get an Oscar nomination (which occurred), and that the cut scene would surely be restored (which it was not). "She felt just great after Jimmy talked to her," said Nick Adams.

Later in the evening, Wood turned around to chat with Lew Bracker. She was now bubbling with excitement at the response the picture had received. All of a sudden, Adams exploded, screaming, "Are you with him or are you with me?" Bracker was startled. "Natalie makes a face Adams can't see," says Bracker. "Jimmy doesn't say a word at all. He just has a smile on his face. Dean wrote Adams off at that point." Despite Adams's typically bad behavior, it was an exhilarating night for all the players at hand. The preview audience's reaction was the first sign that *Rebel* might be everything they hoped it would be. Even Dean dropped his cool façade, asking Bracker what he thought of the film. "It caught me off guard because we never discussed his movies," remembers Bracker. "I said, 'It's very powerful. You're going to be a big star.'"

Surprisingly, *Rebel*'s overprotective director was not on hand that night. Ray was in Europe, where he would remain for more than two months. Warners' European affiliates desperately needed his help with publicity, and they hoped he might be able to head off the censorship problems they anticipated, especially since the British Board of Film Censors banned both *The Wild One* and *Blackboard Jungle*. As it turned out, Ray's presence infuriated rather than placated the British censors. "I'm sorry that I allowed Nick Ray to get into this situation," wrote Warners' British representative Arthur S. Abeles Jr. in a letter to the studio. According to Abeles, Ray "cut absolutely no ice" with the British censors. Ray complained to *Variety* about the British censors, which only made things worse, and he was forced to apologize. To complicate the situation even further, vaudeville comedian George Jessel began a campaign to have *Rebel* banned, and even wrote a letter to Jack Warner excoriating the film, but Warner, who smelled a hit, was baffled by Jessel's interference and dismissed him as an old crank. In the end, the British censors cut five crucial minutes of footage. They edited the knife fight so that it consisted mainly of reaction shots, and eliminated footage of Jim hitting the desk, Judy experiencing exhilaration at the chickie race, and Buzz's landmark line "You got to do *something*." That footage would not be restored for British audiences until 1968.

Before Ray left for Europe, he and Dean had dinner together. The excitement that was building over *Rebel* cemented Ray's working relationship with Dean, especially in light of the actor's problems with *Giant* director George Stevens. Dean missed the organic working methods he and Ray developed together, the creative and personal fusion they experienced. Among other things, they discussed their production company. "We had talked for several hours of many things, of future plans, including a story called *Heroic Love* that we were going to do," said Ray, referring to a novella by author Edward Loomis, which involved a triangle between a novice rancher, his older mentor and that man's much younger wife. Eventually, Dean departed the Chateau. But at three in the morning, he suddenly reappeared in Ray's doorway with an oddly endearing request. His *Giant* co-star Elizabeth Taylor had given him a Siamese kitten and he wanted to borrow a book about cats from Ray. He took the book and headed home. That was the last time Ray would ever see him.

SEPTEMBER 30, 1955

In late September, Natalie Wood and Nick Adams traveled to New York together, to join Sal Mineo on a publicity jaunt for *Rebel*. Dean was supposed to join them after he raced that weekend at Salinas. "I had a secret fantasy: We would all be sitting together in the restaurant in New York, and he would arrive," Mineo remembered. "I'd be a little older now, and maybe we could be really groovy. I was in my city, a child of the Bronx, and now it was my turn, you know? It was that kind of anticipation. And Natalie, too, was all jittery by this time."

On the evening of September 30, Wood, Adams and Mineo attended a performance of Arthur Miller's new play, *A View From the Bridge*, starring Dean's co-star from *East of Eden* Richard Davalos. After the play, they had dinner with Davalos and his wife in Chinatown. Inevitably, the conversation turned to Dean. "We talked about what a great future he had, and how in a few years he'd be the greatest thing that ever hit Hollywood," Wood later remembered. Then, she recalled, Adams blurted out: "With all Jimmy's rodeo riding and his racing, he's not going to live to see thirty."

But Wood immediately shot down this notion, assuring him, "Jimmy's going to outlive every one of us at this table."

As they talked that night, they had no idea that Dean was already dead.

After making two films back-to-back without a break, Dean was exhausted and needed some time off. The first thing he did when he was released from *Giant* was buy a new car and enter another race. The *Los Angeles Herald-Examiner* reported on Dean's plans in a September 16, 1955, article headlined JAMES DEAN PLANS TO GO ON RACING KICK WHEN GIANT ENDS, possibly the last story written about the actor before his death. When a reporter asked Dean whether the studio approved of his racing, he said, "When a man goes home at night, the studio can't tell him not to do what he wants to do."

Ever since Dean's race in Bakersfield, which Johnnie Von Neumann had won in a Porsche Spyder, he had been thinking about trading in his Speedster for the more powerful model. One day in September, Lew Bracker saw a brand-new silver Spyder in the window of Competition Motors, the American distributor of Porsches, which Von Neumann owned. The next day, Dean was there. Von Neumann was reluctant to sell the automobile to Dean. By the car guru's measure, Dean did not have enough experience. The Spyder was not easy to handle. Von Neumann and Joe Playan, both experienced racers who beat Dean at Bakersfield, had nearly lost their lives driving Spyders. The only way Von Neumann would sell the car to Dean was if he agreed to take his mechanic Rolf Wütherich with him when he raced. Dean agreed, trading in his Speedster and writing Von Neumann a check for $3,700.

Dean was proud of his new Spyder. He drove it over to the Warners lot and, spotting George Stevens in a conference, went over and offered him a ride. They sped down the studio streets, flying over speed bumps until studio guards stopped them, telling Dean not to drive the car on the lot again because he might kill someone. Dean told Stevens about his plans to race the Spyder in Salinas, and Stevens suggested that Dean take the car up in a truck instead of driving it on the road. Dean assured him that he would.

Over the years, as Dean's final days became shrouded in myth, a number of people would come forward to say that they sensed something ominous about the car. Dean's friends Eartha Kitt, who served as Dean's dance instructor during his early days in New York, and Ursula Andress both claim to have had eerie premonitions about the Spyder. Perhaps the oddest encounter with the automobile occurred when Dean was having dinner with Lew Bracker at the Villa Capri a week before he died. British actor Alec Guinness, spending his first night in Hollywood, walked in and, seeing no free tables, walked out again. Dean noticed Guinness and ran out after him, offering him a seat at his table. Before they went back in, Dean showed him his new car. Guinness would later write in his autobiography that when he saw the Spyder, "I heard myself saying in a voice I could hardly recognize as my own, 'Please never get in it.' I looked at my watch. 'It is now ten o'clock, Friday the 23rd of September 1955. If you get in that car you will be found dead in it by this time next week.'" Of Guinness's Obi-Wan Kenobi–like premonition Bracker says, "It's absolutely true. When Guinness came back he was ashen."

Customizer George Barris also says he had a strange feeling that the car was haunted. Dean took the car to be customized by Barris, who painted the number 130 on the hood and sides and the words "Little Bastard" on the back. ("George Stevens called him a little bastard," says Barris, but he is unsure of the significance of "130.") While the car was being painted, Barris says that it slipped out of gear, smashing the left parking light. Years later, he says, when he was customizing a replica of Dean's car for a movie about Dean, *Race With Destiny,* starring Casper Van Dien, the exact same thing happened to that car—it also slipped out of gear and the left parking light was damaged.

Dean spent hours learning how to race the Spyder from another *Rebel* alumnus, stunt driver Bill Hickman. "In those final days, racing was what he cared about most," said Hickman. "I had been teaching him things like how to put a car in a four-wheel drift, but he had plenty of skill on his own. If he had lived, he might have become a champion driver."

On the afternoon of September 30, Dean prepared to set off for the race in Salinas. Before Dean left, his cold and distant father, Winton, surprised Dean by coming by to see the Spyder. "Nowadays [Jim] lives in a world we don't understand too well—the actor's world," said Winton Dean in an interview he gave that summer. "He's not easy to understand. But he's all man, and he'll make his mark." Dean offered to take his father for a ride, but Winton declined.

Wütherich, Hickman and photographer Sanford Roth planned to ride with Dean in a station wagon hooked up to a trailer containing the Spyder, as Dean had promised Stevens. George Barris, who saw them off at a gas station where they filled up the tank, says Dean suddenly decided he needed more experience driving the Spyder. Barris did not think it was a good idea to put 350 miles on the car before he raced it. But Dean insisted, so they unloaded the Spyder from the trailer. (According to a persistent *Rebel* rumor, Dean supposedly threw one of the red jackets in the back-seat—although no trace of it was ever found.) Then Dean hopped behind the wheel of the Spyder, with Wütherich in the passenger seat. Hickman and Roth followed in the station wagon, pulling the empty trailer.

As they sped down Highway 99, Dean kept pestering Wütherich with questions: "What's the rev number? How's the oil temp? You sure this is the right road?" He chain-smoked Chesterfields, which Wütherich was forced to light while hunching down out of the wind. At 3:30 p.m. Dean was stopped by a California highway patrolman for speeding—which would add to the rumor that he was being reckless that day—although he was clocked at only 65 miles per hour. At 5 p.m., the team stopped at a grocery store so that Dean could call a friend he met while making *East of Eden*, Monty Roberts, who would later be the basis of the title character in *The Horse Whisperer*. Dean was planning to spend the night at his ranch.

At 5:45, at the intersection of routes 466 and 41 near Cholame, California, Donald Turnupseed, a student at California Polytechnic driving a 1950 Ford, suddenly turned left into the path of Dean's oncoming car. "That guy up there's gotta stop," Dean said. "He'll see us." But apparently, Turnupseed did not see them. Although an investigator would conclude that Dean was not speeding at the time, when he tried to swerve out of Turnupseed's way, he smashed into the Ford. Wütherich was thrown clear of the car and suffered a broken jaw and leg. Turnupseed was barely in-jured. The Porsche was completely crushed.

From the station wagon trailing the Spyder, Hickman saw "an explosion and a great cloud of smoke and dust" up ahead. When Hickman and Roth ar-rived on the scene, they ran up to the Porsche and found Dean trapped behind the steering wheel. "I thought he was alive because there seemed to be air coming out of his nostrils," said Hickman. "They told me later he had died instantly. His forehead was caved in and so was his chest." Roth got his camera and began taking pictures. When Hickman saw the flashes, he screamed at Roth, "You son of a bitch! Help me, come here, help me!" But it was too late. The air Hickman saw coming out of Dean's nostrils was the last breath emptying from Dean's lungs. Hickman cradled the actor in his arms until the ambulance drivers arrived on the scene. They pried Dean's foot loose from the wreckage, lifted his lifeless body onto a gurney and covered him with a blanket. Roth snapped another picture as they put him in the ambulance. Suffering from a broken neck, multiple fractures of his jaw and both arms, and internal injuries, Dean was pronounced dead on arrival at Paso Robles War Memorial Hospital at 6:20 p.m.

"THE BOY IS DEAD!"

There was shocked silence on the other end of the phone when boxer Roger Donoghue called Nicholas Ray in London to tell him about Dean's accident. "Jimmy's dead," said Donoghue. After a long pause, all Ray could finally ask was "Are you sure?" Donoghue assured him that he had called the wire services to verify the news. Ray hung up the phone after simply saying, "I'll talk to you tomorrow."

Instead of returning to Hollywood, Ray took off for Germany to stay in the remote country house of an old lover, Hanna Axmann, an actress who would later appear in several Rainer Werner Fassbinder films. "He cried and cried," remembered Axmann, who had never heard of Dean. "Jimmy is dead, Jimmy is dead," he repeated over and over again. After two weeks, he returned to London to watch *Rebel* with the head of the British censor board, Arthur Watkins. "Much as I love the picture," he wrote to Steve Trilling, "it's a little like going to a funeral."

Sal Mineo learned of Dean's death from Natalie Wood's studio chaperone, after he and Nick Adams had taken Wood back to her New York hotel room that night. The chaperone handed Adams a note when Wood was out of the room, instructing him not to tell her so that she could get some sleep before her scheduled taping of *Heidi* for television the next day.

Wood did not receive the news until the next morning, when she was on her way to the television studio with co-stars Jo Van Fleet, who played Dean's mother in *East of Eden*, and actress Jeannie Carson. Their limousine driver asked them if they had heard about Dean's death. "They were absolutely stunned and could hardly speak during the drive to Brooklyn," Carson said of Wood and Van Fleet. According to Wood, "Everyone was in hysterics, as you can imagine, and it was really Jo Van Fleet being so strong and saying, 'Come on, we have to do this,' that made me able to do it." After the taping, Wood returned to her hotel. Sal Mineo called and the two grieved together on the telephone.

For the supporting cast members of *Rebel*, who were excited by the imminent opening of what for many of them would be their first important film, the news was too shocking to believe. They all remember where they were that day. Steffi Sidney had just received a package of photographs of her and Dean taken at the Villa Capri the week before. Corey Allen had just gotten back from his first trip to Europe, paid for by his *Rebel* earnings. Beverly Long was planning to elope to Las Vegas that day, but she immediately put the wedding off. Frank Mazzola was driving in his car when he heard the news on the radio. "This whole thing that I was gonna be a part of with Nick and Jimmy," he says, referring to his potential role in their independent company, "it was like the world was pulled out from under me. I thought he was immortal."

Dennis Hopper and his agent were watching a play as the news spread. His agent was called into the lobby, and when he returned, he told Hopper he had bad news, which he would not relate unless Hopper promised to stay and sit through the play. According to Hopper, "When he told me that James Dean had died in a car accident, I hit him, muttered the word 'liar.' The lights in the theater went off and a single spotlight came up on an empty stage. It seemed like an eternity before I ran from the theater."

Stewart Stern was staying at Arthur Loew Jr.'s house when *Giant* producer Henry Ginsberg called. "The boy is dead!" Ginsberg said. Immediately, Stern knew whom he was talking about. "I was smoking a cigarette and it turned to shit in my mouth," Stern remembered. "Then, I just wandered around. I wanted to be alone. I couldn't believe it. I turned on the radio. There was nothing on the radio. There was no confirmation in the real world that this had happened. I thought it couldn't have. I walked up and down Hollywood Boulevard. I went to Googie's and had coffee. I looked around. Here were all these faces that were there when Jimmy would go in. Nobody knowing anything. I was afraid to say anything. I was afraid I'd be wrong. Then sometime during the night, there was an announcement. And you could tell. You could tell in the way it was when Kennedy had been shot. Cars pulling off the road. Traffic stopping so people could control their agitation while they heard the news. It was like a strange wind that came right through the streets of Hollywood. People's rhythm changed. They began to pull into little groups like mercury rolling across a tabletop, collecting other little pieces of itself. Consoling each other. These eerie sounds, these cries would come up from places. It was a nightmare. But at least then I knew that the world knew and that it had really happened. I've had better friends. I've certainly known people longer—it was only months that I knew Jimmy. I don't know what it is that makes his disappearance as much of an ache as it is. It's never abated."

Dean's body was sent back to Fairmount, Indiana, for the funeral, which took place on October 8 at Back Creek Friends Church, the church Dean attended growing up. Stern, Jack Simmons, Lew Bracker, Dennis Stock and *Giant* producer Ginsberg were among the few friends from Hollywood who attended in person. Elizabeth Taylor sent flowers. Dean's childhood mentor, the Rev. James DeWeerd, delivered the eulogy, calling Dean "a boy who knew how to seek counsel from men older and wiser than himself."

On the train back to Los Angeles, Stern wrote a letter to Dean's uncle, Marcus Winslow. "I shall never forget that silent town on that particular sunny day, and I shall never forget the care with which people set their feet down so carefully on the pavement, as if the sound of a suddenly scraped heel might disturb the sleep of a boy who slept soundly," he wrote. "Our world doesn't seem equipped to contain its brilliance too long. . . . In a world where much is synthetic and dishonest and drab he came and rearranged our molecules. . . . His influence didn't stop with his breathing. It walks with us, and will profoundly affect the way we look at things. From Jim, I have already learned the value of a minute. He loved his minutes and I sure do love mine." To this day, Stern cannot speak about Dean's death without breaking down in tears.

• • •

Any tears that may have been shed on the Warners lot were quickly wiped away by a slew of practical problems that had to be considered and rapidly addressed. The studio now had two major unreleased films with a dead star, *Rebel* and *Giant.* "Nobody will come and see a corpse," Jack Warner said. In fact, the track record for posthumously released films had been mixed. Films by Will Rogers and Jean Harlow released after their deaths had done well, while Carole Lombard's last film, *To Be or Not to Be,* had been a box-office disaster. "What's going to happen to the film? What's going to happen to us?" *Rebel* cast member Jack Grinnage wondered at the time.

Eventually, Warners decided to go ahead with the release of the film as scheduled. "Death of James Dean in an auto accident on the Coast over the weekend has not upset Warner Bros. plans for the release of the two pictures in which the 24-year-old actor had starring assignments," *Variety* announced on October 5. "After conferring with circuits which had booked *Rebel,* Warners decided to go ahead with the ads which prominently feature Dean in both art and copy. Only change in the ads will be the elimination of a line of copy which reads: 'The overnight sensation of *East of Eden* becomes the star of the year!'"

The official premieres in New York and Los Angeles went on as scheduled, but without much fanfare. On October 25, Ray returned to New York to attend the premiere of *Rebel* the next evening at the Astor movie theater in Times Square. Roger Donoghue picked him up at the airport and although it was only ten in the morning, Ray was drunk. "He had fallen off the wagon before that, but I think it was all over on that September night of 1955," Donoghue said. At a press screening, Natalie Wood broke down in tears.

In Los Angeles, *Rebel* premiered at Grauman's Chinese Theatre. "There was something bizarre about the moment," Mazzola remembers. "An empty feeling because Jimmy wasn't there." Overall, the studio showed remarkable restraint. The Los Angeles premiere was a muted affair. "It wasn't as big a kickoff as it normally would have been," says cast member Tom Bernard, who does not recall a single party given afterward.

Reviews of *Rebel* were generally supportive, but at the time few critics realized the impact the film would have on American—and world—culture. Many reviewers were struck by the parallels between Dean's death and

237

the film's chickie run ("James Dean Cheats Car Death in Bit of Film Irony," was the headline on Phillip Scheuer's review in the *Los Angeles Times.)* But the film's heightened realism puzzled many critics. *Variety* called it a "fairly exciting, suspenseful and provocative, if also occasionally far-fetched, melodrama." The *New York Times*'s stodgy critic Bosley Crowther complained that the film had "a pictorial slickness about the whole thing in color and CinemaScope that battles at times with the real-ism in the direction of Nicholas Ray." Yet even Crowther sensed *Rebel's* emotional impact, calling it "a picture to make the hair stand on end." And audiences responded to the film immediately. It outgrossed *East of Eden* in its first week.

After the many blind alleys, the constant rushing against time, the fa-tiguing piling on of inspiration after inspiration, Ray's demands for rawer and ever more truthful emotion, and all the personal trauma that siphoned directly into the film, *Rebel Without a Cause* was an instant box-office suc-cess, but it was destined to become more than the movie of the week, or the year. It created ripples that would continue to open out for decades. Ray and company offered up a romantic, charismatic, sexually charged ar-chetype—a heroic ideal of what being a teen might mean. The film took teenagers as seriously as they took themselves. And now with the passing of Dean, *Rebel* would become a monument of sorts—inseparable from, as critic Geoffrey O'Brien wrote, "the cult of the dead teenager."

Dean and the role he played in *Rebel* became immediately indistin-guishable. His performance and his death may have been the engines that initially drove *Rebel* deep into the culture, but without *Rebel,* Dean would not have become an icon. That certainly would not have happened on the strengths of *East of Eden* and *Giant,* two well-made films that existed far-ther from the Zeitgeist. "To us teenagers," one fan wrote to *Life* magazine, "Dean was a symbol of the fight to make a niche for ourselves in the world of adults. Something in us that is being sat on by convention and held down was, in Dean, free for all the world to see."

A year after *Rebel's* release, the studio continued to receive sacks of mail for James Dean, up to eight thousand letters a month. He received more letters than any living star in Hollywood. "Many of them say they don't believe he is really dead," said the head of a fan mail service. Natalie Wood also sprang into the top ten stars receiving fan mail. Even Jim Backus was inundated with fan mail from teenagers asking him about James Dean or requesting something Dean had touched. "Most of them were very intelligently written and very serious—not the usual fan stuff," said Backus. *Life* magazine called the obsession with Dean "a movie fan craze for a dead man that surpasses in fervor and morbidity even the hysterical mass mourning that attended the death of Rudolph Valentino." Author Jack Kerouac—a fan of *Rebel*—likened the phenomenon to the kind of religious mysticism surrounding Saint Theresa.

Fan magazines helped fuel the Dean cult with endless tributes and bizarre rumors. Some magazines claimed Dean had a death wish. There were rumors that Dean's death was the result of a communist plot hatched because of Dean's "anti-Communist activities." Some fans even believed that Dean was not really dead but was so horribly disfigured in the accident that he went into hiding.

Some allege that Warners had a hand in launching the mania over Dean, in order to save its investment in the actor's films. Jack Grinnage contends that the studio set out to create a "mystique" about Dean's death. The scandal magazine *Inside Story* claimed that Warner Brothers executives held a secret meeting to decide how to sell Dean's unreleased films. According to the magazine, the studio recruited fan club members to hold memorials for Dean and make pilgrimages to his grave and even spread rumors that he was still alive by planting items in gossip columns. There were also stories that Warners was consulting psychologists for advice on how to manipulate the market for Dean's last film, *Giant,* stories that director George Stevens vehemently denied.

Whatever role Warners played in the mythmaking, it started almost immediately. A mere two days after Dean died, a front-page story appeared in the *Los Angeles Times* under the headline DEATH PREMONITION BY DEAN RECALLED: "Hollywood friends, shocked and saddened by the death of James Dean . . . recalled yesterday that he was always in a hurry because he believed he might not live very long. The actor, a nonconformist in his private life, spoke often of this 'premonition of death' and it came to be an accepted part of his unpredictable character, they said."

"The way he died . . . was grim fatalistic proof of everything people were saying about him," said Bill Hickman. "The myth-makers had what they wanted."

In 1956, with the culture's Dean obsession showing no signs of abating, Warners announced it was producing a documentary about Dean, *The James Dean Story*, with a script written by Stewart Stern and co-directed by George W. George and Robert Altman (who in 1982 would direct the film *Come Back to the Five and Dime, Jimmy Dean, Jimmy Dean*). Warners also rereleased *Rebel Without a Cause* in March 1956, the same month that saw the release of Nicholas Ray's personal disappointment, *Hot Blood*.

Rebel had ultimately cost the studio $1,500,000 to produce. In its first year of release, it would take in $4,500,000, making it the eleventh-highest-grossing movie of 1956, the year in which its grosses were calculated. That put the movie just behind *The Searchers*, the film with which Natalie Wood followed *Rebel*. The number one film of that year was *Guys and Dolls*, starring Dean's idol Marlon Brando.

In 1956, Sal Mineo and Natalie Wood would be nominated for Oscars for their work on *Rebel*, as would Ray for Best Motion Picture Story. (Screenwriter Irving Shulman protested Ray's solo nomination for *Rebel*'s story, but the Academy refused to act on his complaint). Surprisingly, Dean was not nominated for *Rebel* but was nominated that year for *East of Eden* and would be nominated again the following year for *Giant*. Although none of the *Rebel* nominees went home with an Oscar—Wood lost to Jo Van Fleet for *East of Eden;* Mineo, to Jack Lemmon for *Mr. Roberts;* and Ray, to Daniel Fuchs for *Love Me or Leave Me*—the movie continued to have a profound and enduring effect on Wood, Mineo and Ray. They had poured themselves into the film, and they would be forever identified with it. Perhaps it's no surprise that the film they crafted through their own hurt and passion should shadow them for the rest of their lives.

In one of the many prescient quotes that haunt the history of *Rebel Without a Cause*, Sal Mineo would say, many years later, "When we were shooting *Rebel*, we became good friends. Jimmy really believed in this stuff: 'We're all cursed. We are the young ones put on earth to make the old ones wake up.' He had some sort of odd idea that since Natalie and I were getting close to him, we would be cursed too . . . [and] all die violent deaths."

CHAPTER SIXTEEN

The Leading Lady

Of all the major players in *Rebel Without* *a Cause,* Natalie Wood seemed to be the least likely to succeed on her own. During the making of *Rebel,* she was plagued with bouts of insecurity and anxiety. She needed to be coached and coddled into hitting her highest marks. But ironically, it would be the shy, uncertain Wood who would end up having the most successful movie career of all the *Rebel* players, including Ray. As she hoped, the movie made her a star, and she would remain a star. Ironically, it was the very quality that made Ray and Dean doubt her suitability for *Rebel*—her Hollywood DNA—that helped her triumph. Wood's savviness at navigating the movie business, and her unrelenting need to stay in the game, would save her time and again.

It wasn't long after finishing *Rebel* that Wood realized her status at Warners had changed. Accompanied by her friend and former double, Faye Nuell Mayo, Wood drove onto the Warners lot for one of the many looping sessions on the film. But when she tried to park near the Warners commissary for lunch, sawhorses blocked all the spaces. A security guard spotted her and said, "Wait a second, Miss Wood. Let me move this," and he cleared a place for her car. According to Mayo, "Natalie looked at me and said, 'Now it starts.'" At that moment, she knew her life had changed forever.

At first, like everyone associated with *Rebel,* Wood found that her career was inextricably tied to the ever-burgeoning Dean death cult. "It's a gruesome thought that she owes her stardom to James Dean's bad driving, but it's certainly true that his death helped establish him as an icon and that her association with him benefited her," said film critic Stanley Kauffman. Almost overnight, she became a fixture in movie fan magazines, but she was usually mentioned in tandem with Dean. And she was constantly pummeled with questions about a romance between them, which she always denied existed. "I was embarrassed," she said, "because it made me look as if I were capitalizing on his fame."

That feeling of guilt was not shared by cast members Dennis Hopper and Nick Adams, who were Wood's constant companions for a few years after the film wrapped. Some in the *Rebel* cast were disgusted with Hopper and especially Adams for the way they behaved in the aftermath of Dean's death, exaggerating their connection with him. "When Jimmy died, we all got furious with Nick Adams," says Mayo. "He did every story in every movie magazine. It was pretty gross. He used it as a stepping-stone for his own career. Dennis did that, too, to a lesser extent." Some speculated that the ambitious young actors were also exploiting Wood. According to Jack Grinnage, either Hopper or Adams—he doesn't remember which—said of Wood on the set of *Rebel,* "I'm going to hold onto her bra strap as long as I can." Obviously, they had recognized her incipient star quality.

Whether they were using her or not, Wood enjoyed playing the star with Hopper and Adams, who became roommates after *Rebel.* The trio saw themselves as heirs to the great, glamorous Hollywood past. "We were always envious of the generations before us," said Hopper. "People think that we were wild, but man, we had a lot to come up to, in our opinion, from the generation that had just, like, disappeared—the John Garfields and the Lana Turners, Ava Gardners. In a strange way, we were trying to emulate some sort of past glory." One night, they decided to stage a champagne orgy, because Wood heard that Jean Harlow had once had one. They filled a bathtub with champagne, but when Wood climbed in, the alcohol burned her vagina and she leapt out of the bath screaming, bringing a quick end to the event. Living the decadent Hollywood lifestyle was harder than they had imagined.

Meanwhile, Wood was still having an affair with Hopper, dating him through the next year, although things between them had become very casual. "We got into a relationship where we were going out to parties together and we would score for each other," explained Hopper. "She'd say, 'I'd really like to have a date with him,' and I'd say, 'I'd really like to have a date with her,' and we had great fun procuring for each other. We weren't blind to the fact that we could see other people, but we were having sex all through our relationship." Wood was also seen arm in arm with Nick Adams, though most agree their relationship was not sexual. "They were just good friends," says Wood's friend Jackie Perry. "She even commented to me, 'Can you imagine Nick and I trying to have sex?'"

Almost immediately after *Rebel,* Wood's dating career became a hot topic in the press. And she continued to give them plenty to write about. Through Adams and Hopper, Wood met and dated Elvis Presley, who was new to Hollywood and was yearning to connect with the James Dean myth. When Nick Ray ran into Presley at the MGM cafeteria, he experienced firsthand the singer's obsession with Dean. "He knew I was a friend of Jimmy's and had directed *Rebel,*" said Ray, "so he got down on his knees before me and began to recite whole passages of dialogue from the script. Elvis must have seen *Rebel* a dozen times by then and remembered every one of Jimmy's lines." When Presley followed his idol into the movies, the producer of his first film, *Love Me Tender,* was none other than *Rebel*'s producer David Weisbart.

The gossip columns went wild over the idea of a Wood-Presley romance. An alliance between the heirs of the Dean myth was almost too good to be true. Louella Parsons demanded and got an interview with Wood and Presley, who dropped by her house with his entourage in tow. Parsons reported that hundreds of Presley's female fans were writing her angry letters about Wood, afraid that she might marry Presley. But in reality, Wood found Presley to be almost exotically straight and narrow. She had never met anyone so religious or straitlaced. "He didn't drink. He didn't swear. He didn't even smoke. It was like having the date I never had in high school. I thought it was really wild!" she said. Wood made a pilgrimage to Graceland, where hundreds of Elvis fans waited outside the gates, and she rode around Memphis on the back of Presley's motorcycle, pursued by fans and photographers. She was shocked at the way Presley allowed his public to get so close to him. "He felt he had been given this gift, this talent, from God," said Wood. "He had to be nice to people. Otherwise, God would take it all back." Presley-mania was too much for Wood to handle, and she made a quick getaway back to Hollywood, ending the brief courtship, to the relief of Presley's devotees.

Presley and Hopper were not the only men Wood dated during her first flush of *Rebel* success. Two days after Dean died, Walter Winchell reported that she was dating her tutor from *Rebel,* Tom Hennesy. "Says he's The One, no matter what items you read," reported Winchell. Hennesy says that he would sometimes take her out to dinner or have lunch with her at the studio commissary but denies they were dating. "I was engaged to be married," he says. "Natalie was always flirtatious. I didn't encourage that at all." The long list of other men Wood reportedly dated over the next two years includes Frank Sinatra, Tab Hunter, Nicky Hilton, Martin Milner, Robert Vaughn, Perry Lopez (who worked as Ray's assistant on *Rebel*) and Raymond Burr. Gossip columnists became Wood's eager codependents, selling more magazines by excitedly hyping every new date—even the ones they knew were studio setups. Then as the self-appointed guardians of Hollywood morality, they would slap her down for being promiscuous.

By the end of 1956, Wood had won a Golden Globe as Outstanding Newcomer (along with Carroll Baker and Jayne Mansfield, both of whom had tested for the role of Judy in *Rebel*) and she was named Most Popular New Star of 1956 by *Modern Screen.* At a party after the ceremony, she ran into her future husband, actor Robert Wagner, a man she would marry not once but twice.

Wagner could not relate to Wood's friends. He was eight years older than her and felt more comfortable socializing with Hollywood royalty like Humphrey Bogart, Lauren Bacall, Spencer Tracy and Katharine Hepburn. "She was running around with Jimmy Dean and those guys—you know, part of the rebel movement," said Wagner. "Me, I was around the elite of Hollywood. It was a whole new world to her." This new world had an obvious attraction for Wood.

Wood's friends from her *Rebel* days fell by the wayside as she traveled in Wagner's glittering circle. She lost touch with Hopper after he was fired from Warners and blackballed for a time from the industry in 1958 for tangling with director Henry Hathaway on the film *From Hell to Texas.* And she was bitterly betrayed by Nick Adams. He had asked her for a loan and when she rebuffed him, he threatened to blackmail her, saying, "I know a lot of stuff about you that I could sell to get the money I need." Shocked by his treachery, she ended their friendship. A year later, in 1961, his television series, ironically called *The Rebel,* was cancelled and Adams would begin a long descent into drugs and alcoholism. On February 7, 1968, Adams died of a prescription drug overdose at thirty-six. The coroner could not determine if his death was an accident or suicide. Some conspiracy theorists even claimed he was murdered, but the exact circumstances of his death would always remain a mystery.

On the first anniversary of their first date, Robert Wagner proposed to Wood—and in grandly old-fashioned Hollywood style. He and Wood celebrated their anniversary by opening a bottle of Dom Perignon. Wood discovered a diamond-and-pearl engagement ring submerged in the champagne at the bottom of her glass. It was engraved with the words "Marry me?" A few weeks later, in December 1957, nineteen-year-old Wood and twenty-seven-year-old Wagner wed.

THE GOLDEN WORLD

The marriage of the handsome Wagner and the beautiful Wood provided more irresistible fodder for the film magazines, which celebrated it as a storybook romance. They bought a mansion in Beverly Hills and garishly decorated it with marble floors, crystal chandeliers and a bathroom with a marble tub that was so large the ceiling began to crack beneath it. But as Wood's glamour quotient continued to rise, her acting career was, once again, becoming a source of high anxiety. In order to get the part in *Rebel*, Wood had been forced to sign a long-term contract with Warner Brothers. But her contract kept her virtually enslaved to Jack Warner for years afterward. When she found out she had won an Oscar nomination for *Rebel Without a Cause*, she was in the midst of shooting *Burning Hills*, a low-budget Western, playing the unlikely role of a Mexican girl opposite another young new Warners star, Tab Hunter. Even after her Oscar nomination, the studio seemed to have no idea what to do with Wood, putting her in one mediocre low-budget picture after another, often in ethnic roles.

Dissatisfied with the films she was forced to make, Wood began fighting back, refusing to do certain films and getting placed on suspension. One suspension lasted eighteen months, which, according to Hedda Hopper, was the longest ever suffered by an actress. She got out of another film by having a tonsillectomy. "I was saving my appendix for a really horrible film," she joked.

Wood was hungry for a project that would match her experience on *Rebel*. "Later in life she often described *Rebel Without a Cause* as the experience that fired her to become a serious actress," said her friend and biographer Gavin Lambert. Before *Rebel,* Wood might have been satisfied with just being a star. But after *Rebel,* after Dean and after Ray, she knew that acting could be riskier and more thrilling. That sometimes proved to be a dangerous realization for her, considering her insecurity and the fact that she did not have complete control over her gifts. For the public, Wood would be able to turn on "The Badge," as she called her star persona, at a moment's notice, while in private she would often sink into the depths of depression, becoming emotionally unhinged in ways that could sometimes be glimpsed in the boundless hysteria of her finest performances.

Five years after Wood made *Rebel,* she finally got a chance to make a movie that had as much artistic potential. *Splendor in the Grass* was directed by Ray's mentor, Elia Kazan, and co-starred Warren Beatty in his first movie role. "Natalie knew she had made a lot of bad pictures, and that her career was in danger," said Kazan. "She wanted to right it before it was too late." Wood desperately needed the help of a director to bring out her talents, and Kazan would provide that guidance. The film would usher in the greatest period of her post-*Rebel* acting career.

Wood was thrilled to have entered Kazan's sphere. Like Ray, Kazan set about remaking her. "I put paint remover on her, took off her glamorous clothes, and put her up there naked and gasping," he said. In fact, working on *Splendor,* Wood later said, "was like being reintroduced to that golden world that Nick Ray had given me a glimpse of . . . Nick was sort of his disciple. So here I was with Kazan, the real number one director."

The role of Deanie seemed perfect for Wood. Like Wood, she has a loving but weak father and a controlling mother who fills her head with horror stories about sex. When her boyfriend (played by Beatty, a James Dean disciple) leaves her because she won't go to bed with him, she tries to commit suicide in a fit of sexual panic and is sent to a sanitarium. As Kazan said of Wood, "When the persona fitted the role, you couldn't do better." In fact, Wood's role would build on Judy, her *Rebel* character, in a provocative way. After *Splendor,* she would play many women who ran up against the sexual morality of their time. When the audience saw Wood's name above the title, it often meant that the movie pushed against the edge of serious sexual content.

At first, Kazan was an insightful and considerate teacher, helping Wood by giving her some foundation in basic acting techniques the way he did with Dean in *East of Eden,* telling her to break the character down into "beats" and look for the turning points. "Kazan showed me different ways to play a scene," said Wood. "He said, 'Try things, risk it, don't worry about making a fool of yourself; be bold; be brave; don't be afraid; don't play it safe. What's the worst that can happen?' . . . He was trying to get me to be free. To loosen up. His teaching was a wonderful gift."

Not all of his lessons stuck, however. Wood confessed her unabated fear of crying on cue to Kazan, but instead of teaching her how to do it step by step, he told her that it wasn't the crying that was important but the emotion that was projected. To demonstrate, he had another actress cry in a scene where crying wasn't necessary. "He tried to impress on me how unimportant the ability was, that it didn't fit, that just crying itself was not the ultimate goal," said Wood. "But I was so neurotic I took it as a further example of my failure as an actress."

Nevertheless, Wood's performance in *Splendor* was her best since *Rebel.* Once again, you can see her tearing compellingly at the limits of her abilities and often breaking through. For her forceful work, she garnered a second Oscar nomination (though she lost to Sophia Loren for *Two Women*). But the role was emotionally draining and came at great personal cost. "I always had a bit of inner resistance to doing that part because I felt that in order to play some of those scenes I would have to open doors and relive a lot of feelings I had put a lid on," said Wood. "I had a hunch that it wasn't going to be good for me to do that part in terms of my emotional life; and I was right. It did open up a lot of wounds and led to the marriage breaking up."

Wood and Wagner's fairy-tale marriage reached the breaking point just as she was finishing *Splendor in the Grass.* When they announced they were separating, the movie industry was shocked. Reportedly, Elizabeth Taylor was so upset that the Hollywood dream couple had separated that she was put under sedation. Wood began showing up in public with Warren Beatty even before the divorce was final, and there were rumors that he had precipitated the breakup. For the rest of her life, Wood seemed torn between men who promised danger—like Dean, Ray and Beatty—and the more stabilizing influence that Wagner exemplified.

FOUR IN A ROW

Between 1961 and 1962, beginning with *Splendor in the Grass*, Wood made four films that came closest to recapturing her *Rebel* past—and she became a bigger star than ever. While Wood was still making *Splendor*, Jerome Robbins and Robert Wise were shown footage and decided to cast her in *West Side Story*, which would go on to win ten Oscars, including Best Picture. Once again Wood found herself in familiar territory, starring in a film that was in part inspired by *Rebel*. Like *Rebel*, it's a story of juvenile delinquency, gangs and misunderstood youths whipped up into a mythic, dreamlike frenzy. Wood rehearsed the role with obsessive tenacity, spending grueling hours learning the dance numbers and trying to learn how to speak with a Puerto Rican accent. While she is often affecting as a lovesick teenager, she is less convincing as a Puerto Rican. And she was dealt an ego-shattering blow when she discovered that despite the reassurances of the director, her voice was being dubbed on all the songs by Marni Nixon.

Wood's singing talents were featured in her next film, *Gypsy*, where her untrained voice was perfectly suited to her character, stripper Gypsy Rose Lee. Playing the daughter of the ultimate stage mother, Wood got the chance to confront her feelings about her own mother in a role that seemed almost autobiographical. In fact, even at this late date, her mother continued to watch her from the wings. Mrs. Gurdin was still included in all of Wood's contracts as the employee in charge of answering Wood's fan mail.

Wood earned her third Oscar nomination, her second in two years, for her next film, *Love With the Proper Stranger*. "I think *Love With the Proper Stranger* was Natalie's real breakthrough," said actor George Segal. "In *Rebel Without a Cause* she was very promising but not completely secure." In the film, which dealt with the hot-button issue of abortion, Wood plays a woman who becomes pregnant after a one-night stand with a musician and tracks him down to get the money to end the pregnancy, but then falls in love with him. The musician was played by Steve McQueen, yet another actor touted as the "New James Dean." He shared Dean's fascination with motorcycles and fast cars and even worked at one point as Dean's mechanic. Wood, who broke up with the commitment-adverse Beatty while making the film, was clearly attracted to McQueen, who was married at the time, and their chemistry shows on-screen. Years later, they would have a brief affair.

But despite Wood's success and apparent power, she was still not free of the stranglehold Jack Warner had on her career. He forced her to make two insipid comedies, *Sex and the Single Girl* and *The Great Race,* before he would release her to make two films that she wanted—*Inside Daisy Clover,* based on a novel by Gavin Lambert; and *This Property Is Condemned,* based on a play by Tennessee Williams. Finding herself once again swinging rapidly from a high point to a low point in her career, and devastated by the failure of her relationships with Wagner and Beatty, she briefly found solace in Stewart Stern's cousin, and James Dean's friend, Arthur Loew Jr. He was still the life of the party and had taken to dating women on the rebound, such as Debbie Reynolds after Eddie Fisher left her for Elizabeth Taylor. Though Loew bought Wood a fourteen-karat diamond engagement ring, Wood broke the engagement a week after losing the Oscar for the third time.

The twenty-seven-week shoot of *The Great Race,* on location in Europe, was a difficult one for Wood, who did not get along with director Blake Edwards. One night in the midst of shooting, she tried to commit suicide by taking an overdose of sleeping pills. What specifically triggered her suicide attempt remains a mystery. That night, she had run into Beatty at a restaurant and he dropped by her house later that evening, but he left after a few minutes. She never discussed what happened with anyone but her analyst. Hospitalized over the weekend, she returned to the set on Monday as scheduled, ever the professional. "I'll get by," she explained. "There aren't any close-ups scheduled."

SAFE HARBOR

In the mid-1960s, Wood finally broke her contract with Warner Brothers, paying the studio $250,000 to let her go. Wood closed out the 1960s, her best decade as an actress, with a film that showed she was still willing to take chances—*Bob & Carol & Ted & Alice*. The director, Paul Mazursky, had never directed a feature film, and Wood was the only star in a cast of then little-known actors, including Elliott Gould, Robert Culp and Dyan Cannon. A satire on the New Morality, the film demonstrated that Wood could change with the times and make a film that was as relevant to 1969 as *Rebel* was to 1955. Featuring encounter groups, dope smoking and mate swapping, the film included many scenes that were improvised, and the risk-taking energized Wood. "Now is the most exciting period of film," she said. "It's the end of the studio production made by numbers. Studios are being sold. That's healthy. Let the director shoot on the street." Though she had taken a cut in salary offset by a percentage of the profits to make the film, the gamble paid off. It made her rich—and just in time. Soon after *Bob & Carol & Ted & Alice*, she would find herself hitting Hollywood's glass ceiling for aging actresses, especially actresses who were as identified with sex as Wood was.

In 1972, with her professional life once again on the wane, Wood retreated to a safe harbor. She and Robert Wagner, whose career had been revived with the TV series *It Takes a Thief*, remarried on a boat off Catalina Island on July 16. Two years later, she gave birth to her second daughter, Courtney. (Her first daughter, Natasha, was born two years earlier, during her brief marriage to British talent agent Richard Gregson.) For a few years, Wood settled into a comfortable pattern. While she remained a certifiable star, she was offered fewer movie roles. So she embraced television, making a TV movie with Wagner called *The Affair*, playing opposite Wagner and Laurence Olivier in a television production of *Cat on a Hot Tin Roof* and earning an Emmy for the miniseries *From Here to Eternity*. And then, in 1981, she was cast in the science fiction film *Brainstorm*, directed by Douglas Trumbull, who had been the special-effects supervisor for Stanley Kubrick's groundbreaking *2001: A Space Odyssey*.

When she was offered the role in *Brainstorm*, she joked that it was the modern equivalent of casting aging actresses in horror films. But despite a director who was more concerned with technology than acting, she found a co-star who would kick up some of those old *Rebel* memories. Christopher Walken, who had just won an Oscar for *The Deer Hunter*, had many of the qualities that so enamored her of James Dean. He had studied at the Actors

Studio. He was attractive, just a little crazy and dangerous. "Right before a scene would start," said co-star Louise Fletcher, "he would do something completely different to get the energy going, like he'd drop his pants or something." Walken rewrote dialogue at script meetings that recalled the rehearsals for *Rebel*. And according to some who worked on the film, he began to take over the movie from Trumbull. Wood fell under his spell. According to Wagner's onetime stepson Josh Donen, "In spite of her love for RJ [Wagner] and her daughters, Natalie had been fired by Walken's talk of freedom and dedication to art." Working with Walken rejuvenated the forty-three-year-old Wood in a way that no project had in years. Reportedly, Wagner had been hearing rumors that Wood was infatuated with Walken and he began to grow jealous, suspecting they were having an affair.

The day before Thanksgiving, Wood's friend Faye Nuell Mayo visited her on the set of *Brainstorm* and the two reflected on the more than twenty-five years that had passed since they worked on *Rebel* together. "We got into this very nostalgic conversation about everyone who'd died," she remembers. "She said, 'Yeah but we're still here,'" Mayo remembers. "And I said, 'Yes we are.'"

Wood and Wagner planned to spend the weekend after Thanksgiving together on their yacht *Splendour*, named after *Splendor in the Grass*, and Christopher Walken accepted an invitation to join them. The sea was rough on the Friday after Thanksgiving, November 27, 1981, the first day Wood, Wagner and Walken spent on the *Splendour*, off Santa Catalina Island. Walken got seasick as soon as they left the port and remained in his cabin bedridden, while Wood and Wagner argued over whether to take the boat to calmer waters. When they couldn't agree where to anchor the vessel, Wood angrily took the dinghy (named *Valiant* after Wagner's role in *Prince Valiant*, a film he professed to find embarrassing) and went ashore with the boat's captain to spend the night in a hotel. But by the next day, everything seemed to have been patched up. Wood, Wagner and Walken had dinner together at a restaurant at Isthmus Cove on the island. They had started drinking early that evening and grew increasingly drunk and raucous as the night wore on. At one point after making a toast, they smashed their glasses on the floor, causing heads to turn in the restaurant. By the time they left around 10 p.m., they were so drunk that the restaurant's manager called the Harbor Patrol office to make sure they got back to their boat safely.

When they were back on board the *Splendour,* they continued drinking, and Walken and Wagner began arguing about Wood. "Walken kept encouraging Natalie to pursue her career as an actress, to follow her own desires and needs," according to Wagner. "He talked about his 'total pursuit of career,' which was more important to him than his personal life, and it was obvious I didn't share his point of view. It struck me as some kind of put-down, and I got really angry. I told him to stay out of it, then picked up a wine bottle, slammed it on the table, and smashed it to pieces." Walken later told police that Wagner complained that Wood "was away from home too much . . . away from the kids." Walken had taken Wood's side, saying that "she was an actress, she was an important person, this was her life." But realizing he was getting in the middle of a family argument, Walken stepped outside to get some air. When he returned, everyone had calmed down and apologized.

Wood went down to bed soon afterward and wrote in her diary, "This loneliness won't leave me alone," a line that appeared in two songs at the time: Otis Redding's "(Sittin' on) The Dock of the Bay" and Jimmy Cliff's "Many Rivers to Cross." Walken went to bed soon thereafter. Wagner continued drinking with the boat's captain, and later went down to the bedroom to check on Wood. But he discovered that Wood had disappeared and the dinghy was missing from the side of the boat. At 1:30 a.m., Wagner called Harbor Patrol and a search for Wood was launched. The search went on all night and into the morning. It wasn't until 7:45 a.m. on November 29 that the body of the forty-three-year-old actress was found floating in a lagoon off Santa Catalina Island, with the empty dinghy nearby.

As soon as her body was found, wild speculation raged as to what happened that night. The Los Angeles County Coroner, Thomas Noguchi, felt compelled to call a news conference to put an end to the rumors. He revealed that Wagner and Walken had had an argument, but concluded, "It was not a homicide. It was not a suicide. It was an accident." An autopsy showed that she was "slightly intoxicated" and bruises were consistent with the fall overboard. Noguchi speculated that Wood fell into the water when she was trying to get into the dinghy, perhaps to head back to the island. It seemed unlikely, however, that Wood would leave the boat alone dressed only in a red parka, floral nightgown and blue socks and without the bracelet she always wore in public. Later, in the 1986 biography *Heart to*

Heart with Robert Wagner, the actor would offer another theory: that the dinghy kept Wood awake by banging against the side of the boat and she was trying to retie it to stop the noise when she fell in.

The fact that Wagner and Walken at first denied to police that they had had an argument that night and were unclear about the timing of events, added fuel to the rumors that Wood's death was not an accident. Although Wagner and Walken eventually told police about the argument, a homicide investigator publicly chastised Noguchi, saying, "There was no indication that there was any argument. I think [Noguchi] was juicing it up a little bit." Later, some would point to this discrepancy as evidence of a cover-up by police. Despite the coroner's conclusion that it was an accident, and no evidence of foul play, many would remain unconvinced. In an article about her death, *Time* magazine noted the irony that in an interview given just before she drowned Wood had said, "I'm frightened to death of the water. I can swim a little bit, but I'm afraid of water that is dark."

Just as James Dean's friends would speak of his premonitions of death, many who knew Wood would recall her fear of drowning in dark water. In the minds of the media and the public, Wood's sudden shocking death would immediately recall the tragic events surrounding the release of *Rebel Without a Cause.* It was a sad coincidence, one of the many ironies in the *Rebel* story, and it would contribute to the preposterous but persistent intimations of a *Rebel* curse.

Years after she died, screenwriter Stewart Stern was packing his possessions for a move and came upon two copies of his script for *Rebel Without a Cause.* He opened them and discovered that, without telling him, Wood had autographed both copies one night when she and Wagner had come to dinner. "Stewart, thank you for giving me my beginning," she had written. "I hope I get to say your words again. This was the first time it mattered. I love you, Natalie Wood, 1972."

CHAPTER SEVENTEEN

The Erotic Politician

Like his on-set classmate Natalie Wood, Sal Mineo became an instant star after *Rebel*'s release. Only seventeen years old, the sad-eyed kid from the Bronx was breathlessly catapulted to a heady career peak. But unlike Wood's, Mineo's position would prove far more precipitous and short-lived. His persona—and his personal life—would make it far more difficult for him to maintain Hollywood's interest, especially once he began cracking open the closet on his sexuality. As he once quipped to an interviewer who mentioned that he began his career at the top: "And I've been working my way down ever since."

Dazzled by his immediate success, Mineo followed *Rebel* by securing roles in two prestigious studio projects: George Stevens's *Giant* and Robert Wise's *Somebody Up There Likes Me,* both set to star James Dean. Together, these films should have solidified Mineo's standing as a serious actor and Dean's on-screen partner. In fact, having taken Mineo under his wing, Dean was the one who insisted his *Rebel* co-star be given a part in *Giant*. But Mineo's role—that of young soldier Angel Obregón—was almost entirely excised by Stevens. And Dean did not live to play the role of boxer Rocky Graziano in MGM's *Somebody Up There Likes Me.* Warners had agreed to lend Dean to MGM in exchange for MGM contract player Elizabeth Taylor's work in *Giant,* but after Dean's fatal crash, he was replaced by Paul Newman. Dean's absence from the film had a compromising effect on Mineo's performance. In his acting, Mineo continued to demonstrate the influence of Dean—and Nicholas Ray. He brought everything he had to the part of Graziano's best friend, tossing in seemingly improvisatory moves, and working a raw nerve. But as a result, he stood out from the general tone of the film. His approach was too feverish and fidgety. Mineo seemed to be fighting against the film's simplicity as he tried to inject the same ambiguous level of hero worship between his character and Rocky as existed between Plato and Jim Stark. The film refuses to bend toward either his intentions or his acting style.

According to actor Ken Miller, who was originally cast in *Rebel* and appeared with Mineo in the 1957 film *Dino,* "He was so emotional that the director would have to stop shooting and take him over to the side and say that was too much. The tears came too quick. Because Sal could make tears quick, believe me. He was getting too emotional and he was becoming too stage-actorish. In films less is more. Sal was getting the emotion before it was time because he knew it was coming." Instead of accommodating his intensity, as some of Natalie Wood's best movies did, Mineo's films tended to shove him to the margins. There he would find himself stranded again and again.

TEEN IDOL

As Mineo would soon realize, the collective Hollywood brain trust had something very different in mind for him. Instead of continuing in films of stature, Mineo suddenly became part of Hollywood's experiment in crafting and selling teen idols. His image and persona would be targeted to kids who, immediately following *Rebel,* found themselves drowning in a flood of product. Without James Dean around, Mineo was the only sexy young man available who could credibly carry the *Rebel* banner into the new adolescent market. In a way, he became a victim of what *Rebel* had wrought—but not before he rode a wild wave of popularity.

Throughout the mid-1950s, Mineo was constantly featured in movie magazines where he could be seen playing bongos or tinkering with his car, where he was the prize in a "Win a Date with Sal Mineo" contest and where he was sold as a red-blooded American boy. ("He doesn't like to date the same girl more than three or four times," according to *Photoplay.*) More authentically, the magazines played up his love of family. Between films, Mineo continued to go home to his parents in the Bronx, where adoring fans could be a big problem, making it hard for him to walk the neighborhood streets, and at one point turning his cousin's wedding into a media circus. *Photoplay* magazine reported that Mineo bought his family a $200,000 house in Mamaroneck, New York.

As the studios continued to refine their sense of what the teen market could bear, Mineo found himself being sold as a pop-music star. He recorded two singles that landed on the *Billboard* charts: "Start Movin' (In My Direction)"—which sold over a million copies—and the less successful "Lasting Love." And he was used to bring his credibility to a score of B-level teen movies. In a breakneck succession of films—*Crime in the Streets, Dino, The Young Don't Cry* and *Rock, Pretty Baby*—the young actor found himself typecast in fairly low-budget films as a troubled teen, earning him the nickname "The Switchblade Kid." And over and over, the publicity for these films played the *Rebel* card. The press book for *Crime in the Streets* (1956) cried: "SAL MINEO, sensation of *Rebel Without a Cause* rages to stardom!" Publicity for *Rock, Pretty Baby* (1957) promised moviegoers they would find Sal "as great as he was in *Rebel* . . ."

When Universal-International produced *Rock, Pretty Baby,* the story of a fledgling rock band, the studio injected *Rebel* links throughout the film, not just as part of the advertising campaign. The studio gave Mineo top billing although he played a secondary character, the band's drummer, Angelo Barrato. The film's true hero, played by handsome John Saxon, is given the Dean-like name Jimmy Daley, and his band logo is a large, attention-getting "JD." As in *Rebel,* Mineo plays Jimmy's sidekick. The setting was the middle-class suburbs. Parental tensions and young love were the plot drivers. But try as they might to follow the *Rebel* template, *Rock, Pretty Baby* is nearly the anti-*Rebel* in its overall squareness. In one quick year, Hollywood had taken the honesty of *Rebel*—and of its precursor *Blackboard Jungle*—and mulched it into demographically targeted product.

But even in a one-note project such as *Rock,* Mineo could not hide the fact that there was something different about him, which lends an element of sexual ambiguity to almost every film he's in, even though *Rock's* insistence on Angelo's hungry eye for girls tries to erase any lingering unease concerning Mineo's preferences. Mineo's dark intensity, his overeager acting style and cackling laugh are discordant with the film's general mood of

Leave It to Beaver blandness. Without Ray or Dean to ground him, Mineo continued to ride his highly charged current all by himself.

Coincidentally, the first words spoken to Mineo in *Rock, Pretty Baby* are "Where's Jimmy?" And Mineo may have been asking himself that same question. Mineo was very callow and impressionable when he fell under Dean's intense influence. So it is not surprising that he patterned much of his personal life after Dean. It may have been an effective way to deal with grief. "There are a lot of things Sal did to emulate James," according to Mineo's friend and biographer, H. Paul Jeffers. "Jimmy Dean liked to play the bongos; Sal became a drummer. Dean was interested in bullfighting; Sal got interested in bullfighting. James Dean had an MG sports car; Sal got an MG sports car. James Dean liked to speed; Sal liked to speed. In fact, he got stopped a number of times on the Henry Hudson Parkway for speeding." One of those incidents prompted a fan magazine to suggestively ask: "Is Sal Mineo Too Fast for His Own Good?"

Throughout his life, Mineo always remained cagey with the press about whatever romantic and sexual feelings he might have had for Dean. But he was frank with Jeffers, whom he hoped would write his life story someday. "Sal told me that he realized he was in love with Dean," says Jeffers. "There's no question he was head-over-heels in love with him.

"Dean also had a lot of influence on him in terms of body and physical conditioning," says Jeffers. And over the years, Mineo's concentration and pride in his physique would become ever more apparent in his way of dressing and his provocative inclination to display his body both on-screen and onstage.

Although Jeffers does not feel that Mineo could ever be called a Method actor, Mineo continued to manifest Dean's intensity in tackling roles, at least in the years just following *Rebel*. But from the evidence of his performances after 1958, he eventually learned how to modulate his screen acting to fit the project at hand. And his new confidence on-screen coincided with his intense desire to escape from the teenscape to which he had been exiled.

EXODUS

In 1959 and 1960, Mineo secured two back-to-back parts that, like *Giant* and *Somebody Up There Likes Me,* should have ensured his transition from teen idol to serious adult actor. First, he played the title role in *The Gene Krupa Story,* the dramatic biopic of the famous swing-era drummer, in which Mineo got to play drums (although Krupa's playing is what is heard on the soundtrack). Ironically, it was Gene Krupa's drumming that inspired Marlon Brando's bongo playing, which inspired Dean's bongo playing, which, in a final turn of the wheel, inspired Mineo.

The Gene Krupa Story was a hit and it would become one of Mineo's favorite films. "He was gung-ho in this picture," says the film's assistant director, Ray Gosnell Jr., who also worked as an assistant director on *Rebel.* "He would frequently be there even when he wasn't called to the set. He really spent a lot of time rehearsing with the drums." But it was his next project that truly promised to change his career forever. He landed the part of Dov Landau, the fledgling Israeli terrorist in director Otto Preminger's epic *Exodus.* After Plato, Dov is the role for which Mineo is best remembered.

Exodus was a sprawling story with a huge cast that included Paul Newman, Eva Marie Saint, Ralph Richardson and Lee J. Cobb, all listed in the cast before Mineo. Based on a best-selling novel by Leon Uris—who had once taken a crack at the *Rebel* script—it tells the story of the reclaiming of Israel by the Jews after World War II. It's the kind of monumental movie that can benumb an audience with its scale. But Mineo's Dov Landau supplies the film with a taut and heartbreaking emotional center.

Preminger was known for pushing the envelope when it came to adult themes in American film. "He helped end movie censorship," said Mineo of the director, whose 1953 film *The Moon Is Blue* was the first Hollywood film released without the approval of the Production Code Administration. Preminger had something decidedly risky in mind for his actor, something that might explain why he wanted Mineo so badly for the part. In his all-important interrogation scene, Dov is forced to reveal that he was repeatedly raped by Nazi soldiers while he was held in a concentration camp. It's a pain-wracked revelation that stands as one of Mineo's most powerful moments on film, perhaps his best work since Plato asked, "What does he know about Man alone?"

"The word *homosexual* had hardly been mentioned in anything then," said Mineo, "and when I said that speech, you could hear the shock."

The role made such an impression that Mineo was nominated for his second Academy Award for Best Supporting Actor. He was sure he would win it. He had won the Golden Globe. He had certainly found his footing as a film actor. And if anything, he had become more handsome, finally outgrowing his "wheat-flour dumpling" looks, as he called them. On Oscar night, he was seen praying in his seat when his category was announced. But once again, the Academy passed him over.

Years later, Joe Bonelli, a young actor who became Mineo's friend, asked him who had won that evening.

"Fucking Peter Ustinov," said Mineo.

"Goddamn, Sal," responded Bonelli. "Suppose it had been the next year and you lost to George Chakiris. Peter Ustinov is a great actor at least."

"It was my fucking Oscar," Mineo insisted, and walked off.

The loss not only devastated Mineo, but also seems to have had a detrimental effect on his career overall. Suddenly, after *Exodus,* the studios stopped calling—and that fact remains one of the great mysteries of Mineo's life.

Was it his short size? Was he too much of a 1950s icon? Was it his ethnicity? Did he rely too much on his decidedly un-showbiz family to steer his career decisions? All of these reasons have been offered to explain the sudden and surprising downturn in Mineo's fortunes. But there is a very good chance that after playing Plato and Dov, Mineo might have been the victim of something less freely discussed back then. A homophobic Hollywood could easily have sensed something about the actor—as Ray and Dean had—that Mineo himself was not prepared to face. That was all about to change.

COMING OUT

Mineo would often tell an anecdote that amounted to his official coming-out story: He had lost the Oscar. No offers were coming in. And he suddenly discovered he was broke. At the time, he was living with his *Exodus* co-star Jill Haworth in a house in Malibu. Then, one night, while Haworth was making a movie in France, he went out walking alone on the beach. He saw a young man and they started talking. Sal invited him back to his empty house. And from that point on, as H. Paul Jeffers says, "Sal knew what was going on in his life. That was the first time."

While this story might be seen as marking an overly neat break with the past, having all the earmarks of a personal myth, the years of Mineo's increased openness about his homosexuality certainly coincided with his disenchantment with Hollywood. Before losing the Oscar for the second time, he had always put his career first, finding his deepest satisfaction in the thrill of being and playing the star. He enjoyed spending money, enjoyed the parties, enjoyed the status. But now the ways of celebrity were not working so well for him. Mineo developed a more cynical attitude toward Hollywood and that apparently freed him to explore other, more authentic aspects of his character. Then again, maybe by the age of twenty-two, and at a time when American culture, including the media, was moving toward a period of sexual experimentation, Mineo was merely looking for a good excuse to come out of the closet.

(A particularly ludicrous *Rebel* myth—one that marks a height of *Rebel* obsessiveness—tells a different story about Mineo's sexual revelations. One misty night in Hollywood, Mineo was supposedly in a car wreck. And while trapped in the car, handwriting appeared on the foggy windshield. The invisible hand spelled out the name: JAMES DEAN. And from that moment on, Mineo understood he had to be more open about his sexuality.)

In 1965, Mineo would take a role that marked his break with the studio system and certainly his break with the mainstream. Shot on a shoe-string budget in Manhattan, *Who Killed Teddy Bear?* was a lurid thriller directed by Joseph Cates (father of actress Phoebe Cates and brother of director Gilbert Cates). Mineo played a character who in his shyness and self-effacing quality seemed like a grown-up Plato—a young closeted Plato who had grown up to become a waiter in a 1960s Manhattan discotheque. But Mineo's character, Lawrence, had a dangerously psychotic dark side. He was a voyeur, a rapist and a murderer. The movie followed *Psycho*'s lead in combining a self-conscious use of cheap TV-derived production values with a new frankness about sexual perversion, all in the name of driving a thriller plot.

But *Teddy Bear* did not come with Hitchcock's imprimatur. The film developed a cult following over the years for its pulpy, fever-dream qualities, its gauzy close-ups of Mineo in his underwear, and for its colorful, off-Hollywood cast including Rat Pack moll Juliet Prowse (as the harassed heroine), Broadway diva Elaine Stritch (as a lesbian club owner) and TV game show host Jan Murray (as a cynical cop whose beat is the perverse). The film looks forward to the independent-minded films of the 1970s such as *Taxi Driver* (whose cinematographer, Michael Chapman, was assistant cameraman on *Teddy Bear*). Whatever cult status the movie may have achieved over the years and however interesting it looks in retrospect, it was career suicide at the time. "I found myself on the weirdo list," said Mineo.

"You see, in some of the shots," as Sal told an interviewer in 1976, "while I was on the phone they wanted to sort of suggest that I was masturbating, but I couldn't be naked. This was '67 or '68. So I was just wearing jockey shorts. It turned out that that was the first American film where a man wore jockey shorts. They always had to wear boxer shorts on screen. So I got hit with all of this, and I'm laughing about all this controversy about what is considered obscene! Imagine! And only a few years later we've got *Deep Throat*!"

After *Teddy Bear*, a new phase began in Mineo's life and career, one that would find him becoming more open, daring—and playful—regarding his sexuality, and one that would also find him returning to his roots in the theater. In 1968 and 1969, he directed L.A. and New York productions of John Herbert's play about life in prison, titled, after a line in Shakespeare, *Fortune and Men's Eyes*. According to Jeffers, "*Fortune and Men's Eyes* was originally set in a men's prison. Sal wanted to do it with young guys, make it a young man's prison, young good-looking guys. And move the play's offstage rape onstage. That was Sal Mineo saying 'Hey world, Plato really was gay.'"

The New York program for the play included a dedication to James Dean and a biography of Mineo in which his friend, press agent Elliot Mintz, provocatively referred to Mineo as "an erotic politician." But Mineo had still not completely come out of the closet. In an interview given to

Avanti magazine around the time of *Fortune,* he is very defensive about the play's gay content, saying, "I don't consider the play to be about homosexuality." In the same interview, he denies that he is gay.

Fortune and Men's Eyes had been mounted in New York before, but Mineo's homoeroticized version was something different. He altered the play so much that, perhaps in the spirit of *Fellini Satyricon* (which also appeared in 1969), the play was advertised as *Sal Mineo's Fortune and Men's Eyes.* The production was blasted by *New York Times* theater critic Clive Barnes. In a spirit of high moral dudgeon, Barnes challenged the show's potential audience by writing: "I suggest that if this does sound like the kind of play you would like, you need a psychiatrist a lot more than you need a theater ticket." Barnes's scathing yet excitable review underscored many of the show's sexy and sensationalistic aspects, and went a long way toward securing its infamous status and healthy run.

P.S.

Despite the controversy surrounding *Fortune,* once it closed, Mineo still found himself in career limbo. Throughout the early 1970s, he was relegated to guest spots on TV shows such as *Hawaii Five-O, My Three Sons* and *Columbo.* Through his friend Roddy McDowall, he eventually landed the rather ignominious role of a chimpanzee in the low-budget *Escape from the Planet of the Apes,* the second sequel in the series. Throughout this ego-denting period, Mineo reportedly maintained good humor, a forward-looking attitude and a generous spirit, but money remained tight.

"When I first met him he had a Bentley," said his friend director Peter Bogdanovich. "The last time I saw him he was driving a VW. I said I had some furniture I was getting rid of. He took it." By this point, according to Bogdanovich, Mineo was less like a Hollywood star than "an unconventional Greenwich Village artist type. He wasn't like anybody else."

In 1974, Mineo was momentarily reunited with his old director Nicholas Ray, who had also fallen on rough times. According to Susan Ray, the director's wife at the time, "Sal and Nick came together again at the house we had on 12th Street in Manhattan. I think that Sal looked Nick up. I remember he wore very pale clothes, beiges, very slick clothes. He looked very pretty. He was smooth-featured. I remember Nick making a comment to the effect that Sal was a little lost."

Despite Ray's comment, Mineo had certainly found a more honest, authentic approach to living his personal life. During this period, he forged a long-term relationship with actor Courtney Burr. And for a while, Mineo and Burr resided in London. Throughout those years, Mineo tried to get various productions going, many of which were gay-themed. At one point, he was interested in buying the rights to James Leo Herlihy's novel *Midnight Cowboy*. Eventually, the film was made—without him—and went on to be the first X-rated film to win the Academy Award for Best Picture. He even talked about resuscitating his old music career by putting together a music group inspired by director Peter Watkins's prescient 1967 cult movie *Privilege,* which is about a sexy young rock star whose violent stage act is used by a fascist state to control the country's youth. But like most of Mineo's projects of this period, it never came to fruition.

Invariably, references to *Rebel Without a Cause* kept reappearing in Mineo's life. Eventually, he would comically refer to the film as *"Rebel Without a Pause."* Joe Bonelli remembers the evening Mineo appeared as a guest on *The Joey Bishop Show,* one of the first late-night talk shows to go up against *The Tonight Show with Johnny Carson.* "Sal went down to tape it. And when he came out, he said, 'You won't believe what happened. We've got to go to the bar and watch me on the show'—which was broadcast later that night. There was a bar that connected to the Coronet Theater in L.A. and we all used to run in there and hang out. Sal said that when he arrived at the taping, host Joey Bishop told him that they had gotten a clip of *Rebel* to show, if that was all right with Sal. And Sal said, 'Yeah. As a matter of fact, I have not seen *Rebel* since it came out.' So they showed a scene that ends with a close-up on Sal with those big eyes looking at Jimmy Dean's character with absolute adoration. They finished on that close-up and faded into his face watching the monitor. 'The look was exactly the same,' Sal said. 'My soul was bared on nationwide television.'"

After a long dry spell, Mineo found his next major project once again in the theater. In San Francisco, he took a lead role in *P.S. Your Cat Is Dead,* a play that seemed to mark a change in his fortunes—and a definite change in the kind of gay material with which he had been involved. *Fortune and Men's Eyes* was both sensationalistic and hard-edged in its treatment of gay themes. Like Mart Crowley's breakthrough play *The Boys in the Band*, it was the product of more self-loathing times. But by the mid-1970s, gay life had taken another leap into general acceptance—and *P.S. Your Cat Is Dead* reflected those changes. The play might have caged its gay themes in a fog of bisexuality but, essentially, it's a sweet love story between two men, albeit a house thief and his victim. It was written by James Kirkwood, who would eventually write the gay-positive book for *A Chorus Line*.

The San Francisco production had been a big hit, and Mineo received his best reviews in years. Picking up Keir Dullea as a co-star, the play moved to Los Angeles. Looking back, many of those closest to Mineo remember his excitement about the L.A. opening. Mineo felt that the sexy yet audience-friendly *P.S. Your Cat Is Dead* might be just the thing to get his career back on track. He rented a temporary apartment in West Hollywood and began rehearsals at the Westwood Playhouse. But sadly, Mineo would never open in L.A. On February 12, 1976, just one week into rehearsals, thirty-seven-year-old Sal Mineo was murdered near his newly rented apartment. According to the coroner's report, he died of a massive hemorrhage. He had been stabbed repeatedly in the heart with a heavy knife. A white male with long hair and wearing dark clothes was seen running from the scene of the crime. Unavoidably, Sal Mineo's abrupt and violent demise would be seen as further proof of a *Rebel* curse.

THE MURDER MYSTERY

Despite his years of relative obscurity, Mineo's death made headlines across the country. The crime generated a wealth of media speculation about Mineo's lifestyle, furthered by the fact that the mystery of his death went unsolved for more than a year. In a 1978 article in *Esquire*, Bogdanovich imagined his self-mocking friend reacting to the news frenzy by saying, "A lotta good that does me."

Like the media, the police were seemingly distracted by the issue of Mineo's gayness. According to former L.A. detective Dan Tankersley, "During the investigation that night we found out he was a homosexual. Then that opened a whole new field. Is this a disgruntled lover? Is this a male prostitute he picked up off the street?"

Many years later, Tankersley asked himself, "Why didn't we pursue the robbery angle more? We might have solved it a lot sooner."

In fact, the crime might have remained unsolved to this day if the wife of twenty-two-year-old Lionel Williams had not informed the police in May 1977 that her husband—a former pizza delivery man—had come home on the night of the killing, saying that during an attempted robbery he had murdered Sal Mineo with a hunting knife he bought for $5.28. Police were able to purchase a knife identical to the one she described and match it exactly to the wound in Mineo's chest, which had been preserved after the autopsy.

On February 14, 1979—almost three years to the day after Mineo was killed—Lionel Williams was found guilty of a cluster of crimes: the second-degree murder of Sal Mineo, as well as ten other "strong-armed" robberies committed in Los Angeles around the time of Mineo's murder. Some would continue to doubt that the prosecution, whose case was based on circumstantial evidence, had proven Williams's guilt. According to the *New York Daily News*, "Three witnesses who believed they saw Mineo's killer said that the assailant was white. Williams is black. All witnesses who testified about the killer's height said that he was 5 feet 8 or taller. Williams is 5 feet 5." But the prosecution argued that it was too dark to properly identify the perpetrator, and two witnesses testified that Williams had bragged about the murder. Williams was sentenced to serve fifty-one years to life. He was paroled in 1994 after serving fifteen years in prison.

The day after Mineo's stabbing, his body was returned to New York and his family. His funeral took place at a Catholic church in Mamaroneck, near the home Mineo had bought for his family nearly twenty years earlier. Nicholas Ray attended the funeral. No one else from *Rebel* was reportedly in attendance. The *New York Times* would begin its coverage with an immediate evocation of Mineo's classic role: "When Plato, the alienated teenager played by Sal Mineo, died at the end of the 1956 film *Rebel Without a Cause*, he was mourned only by the family housekeeper and two high-school friends. At Sal Mineo's funeral today, about 250 people crowded into Holy Trinity Roman Catholic Church, and dozens more stood outside. Most were curious spectators."

By the end of his life, Mineo seemed to have come to much better terms with his identity—and his sexuality. He took great pride in having portrayed gay characters. "It meant a lot to him to be a gay icon," says Joe Bonelli. "He was proud to say he was the first gay teenager in the movies," says H. Paul Jeffers. Given the repressive tenor of the times, Mineo continued to remain cagey with the press. But many of his choices were extremely brave, audacious and indeed rebellious for a Hollywood star of that era. Ultimately, he wore his sexuality casually. And it remains one of *Rebel*'s greatest legacies—and a primary reason for the film's continued freshness and resonance—that the origins of Mineo's evolution might be traced to Plato.

CHAPTER EIGHTEEN

Elegy for a Director

During the shooting of *Rebel*, James Dean had become an essential part of Nicholas Ray's imagined future. "Jimmy was the key," according to Frank Mazzola. "Nick and Jimmy were going to take something out into the world." They planned to form the kind of independent production company that had begun to thrive in the wake of the weakening studio system. And Ray looked forward to the day he could have it both ways: when he could continue to rely on the big studios and all the support they provided, while calling his own shots. "We would have done both feature pictures and a TV series, which would have allowed Jim to break in as a director," said Ray to a reporter soon after Dean's death, indicating the level of control over their own destinies they hoped to achieve.

Dean and Ray discussed plans to adapt various projects, including a story about a Mexican road race, an adaptation of Edward Loomis's *Heroic Love*—which centered on a complex mentor relationship between two men—and a novella by Italian author Alberto Moravia titled *Agostino*. Moravia's story concerned a thirteen-year-old Italian boy who has a nearly incestuous relationship with his mother, and who experiences his first glimmers of sexual awakening when he falls in with a gang of kids led by an adult pederast. Clearly, Ray and Dean planned to continue pushing at the edge of sexual candor and studio standards, which would certainly provide the friction they required for inspiration and allow them to continue to explore their own characters. But with Dean's death, none of these projects would ever see the light of day, and neither 267 would Ray's dream of an unassailable power base in Hollywood. Instead, Ray would slip deeper into dissatisfaction, into drug abuse, alcoholism and gambling.

By the mid-1950s the kind of intimate films Ray made at RKO—and planned with Dean—were seldom being made by the studios any longer. But for a while, Ray found a way to adapt to Hollywood's new order, given his comfort with CinemaScope and an ardor for color and movement that rivaled his passion for psychologically rooted drama. Ray's post-*Rebel* films reflect the studio's new taste for gigantism in the face of the continued threat from the small screen. As he had demonstrated in *Rebel*, Ray instinctively knew how to invest the often stifling CinemaScope format with energy. For a while, he was able to ride along as Hollywood hit its mannerist phase.

Hot Blood, Bigger Than Life, Bitter Victory—these were the titles of some of the films he made after *Rebel*, and like his earlier movies—*They Live By Night, In a Lonely Place, On Dangerous Ground*—they read like chapter headings in his biography. Along with directors Vincente Minnelli (*The Cobweb, Some Came Running*) and Douglas Sirk (*Written on the Wind, Tarnished Angels*), Ray was one of the few filmmakers who could effectively harness melodrama writ large. He found a way to turn even the most overblown and tawdry projects into "indisputable records of a very personal anguish," according to critic Andrew Sarris, who notes that "Ray's characters are inflicted with all the psychic ills of the fifties." Paranoia, violence, jealousy, disillusionment and isolation continued to be earmarks of Ray's films and, ever more demonstrably, his life.

During his last years in Hollywood, Ray never got back to the subject of youth, for which his sensibility was ideally suited. As he drifted from project to project, from Warners to Fox to MGM, he would never craft another sizable hit; he certainly never created a film that would strike at the Zeitgeist like *Rebel*. Toward the end of his life, Ray would say, "If *Rebel* has been playing for the last twenty years (and it has), then it can stand as my epitaph." As Ray predicted—and perhaps feared—*Rebel* would represent the apex of his career.

DOWN AND OUT IN HOLLYWOOD

In the last writings of his life, Ray would speak of a decades-long personal blackout that began in 1957, just about the time *Rebel* receded from his life, after having made its way around the world. Ray was always a heavy drinker, given to starting his day with a brisk vodka. But increasingly after *Rebel*, and especially after the death of Dean, Ray's alcohol intake took a toll on his work.

While on the set of 1956's *Bigger Than Life*, Ray's alcoholism worsened, according to his friend Gavin Lambert, the writer and film critic. He had met Ray in London while the director was there promoting *Rebel*. Lambert had been a Ray aficionado since the director's first film, *They Live by Night*, British critics being some of the first to appreciate Ray's work. After spending the night with Ray at his hotel suite, Lambert agreed to follow him back to Hollywood. "I could see him on the set when he had a particularly heavy night of drinking," remembered Lambert, who worked on the script for *Bigger Than Life*. "His responses were not as good. It did not happen very often but there were definitely a few days when he was slow and really couldn't make up his mind what he wanted to do that day, where he wanted the camera." Lambert also discovered that Ray's medicine cabinet was filled with prescription drugs.

By his next film, Ray's drinking had grown worse. Just before beginning work on one of his slightest projects, *The True Story of Jesse James*, a drunken Ray fell down the steps outside Bungalow 2 at the Chateau Marmont and needed to use a cane for several weeks. It was one of the first outward signs of the physical abuse he would inflict on himself over the years.

Jesse James gave Ray a chance to work for the first time with his son Tony, who was cast in a small role as Bob Younger, a member of the James Gang. But it was a particularly bitter project for Ray. For the lead, he hoped to hire Elvis Presley, who had just had a major hit with his first film, *Love Me Tender*. Ray was always searching for a new Dean, and he thought he had found one. According to Lambert, who did uncredited work on the script, Ray "wanted to dramatize parallels between the post–Civil War adolescent bandit and the delinquent youth of today," hoping to turn Jesse James into a gun-slinging rebel without a cause. Ray also planned to shoot the Western in an audacious manner, underscoring the notion of the myth of the West by telling the story with a series of tableaus. "I'd do it entirely as a ballad, stylized in every aspect, all of it shot on a stage, including the horses, the chases, everything, and do it in areas of light." It was a fascinating idea—but the studio fought him all the way. He would get none of what he wanted. He was forced to make a fairly straitlaced film with a very straitlaced actor, Robert Wagner, the future husband of Natalie Wood.

Ray was desperate to branch out, to expand his working canvas beyond the reach of the studios, which were suffocating him. His next project—a World War II movie titled *Bitter Victory*—was his first international co-production. The film was shot in Libya, with money raised by international businessman Paul Graetz. Ray took Gavin Lambert along for company and to help work on the script. During a rare golden moment, they visited the Roman amphitheater at Sabratha. Ray looked down into the vast semicircular arena from the very top row, and said, "Do you realize the Romans built in CinemaScope?"

Sadly, *Bitter Victory* did not represent a new beginning for Ray. The shoot was plagued by money problems and interference from Graetz, who fired Lambert when he would not spy for him and reveal whether Ray was drinking or taking drugs. Lambert's loyalty was laudable, in light of his own problems with Ray. Ray was careering out of control. He gambled incessantly and took up with a young female heroin addict. After a stormy two years, Lambert had had enough. Brokenhearted, he left Libya and Ray. And yet, like so many others who escaped the wreckage of Ray's life, Lambert remembers the director with vividness and empathy.

"He was a very dear man in many ways, very generous, very creative," says Lambert. "But he couldn't work out his life. He never quite made up his mind about his sexuality. He was very conflicted, very lonely. He wanted total independence, his own projects away from major studios. At the same time, he wanted to be put up in a five-star hotel. Of course, there was no independent film movement at the time. And the kind of projects he wanted to do did not have low enough budgets for him to be free. He wanted the big stars and he wanted it all his own way. He didn't even want the studio to know what he was doing. All these conflicts led to him drinking and, eventually, that got around."

In late 1957, Ray—whose life would now become increasingly, desperately peripatetic—found himself in Florida making *Wind Across the Everglades* with writer Budd Schulberg (*On the Waterfront*). But Ray fought with Schulberg over control of the project, and bad weather and Ray's drinking and ill health doomed the film. By early 1958, Ray was back in Hollywood directing the CinemaScope gangster picture *Party Girl* for MGM, starring Cyd Charisse. *Party Girl* would be his last official Hollywood studio project and, with its dance sequences, the closest he would get to making a musical, a genre that always appealed to him.

During these years, Ray married again, for the third time. On October 13, 1958, he wed an actress and dancer named Betty Utey, who played a small role in *Party Girl* and had also appeared with Charisse in *Silk Stockings* and in Douglas Sirk's *Tarnished Angels*. After their wedding in Maine, Ray and Utey returned to Hollywood and, despite Ray's string of nonhits, he received a welcome reception. "There were people in high places who believed in him," said Utey, "especially if he wasn't drinking." During this period, Ray seems to have turned some attention toward issues of family. He and Utey would have two daughters, Julie Christina and Nicca.

In 1960, Ray's ex-wife Gloria Grahame and his son Tony ripped open the wounds of the past by marrying each other. Reportedly, upon hearing the news, the director threw up. Years later, Ray would pour his unresolved anger into an aborted screenplay called *The Cain and Abel Story,* feverishly mistyped as *The Cain and Abke Stiry.* In the violent four-page manuscript, Ray writes of a man living in Madrid named Nick, who has two sons named Tim and Sim. In a rage, Nick accuses Sim of sleeping with his wife and punches him in the mouth, knocking out his teeth. Then he grabs a knife and, in Oedipal fury, he threatens to put out Sim's eyes.

Soon after Grahame and Tony got married, Ray's thirteen-year-old son Tim left his mother and joined his father's new family, at Betty Utey's urging. At the time, Ray was residing in Europe, where he had gone to make *The Savage Innocents*—a Paramount picture about the Inuit, shot in Ottawa, London and Italy. Ray taught Tim about filmmaking, giving him a camera to make a film about "the 'uncomfortableness' of being a teenager." But things did not work out well for them. Ray gambled away the villa where they were living. Eventually, Tim found himself stranded without funds, the victim of his father's resentment and torturous personality. In a sadly familiar scenario, Ray was rumored to have seduced one of Tim's girlfriends. For several years, father and son had no communication.

Ray's life was in constant chaos now. He always prided himself on taking leaps into the void, but now it seemed he had developed an unavoidable instinct for self-destruction. He must have perceived that his career was slipping away. And with *Wind Across the Everglades, Party Girl* and *The Savage Innocents* added to his list of financial disappointments, Hollywood suddenly lost interest in him.

Badly in need of money, Ray joined forces with producer Sam Bronston. A former executive at Columbia Pictures, Bronston had built huge soundstages in Spain, where he planned to turn out historical spectaculars, including *King of Kings,* the story of Jesus Christ. Moving toward large epic productions was not the best idea for Ray. He was getting too far from the original sources of his inspiration. And he urgently needed a project to believe in, not just another work-for-hire.

Working for Bronston proved every bit as frustrating as working for the studios. Surprisingly, *King of Kings* was Ray's first box-office hit since *Rebel.* It was the seventh-highest-grossing film of 1962, taking in seven and a half million dollars. And, despite the daunting challenge of its scale, *King of Kings* was exquisitely directed by Ray, who seemed to be operating at full strength despite his personal problems. With the help of Philip Yordan's script, Ray crafted an intelligently dispassionate Passion, short on religious kitsch and sentimentality. Starring callow, blue-eyed Jeffrey Hunter as a Christ who is something of a political rebel, the film was dubbed "I Was a Teenage Jesus" by the industry, according to *Time* magazine. Critic Jonathan Rosenbaum would also note how the film hearkens back to Ray's earlier triumph: "The flaming red garments and rebellious stances of its Jesus take us right back to James Dean in his leather jacket."

The financial success of *King of Kings* might have gone a long way to restore Ray's stature. But just when he seemed ready for his second act, his career did what it was threatening to do for so long. It ruptured.

Ray made a Faustian bargain when he accepted yet another project from Bronston. He agreed to direct a second epic, *55 Days at Peking,* the story of the Boxer Rebellion in China. Ray was clear-eyed about why he took the project: "I made the mistake common to the journalist who says to his wife, 'Darling, I've just had an offer from an advertising agency to become their chief writer for commercials. It'll bring me $200,000 a year, and that will give me the chance to move to Connecticut and write the Great American Novel.' This gave me a lot more than $200,000, and I thought, 'All right, for the last time I'll break my promise to myself never to do anything I don't want to do.'" But these kinds of compromises had been damaging Ray throughout his career.

Just as he entered production on *55 Days at Peking*, Ray had a nightmare that would haunt him for the rest of his life. He awoke, startled, and turned to Betty. "Something has come to me in the night," he said, "and told me that if I do this film I will never make another film."

Ray described the situation on *55 Days at Peking* as similar to the "worst of Hollywood." He accused Bronston of deceit, stealing and cheating. "The pressure was tremendous," Ray said. "On a $6 million production, I had no production manager, and a 21-year-old assistant director. No script. I had two artists in my office, one Chinese and one Spanish. I'd describe the scene to them, they'd draw it and then I'd give it to the so-called writers and say, 'Write a scene around this?'"

Then on September 11, 1962, Ray had a heart attack on the set. "It wasn't a major heart attack," according to Betty Utey. But it sent Ray to the hospital and gave Bronston the opening he needed. He brought in Andrew Marton, a second-unit director who had worked on the celebrated chariot sequence in the Oscar-winning *Ben-Hur* and the battle sequences in *Cleopatra*. Ray was off the picture. He would never direct a major Hollywood feature again.

THE AUTEUR

After the debacle of *55 Days in Peking*, Ray began a period of intense drift. He and Betty separated, and Ray began migrating from one European capital to another, one aborted project to another, adding a taste for amphetamines to his other vices. At one point, according to his old friend and mentor John Houseman, "He retired to a small, isolated island in the North Sea, from which he reappeared in his late fifties—penniless, with his health seriously damaged."

But ironically, as Ray's career died, his reputation grew. In the pages of

273

the French film journal *Cahiers du Cinéma,* a sea change had occurred in film criticism. A new idea about filmmaking had emerged, which would become known as the "auteur theory." The auteur theory views film as the creation of a single individual, the director. It would celebrate movies driven by an individual style or a personal obsession. It would crown new geniuses—Hitchcock, Hawks, Minnelli—who were seen to have heroically circumvented the strictures of the studio system to produce films according to their own vision. These directors were considered aesthetically and morally driven subversives, whether they actually were or not. And very few directors filled this bill better than Nicholas Ray. He would be called the theory's "test case" and its "cause célèbre." As he continued to flounder personally and professionally, his reputation swelled until he came to be seen as *the* auteur.

At the beginning of the 1960s, many of the young critics of *Cahiers du Cinéma* became major directors in the French New Wave, and their words would carry special weight as they lined up to pay homage to Nicholas Ray. François Truffaut would dub him "the poet of nightfall." Jacques Rivette would extol Ray as the best director of the period following World War II. But most famously of all, in 1958, Jean-Luc Godard would proclaim, "There was theater (Griffith), poetry (Murnau), painting (Rossellini), dance (Eisenstein), music (Renoir). Henceforth there is cinema. And the cinema is Nicholas Ray." Those last five words would follow the director for the rest of his life—and they would sustain him through very rough times.

Eventually, Ray would see almost all his films reevaluated upward. His estrogen-driven Western *Johnny Guitar* would come to be viewed as "dream-like, magical . . . delirious" by Truffaut. It would become a major cult film, even spawning a musical in 2004. Two of Ray's most mature and least compromised adult projects, *In a Lonely Place* and *The Lusty Men,* would be duly placed in the pantheon of great American films. In more recent years, *Bitter Victory* has been rediscovered, while *Run for Cover*—his 1955 Western—remains ripe for reevaluation. Even good but lesser films such as *Party Girl* and *Hot Blood* have found their supporters, while *Bigger Than Life,* his story of cortisone addiction in a middle-class father and husband, now looms as one of his greatest achievements. It would be seen as a corrosive portrait of the "ingrowing sickness of the good life," according to critic David Thomson, much like an adult version of *Rebel.* Of course, critical consensus remained high about *Rebel*, the one film of Ray's that did not need the auteur theory.

During the 1960s, Ray was the subject of retrospectives and served as a juror at film festivals. He came to know all the young directors of the French New Wave and stood with them at the barricades when Henri Langlois was fired from his position as head of the Cinémathèque Française in 1968. And yet Ray could not get any projects off the ground, and his personal life continued to spin out of control. His embrace by young filmmakers only worsened his penchant for self-destruction, according to Houseman, giving him "megalomaniacal fantasies that caused him to blow one film deal after another; haunted by a deepening, neurotic fear of losing his creative ability, he became increasingly reluctant to risk his reputation on a new film."

In 1957, Jean-Luc Godard had insightfully written: "It is difficult to see [Ray] doing anything but make films. . . . Were the cinema suddenly to cease to exist, most directors would be in no way at a loss; Nicholas Ray would."

During this period of drift, a deepening chasm formed between Ray's past and his present, his reputation and his current career. At Cannes, director Alan J. Pakula would bow and call him "maître," while director Hubert Cornfield would accost Ray, acerbically telling him, "You know, instead of drinking yourself to death, you could still make a great low-budget film and get back in the running."

Finally, a tangible and inspiring new project did emerge. It had all the elements necessary to lift Ray out of his dolor. It would return him to the United States and, most importantly, thrust him back into the vital center of American youth culture, just as that culture was once again erupting.

It began as a project called *The Defendant,* concerning a boy who was arrested for possession of marijuana and persecuted, in true Ray fashion, for "freedom of the mind." It was a perfect fit for the director of *Rebel,* who had hit a point in his life where he was driven to repeat the *Rebel* experience. Once Ray arrived back in the U.S. in 1969, he was thrilled to witness what was going on. The Vietnam War had kicked off a period of great dissent, driven by college-age kids. And at the same time, the culture seemed to have caught up with Ray's own penchant for drugs and sexual experimentation. It was as if he were experiencing the youthful rebellion that he himself had forecast. As critic David Thomson would write, *Rebel* "now looks like the first film to catch the revolutionary unease of the younger generation." Ray threw himself into the heart of the youth movement, newly inspired, hoping for rebirth. As a result, and like "The Blind Run," *The Defendant* began to expand and change, crashing directly into reality.

Ray began shooting documentary footage of antiwar marches to use in *The Defendant,* but eventually he decided to focus instead on the case of the Chicago Seven, a group of antiwar organizers and demonstrators who were arrested at the 1968 Democratic National Convention and tried for conspiracy. He called the trial "the greatest circus of bigotry I'd ever heard directed at young people who were the now 32- and 33-year-old equivalents of James Dean."

The Chicago Seven trial included such 1960s icons as Black Panther Bobby Seale, Jane Fonda's future husband Tom Hayden, and Yippie leaders Jerry Rubin and Abbie Hoffman. They were thrilled to have Nicholas Ray on board. "We were all . . . well, honored," said Abbie Hoffman, who described Ray as "a rebel with a cause, an independent minded free spirit," adding, "anybody who'd met Jimmy Dean, what the hell, gonna let him in the door!"

Using what he described as "the privilege of a $30,000 overdraft at my bank," Ray began to shoot. "We couldn't get cameras into the court. I tried a couple of times, but they made too much noise. So we shot everything that happened outside the courtroom. I sent camera crews with the guys when they were speaking at news conferences, doing karate exercises. . . . We shot 30,000 feet of film, and 540 hours of tape which I bribed from an official of the court. The tape was delivered to me by a lieutenant in Chicago's finest, delivered to me like a gangster, off an alley, from under his leather jacket." These guerrilla tactics energized Ray. But despite his enthusiasm and the fact that the winds of history were with him, this project, like so many others, fell apart.

Ray blamed the caprice of his financial supporters: Grove Press, Hugh Hefner, and Michael Butler, producer of the original Broadway production of *Hair.* Ray would simply say, "The three great pornographers of the United States . . . backed out." But Susan Ray, then an eighteen-year-old student who met Ray in Chicago and would become his fourth wife, says,

"The money was withdrawn for political reasons," a point of view backed up by film historian James Leahy, who was working with Ray at the time. He insists that certain government contracts held by one of the film's backers "had come under threat."

The death of this project could not have been worse for Ray. The Chicago Seven movie represented too many things to him: his return to form, his triumphant return to America, his realignment with the current events, his career vindication. Its demise hit him hard, and left a physical mark.

When the Chicago Seven project fell apart, Ray reacted less in anger than with depression—"which exacerbated the problem," according to Susan Ray. It was 3 a.m. when Ray found out he had lost his backing. Immediately he became despondent. This scenario of failure had replayed too many times. He dismissed his staff and, clearly overwhelmed, he fell asleep at his editing table. Suddenly he was awakened by a strange feeling. "My eye was kind of heavy," Ray said. Over the next six hours, as he struggled to find a doctor, the pain and discomfort grew worse. Eventually, he was taken to the hospital but it was too late. According to Ray, "If I had made it 20 minutes sooner, they would have been able to inject nicotinic acid and save the eye." But instead, Ray experienced an embolism in his right eye and would begin wearing what would become the trademark of his later years: a black eye patch.

No longer the handsome young swain or the distinguished silver-haired maestro, Ray would become a ragged pirate on the stormy seas of cinema. And he took pride in his startling new accessory. "He would buy eye patches by the box," says Susan Ray, "because he was always sweating quite a lot from the vitamin B and the methamphetamine."

But over the years, the eye patch developed its own aura of mystery. Ray insisted he needed the patch, but according to Susan Ray, "There's some question as to how much of his sight he lost. At a certain point, he did stop wearing the eye patch and could see well. He never had very good depth perception, although in the early days I frequently saw him scooping up some cocaine off the floor. He had no trouble seeing that. He did have an embolism in the eye but I don't think it completely destroyed his sight. I think it was partly hypochondria. Partly vanity. It suited his rakish nature."

Maybe Ray was thinking of the romantic solitude of Chicamaw, the old one-eyed bank robber in his first film, *They Live by Night,* who portentously said, "I'm better off alone. And I always was." The eye patch certainly contributed to the sense of a man falling apart one piece a time. Yet Ray continued to keep moving, like some kind of real-life Terminator, propelled by cinema and his insatiable curiosity despite the fact that his body was deteriorating. Shooting speed at this point, Ray never stopped lurching forward, toward no particular goal. Blindly (or half-blindly), he continued to pitch himself into space, hoping to reach the next realm of inspiration. There was simultaneously something pathetic and heroic about his efforts.

WE CAN'T GO HOME AGAIN

With the collapse of the Chicago project, Ray was in drastic financial straits, and desperately needed some kind of project to focus his energies. Then in 1970 at a Grateful Dead concert at the Fillmore East, Ray ran into Dennis Hopper. Hopper at the time was living out Ray's dream. Having helped kick-start the independent, director-driven cinema of the 1970s by co-directing *Easy Rider* (itself a child of *Rebel Without a Cause*), he had become a major player in the new, hipper, looser, drug-fueled Hollywood scene. Hopper could see Ray needed help. So, with their old jealousies over Natalie Wood far behind them, Hopper embraced his old director. He asked Ray to join him at his ranch in Taos, New Mexico, where he was editing his new film, *The Last Movie.* "Nick was unemployed, about to turn sixty and methamphetamine had just been made illegal. It was a good time for him to get out of town," said Susan Ray. "In Taos, Dennis provided shelter, food, drink, entertainment, new faces, wide vistas, guns, horses: a deluxe outlaws' den where Nick could rage freely."

Hopper also gave Ray a chance to get back in touch with cinema. Ray sat in with Hopper at the editing table as he tried to wrangle a coherent film out of the thirty-eight hours of footage he shot for *The Last Movie* during the chaotic, cocaine-fueled production in Peru. *Rebel* screenwriter Stewart Stern had written the screenplay, but Hopper threw it out and improvised a new script on location, which caused a "big falling out" between them, according to Stern. The film was being financed in part by Universal under Ray's former agent—and the man who had arranged the deal for Ray to direct *Rebel*—Lew Wasserman.

In Taos, Ray proposed to Susan, and through Hopper, Ray would make an important change in his career, one that would sustain him throughout the last period of his life. "With him living at the house and running up a $30,000 phone bill every month, I was forced to get him a job teaching school," said Hopper. Hopper helped Ray secure a position at Harpur College of Arts and Sciences at Binghamton University in upstate New York. Ray had always been a generous imparter of wisdom. His gurulike quality was one of the reasons kids were drawn to him. He was a teacher by nature. Now he would be able to earn a paycheck doing what came naturally. The college signed him to a two-year contract.

Despite a slew of hard knocks, his age and his deteriorating physical shape, Ray did not arrive at Harpur in a state of defeat or as a beaten soul, a semiretired filmmaker attempting to shore up his later years. If anything, Ray was as feisty and hungry as ever. He approached his new work as he had his old work—with dedication, defiance and his own agenda.

Ray felt that the best way to teach his students about filmmaking was actually to make a film. "I was sure as hell going to get them off their asses—not lecture to them," Ray said. But instead of allowing his students to develop their own projects, he decided that they would make a film *with him;* they would essentially help him make a film of his own. He quickly pulled together a script he titled *The Gun Under My Pillow,* echoing his memory of James Dean living in his Warners dressing room with a .45 under his pillow, and Plato retrieving the pistol from his mother's bedroom in *Rebel.* "It describes a psychological state that Nick lived in," says Susan Ray, "and what he identified with in Dean."

The film, which would eventually be called *We Can't Go Home Again,* became the most experimental film he would ever undertake. He simultaneously shot the movie in various formats and edited the footage together into a barrage of split-screen images. Ever responsive to the avant-garde, Ray employed video artist Nam June Paik's brand-new video color synthesizer to give the images a distorted, psychedelic look. He overlapped footage and ran strips of film—including some of his Chicago footage—down the sides of the central image, producing a rattling, visually cacophonous collage effect. He said, "I dreamed for years about breaking the rectangular frame," the frame being the ultimate boundary for the now self-conscious iconoclast. As a result, the film feels like a fierce download-ing direct from its director's mind, as if he was projecting the film straight from his nervous system onto the screen.

For the next two years, Ray and his class would dedicate themselves to the film. They were thrilled to be working hand-in-hand with the director of *Rebel Without a Cause*, which "was still very much a part of our culture," says Ray's student Tom Farrell, who would become one of the director's closest companions in his last years. But Farrell and the other students had no idea how close their experience would come to the experience of mak-ing *Rebel*.

Like *Rebel*, the film's free-form plot centers on a trio of young people played by Farrell, Leslie Levinson and Richie Bock. Ray, wearing a red jacket throughout the film, plays a teacher who inspires and manipulates his students. "I play the part of a betrayer," he said, "typical of my genera-tion . . . The betrayals that I engage in [in the movie] are like asking your kid to jump into your arms and then pulling your arms away, the kind of betrayals that lie behind the wars, the assassinations, the Watergates." Throughout the film, Ray looks horribly haggard, but he maintains a ragged grace and a burned-out hipster edge.

At one point in the film, the three students pay Ray a visit and proceed to taunt him. One of the students somersaults into the room, looks up at Ray from the floor and says, "Aren't you too old to be a new professor?" while another asks, "Didn't you direct *Rebel Without a Cause*?" Ray con-cocted this scene as a private reenactment of the night that James Dean showed up at the Chateau Marmont with Vampira and Jack Simmons, the night he decisively moved toward casting Dean in *Rebel*.

"Nick was very manipulative," says Levinson. "I think any director is ma-nipulative. Why else would we work with him? He wasn't paying us. He was ruining our lives. No one would talk to me. They thought I was killing my-self." But Levinson is quick to add, "He loved me. I knew that. I loved him." In *We Can't Go Home Again*, Levinson's character claims that she deliberately slept with a man who had a venereal disease and prostituted herself to raise funds for the movie—although the actress refuses to say if these scenes were directly based on true experiences.

Driven, it seems, to conjure the past, Ray repeated his *Rebel* pattern by folding his young actors under his wing and engaging them in agonizing psychodrama in the name of cinema, an experience that many of them still recall with mixed emotions.

"Nick taught us that acting is living," says Farrell. "He invited people to write and present stories of personal experiences. It had to be a personal experience that came from the gut. I can imagine how he directed James Dean and Natalie Wood and Sal Mineo because he could be very tender like a father, like he's trying to bring out the best in you, trying to console you and show you how it's important to let this part of yourself out to reveal yourself. I was able to dredge up things I didn't know I had with his comforting words." During his best scene in the final film, Farrell discusses his tortured relationship with his policeman father as he tearfully cuts off his beard.

Ray's working methods proved too intense for a number of his students. "Some people had dropped out. They couldn't take Nick anymore," says Farrell. "We often had to film all night and students were involved in other classes. We got in the habit of drinking and smoking pot and filming together." Although Farrell says he was "guilty of venerating him as a god," he also witnessed a dark side of Ray. Apparently after being rebuffed when he made a pass at one of the female students, Ray cut her out of the film, obliterating her image in some of the footage with the video color synthesizer. "His behavior was often bizarre," says Farrell.

Soon, Ray's working methods began to alarm the college. In the spring of 1972, Ray was asked to show some footage from the film at a conference on independent filmmaking that was being held at Harpur. "Nick says, 'We just got something back from the lab. Let's put it in the projector,'" remembers Farrell. The audience was shocked to see footage of Ray and his students smoking pot together. "The director of the film department had a fit," says Farrell. "That was the beginning of the end of Nick at Harpur."

After the school year ended, Farrell stayed with Ray at the isolated farmhouse where Ray was living. One day, in an incident that recalls one of Ray's own early experiences with a college professor, Farrell says Ray "came on to me in a way, not in a sexual way, but he wanted affection from me and I couldn't give it to him. I was taken aback. I wasn't expecting it at all. He started to say things like, 'Oh sometimes you just need someone to talk to' and he would be very tender. It wasn't an overt pass. I think Nick was fundamentally a lonely man. I think he needed attention. He needed to have people around him. He didn't like to be alone for long. I couldn't believe it when he wanted some display of affection coming back from me and I couldn't give it to him in a physical way. I'm not like that at all. I couldn't understand how someone who had three wives and four children might have homosexual inclinations."

After leaving Harpur, Ray continued working on the film, and by 1973 he believed in his new movie so much that he took the brave and potentially humiliating move of trying to raise capital in Hollywood. He called Gene Kelly and even tried, unsuccessfully, to contact his old boss Howard Hughes for funding. He felt he had been given another opportunity to recapture or at least reactivate the past. With a small crew in tow, he moved once again into the Chateau Marmont, actually managing to secure his old space, Bungalow 2. The bungalow still looked as it did in 1955, and, Farrell says, Ray pointed out a couch where he said he had sex with Natalie Wood. According to crew member Charles Bornstein, "The simple fact that this guy, who was completely indigent, could get an expensive bungalow at the Chateau Marmont, run up enormous bills—just the phone bills alone!—and never pay them, was a great experience."

To get around town, Ray borrowed a car from a friend, although "it wasn't in very good shape," says Frank Mazzola. "He called me and wanted to know if I could push the car to kick it over," says Mazzola. "The car slid over the bumper of my car and it hit my grille. And it was a new car. But Nick was Nick. I didn't care. I always thought it was kind of a sad state for him because Nick was a great inspiration to all of us."

For the last time, Ray would organize one of his Chateau Marmont parties to raise money in order to take his movie to the Cannes Film Festival. Novelist Ken Kesey showed up with his friend Wavy Gravy, who brought kegs of laughing gas. But sadly, few of his Hollywood friends attended, which only fueled his sense of betrayal. Natalie Wood and Robert Wagner were among the few of his old friends to show up. They offered a token contribution of a thousand dollars.

Despite the lack of funds, Ray did manage to show a version of *We Can't Go Home Again* at Cannes in 1973. If he could not count on Hollywood, he hoped that the French would once again come through for him. But even his staunchest supporters greeted the film with bewilderment.

And perhaps in reaction, he turned the experience into an even bigger disaster, gambling away what little money he had.

Despite his film's reception at Cannes, Ray never stopped believing in *We Can't Go Home Again.* Largely plotless and formally open-ended as it was, the movie may have been subconsciously fashioned as a project that could never truly reach its endpoint. Ray would continue to edit and reedit the film for the rest of his life.

LIGHTNING OVER WATER

"It was hell," says Susan Ray about the period following their visit to Cannes. Ray, who had always been able to hold his liquor, was now imploding under its influence. "He was falling down drunk and he was hallucinating and deeply, deeply depressed," according to Susan, who eventually reached the point where she could no longer abide the situation. Following the advice of a social worker who told her that she was actually enabling Nick, Susan left him. But soon after Susan's departure, Ray would experience a nearly miraculous turnabout, one that would lead to a grace period in his life, much like the kind of grace period he would often provide for his heroes—à la *Rebel*'s mansion sequence—before doom resurfaced.

Within a week of Susan's leaving, Ray fell down the stairs that led to the loft he and Susan then shared in the SoHo district of Manhattan. Finally shocked into action, he checked into detox and joined Alcoholics Anonymous. For the first time in decades, he seemed to be on the road to recovery. Susan Ray quickly reentered her husband's life with new determination, even accompanying Ray to AA meetings. Then, in early 1977, the newly sober Ray secured teaching jobs at the Lee Strasberg Institute and New York University, with the help of old mentors Elia Kazan and John Houseman. This time, there would be no private agenda, no films of his own to press upon his students. Ray found that he loved teaching, pure and simple.

Just as Ray's career once served as a beacon to the French New Wave directors, now he would have a direct influence on the new generation of American independent directors. While at NYU, he would teach young filmmaker Jim Jarmusch, who considered Ray a "hero" and whose 1983 film *Stranger Than Paradise* would represent the opening salvo of the indie revolution. Ray continued to work on *We Can't Go Home Again* and even acted in two films: German filmmaker Wim Wenders's *The American Friend*, co-starring Dennis Hopper, and Milos Forman's *Hair*. But in the fall of 1977, after just a few years of clarity and renewed strength, Ray was diagnosed with lung cancer.

"Of course there was a kind of denial," says Susan Ray, remembering the period in tears. "But then a tremendous spirit. And he kept working." Ray would undergo two bouts of surgery, but they did not achieve the miracle he hoped for. He would continue to deteriorate over the next two years, his condition further damaged by painkillers and the depression they caused. Even at this late date, with very little strength left, the cinema was not through with him—and he was not through with it.

Ray wanted to make a film that centered on illness, which he discussed with his son Tim, who had drifted back into his life. Soon afterward, Wim Wenders made the film happen. Wenders proposed a collaboration between himself and Ray on a film about a dying painter whom Ray would portray, the same character he played in Wenders's *The American Friend*.

According to Wenders, Ray was "afraid he might not have all that much longer to live and the one desire he would have would be to make another movie and project a different image of himself to the world. He was still suffering from the fact that, for most of the film community in America . . . he was considered somebody who had to abandon his last film, *55 Days at Peking*, and had to dishonorably leave Hollywood."

Ray was in good spirits when Wenders arrived at his loft on the corner of Spring Street and West Broadway in SoHo, then the center of New York's art scene. At that time, April 1979, Wenders found Ray to be "clean, sharp, witty and mentally completely on top of things." But as the film progressed, Ray rapidly deteriorated. "The cancer in his body proved stronger than any of our attempts to fight it with fiction," said Wenders.

At one point, Ray suggested making the film about a dying old man spending his last days with his family, including a son who is married to his former wife, a clear reference to his son Tony's marriage to Ray's ex Gloria Grahame. But eventually, the film evolved from autobiography to documentary. It became more about the dying of Nick Ray, for better or worse.

"I don't think Nick thought in terms of this is a good thing to do or not a good thing to do," says Susan Ray. "It was an opportunity to make a film. That simple. Once he was in, he was in." According to Tom Farrell, who shot the video sequences in the film, "Nick looked at dailies with us and said, 'I look horrible.' And it hit him. He felt the film was slipping out of his hands because he was getting ill. Wim would decide the fate of the movie and I think it scared him."

The movie Ray and Wenders made, *Lightning Over Water,* is often difficult to watch. Susan Ray felt that, ultimately, Wenders was not very generous to Ray. John Houseman called the film "repulsive." Elia Kazan was shocked to come across the film crew when he visited Ray in the hospital. "I found it grotesque: a man cooperating in putting his own death on film," said Kazan. "I thought Wenders ghoulish, but I also thought that this might be what Nick himself would most wish to do." The film is remarkably faithful to Ray in its stubborn, raw-nerved quest for something confrontational, honest and true. In some ways, it is the ultimate Nick Ray cinematic experience. If Ray wanted to make a film of his own personal anguish, Wenders helped him achieve his goal in almost unbearably direct form.

Much of the movie takes place in the loft where Nick tends to his pain while continuing to work on the editing of *We Can't Go Home Again.* Throughout, Ray is clearly in agony. You hear his groans and yells and see the pain tugging at the side of his mouth. You can feel it deep inside his bones. His wisps of white hair, cadaverous face and creaking body movements are heartbreaking, although he still manages to rise to moments of dignity and grace, especially while watching his unfinished film, one leg languorously draped over the other, the still-present cigarette delicately dangling from his hand.

The final scene—the last Ray would ever shoot—was done on a set made to look like a hospital room. Ray is in bed. A black cat sits on the floor beside him. His son Tim is present, acting as assistant cameraman. Dressed in a red shirt, Ray weakly discusses his condition and recites some lines from *King Lear.* His breathing is labored, and he moans, less, it seems, in pain than as an actor's exercise, an attempt to free himself up, still trying at this late date to conjure something for the camera. Suddenly, he decides that enough is enough. He has no more to give. Wenders agrees. But he insists that Ray be the one to say "Cut." He wants him to draw the cinematic curtain on his own life. Ray weakly, distractedly, obeys. Then he asks Ray to say "Don't cut" and Ray once again follows direction. But then Ray's slack and sickly face pulls together. He looks defiantly into the camera. With all the authority he can muster, he finally says "Cut!" as if he means it, as if he wills it. And the screen goes black.

Nicholas Ray died on June 16, 1979, roughly a month after completing his work on *Lightning Over Water*. Years earlier, he dreamt that he would never finish another film—but he beat that prophecy, insofar as *Lightning Over Water* is his film. And while *We Can't Go Home Again* remains incomplete, a new version of the film exists in a work print, sitting in Susan Ray's garage in upstate New York, and it may still see the light of day. Meanwhile, since Ray's death, the Cannes version of *We Can't Go Home Again* has only gained in emotional impact.

Ray's personal life did not end with anywhere near as much closure. He remained estranged from his son Tony, even after Tony's divorce from Gloria Grahame in 1976, and even though Tony had followed in his father's footsteps, becoming a relatively successful assistant director who worked on several films with Paul Mazursky. Although Ray experienced some reconciliation with his second son, Tim, their relationship remained strained. "Nick always seemed hard on him for some reason. He snapped at him a couple of times and I couldn't understand it," says Tom Farrell, who once told Tim that Ray was like a father to him. "I didn't realize how crushing that would be for Tim to hear that. He said to me, 'I didn't feel like he was my father.' Nick was absent for much of his life."

"To his own sons, he was a terrible father," says Susan Ray. "I don't think he knew how. I don't think he was able." Ironically, while Ray was never able to resolve his issues about being a father—or a son—he would become a paternal figure to so many. "You become what you need," believes Susan.

"I think he felt guilty for his gifts," she says. "It's like Prometheus stealing the fire. He had so much talent, it was a huge theft. It was a theft from the gods. And there's a kind of natural guilt that goes along with that. Plus there was a dead father. A father who died of alcoholism. That really leaves a mark."

Throughout his life, Ray abandoned himself to his more passionate instincts. And despite his many failings, he defined a certain kind of bravery. "He didn't give in, not a minute, not on an inch of film," said Elia Kazan. "Even in his last terrible misery, he clung to every 'foot' of life, the film on which his living was being preserved. You may call it phony, and I will understand why. But I call it heroic. In a way, I thought, he was speaking for all artists." Ironically, many critics would come to see Ray as a greater filmmaker than his old friend and rival Kazan, and Kazan did not disagree: "He went 'all the way,' and I did not. I was more disciplined, more in control, more cautious, more bourgeois. Perhaps, I thought, he's been more of an artist, more of a gambler."

In some ways, Ray was the Melville hero that actress Betsy Blair saw in him back in the days of her great Hollywood parties. He became his own Romantic figure, flinging himself recklessly through time, creating and destroying all along the way. He maintained an intense, self-dramatizing regard and respect for his feelings. If *Rebel* aches like kids ache, that's because Ray ached that way. He worked off his pain, struggled against authority and refused to "mature" if that meant feeling less.

During his last years, as he worked on an autobiography, Ray seemed to be testing out elegies for himself. In a fragment titled "I Am Concerned with the State . . ." he told of a schoolteacher he met while preparing the script for *Rebel*. The teacher explained that a juvenile delinquent was "merely a boy or girl who has fallen out of attention." With humor, regret and pride, Ray added, "Sixty-some years is a long time to be a juvenile delinquent."

The *Rebel* Effect

It has been half a century since *Rebel Without*
a Cause was released. Yet amazingly, the movie's presence can still be felt, not only in the U.S. but around the world. In the years after its debut, *Rebel* became "a worldwide cult phenomenon," according to critic Elliott Stein, and it remains so. Even the most impressionistic attempt to trace the *Rebel* effect is a daunting project, considering the film's wide-ranging and incalculable influence. To this day, even the movie's surface imagery is ubiquitous. Portraits of Dean in his red jacket pop up on the walls of diners, record shops, clothing stores, anyplace that wants to designate itself as hip and youth-oriented, or wants to cloak itself in the glamour of the 1950s or Hollywood. In many ways, Dean's image, like those of Marilyn Monroe and Elvis Presley, has become a Hollywood-bred symbol of the world's common culture.

Even the movie's title has become part of everyday vernacular. According to *Brewer's Twentieth-Century Dictionary of Phrase and Fable,* "the label 'rebel without a cause' is resuscitated by the press with each new wave of teenage rebellion. . . . It was even used by the National Westminster Bank in an attempt to persuade teenagers that opening a bank account is a cool thing to do." It has become shorthand to describe everyone from Colombian guerrillas to Hezbollah suicide bombers to impoverished South African teenagers to recalcitrant movie stars.

Tracing the *Rebel* effect is further complicated by the fact that each successive generation has adopted and adapted the film to suit its own rebellious needs. Columnist George Will blamed *Rebel* for the youthful unrest that convulsed the country in the 1960s. "In *Rebel*," he wrote, "Dean played himself—a mumbling, arrested-development adolescent—to perfection. Feeling mightily sorry for himself as a victim, his character prefigured the whiny, alienated, nobody-understands-me pouting that the self-absorbed youth of the sixties considered a political stance." Director Peter Bogdanovich believes that *Rebel* was "pretty irresponsible" and "gave birth to an entire generation of self-indulgent teenagers. It had tremendous impact."

In some ways, Will and Bogdanovich are right. *Rebel* did presage the protests of the 1960s. "It gave voice to something that was in the adolescent behavior that had not been heard by the older generation," says director Arthur Penn. "It was ten years in advance of what would happen in the sixties between youth and parents," says director Bernardo Bertolucci, who showed *Rebel* to his trio of young actors in *The Dreamers*—a film about the 1960s—to help prepare them for their roles.

As the 1960s gave way to the '70s and '80s, *Rebel* also connected to the self-possession of the time. It forecast the softening of gender lines in the 21st century. And it was embraced by slackers in the '80s and '90s, who were defiantly opposed to getting up from their couches, making them modern equivalents of causeless rebels. As the director of *Slacker*, filmmaker Richard Linklater, once mused: "Maybe teenager land hasn't changed much at all in the 40 years since the moment in Nicholas Ray's *Rebel Without a Cause* where Jim and Buzz stare over the edge of the cliff."

Of course, *Rebel Without a Cause* did not emerge in a vacuum. Hollywood was already taking a few tentative steps in exploring the phenomenon of a burgeoning youth culture. *Blackboard Jungle* and Marlon Brando's motorcycle film *The Wild One* preceded *Rebel*, but both films represented a repressive response to the new generation that was emerging. *Rebel* was—and always will be—something more. *Rebel* captured America on the cusp of a new age. It played a key role in the transformation and elevation of adolescents to rebels in their own mind, even making room for gay people in its vision. (Ironically, psychologist Robert Lindner, the author of the book *Rebel Without a Cause*, saw homosexuality as "a reaction of nonconformity, a rebellion of the personality," tying gayness directly to the concept of the rebel.) Sociologist Orrin Klapp wrote that in *Rebel*, Dean would "crystallize a social type," becoming the embodiment of the alienated teenager. According to writer David Dalton, Dean was "the Abraham

Lincoln of adolescence. He freed the teens. He portrayed a teenager so realistically that he became the model for all of the pop culture that followed."

Although teen movies were relatively rare before *Rebel,* a flood of "teensploitation" films followed hot on its heels. Some of these films would provide paychecks for the young cast members of *Rebel.* Sal Mineo played young delinquents in *Crime in the Streets* (1956), *Rock, Pretty Baby* (1956), *Dino* (1957) and *The Young Don't Cry* (1957). Corey Allen reprised his role as a Buzz-like gang leader in *Juvenile Jungle* (1958); Jack Grinnage played a teenage inmate in *Riot in Juvenile Prison* (1959) and saved Elvis Presley's life in *King Creole;* and Steffi Sidney portrayed a teenage gang member in *The Hot Angel* (1958). As Hollywood scrambled to exploit the suddenly lucrative teen market, it would grind out one low-budget movie after another from lurid "JD" movies (*The Delinquents, The Young Stranger, High School Confidential*) to hot-rod movies (*Dragstrip Riot, T-Bird Gang, The Wild Ride*), "bad girl" movies featuring conflicted gang molls like the one Natalie Wood played in *Rebel* (*Dragstrip Girl; Hot Rod Girl; Eighteen and Anxious; Live Fast, Die Young*), rock and roll musicals (*Don't Knock the Rock, Untamed Youth, Rock Around the Clock*) and even teenage horror and science fiction (*I Was a Teenage Werewolf, Teenagers from Outer Space, The Blob*).

But while none of these cheap knockoffs would come close to scaling the poetic heights of *Rebel Without a Cause,* the movie would inspire the filmmakers who later reinvigorated American cinema with the director-driven films of the 1960s and 1970s. Dennis Hopper's *Easy Rider* evoked the counterculture of the late 1960s the way *Rebel* had captured the restless youth of the 1950s. *The Graduate* and *Bonnie and Clyde* both owe their style and attitude to *Rebel.* ("Clyde would have been a perfect part for James Dean," says critic J. Hoberman, who points out that *Bonnie and Clyde* has "everything to do with 1950s delinquency films like *The Wild One* and *Rebel Without a Cause.*") Martin Scorsese, whom critic Anthony Lane calls "Ray's most forceful heir," brought the frenetic energy, ritualized violence and bravura camera work of *Rebel* to many of his films, from *Mean Streets* to *Gangs of New York.* The influence of *Rebel* can be seen in Bogdanovich's *The Last Picture Show,* which ends with an homage to Plato's death; in the aimlessly cruising teenagers in George Lucas's *American Graffiti;* and the teenage gangs inhabiting a world of their own in Francis Ford Coppola's *The Outsiders* and *Rumblefish.* Terrence Malick's 1973 film *Badlands* (featuring a Dean-like performance by Martin Sheen) was based on the murder spree of Charlie Starkweather, a serial killer who imitated and idolized James Dean, and in turn inspired the song "Nebraska" by Dean fan Bruce Springsteen—just one example of how Dean's influence almost genetically passes down through the culture.

As a teacher of director Jim Jarmusch (*Stranger Than Paradise*), Nicholas Ray himself would have a direct influence on the independent film movement that arose in the 1980s, but *Rebel*'s influence can be seen most specifically in the films of directors who are drawn to youth the way Ray was. The relationship between Keanu Reeves and River Phoenix in Gus Van Sant's *My Own Private Idaho* echoes the bond between Jim and Plato in *Rebel.* (Reeves also plays Dean's role in Paula Abdul's video "Rush Rush," a takeoff on *Rebel*, with Abdul as Natalie Wood.) *Elephant,* Van Sant's empathetic take on high school life, was created through hours of rehearsals and improvisations with its young cast, recalling Ray's sessions at the Chateau Marmont. At one point, photographer and filmmaker Larry Clark (*Kids, Bully*)—whose films mirror *Rebel*'s methods with a fin de siècle twist—considered directing a biography of Ray. When screenwriter Kevin Williamson produced a show about teens for television, he alluded to the huge influence *Rebel* had on all teen culture to follow when he called the series *Dawson's Creek* after *Rebel*'s Dawson High School. And more recently, *The O.C.*'s Ryan (Benjamin McKenzie), the troubled new kid in town, whom we meet in Juvenile Hall on the premiere episode, appears to have borrowed his white T-shirt—and rebellious attitude—directly from James Dean.

Ironically, though *Rebel* had no rock music on its soundtrack, the film's sensibility—and especially the defiant attitude and effortless cool of James Dean—would have a great impact on rock. The music media would often see Dean and rock as inextricably linked. The industry trade magazine *Music Connection* even went so far as to call Dean "the first rock star." Elvis Presley saw *Rebel* so many times he had memorized the dialogue. He often seemed to be channeling Dean's persona with his shy, mumbly, sexually charged swagger. Among the rockers who also borrowed some of their style from Dean were Gene Vincent and Eddie Cochran (who died in a car crash in 1960).

As rock music became the defining expression of youth in the 1960s, the influence of *Rebel* was conveyed to a new generation. Growing up in the 1950s, Bob Dylan repeatedly saw *Rebel* and once showed up unannounced at one o'clock in the morning at the Winslows' farm in Fairmount, Indiana, to see where Dean grew up. (In Don McLean's song "American Pie," a coded history of rock and roll, "the jester," usually interpreted as Dylan, wears "a coat he borrowed from James Dean.") On their car-culture concept album *Little Deuce Coupe*, the Beach Boys mythologized Dean as a hot-rod martyr in the song "A Young Man Is Gone" ("And they say that he'll / Be known for evermore / As the Rebel Without a Cause"). In England, where *Rebel* was banned for teens until 1968, Dean's persona in the film would inspire British teen idols Cliff Richard, Billy Fury and Adam Faith. "I just felt I wanted to be James Dean," said Faith after seeing *Rebel*. Even John Lennon said of one of the original members of the Beatles: "[Stuart Sutcliffe] was really our leader, and he was really into the James Dean thing. He idolized him. Stuart died young before we made the big time, but I suppose you could say that without Jimmy Dean, the Beatles would have never existed."

In the 1970s, Springsteen, who shared Dean's love of cars and rebellion, was marketed to the next generation of rock fans as "a '50s hood in the James Dean mold," according to *Time* magazine, and reportedly carried a biography of Dean on the road with him for a year. When David Bowie, who idolized Dean, created his decade-defining character of Ziggy Stardust, he was dubbed "James Dean with a guitar." In "Walk on the Wild Side," Lou Reed would sing of Warhol superstar Jackie Curtis, who "thought she was James Dean for a day." David Essex turned Dean's name into a rock and roll chant in his anthem "Rock On." The chorus of the Eagles' 1974 song "James Dean"—"You were too fast to live, too young to die"—alludes to a line from Nicholas Ray's *Knock on Any Door* that would forever be associated with Dean after he died. Malcolm McLaren and Vivienne Westwood's King's Road fetish clothing shop Sex, which set the style for British punk, was actually called "Too Fast to Live, Too Young to Die" when they first opened it.

In the last few decades, Dean would persist as a symbol of rebellion for alternative rock and hip-hop. Morrissey filmed his video for "Suedehead" in Dean's hometown of Fairmount and wrote a worshipful biography of the actor called *James Dean Is Not Dead*. Kurt Cobain, who sputtered the halting lyrics of "Smells Like Teen Spirit" like a tongue-tied Jim Stark, would be compared to James Dean even before he joined the pantheon of stars who died young. Chuck D of Public Enemy (whose song "Rebel Without a Pause" appears on his pioneering rap album *It Takes a Nation of Millions To Hold Us Back*) called fellow rapper Tupac Shakur "the James Dean of our times. Basically a rebel without a cause." Film critic Andrew Sarris wrote of Eminem, who was given *Rebel* to watch in preparation for his performance in *8 Mile*, "I have to go back to James Dean in Elia Kazan's *East of Eden* and Nicholas Ray's *Rebel Without a Cause* in 1955 to find a comparably jolting piece of male aggressiveness coupled with bottled-up vulnerability."

Over the decades since its release, *Rebel*'s effect has spread far beyond the borders of America's popular culture. The influence of *Rebel* can be seen in a number of French films from François Truffaut's *400 Blows* to Jean-Luc Godard's *Breathless* as well as in the personas of such Gallic pop stars as Johnny Hallyday and Sylvie Vartan. Reflecting on the characters in *Rebel*, French critic and director Eric Rohmer wrote: "Their reasons are our reasons, their honor our honor, their madness ours. . . . By merit, they have acquired the dignity of tragic heroes." At one time, France even had a cable channel called Canal Jimmy, inspired by Dean—whose influence can never be separated from *Rebel*. According to the channel's owner, Michel Thoulouze, he named the channel after Dean "because he was the symbol of . . . jeans, T-shirts, muscle cars, the road." Thoulouze underscored the binding effect *Rebel* had on several generations when he said, "Today's fathers and sons share the same dream, wear the same T-shirt, so I created the T-shirt channel." In postwar West Germany *Rebel* inspired such films as *Die Halbstarken* (1956), starring Germany's James Dean, Horst Buchholz, in which leather-jacketed gang members rode bicycles instead of cars. "Every time I go to Europe I remember that James Dean never saw Europe, but yet I see his face everywhere . . . windows of the Champs Elysées, discos in the south of Spain, restaurants in Sweden, T-shirts in Moscow," said Dennis Hopper.

In Brazil, *Rebel*'s Portuguese title *Juventude Transviada* (Wayward Youth) would enter the language as a term to describe troubled kids. In Asia, James Dean would be idolized with feverish devotion. There is a Japanese brand of cigarettes called "Dean," and Dean's image has been used to sell electronics and welcome visitors to an international AIDS conference. Japanese businessman Seita Ohnishi, said to be the world's biggest James Dean fan, erected a $50,000 monument to Dean in Cholame, California, near the site of his death. Japanese director Nagisa Oshima's film *Cruel Story of Youth* has been called a Japanese *Rebel Without a Cause*. The title of Hong Kong filmmaker Wong Kar-Wai's *Days of Being Wild* (1990) is borrowed from the Chinese release title of *Rebel*. The groundbreaking films of Taiwanese director Tsai Ming Liang, which evoke the feelings of that country's disaffected youth, revive the image of Dean. In Liang's 1992 film *Rebels of the Neon God*, an adolescent antihero stares admiringly at a life-size cardboard cutout of Dean from *Rebel*, and in *The River* (1997), the troubled young protagonist has pictures of Dean plastered on his bedroom wall.

Of course, *Rebel*'s effect cannot be separated from the grinding wheels of marketing. *Rebel* would also have a big impact on commerce as well as art. *Rebel*'s box-office success helped identify a teen market that would soon have advertisers salivating for the chance to sell them everything from pop music to cars to clothing. The word *teenager*, coined originally as a marketing term, had existed for only a little more than a decade when *Rebel* was made, and advertisers had no idea at first how to sell to these suddenly prosperous new consumers. *Rebel* not only helped to define the tastes of this market but also to drive them. It was one of the first films to successfully use product placement aimed at teenagers—one of its more unfortunate legacies. After an Ace comb showed up in the film, sales skyrocketed. *Rebel* is said to have also caused a surge in sales of T-shirts and blue jeans.

After his death, Dean's image became a staple of advertising that continues to this day. *Forbes* magazine ranked Dean as one of the top money-makers among dead celebrities, still raking in more than $5 million in licensing and merchandising fees a year, even though his estate gets no royalties from his films. According to Forbes, "Were it not for the worldwide licensing of Dean's image to sell everything from jeans to eyewear to watches, pop culture might have forgotten this '50s icon. After all, Dean only made three major Hollywood movies. But his look, timeless in its coolness, is a major draw for advertisers looking to reach both a young demographic and nostalgic baby boomers." Dean's image has been used to hawk Hamilton watches, Lee Jeans, Franklin Mint collectibles, American Greetings cards, Converse sneakers, and clothes by the Gap and Barneys. A James Dean commemorative stamp issued by the U.S. Postal Service in 1996 was one of the best-selling stamps of all time.

• • •

Many aspects of *Rebel* and the Dean persona remain the object of fascination, mystery and fetish. His red jacket is an especially potent symbol, and like the movie, its meaning shifts with each new decade. While the jacket may have once represented Dean's passion, as the decades passed the jacket came to represent a quieter kind of rebellion, a hipper dispassion. It became the outward sign of an unruffled interior, an ironic detachment, a sexy superiority. In the 1980s, it transmogrified into Michael Jackson's red leather jacket in his "Beat It" video, which notably focused on street gangs.

Although costume designer Moss Mabry claims three red jackets were made for the film, no one knows where they are now. Dean ceremoniously gave one to Natalie Wood on *Rebel*'s last day of shooting. *Rebel* composer Leonard Rosenman says that Dean gave him one. Another friend of Dean's, performer Sammy Davis Jr., claimed that he had one. And there was the wild rumor that Dean threw one in the back of his Porsche Spyder on the afternoon he crashed. But apparently none of these jackets has survived.

As for the Porsche Spyder itself, it too became an object of nearly cult devotion. After Dean's accident, car customizer George Barris purchased the wreckage of Dean's silver Porsche Spyder for $2,500 and sent it around the country as a lesson in car safety. Ominous occurrences connected with the car gave rise to the idea that it was cursed. "We called it the curse of the James Dean Death Car," says Barris. A fire broke out in a garage where it was being stored. A driver of a truck transporting the car was reportedly crushed to death when it fell off the back on top of him. A man who bought the car's transmission was supposedly killed in an accident. At one show, the car rolled off the platform and broke someone's leg, and someone trying to steal the steering wheel broke his arm. Finally, after appearing at a show in Florida, the car was loaded on a truck to take it to Los Angeles, but when the truck arrived on the West Coast, the Spyder was gone. Its mysterious disappearance has never been resolved.

Even after fifty years, Dean still inspires legions of devoted fans, the most extreme of which are often called "Deaners." James Hopgood, an anthropologist who has studied the Deaners, has compared the phenomenon to a religious cult with its own "theology." The Deaner belief system, according to Hopgood, is based on certain core values devotees identify with Dean, including "creativity in the arts, courage and daring, eternal youth and beauty, rebellion against authority, individualism and 'lone-wolfism,' self-seeking introspection, and the 'common person.'" Every year on the anniversary of Dean's death, thousands of Deaners from around the world make pilgrimages to his hometown of Fairmount, Indiana, to take part in rituals celebrating his life and work.

Dean would also inspire reverence from a wide range of artists and writers, especially those who were blurring the divide between high and low culture, such as Ray Johnson and Andy Warhol. "James Dean was the perfect embodiment of an eternal struggle," wrote Warhol, who painted Dean in his *Rebel* pose. "It might be innocence struggling with experience, youth with age, or man with his image. But in every aspect his struggle was a mirror to a generation of rebels without a cause. His anguish was exquisitely genuine on and off the screen; his moments of joy were rare and precious. He is not our hero because he was perfect, but because he perfectly represented the damaged but beautiful soul of our time." Poet Frank O'Hara shocked the public when he published a series of elegies for James Dean after his death. "The James Dean necrophilia had penetrated even the upper levels of culture," wrote poet Turner Cassity in a letter to *Life* magazine.

After Dean's death, one actor after another was crowned by fan magazines as the "new James Dean," including Dennis Hopper, Steve McQueen, Paul Newman, Dean Stockwell, Anthony Perkins and Warren Beatty. In 1983, *Rolling Stone* put Sean Penn on its cover and declared him "the next James Dean." There have also been female James Deans (as Angelina Jolie has been called), French James Deans (Gérard Philipe, Alain Delon), British James Deans (Christopher Jones, Terence Stamp, David McCallum), Polish James Deans (Zbigniew Cybulski), Brazilian James Deans (Caio Blat), Mexican James Deans (Gael García Bernal), Kazakh James Deans (Olzhas Nusuppaev) and Japanese James Deans (Akagi Keiichiro, Yujiro Ishihara). Of course, Dean's influence on actors goes beyond mere labeling. "James Dean's acting flies in the face of fifty years of filmmaking; each gesture, attitude, each mimicry is a slap at the psychological tradition," said François Truffaut. Many actors have specifically pointed to Dean as an inspiration. Johnny Depp once stayed in the room at the Iroquois Hotel where Dean once lived in an attempt to channel his spirit (just as Dean once stayed in a room Sarah Bernhardt occupied hoping to feel her presence). "If Marlon Brando changed the way people acted, then James Dean changed the way people *lived.* He was the greatest actor who ever lived. He was simply a genius," said Martin Sheen. "I grew up with the Dean *thing*," said Al Pacino. *"Rebel Without a Cause* had a very powerful effect on me."

In the fifty years since its release, *Rebel's* potency shows no signs of diminishing. *Rebel* was named one of the Top 100 films of all time by the American Film Institute, whose criteria included cultural impact, historical significance and critical recognition. It was among the first fifty films added to the National Film Registry by the Library of Congress. It is popularly cited in most polls of significant films in the popular press: one of the "50 Greatest Movies on TV and Video" according to *TV Guide,* and one of the "100 Greatest Movies" of all time, according to *Entertainment Weekly,* whose critic called it "the arrival of a true teenage sensibility in the pop culture" and "the film that lives up to the James Dean mystique." Dean himself was chosen by the American Film Institute as one of the 25 Greatest Male Screen Legends.

When asked to explain the movie's enduring power, screenwriter Stewart Stern said that the film was "a plea for compassion. That's why kids love it." According to Stern, "I think one of the things that [*Rebel*] talked about was love, a real need for connection. And for the recognition that everything that people condemn in us as some kind of nefarious behavior—experimental behavior, dangerous behavior—is absolutely pure, sweet, innocent reaching out."

New Yorker critic Anthony Lane wrote that *Rebel* "is not just a portrait of adolescence; it breathes haltingly, with adolescent lungs," and that was true of Nicholas Ray's best films: they are living, breathing entities. They seem to have nervous systems. Clearly, something remarkable happened on that *Rebel* set, especially between Ray and Dean. They gave each other the courage to strike out for something they had only sensed, and they succeeded in giving form to the dream life of teenagers. Despite their lapses in judgment, their power plays and manipulations, Dean and Ray set out to find something new and true—without a clear direction, perhaps, but never without a cause.

Notes

CHAPTER ONE. *Birth of a Rebel*

PAGE

1 *In the early 1950s:* Norman Lloyd, authors' interview, 11/7/03; Saul Chaplin, *The Golden Age of Movie Musicals and Me,* pp. 64–68; and Betsy Blair, *The Memory of All That: Love and Politics in New York, Hollywood, and Paris,* pp. 145–60.

1 *Blair remembers:* Betsy Blair, authors' interview, 7/23/03.

1 *"There was a little slope":* Betsy Blair, authors' interview, 7/23/03.

2 *Earlier that summer:* Bernard Eisenschitz, *Nicholas Ray: An American Journey,* p. 187.

2 *He found Grahame and his barely teenage son "in bed together":* Gavin Lambert, authors' interview, 9/19/03.

2 *Ray exploded in fury:* Vincent Curcio, *Suicide Blonde,* p. 96.

2 *Ray claimed he married Grahame:* Eisenschitz, *Nicholas Ray,* p. 109.

3 *he forced Tony:* Curcio, *Suicide Blonde,* p. 98.

3 *In the end:* Eisenschitz, *Nicholas Ray,* p. 192.

3 *Ray never played the recording:* Curcio, *Suicide Blonde,* p. 98.

3 *"In the circle":* Norman Lloyd, authors' interview, 11/7/03.

3 *"I remember asking him":* Gavin Lambert, authors' interview, 9/19/03.

3 *"It was all":* Betsy Blair, authors' interview, 7/23/03.

4 *Throughout the development of the script:* Stewart Stern, authors' interview, 9/6/03.

4 *"He should never":* Gavin Lambert, authors' interview, 9/19/03.

4 *"Turn trauma into drama":* Patricia Bosworth, *Marlon Brando,* p. 57.

4 *His family was part:* Michel Ciment, *Conversations with Losey,* p. 11.

4 *Ray's father was a contractor:* Susan Ray, ed., *I Was Interrupted: Nicholas Ray on Making Movies,* pp. 22–23.

5 *"Nick didn't have a father":* Susan Ray, authors' interview, 12/29/03.

5 *In the year Tony Ray was born:* Eisenschitz, *Nicholas Ray,* pp. 39–45.

6 *Kazan was impressed:* Elia Kazan, *A Life,* p. 790.

6 *"For a man who had not always shown himself":* John Houseman, *Front and Center,* p. 205.

6 *Schary's girlfriend had already been cast:* Maureen O'Hara, authors' interview, 2/10/05, and O'Hara, *'Tis Herself,* p. 126.

7 *"Brought up in the Depression":* Houseman, *Front and Center,* pp. 178–79.

8 *Ray later told Gavin Lambert:* Gavin Lambert, *Mainly About Lindsay Anderson,* p. 87.

PAGE

8   *After nearly a decade in Hollywood:* Stewart Stern, authors' interview, 9/6/03.

8   *As he explained to his agent:* "Interview with Nicholas Ray," *Camera Three*, CBS, 1977.

8   *In Memphis:* "Our Vicious Young Hoodlums: Is There Any Hope?" *Newsweek*, 9/6/54, p. 43.

8   *Between 1948 and 1953:* Richard Clendenen, "Why Teen-Agers Go Wrong," *U.S. News & World Report*, 9/17/54, p. 80.

8   *"We have the spectacle of an entire city terrorized":* Victor Navasky, *Naming Names*, p. xi.

9   *"the glitter of fulfillment":* Geoffrey O'Brien, *Hardboiled America: Lurid Paperbacks and the Masters of Noir*, p. 166.

9   *The word* teenager: Thomas Hine, *The Rise and Fall of the American Teenager*, p. 8.

9   *"The celluloid strip":* "Interview with Nicholas Ray," *Camera Three*.

9   *His growing passion:* Eisenschitz, *Nicholas Ray*, p. 231.

10   *"There are six films":* "Interview with Nicholas Ray," *Camera Three*.

10   *"I wish Buñuel":* Michael Goodwin and Naomi Wise, "Nicholas Ray: Rebel!" *Take One*, Jan. 1977, p. 10.

10   *"slum area rationalizations":* Nicholas Ray, "The Blind Run," 9/18/54, files on *Rebel Without a Cause*, Warner Bros. Archives, Cinema-Television Library, University of Southern California, Los Angeles, p. 11.

10   *Instead, he wanted to focus:* "Interview with Nicholas Ray," *Camera Three*.

10   *Warner Brothers had just begun:* Thomas Pryor, "Warners to Seek Fresh Film Faces," *New York Times*, 2/4/55, p. 17.

10   *The studio suggested:* Eisenschitz, *Nicholas Ray*, p. 231.

11   *Warners then handed:* "Interview with Nicholas Ray," *Camera Three*.

11   *Ray drove to the Warners lot:* Eisenschitz, *Nicholas Ray*, p. 232.

11   *For forty-five minutes:* Eisenschitz, *Nicholas Ray*, pp. 231–32.

11   *After he had performed:* "Interview with Nicholas Ray," *Camera Three*.

12   *At 9 a.m.:* "Interview with Nicholas Ray," *Camera Three*.

12   *Ray chose thirty-nine-year-old David Weisbart:* Nicholas Ray, "Story into Script," *Sight and Sound*, Autumn 1956, p. 70.

12   *"He was a gentleman":* Dennis Stock, authors' interview, 3/31/05.

13   *But when Weisbart first encountered:* Ray, "Story into Script," p. 70.

13   *According to Gavin Lambert:* Gavin Lambert, authors' interview, 9/19/03.

13   *Lindner had been paid:* memo from Albert Taylor to Jake Wilk, 2/8/54, files on *Rebel Without a Cause*, Warner Bros. Archives.

13   *As far back as 1947:* files on *Rebel Without a Cause*, Warner Bros. Archives.

13   *But Ray continued to feel:* Eisenschitz, *Nicholas Ray*, p. 231.

13   *While working on* Rebel: Ray, "Story Into Script," p. 74.

CHAPTER TWO. *Seducing Dean*

15   *nobody specific in mind:* "Interview with Nicholas Ray," *Camera Three*, CBS, 1977.

15   *"conflict of violent eagerness":* Donald Spoto, *Rebel*, p. 212.

15 *Right on the Warners lot:* Susan Ray, ed., *I Was Interrupted: Nicholas Ray on Making Movies,* p. 112.

15 *One afternoon, Kazan invited Ray:* "Interview with Nicholas Ray," *Camera Three.*

15 *he was introduced both to Rosenman:* Susan Ray, *I Was Interrupted,* p. 108.

16 *Although Ray hardly spoke:* Susan Ray, *I Was Interrupted,* p. 108.

16 *And as far as the critical:* David Dalton, *James Dean: Mutant King,* p. 172.

16 *Ray began hearing stories about Dean:* Susan Ray, *I Was Interrupted,* p. 108.

16 *Dean exacted his revenge:* Susan Ray, *I Was Interrupted,* p. 108.

16 *One day, he asked Ray:* Susan Ray, *I Was Interrupted,* p. 108.

16 *"I didn't pick Jimmy for Rebel":* Dalton, *James Dean,* p. 222.

17 *Dean later claimed:* Dalton, *James Dean,* p. 9.

17 *"His father was a monster":* Spoto, *Rebel,* p. 172.

17 *During a statewide oratory contest:* Howard Thompson, "Another Dean Hits the Big League," *New York Times,* 3/13/55, Section II, p. 5.

17 *He would go on to appear regularly:* Paul Alexander, *Boulevard of Broken Dreams,* p. 37.

17 *"Why don't you become a lawyer":* Richard Moore, "Lone Wolf," *Modern Screen,* August 1955, p. 75.

17 *So he took the advice:* Joe Hyams, *James Dean: Little Boy Lost,* p. 43.

18 *For the rest of his life:* Spoto, *Rebel,* p. 160.

18 *In a revealing interview with a New York Times reporter:* Thompson, "Another Dean Hits the Big League," p. 5.

18 *"I don't know what's inside me":* William Bast, *James Dean,* p. 66.

18 *"Dean was scarcely at the Studio at all":* Dalton, *James Dean,* p. 92.

19 *"He dropped his voice to a cathedral hush":* Elia Kazan, *A Life,* p. 538.

19 *Dean bought his first cycle:* Alexander, *Boulevard of Broken Dreams,* p. 38.

19 *He left countless messages:* Truman Capote, "The Duke in His Domain," *New Yorker,* 11/9/57, p. 87.

19 *"Be who you are, not who I am":* Marlon Brando, *Songs My Mother Taught Me,* p. 224.

19 *Dean appeared in sixteen television plays in 1953 alone:* Spoto, *Rebel,* p. 123.

19 *"He would do his homework":* Betsy Palmer, authors' interview, 2/21/05.

20 *"The movies were still portraying kids":* Dalton, *James Dean,* p. 105.

20 *"quality of adolescent boil":* Arthur Penn, authors' interview, 5/25/04.

20 *Leonard Rosenman was a serious avant-garde composer:* Leonard Rosenman, "Jimmy Dean: Giant Legend, Cult Rebel," *Los Angeles Times Calendar,* 12/18/77, p. 70.

20 *According to the composer: James Dean: The First American Teenager,* film directed by Ray Connolly, ZIV International, 1975.

20 *He asked for piano lessons:* Rosenman, "Jimmy Dean: Giant Legend, Cult Rebel," p. 70.

21 *"Jimmy had a severe identity problem": James Dean: The First American Teenager.*

21 *"Their crazy world":* Stewart Stern, authors' interview, 9/6/03.

21 *Then, on opening night:* Dalton, *James Dean* p. 152.

Notes

PAGE

21 *After Brando turned down:* Patricia Bosworth, *Marlon Brando,* p. 93.

21 *Kazan found the actor dressed:* Kazan, *A Life,* p. 534.

22 *"He had a grudge against all fathers":* Dalton, *James Dean,* p. 162.

22 *Together they explored:* Randall Riese, *The Unabridged James Dean,* p. 281.

22 *Once when a scene was not going particularly well:* Kazan, *A Life,* p. 535.

22 *When Dean was having difficulty:* Hyams, *James Dean,* p. 152.

22 *"Directing him was like directing the faithful Lassie":* Spoto, *Rebel,* p. 165.

22 *what he called Kazan's "gimmicks":* Ronald Martinetti, *The James Dean Story,* p. 93.

23 *"A director shows the way":* Dalton, *James Dean,* p. 232.

23 *Dean and Ray's mutual seduction shifted into higher gear:* Susan Ray, *I Was Interrupted* p. 109.

23 *As soon as Ray opened his door:* Tom Farrell, authors' interview, 9/20/04.

23 *From the ground:* Susan Ray, *I Was Interrupted,* p. 109.

24 *"Kazan had told Dean":* "Interview with Nicholas Ray," *Camera Three.*

24 *Director Vincente Minnelli wanted him:* John Houseman, *Front and Center,* pp. 456–57.

24 *Meanwhile, the magazine press:* Alexander, *Boulevard of Broken Dreams,* p. 180.

24 *"I leveled with him all the time":* Martinetti, *The James Dean Story,* p. 121.

25 *"Started at 1 p.m. with Bop":* Army Archerd, "Just for Variety," *Daily Variety,* 11/23/54, p. 2.

25 *"To work with Jimmy meant exploring his nature":* Susan Ray, *I Was Interrupted,* p. 109.

25 *"It was exploratory on both sides":* Val Holley, *James Dean: The Biography,* p. 244.

25 *One afternoon, he told playwright Clifford Odets:* Susan Ray, *I Was Interrupted,* p. 110.

25 *But Dean was disappointed to discover that Shulman's car:* Martinetti, *The James Dean Story,* p. 122; Ray, "Story into Script," pp. 72–73.

26 *When he arrived in New York:* Susan Ray, *I Was Interrupted,* pp. 110–11.

26 *Dean was known:* Mike Connolly, "This Was My Friend James Dean," *Modern Screen,* Dec. 1955, p. 80.

26 *"automobile posters":* "Interview with Nicholas Ray," *Camera Three.*

26 *Dean also owned:* Connolly, "This Was My Friend James Dean," p. 80.

26 *Dean's apartment also featured a small porthole window:* John Gilmore, *Live Fast—Die Young: My Life with James Dean,* p. 103.

26 *"pathological desire for tension":* Eisenschitz, *Nicholas Ray,* p. 247.

26 *One afternoon when Dean was especially sullen:* Susan Ray, *I Was Interrupted,* p. 111.

27 *"The drama of his life":* Spoto, *Rebel,* p. 212.

27 *The director introduced Dean to Tony:* Susan Ray, *I Was Interrupted,* p. 111.

27 *"We knew he was Nick Ray's kid":* Bob Heller, authors' interview, 3/29/05.

27 *"One day in a restaurant":* Susan Ray, *I Was Interrupted,* p. 112.

28 *"Jim ordered the food":* Susan Ray, *I Was Interrupted,* pp. 112–13.

28 *On January 4, 1955:* Thomas Pryor, "Film Assignment for Jane Russell," *New York Times,* 1/4/55, p. 24.

CHAPTER THREE. *Child Star*

29 *Wood managed to get a copy:* Gavin Lambert, *Natalie Wood: A Life,* p. 86.

30 *when she read it, she wept:* Suzanne Finstad, *Natasha: The Biography of Natalie Wood,* p. 161.

30 *"I felt exactly":* Bob Lardine, "A Star Is Born Again," *New York Sunday News Magazine,* 2/11/79, p. 26.

30 *who filled her daughter's head with paranoid fantasies:* Lambert, *Natalie Wood,* pp. 80–81.

30 *though only after her mother:* Finstad, *Natasha,* p. 43.

30 *"I was playing so many parts":* John Hollowell, "I'm Going to Live My Life," *New York Times,* 3/9/69, p. D13.

30 *Her mother was capable of doing almost anything:* Lambert, *Natalie Wood,* p. 61.

31 *"She was drinking zombies":* Steffi Sidney, authors' interview, 9/5/03.

31 *In 1954, the summer Natalie Wood turned sixteen:* Finstad, *Natasha,* p. 150.

32 *Wood took a curve:* Finstad, *Natasha,* p. 150.

32 *The producers had wanted:* Dick Moore, *Twinkle, Twinkle, Little Star: But Don't Have Sex or Take the Car,* p. 245.

32 *"Like everybody else in Hollywood":* David Dalton, *James Dean: Mutant King,* p. 206.

33 *Wood found Dean attractive:* Finstad, *Natasha,* pp. 158–59.

33 *"Natalie was young":* Val Holley, *James Dean: The Biography,* p. 243.

33 *Despite her inexperience:* Lambert, *Natalie Wood,* p. 85.

33 *But if she thought:* Finstad, *Natasha,* p. 160.

34 *"It was difficult":* Mary Ann Brooks, authors' interview, 1/23/04.

34 *She threatened: Intimate Portrait: Natalie Wood,* Lifetime Television, 1996.

34 *"She thought":* Nick Adams, "The Girl Who Grew Up Too Fast," *Modern Screen,* May 1956, p. 96.

34 *When she finally had her meeting:* Finstad, *Natasha,* p. 164.

34 *Ray was not impressed:* Dalton, *James Dean,* p. 227.

35 *She and her friend:* Jackie Perry, authors' interview, 12/10/03.

35 *One afternoon at the commissary:* Jackie Perry, authors' interview, 12/10/03.

35 *Later in life, Ray would:* Susan Ray, ed., *I Was Interrupted: Nicholas Ray on Making Movies,* p. 9.

35 *According to Gavin Lambert:* Gavin Lambert, authors' interview, 9/19/03.

35 *"I would have done anything":* Joan Collins, *Second Act: An Autobiography,* p. 124.

35 *"When she went after this part":* Mary Ann Brooks, authors' interview, 1/23/04.

35 *Ray mentored Wood:* Finstad, *Natasha,* p. 166.

35 *"He opened the door":* Dick Moore, "A Last Visit with Natalie Wood," *McCall's,* October 1984, p. 56.

Notes

36 *Meanwhile, Dean was pushing for his friend:* Carroll Baker, *Baby Doll,* pp. 99–100, 114.

36 *One day, Ray invited Wood and Perry:* Jackie Perry, authors' interview, 12/10/03.

36 *Despite his doubts:* Finstad, *Natasha,* p. 169.

36 *The test took place:* Lambert, *Natalie Wood,* p. 89; Finstad, *Natasha,* p. 169.

36 *According to Jim Nelson:* Jim Nelson, authors' interview, 12/16/03.

37 *Hopper later said he was called:* Dennis Hopper, "James Dean," *Mirabella,* Nov. 1990, p. 184.

37 *The offer from Warner Brothers:* Hopper, "James Dean," p. 184.

37 *"She told me":* Finstad, *Natasha,* p. 170.

37 *Wood told Hopper:* Lambert, *Natalie Wood,* p. 89; Finstad, *Natasha,* p. 170.

38 *Jackie Perry says:* Jackie Perry, authors' interview, 12/10/03.

38 *According to Dennis Hopper:* Finstad, *Natasha,* p. 173.

38 *Her friend Mary Ann Brooks:* Mary Ann Brooks, authors' interview, 1/23/04.

38 *Later that year:* Finstad, *Natasha,* pp. 173–74.

38 *"In those days":* Faye Nuell Mayo, authors' interview, 9/15/03.

39 *"I didn't even put":* Dalton, *James Dean,* p. 227.

39 *However, Hopper, who read with Mansfield:* Finstad, *Natasha,* pp. 171–72.

39 *Faye Nuell Mayo believes:* Faye Nuell Mayo, authors' interview, 9/15/03.

39 *One night, a frustrated Wood:* Jackie Perry, authors' interview, 12/10/03.

40 *In the hallways of the hospital:* Jackie Perry, authors' interview, 12/10/03.

40 *"I kept saying":* I'm a Stranger Here Myself, October Films, 1974.

40 *"I'm sure that the reason":* Finstad, *Natasha,* p. 177.

40 *When Ray arrived:* Jackie Perry, authors' interview, 12/10/03.

40 *"I was trying":* Finstad, *Natasha,* p. 176.

40 *"He opened his home":* Jackie Perry, authors' interview, 12/10/03.

40 *In later years, both Wood and Ray would tell a similar story:* I'm a Stranger Here Myself; Patricia Reynolds, "Natalie Wood's Own Story," *Pageant,* July 1971, p. 56; "Movie Star into Actress: The Story of Natalie Wood," *Newsweek,* 2/26/62, pp. 54–57.

41 *Dennis Hopper doubts that anyone:* Finstad, *Natasha,* p. 177.

41 *"they made up this story":* Gavin Lambert, authors' interview, 9/19/03.

41 *The real reason Wood called Ray:* Lambert, *Natalie Wood,* p. 90.

41 *When Ray left:* Finstad, *Natasha,* p. 176.

CHAPTER FOUR. *The Script*

42 *"This is all I have":* Michael Goodwin and Naomi Wise, "Nicholas Ray: Rebel!," *Take One,* Jan. 1977, p. 13.

43 *He had an uneasy relationship with writers:* Nicholas Ray, "Story into Script," *Sight and Sound,* Autumn 1956, p. 71.

43 *"Nick would change":* Gavin Lambert, authors' interview, 9/19/03.

43 *The treatment is strong on character relationships and theme:* Nicholas Ray, "The Blind Run," 9/18/54, files on *Rebel Without a Cause,* Warner Bros. Archives, Cinema-Television Library, University of Southern California, Los Angeles.

44   *Ray's close friend John Houseman said:* John Houseman, *Front and Center,* p. 178.

44   *Walter Matthau would:* Norman Lloyd, authors' interview, 11/7/03.

44   *"He was known":* Patrick McGilligan and Paul Buhle, *Tender Comrades,* p. 358.

44   *"To call him inarticulate":* Susan Ray, authors' interview, 12/29/03.

45   *Discussing* Rebel's *hero:* Susan Ray, ed., *I was Interrupted: Nicholas Ray on Making Movies,* pp. 119–20.

45   *Even more significantly, Odets contributed one:* Stewart Stern, authors' interview, 9/5/03.

45   *Dean had screen-tested:* Randall Riese, *The Unabridged James Dean: His Life and Legacy from A to Z,* p. 43.

45   *Although Uris was not his first choice:* Ray, "Story into Script," p. 72.

45   *When Ray made:* Penelope Houston and John Gillett, "Conversations with Nicholas Ray and Joseph Losey," *Sight and Sound,* Autumn 1961, p. 184.

45   *"In listening to these adolescents talk":* Ray, "Story into Script," p. 72.

46   *sought out the advice:* credits, *Los Olvidados,* directed by Luis Buñuel, Ultramar Films, 1950.

46   *donned threadbare clothes:* Luis Buñuel, *My Last Sigh,* p. 199.

46   *Among his most outlandish ideas:* memo from Nicholas Ray to David Weisbart, 10/7/54, files on *Rebel Without a Cause,* Warner Bros. Archives.

46   *"There is no incident":* memo from Nicholas Ray to David Weisbart, 10/18/54, files on *Rebel Without a Cause,* Warner Bros. Archives.

47   *In an October 7 memo:* memo from Nicholas Ray to David Weisbart, 10/7/54, files on *Rebel Without a Cause,* Warner Bros. Archives.

47   *Before beginning to write a treatment:* Leon Uris, "Rayfield," 10/13/54, files on *Rebel Without a Cause,* Warner Bros. Archives.

47   *"one of those quiet 'normal' communities":* Ray, "Story into Script." p. 72.

47   *Dated October 13, 1954:* Uris, "Rayfield."

47   *"slum area rationalizations":* Ray, "The Blind Run," p. 11.

47   *"We have provided":* memo from Nicholas Ray to David Weisbart, 10/18/55, files on *Rebel Without a Cause,* Warner Bros. Archives.

47   *"made me vomit":* Bernard Eisenschitz, *Nicholas Ray: An American Journey,* p. 234.

48   *But he did create:* Leon Uris, *Rebel Without a Cause #2,* 11/1/54, p. 11, files on *Rebel Without a Cause,* Warner Bros. Archives.

48   *Uris wrote that she:* Uris, *Rebel Without a Cause #2,* p. 8.

48   *Ray had admired his book:* Gavin Lambert, authors' interview, 9/19/03.

48   *1947's* The Amboy Dukes: Geoffrey O'Brien, *Hardboiled America: Lurid Paperbacks and the Masters of Noir,* p. 160.

48   *In addition, Shulman had been a schoolteacher:* Ray, "Story into Script," p. 73.

48   *Unlike Uris:* Ray, "Story into Script," p. 73.

48   *Shulman and Ray discussed:* Ray, "Story into Script," p. 73.

49   *A friend of Ray's:* Eisenschitz, *Nicholas Ray,* p. 232.

49   *In addition to a scene:* Silvia Richards and Esther McCoy, *Main Street, Heaventown,* undated manuscript, Esther McCoy Papers, Archives of American Art, Smithsonian Institution, Washington, D.C.

Notes

PAGE

49 *Shulman said the theme:* David Dalton, *James Dean: Mutant King,* p. 226.

49 *Shulman wrote from:* Irving Shulman, *Juvenile Story,* manuscript dated 12/3/54 to 1/26/55, Vernon R. Alden Library Archives and Special Collections, Ohio University, Athens, Ohio.

50 *But Ray said that the real breaking point:* Ray, "Story into Script," p. 73.

50 *"I didn't like working with Ray":* Dalton, *James Dean,* p. 226.

51 *"Nick had practically":* Dalton, *James Dean,* p. 226.

51 *The studio considered abandoning the project:* Ray, "Story into Script," p. 73.

51 *After a brutally competitive game of volleyball:* Charles Nafus, "Writing Rebel," *Austin Chronicle,* 6/16/00, http://www.austinchronicle.com/issues/dispatch/2000-06-16/screens_feature2.html

51 *Ray had seen:* Kent Brown, *The Screenwriter as Collaborator: The Career of Stewart Stern,* p. 94.

51 *"Maybe sometime you want":* Stewart Stern, authors' interview, 9/6/03.

51 *Growing up:* Patrick McGilligan, *Backstory 2: Interviews with Screenwriters of the 1940s and 1950s,* p. 277.

52 *Zukor had married the sister:* Stewart Stern, authors' interview, 9/6/03.

52 *Serious and bookish, Stern found himself:* Stewart Stern, authors' interview, 9/6/03.

53 *Later that week:* Stewart Stern, authors' interview, 9/6/03.

53 *Within a week of meeting Dean and Ray:* Adele Essman, authors' interview, 9/13/03.

53 *Irving Shulman was not working out:* Brown, *The Screenwriter as Collaborator,* p. 94.

53 *And Stern agreed with Ray about the finale:* Stewart Stern, authors' interview, 9/6/03.

53 *Ray agreed and on January 5, 1955:* Warner publicity memo, 1/5/55, files on *Rebel Without a Cause,* Warner Bros. Archives.

54 *"Nick was in agony":* Brown, *The Screenwriter as Collaborator,* p. 95.

54 *Ray told him:* McGilligan, *Backstory 2,* p. 287.

54 *who quickly learned that the project:* Stewart Stern, authors' interview, 9/6/03.

54 *"His bewildered adult":* Brown, *The Screenwriter as Collaborator,* p. 95.

54 *"The thought of writing fast":* Stewart Stern, authors' interview, 9/6/03.

55 *He took extensive notes:* undated Stern Research Notes, Papers of Stewart Stern, University of Iowa, Iowa City, Iowa.

55 *"I couldn't figure out":* McGilligan, *Backstory 2,* p. 287.

55 *He spent one day:* Stewart Stern, authors' interview, 9/6/03.

55 *One night as he was staring at a yellow legal pad:* Nafus, "Writing Rebel," *Austin Chronicle,* June 16, 2000, http://www.austinchronicle.com/issues/dispatch/2000-06-16/screens_feature2.html.

55 *One unproductive afternoon:* Stewart Stern, authors' interview, 9/6/03.

55 *Finally, the script:* Stewart Stern, authors' interview, 9/6/03.

55 *Stern wrote three:* Stewart Stern, *Rebel Without a Cause,* first draft manuscript dated 1/17/55, Papers of Stewart Stern, University of Iowa, Iowa City, Iowa.

56 *When he returns home that night:* Stewart Stern, authors' interview, 9/6/03.

56 *"I thought they were"*: Stewart Stern, authors' interview, 9/6/03.

56 *"The kids themselves"*: Brown, *The Screenwriter as Collaborator,* p. 101.

56 *"not only exciting, but realistic"*: memo from Nicholas Ray to David Weisbart, 2/26/55, files on *Rebel Without a Cause,* Warner Bros. Archives.

56 *While Stern gives credit to Ray*: Stewart Stern, authors' interview, 9/6/03.

56 *"You think when the end of the world comes"*: Stewart Stern, *Rebel Without a Cause* screenplay, 3/25/55, p. 37, Papers of Stewart Stern, University of Iowa, Iowa City, Iowa.

56 *"a single revolution"*: Aristotle, *Poetics,* translated by S. H. Butcher, p. 60.

56 *The "crazy compactness" of the time frame*: Brown, *The Screenwriter as Collaborator,* p. 103.

57 *"We wouldn't be locked"*: Brown, *The Screenwriter as Collaborator,* p. 103.

57 *Stern was so excited*: Stewart Stern, authors' interview, 9/6/03.

57 *He said he had originally written a note to Irving Shulman*: Ray, "Story into Script," p. 73.

57 *"a couple of scenes"*: McGilligan, *Backstory 2,* p. 358.

57 *"It's such an antic"*: Stewart Stern, authors' interview, 9/6/03.

57 *"Philip Yordan was quite"*: Gavin Lambert, authors' interview, 9/19/03.

58 *"Without meaning to use"*: Brown, *The Screenwriter as Collaborator,* p. 105.

58 *Dean seemed to like Stern*: McGilligan, *Backstory 2,* p. 290.

58 *But although he told Stern*: Stewart Stern, authors' interview, 9/6/03.

58 *he apparently had doubts*: *Los Angeles Mirror-News,* 3/11/65, page unknown, newspaper clipping, files on *Rebel Without a Cause,* Warner Bros. Archives.

58 *As Stern neared the end of his work*: Stewart Stern, authors' interview, 9/6/03.

CHAPTER FIVE. *Gang Wars*

60 *As early as Christmas Eve of 1954*: Mike Connolly, "Rambling Reporter," *Hollywood Reporter,* 12/24/55, p. 2.

60 *In fact, if the shooting schedule*: John Howlett, *James Dean: A Biography,* pp. 93–94.

61 *Dean was officially announced as Jett Rink*: Thomas Pryor, "Columbia to Film Poems by Jeffers," *New York Times,* 3/17/55, p. 28.

61 Giant *would begin shooting*: Randall Riese, *The Unabridged James Dean: His Life and Legacy from A to Z,* p. 198.

61 *"Contractually no—emotionally yes"*: Howard Thompson, "Another Dean Hits the Big League," *New York Times,* 3/13/55, Section II, p. 5.

61 *"Gordian knot"*: Mark Rappaport, "The Picture in Sal Mineo's Locker," *Senses of Cinema,* July–Aug. 2002, http://www.sensesofcinema.com/contents/02/21/sd_sal_mineo.html.

61 *Like Ray, Dean was given to twinning*: *James Dean: The First American Teenager,* film directed by Ray Connolly, ZIV International, 1975.

62 *When pugnacious*: Frank Mazzola, authors' interview, 9/16/03.

62 *"Basically, the Athenians were a club"*: Syd Field, authors' interview, 1/16/04.

Notes

PAGE

62　*The Athenians were tough guys:* Frank Mazzola, authors' interview, 9/16/03.

62　*The Athenians were also involved in one of the biggest:* Frank Mazzola, authors' interview, 9/16/03.

64　*"We weren't going around with ducktails":* Frank Mazzola, authors' interview, 9/16/03.

64　*"Frank's house was upper-middle-class":* Syd Field, authors' interview, 1/16/03.

64　*Many members of Mazzola's family:* Frank Mazzola, authors' interview, 9/16/03.

64　*"I remember the first time I saw Jimmy":* Frank Mazzola, authors' interview, 9/16/03.

65　*"Nick's secretary":* Frank Mazzola, authors' interview, 9/16/03.

65　*"I was just being honest":* Frank Mazzola, authors' interview, 9/16/03.

65　*for which he was eventually paid:* memo from David Weisbart to Steve Trilling, 3/28/55, files on *Rebel Without a Cause,* Warner Bros. Archives, Cinema-Television Library, University of Southern California, Los Angeles.

66　*"Stewart always used to tell me":* Frank Mazzola, authors' interview, 9/16/03.

66　*An entirely new vernacular was emerging:* Tom Dalzell, authors' interview, 9/30/04.

66　*Stern's list of new phrases:* Stewart Stern, "Juvenile Talk," Papers of Stewart Stern, University of Iowa, Iowa City, Iowa.

66　*"Jimmy was twenty-four":* Frank Mazzola, authors' interview, 9/16/03.

66　*Together with Ray, they would meet:* memo from David Weisbart to Steve Trilling, 3/28/55, files on *Rebel Without a Cause,* Warner Bros. Archives.

66　*"He used to spar":* Frank Mazzola, authors' interview, 9/16/03.

67　*"My main memory":* Syd Field, authors' interview, 1/16/04.

67　*On February 10, 1955, Mazzola even arranged:* memo from David Weisbart to Steve Trilling, 3/28/55, files on *Rebel Without a Cause,* Warner Bros. Archives.

67　*Because of Ray's age:* Frank Mazzola, authors' interview, 9/16/03.

67　*He introduced Ray as his uncle:* David Dalton, *James Dean: The Mutant King,* pp. 243–44.

67　*"Every custom car that went by":* Frank Mazzola, authors' interview, 9/16/03.

67　*"I had a wristwatch":* "Interview with Nicholas Ray," *Camera Three,* CBS, 1977.

68　*Ray came away from the experience:* Dalton, *James Dean,* pp. 243–44.

68　*"We played the bad kids":* Beverly Long, authors' interview, 9/8/03.

68　*"Everyone was being transformed":* Corey Allen, authors' interview, 9/17/03.

69　*Frank Sinatra—the veritable king of Las Vegas—had been denied:* Shawn Levy, *Rat Pack Confidential: Frank, Dean, Sammy, Peter, Joey and the Last Great Show Biz Party,* pp. 295–96.

69　*"I was not a physical young man":* Bernard Eisenschitz, *Nicholas Ray: An American Journey,* pp. 241–42.

69　*"There were about":* Corey Allen, authors' interview, 9/17/03.

69　*"I was twenty":* Corey Allen, authors' interview, 9/17/03.

70　*"He ran us through":* Eisenschitz, *Nicholas Ray,* pp. 241–42.

70　*"He would take the kids":* Stewart Stern, authors' interview, 9/6/03.

70　*"Nick was getting down to brass tacks":* Corey Allen, authors' interview, 9/17/03.

70   *"It didn't matter"*: Eisenschitz, *Nicholas Ray,* pp. 241–42.

71   *"They wanted it to look"*: Jack Grinnage, authors' interview, 9/8/03.

71   *"It was all improvisation"*: Frank Mazzola, authors' interview, 9/16/03.

71   *"In my mind"*: Frank Mazzola, authors' interview, 9/16/03.

72   *"I was standing out in the hall"*: Beverly Long, authors' interview, 9/8/03.

72   *"Nick Ray wanted contrast"*: Steffi Sidney, authors' interview, 9/5/03.

72   *According to his daughter:* Steffi Sidney, authors' interview, 9/5/03.

73   *Skolsky's trademark question:* Vincent Curcio, *Suicide Blonde,* p. 86.

73   *"I learned to play Ping-Pong at Chasen's"*: Steffi Sidney, authors' interview, 9/5/03.

73   *"Then my father came home one night"*: Steffi Sidney, authors' interview, 9/5/03.

73   *"We knew that Steffi"*: Faye Nuell Mayo, authors' interview, 9/15/03.

73   *She was a member:* Steffi Sidney, authors' interview, 9/5/03.

73   *"My character always carried a brush"*: Steffi Sidney, authors' interview, 9/5/03.

74   *Looking for a bonding experience:* Steffi Sidney, authors' interview, 9/5/03.

74   *By late February, the cast of gang members was cut to size:* memo from Nicholas Ray to David Weisbart, 3/1/55, files on *Rebel Without a Cause,* Warner Bros. Archives.

75   *"the most ambitious actor"*: Gavin Lambert, *Natalie Wood: A Life,* p. 116.

75   *Adams got his first role:* Tom Hennesy, authors' interview, 9/18/03.

75   *According to Ken Miller:* Ken Miller, authors' interview, 12/9/03.

76   *As late as March 2:* memo from Nicholas Ray to David Weisbart, 3/2/55, files on *Rebel Without a Cause,* Warner Bros. Archives.

76   *In fact, on March 11:* memo from Solly Baiano to Nicholas Ray, 3/11/55, files on *Rebel Without a Cause,* Warner Bros. Archives.

76   *In a March 1 memo:* memo from Nicholas Ray to David Weisbart, 3/1/55, files on *Rebel Without a Cause,* Warner Bros. Archives.

76   *A March 2 memo:* "Potential Cast List Memo," 3/2/55, files on *Rebel Without a Cause,* Warner Bros. Archives.

76   *"Nick Ray always had Natalie in mind"*: Steffi Sidney, authors' interview, 9/5/03.

76   *In fact, in a March 1 memo:* memo from Eric Stacey to Solly Baiano, 3/1/55, files on *Rebel Without a Cause,* Warner Bros. Archives.

CHAPTER SIX. *The First Gay Teenager*

78   *In his March 1 memo:* memo from Nicholas Ray to David Weisbart, 3/1/55, files on *Rebel Without a Cause,* Warner Bros. Archives, Cinema-Television Library, University of Southern California, Los Angeles.

78   *Frank Mazzola remembers:* Frank Mazzola, authors' interview, 9/16/03.

78   *But although Cavell:* memo from Nicholas Ray to David Weisbart, 3/1/55, files on *Rebel Without a Cause,* Warner Bros. Archives.

79   *Mazzola also recalls:* Frank Mazzola, authors' interview, 7/27/04.

79   *Simmons met Dean:* Val Holley, *James Dean: The Biography,* p. 240.

79   *In 1954, right after Dean appeared:* Holley, *James Dean,* pp. 246–67.

79   *"Jack is always around"*: Sidney Skolsky, "Demon Dean," *Photoplay,* July 1955, p. 78.

80   *"I think Jack"*: Jack Larson, authors' interview, 12/4/03.

Notes

80 *Stern met Dean:* Phil Stern, authors' interview, 12/8/03.

80 *Beverly Long referred to him:* Randall Riese, *The Unabridged James Dean: His Life and Legacy from A to Z*, p. 496.

80 *"I was very worried":* Stewart Stern, authors' interview, 9/6/03.

81 *"I wanted the role to have homosexual overtones":* Riese, *The Unabridged James Dean,* p. 496.

81 *"The loyalty was built in":* Stewart Stern, authors' interview, 9/6/03.

81 *"It was the longest preparation":* Stewart Stern, authors' interview, 9/6/03.

81 *From the top of the staircase:* Holley, *James Dean,* pp. 261–62.

81 *"All of a sudden":* Stewart Stern, authors' interview, 9/6/03.

81 *Although Stern was dead set against Simmons:* Stewart Stern, authors' interview, 9/6/03.

82 *Mineo described his younger self:* Dustin Halliday, "Interview: Sal Mineo," *Avanti,* p. 9, http://salmineo.com/news/avanti.html.

83 *Mineo had one line:* H. Paul Jeffers, *Sal Mineo: His Life, Murder, and Mystery,* pp. 6–9.

83 *the important role:* Jeffers, *Sal Mineo,* p. 12.

83 *"At thirteen":* Victor and Sarina Mineo, "My Brother's Tough—He Is Not," *Motion Picture,* 1956, p. 70, http://salmineo.com/news/tough.html.

83 *Taking the subway:* Peter Bogdanovich, *Who the Hell's in It,* pp. 233–34.

83 *"I had this baby face":* Boze Hadleigh, *Conversations with My Elders,* p. 8.

83 *"I saw this kid":* David Dalton, *James Dean: The Mutant King,* p. 228.

84 *Throughout the development of the script:* Susan Ray, ed., *I Was Interrupted: Nicholas Ray on Making Movies,* p. 111.

84 *"When Nick saw Sal Mineo":* Gavin Lambert, authors' interview, 9/19/03.

84 *"I called him over":* Dalton, *James Dean,* p. 228.

84 *"I was almost sick":* Dalton, *James Dean,* p. 228.

84 *"I'd just like to go over":* Dalton, *James Dean,* p. 228.

85 *"I realize now":* Derek Marlowe, "Soliloquy on James Dean's Forty-Fifth Birthday," *New York,* 11/8/76, p. 46.

85 *"It became quite clear":* Gavin Lambert, authors' interview, 9/19/03.

85 *At one point, Ray asked Mineo:* Jeffers, *Sal Mineo,* p. 26.

85 *"tell Sal Mineo":* Gavin Lambert, authors' interview, 9/19/03.

85 *Beymer, who would later co-star with Natalie Wood:* Gavin Lambert, *Natalie Wood: A Life,* p. 94.

86 *Stewart Stern always felt that this dress rehearsal:* Stewart Stern, authors' interview, 9/6/03.

86 *"I couldn't understand":* Marlowe, "Soliloquy on James Dean's Forty-Fifth Birthday," p. 46.

87 *"the first gay teenager in films":* Hadleigh, *Conversations with My Elders,* p. 12.

CHAPTER SEVEN. *Chateau Interlude*

88 *"If you must get into trouble":* Jean Nathan, "What's Up with the Old Hotel," *New York Times,* 8/1/93, p. V1.

88 *"He enthroned himself"*: Donald Spoto, *Rebel: The Life and Legend of James Dean*, p. 219.

88 *Since it had opened in 1929:* Bernard Eisenschitz, *Nicholas Ray: An American Journey*, p. 235.

88 *Chateau Marmont became a retreat for countless legends:* Raymond R. Sarlot and Fred E. Basten, *Life at the Marmont*, pp. 65, 68, 76, 98, 131, 153, 197.

88 *Jean Harlow trysted with Clark Gable there:* Andre Balazs, *Hollywood Handbook: Chateau Marmont*, p. 124.

88 *Montgomery Clift recuperated there:* Sarlot and Basten, *Life at the Marmont*, pp. 160–63.

88 *In the 1950s:* Sarlot and Basten, *Life at the Marmont*, p. 131.

89 *members of Led Zeppelin:* Nathan, "What's Up with the Old Hotel," p. V9.

89 *Jim Morrison injured himself:* Danny Sugarman and Jerry Hopkins, *No One Here Gets Out Alive*, p. 340.

89 *More recently, in 2004, photographer Helmut Newton:* Jesse McKinley, "Helmut Newton Is Dead at 83," *New York Times*, 1/25/04, p. 1.

89 *And most notoriously, John Belushi:* Peter Biskind, *Easy Riders, Raging Bulls*, p. 412.

89 *The Chateau Marmont rises above:* Sarlot and Basten, *Life at the Marmont*, p. 298.

89 *Percy Marmont experienced:* Ephraim Katz, *Film Encyclopedia*, p. 778.

89 *"It was more like living":* Carroll Baker, *Baby Doll*, p. 106.

90 *"a navel filled with sweat":* Gore Vidal, *Palimpsest*, p. 278.

90 *Actress Shelley Winters remembered:* Shelley Winters, *Shelley II*, p. 48.

90 *Among the women:* Suzanne Finstad, *Natasha: The Biography of Natalie Wood*, p. 171.

90 *Marilyn Monroe:* Eisenschitz, *Nicholas Ray*, p. 276.

90 *Judy Holliday:* Norman Lloyd, authors' interview, 11/7/03.

90 *he was also involved with Edie Wasserman:* Dennis McDougal, *The Last Mogul: Lew Wasserman, MCA, and the Hidden History of Hollywood*, p. 200; Gavin Lambert, authors' interview, 9/19/03.

90 *In his memoir,* Palimpsest: Vidal, *Palimpsest*, p. 278.

90 *Gavin Lambert doubts:* Gavin Lambert, authors' interview, 9/19/03.

91 *Throughout the making of* Rebel: Gavin Lambert, *Natalie Wood: A Life*, p. 89.

91 *Adele Essman, then wife:* Joe Hyams, *James Dean: Little Boy Lost*, p. 239.

91 *Wood's friend Mary Ann Brooks remembered:* Mary Ann Brooks, authors' interview, 1/23/04.

91 *"In order to give her":* Jackie Perry, authors' interview, 12/10/03.

91 *In fact it was in Grahame's first film:* Vincent Curcio, *Suicide Blonde*, p. 76.

91 *He summoned costume designer Moss Mabry:* Moss Mabry, authors' interview, 9/12/03.

92 *To add to the effect of newfound sophistication:* Finstad, *Natasha*, p. 179.

92 *Mabry said that Wood and Ray were ecstatic:* Moss Mabry, authors' interview, 9/12/03.

92 *According to Jackie Perry:* Jackie Perry, authors' interview, 12/10/03.

92 *In a memo on March 31, 1955:* memo from David Weisbart to Steve Trilling, 3/31/55, files on *Rebel Without a Cause*, Warner Bros. Archives, Cinema-Television Library, University of Southern California, Los Angeles.

Notes

PAGE

92 *a vocal coach suggested to him by actor Robert Ryan:* Lambert, *Natalie Wood,* p. 92.

92 *Moise had an intriguing résumé:* Arthur and Barbara Gelb, *O'Neill: Life with Monte Cristo,* pp. 595, 597.

92 *And she had also been a vocal coach:* Lambert, *Natalie Wood,* p. 92.

92 *Moise would be hired:* memo from David Weisbart to Steve Trilling, 3/31/55, files on *Rebel Without a Cause,* Warner Bros. Archives.

92 *"When they offered a certain amount of money":* Harry Clein, "Natalie Wood: On Acting, Nudity, and Growing Up in Hollywood," *Entertainment World,* 1/30/70, p. 7.

93 *"There sat in the corner a little boy":* Eisenschitz, *Nicholas Ray,* p. 526.

93 *He could often be found:* Jackie Perry, authors' interview, 12/10/03.

93 *Roger Donoghue, a young boxer:* Val Holley, *James Dean: The Biography,* p. 262.

93 *Shelley Winters remembered heading down Sunset Boulevard:* Winters, *Shelley II,* pp. 47–48.

94 *"One day we were going to lunch":* Jackie Perry, authors' interview, 12/10/03.

94 *Stewart Stern also remembered seeing Tony:* Stewart Stern, authors' interview, 9/6/03.

95 *As written by Stern:* Stewart Stern, *Rebel Without a Cause* screenplay, 3/3/55, pp. 79–84, files on *Rebel Without a Cause,* Warner Bros. Archives.

95 *"It was beginning to get on my nerves":* "Interview with Nicholas Ray," *Camera Three,* CBS, 1977.

95 *"He was always drinking milk":* David Dalton, *James Dean: The Mutant King,* p. 253.

95 *According to Susan Ray:* Susan Ray, authors' interview, 12/29/03.

96 *"Nick and Stewart Stern would tell us":* Dalton, *James Dean,* p. 231.

96 *Ray would record the actors' efforts on tape:* Lambert, *Natalie Wood,* p. 94.

96 *Wood said that when they rehearsed at the Chateau: I'm a Stranger Here Myself,* October Films, 1974.

96 *"I called the art director in":* Eisenschitz, *Nicholas Ray,* p. 244.

96 *Ray had done this type of thing before:* Eisenschitz, *Nicholas Ray,* p. 144.

96 *As critic David Thomson:* David Thomson, *The Biographical Dictionary of Film,* p. 614.

96 *Eventually, Ray staged an official read-through:* Steffi Sidney, authors' interview, 9/5/03.

97 *Prominent in the pictures:* Winters, *Shelley II,* pp. 48–49.

97 *Nearly everyone in the cast:* Marsha Hunt, authors' interview, 12/7/03.

97 *"It all sounded pretty monotone":* Mitzi McCall, authors' interview, 3/25/04.

97 *"I thought, there's no chance":* Frank Mazzola, authors' interview, 9/16/03.

98 *"She walked in and I was starstruck":* Corey Allen, authors' interview, 9/17/03.

98 *But when the veteran actress greeted the cast:* Beverly Long, authors' interview, 9/8/03; Corey Allen, authors' interview, 9/17/03; and Jack Grinnage, authors' interview, 9/8/03.

98 *"She meant her career was over":* Corey Allen, authors' interview, 9/17/03.

98 *But Hunt herself denies this:* Marsha Hunt, authors' interview, 12/7/03.

98 *"Her whole attitude"*: Beverly Long, authors' interview, 9/8/03.

98 *"My experience was so unusual"*: Patrick McGilligan and Paul Buhle, *Tender Comrades*, p. 306.

98 *And in 1950:* American Business Consultants, Inc., *Red Channels: The Report of Communist Influence in Radio and Television*, p. 85.

98 *"Some I'd never heard about"*: McGilligan and Buhle, *Tender Comrades*, p. 306.

98 *The official reason:* undated publicity memo, files on *Rebel Without a Cause*, Warner Bros. Archives.

99 *"It was a fragmentary role"*: Marsha Hunt, authors' interview, 12/7/03.

99 *Ray was one of the signers: Hollywood on Trial,* October Films, 1976.

99 *"He could be friends with everybody"*: Eisenschitz, *Nicholas Ray*, p. 125.

99 *severely damaging his relationship:* Patricia Bosworth, *Marlon Brando*, pp. 112–13.

99 *According to Ray's old New York friend:* Norman Lloyd, authors' interview, 11/7/03.

100 *Ray came to the attention of the FBI:* Report dated 11/2/42, Files on Nicholas Ray, U.S. Department of Justice, Federal Bureau of Investigation.

100 *Although the investigation:* memo from Lawrence M. C. Smith to J. Edgar Hoover, 10/6/42, Files on Nicholas Ray, U.S. Department of Justice, Federal Bureau of Investigation.

100 *signed off on by J. Edgar Hoover:* memo from J. Edgar Hoover, 10/27/42, Files on Nicholas Ray, U.S. Department of Justice, Federal Bureau of Investigation.

100 *"There were certain traps that every studio had"*: Michael Goodwin and Naomi Wise, "Nicholas Ray: Rebel!," *Take One,* Jan. 1977, p. 11.

101 *Eventually, Ray managed to charm:* Goodwin and Wise, "Nicholas Ray: Rebel!," p. 12.

101 *He reshot parts of several troubled films:* Bernard Eisenschitz, "A Biographical Outline," in Susan Ray, ed., *I Was Interrupted: Nicholas Ray on Making Movies*, p. xlv.

101 *"It was in his stable of anecdotes"*: Susan Ray, authors' interview, 12/29/03.

101 *"Hughes certainly had the power"*: Gavin Lambert, authors' interview, 9/19/03.

101 *During his lifetime, Ray also offered another reason:* Goodwin and Wise, "Nicholas Ray: Rebel!," p. 17.

101 *Ray's first wife, Jean Evans:* Eisenschitz, *Nicholas Ray*, p. 508.

102 *According to Bill Davis:* House Un-American Activities Committee Files, Records of the U.S. House of Representatives, Center for Legislative Archives, National Archives, Washington, D.C.

102 *Ray's often expressed feeling that his was a generation of "betrayers"*: Susan Ray, *I Was Interrupted*, p. xxii.

102 *"I don't particularly care"*: "Interview with Nicholas Ray," *Camera Three.*

CHAPTER EIGHT. *The Red Jacket*

104 *But it was disconcerting:* Gavin Lambert, *Natalie Wood: A Life*, p. 95.

104 *"Warners was frantic"*: David Dalton, *James Dean: The Mutant King*, p. 232.

PAGE

104 *The studio contemplated suspending Dean:* Lambert, *Natalie Wood,* p. 95.

104 *Driving the Porsche Speedster:* Randall Riese, *The Unabridged James Dean: His Life and Legacy from A to Z,* p. 74.

104 *Dean placed first in the Palm Springs Road Race:* Ronald Martinetti, *The James Dean Story,* p. 123.

104 *The following day, he placed second:* Riese, *The Unabridged James Dean,* p. 74.

104 *A few days after Dean's disappearance:* Lambert, *Natalie Wood,* p. 95.

104 *In looking back on* East of Eden: Stewart Stern, authors' interview, 9/6/03.

105 *"I could understand Jimmy's doubts":* Lambert, *Natalie Wood,* p. 95.

105 *"Do you want me to come back":* Patrick McGilligan, *Backstory 2,* p. 289.

105 *"I can't say I don't want you to come back":* Stewart Stern, authors' interview, 9/6/03.

105 *"If you did it and were miserable":* Dalton, *James Dean,* p. 233.

105 *He did not even say hello:* Stewart Stern, authors' interview, 9/6/03.

105 *Staring at a blank wall:* Dalton, *James Dean,* p. 233.

105 *Dean would pull a similar stunt:* Riese, *The Unabridged James Dean,* p. 202.

106 *Hanging out at Arthur Loew Jr.'s house:* Stewart Stern, authors' interview, 9/6/03.

106 *"I knew it would be disaster":* Kent Brown, *The Screenwriter as Collaborator: The Career of Stewart Stern,* p. 106.

106 *Dean had worked at the observatory:* Riese, *The Unabridged James Dean,* p. 306.

106 *It had served as Jor-El's Krypton castle:* K. C. Cole, "Ed Krupp's Star-Studded Cosmic Extravaganza," *Los Angeles Times,* 2/14/99, p. 10.

107 *Located on the south slope of Mount Hollywood:* David Wallace, *Hollywoodland,* p. 82.

107 *"the young boy":* Pauline Kael, *I Lost It at the Movies,* p. 55.

107 *"After* East of Eden, *he sometimes":* Susan Ray, ed., *I Was Interrupted: Nicholas Ray on Making Movies,* p. 112.

107 *"In the mornings":* Joe Hyams, *James Dean: Little Boy Lost,* p. 243.

108 *Dean would sometimes race his Porsche:* Beverly Long, authors' interview, 9/8/03.

108 *Dean was also prone:* Beverly Long, authors' interview, 9/8/03.

108 *While waiting endlessly for camera setups:* Dalton, *James Dean,* p. 247.

108 *Dean and Adams claimed:* undated publicity memo, files on *Rebel Without a Cause,* Warner Bros. Archives, Cinema-Television Library, University of Southern California, Los Angeles.

109 *Corey Allen says that Dean:* Ray Nielsen, "Corey Allen in 'Rebel Without a Cause,'" *Classic Images,* No. 216, June 1993, p. 56.

109 *Ray was worried that Dean's acting:* Corey Allen, authors' interview, 9/17/03.

109 *In Ray's original "Blind Run":* Nicholas Ray, "The Blind Run," 9/18/54, p. 8, files on *Rebel Without a Cause,* Warner Bros. Archives.

109 *"We all tended":* H. Paul Jeffers, *Sal Mineo: His Life, Murder, and Mystery,* pp. 34–35.

109 *"He was all":* Riese, *The Unabridged James Dean,* p. 567.

109 *Wood and Mineo's on-set tutor, Tom Hennesy, remembers:* Suzanne Finstad, *Natasha: The Biography of Natalie Wood,* p. 182.

109 *"This man does not know"*: Bernard Eisenschitz, *Nicholas Ray: An American Journey*, p. 247.

110 *But when Ray saw Wood:* Jack Grinnage, authors' interview, 9/8/03.

110 *Ray had sent Wood a dozen roses:* Frank Mazzola, authors' interview, 9/16/03.

110 *"He was crazy about Natalie"*: Hyams, *James Dean*, p. 239.

110 *Hopper told Steffi Sidney:* Steffi Sidney, authors' interview, 9/5/03.

110 *Originally, Ray had wanted to hire:* Eisenschitz, *Nicholas Ray*, p. 242.

111 *"Haller was a brilliant cinematographer"*: Ray Gosnell Jr., authors' interview, 12/15/03.

111 *"The maximum was not achieved"*: memo from Nicholas Ray to David Weisbart, 3/1/55, files on *Rebel Without a Cause*, Warner Bros. Archives.

111 *"Nobody knew exactly"*: Steffi Sidney, authors' interview, 9/5/03.

111 *According to a studio publicity memo:* undated publicity memo, files on *Rebel Without a Cause*, Warner Bros. Archives.

112 *"You watch too much television"*: Stewart Stern, *Rebel Without a Cause* screenplay, 3/25/55, p. 39, Papers of Stewart Stern, University of Iowa, Iowa City, Iowa.

112 *The scene would be considered so brutal:* Richard H. Walters, Edward Llewellyn Thomas, and C. William Acker, "Enhancement of Punitive Behavior by Audio-Visual Displays," *Science*, 6/8/62, pp. 872–73.

112 *"conflict of sex and power"*: Dalton, *James Dean*, pp. 243–44.

112 *Director and critic Eric Rohmer:* Eric Rohmer, "Ajax or the Cid?," in Jim Hillier, ed., *Cahiers du Cinéma: The 1950s: Neo-Realism, Hollywood, New Wave*, p. 113.

113 *"Jimmy knew how to move"*: Dalton, *James Dean*, pp. 246–47.

113 *For help with the scene:* Frank Mazzola, authors' interview, 9/16/03.

113 *Dean's stand-in on* Rebel, *Mushy Callahan:* Corey Allen, authors' interview, 9/17/03.

113 *his 1951 bout with George Flores:* "Flores Succumbs to Ring Injuries," *New York Times*, 9/3/51, p. 18.

113 *He went on to coach Marlon Brando:* Eisenschitz, *Nicholas Ray*, p. 257.

113 *Dean was thinking about accepting the role:* Val Holley, *James Dean: The Biography*, p. 262.

113 *"Nick had all these kids"*: Dalton, *James Dean*, p. 231.

113 *"If this knife-duel"*: memos from Geoffrey Shurlock to Jack Warner, 3/22/55 and 3/31/55, files on *Rebel Without a Cause*, Warner Bros. Archives.

114 *Instead of rubber blades, Dean wanted to use:* Ronald Martinetti, *The James Dean Story*, p. 130.

114 *"We all argued"*: Nick Adams, "Jimmy's Happiest Moments," *Modern Screen*, Oct. 1956.

114 *A Warners publicity memo:* *Rebel Without a Cause* Production Notes, undated, files on *Rebel Without a Cause*, Warner Bros. Archives.

114 *Allen, who describes himself as a "book nerd"*: Corey Allen, authors' interview, 9/17/03.

114 *"The boys circled each other"*: Hyams, *James Dean*, p. 236.

115 *"I was so fucking nervous"*: Dalton, *James Dean*, p. 244.

Notes

PAGE

115   *Allen had been drinking the night before:* Corey Allen, authors' interview, 9/17/03.

115   *"It wasn't coffee":* Henry Vilardo, authors' interview, 2/5/04.

115   *Suddenly, Ray shouted:* Hyams, *James Dean,* p. 237.

115   *"I committed a cardinal sin":* Nielsen, "Corey Allen in 'Rebel Without a Cause,'" p. 43.

115   *In a fury, he turned to the director:* Hyams, *James Dean,* p. 237.

115   *While a first-aid man:* Dalton, *James Dean,* p. 246.

115   *According to Nick Adams, Dean was delighted:* Adams, "Jimmy's Happiest Moments."

115   *One of the invited journalists:* Neil Rau, "The Fight Was for Blood—and They Got It," *Los Angeles Examiner,* 5/22/65, p. 15.

116   *Despite the hype:* Mary Ann Brooks, authors' interview, 1/23/04.

116   *Dean's stuntman:* Hyams, *James Dean,* p. 237.

116   *When they finally wrapped:* Corey Allen, authors' interview, 9/17/03.

116   *Corey Allen was relieved:* Corey Allen, authors' interview, 9/17/03.

116   *"This may shake you":* Nielsen, "Corey Allen in 'Rebel Without a Cause,'" p. 43.

116   *Cast member Steffi Sidney says:* Steffi Sidney, authors' interview, 9/5/03.

117   *"Warners had reported":* Thomas Pryor, "Color Is Required for CinemaScope," *New York Times,* 4/5/55, p. 33.

117   *Bausch & Lomb, which made the lenses:* Ray Gosnell Jr., authors' interview, 12/15/03.

117   *"They didn't know what I was doing":* Dalton, *James Dean,* p. 233.

117   *"THIS IS A VERY IMPORTANT PICTURE":* memo from Jack Warner to David Weisbart, 4/2/55, files on *Rebel Without a Cause,* Warner Bros. Archives.

117   *"We started out making a routine program picture":* Donald Spoto, *Rebel,* p. 214.

118   *"with enough open territory":* Geoffrey O'Brien, *Sonata for Jukebox,* p. 235.

118   *"It was a modern world":* O'Brien, *Sonata for Jukebox,* p. 235.

118   *Immediately after Warners issued its new orders:* Susan Ray, *I Was Interrupted,* p. 57.

118   Rebel *costume designer Moss Mabry:* Moss Mabry, authors' interview, 9/12/03.

118   *After Mabry let the cast loose:* Beverly Long, authors' interview, 9/8/03.

118   *Steffi Sidney ended up with:* Steffi Sidney, authors' interview, 9/5/03.

118   *Tom Bernard's leather jacket:* Tom Bernard, authors' interview, 9/12/03.

118   *The fur collar:* Jack Grinnage, authors' interview, 9/8/03.

118   *"Bette Davis was":* Moss Mabry, authors' interview, 9/12/03.

118   *"The use of primary color in film":* Susan Ray, *I Was Interrupted,* p. 57.

118   *In fact, in later life Ray:* Susan Ray, authors' interview, 12/29/03.

118   *According to the book jacket:* Max Lüscher, *The Lüscher Color Test,* book jacket.

119   *"It was something he was exploring":* Susan Ray, authors' interview, 12/29/03.

119   *In* Rebel, *Ray used color coding:* Susan Ray, *I Was Interrupted,* p. 58.

119   *According to Ray:* Dalton, *James Dean,* p. 234.

119   *Others say:* Randall Riese, *The Unabridged James Dean,* p. 260.

119   *Frank Mazzola accompanied Dean:* Frank Mazzola, authors' interview, 9/16/03.

119   *where, as Jack Grinnage remembers:* Jack Grinnage, authors' interview, 9/8/03.

119   *"The red jacket was really":* Frank Mazzola, authors' interview, 9/16/03.

119 *After* Rebel *was released, Warners referred fans:* Ezra Goodman, "Delirium Over Dead Star," *Life,* 9/24/56, p. 79.

119 *Moss Mabry tells a completely different story:* Moss Mabry, authors' interview, 9/12/03.

120 *And, although Stern says he didn't realize it:* Stewart Stern, authors' interview, 9/6/03.

120 *"When you first see":* Dalton, *James Dean,* p. 234.

120 *"After the movie came out":* Steffi Sidney, authors' interview, 9/5/03.

120 *Bob Dylan, who saw* Rebel Without a Cause: David Hajdu, *Positively 4th Street: The Lives and Times of Joan Baez, Bob Dylan, Mimi Baez Fariña and Richard Fariña,* p. 67.

120 *Almost thirty years later:* Moss Mabry, authors' interview, 9/12/03.

121 *In 1957 the* New York Times *reported:* Thomas Pryor, "Busy Hollywood," *New York Times,* 9/15/57, p. X7.

121 *And in 2003 a poll of Irish movie theatergoers:* Anthony Barnes, *"Rebel Without a Cause* Named Most Stylish Film Ever," *Irish Examiner,* 5/2/03, http://archives.tcm.ie/irishexaminer/2003/05/02/story437776418.asp.

CHAPTER NINE. *Starting Over*

122 *"Dawson" was picked:* memo from Carl Milliken Jr. to David Weisbart, 3/21/55, files on *Rebel Without a Cause,* Warner Bros. Archives, Cinema-Television Library, University of Southern California, Los Angeles.

122 *"Until they got that done":* Steffi Sidney, authors' interview, 9/5/03.

122 *Ray spent the entire morning:* "Daily Production and Progress Report," 4/2/55, files on *Rebel Without a Cause,* Warner Bros. Archives.

122 *"it was in California":* Stewart Stern, authors' interview, 9/6/03.

123 *"More money!":* Steffi Sidney, authors' interview, 9/5/03.

123 *Actor Ken Miller:* Ken Miller, authors' interview, 12/9/03.

123 *Tom Bernard, who remained in the film:* Tom Bernard, authors' interview, 9/12/03.

123 *"Les jeux de courage!":* Stewart Stern, *Rebel Without a Cause* screenplay, 3/25/55, p. 40, Papers of Stewart Stern, University of Iowa, Iowa City, Iowa.

123 *"She was supposed to be taking French in school":* Stewart Stern, authors' interview, 9/6/03.

123 *"Forever after, Corey Allen would call me":* Beverly Long, authors' interview, 9/8/03.

123 *"All the things that Nick Adams":* Steffi Sidney, authors' interview, 9/5/03.

124 *Once, while Adams was trying to entertain the cast:* Beverly Long, authors' interview, 9/8/03.

124 *Their tutor was sometime actor and stuntman Tom Hennesy:* Tom Hennesy, authors' interview, 9/18/03.

124 *"Natalie was a little bit difficult":* Tom Hennesy, authors' interview, 9/18/03.

125 *At one point he became so concerned about the gang's influence:* Suzanne Finstad, *Natasha: The Biography of Natalie Wood,* p. 186.

Notes

PAGE

125 *"He tried to hang out":* Tom Hennesy, authors' interview, 9/18/03.

125 *Beverly Long agrees:* Beverly Long, authors' interview, 9/8/03.

125 *"If anyone was a bit closer":* Gary Nelson, authors' interview, 1/8/04.

125 *His makeup man:* Henry Vilardo, authors' interview, 2/5/04.

126 *"Nick wouldn't go":* Bernard Eisenschitz, *Nicholas Ray: An American Journey,* p. 246.

126 *"He and Nick had an understanding":* Ray Nielsen, "Corey Allen in 'Rebel Without a Cause,'" *Classic Images,* No. 216, June 1993, p. 56.

126 *"I think Jimmy interpreted his own part":* Tom Bernard, authors' interview, 9/12/03.

126 *"Jimmy ran that film":* Dennis Stock, authors' interview, 3/31/05.

126 *"In my opinion":* Dennis Hopper, "James Dean," *Mirabella,* Nov. 1990, p. 188.

126 *Gavin Lambert once asked Wood:* Gavin Lambert, authors' interview, 9/19/03.

126 *Before every scene:* Corey Allen, authors' interview, 9/17/03.

127 *"He was very fatherly":* Jack Grinnage, authors' interview, 9/8/03.

127 *"Nick was way before his time":* David Dalton, *James Dean: The Mutant King,* p. 231.

127 *Actor Jack Larson:* Jack Larson, authors' interview, 12/4/03.

127 *"Crews were in their forties and fifties":* Gary Nelson, authors' interview, 1/8/04.

127 *Makeup man Vilardo:* Henry Vilardo, authors' interview, 2/5/04.

127 *Nelson, who worked on* The Searchers *with John Ford:* Gary Nelson, authors' interview, 1/8/04.

128 *"We refused to come":* Steffi Sidney, authors' interview, 9/5/03.

128 *"the talkies, of course":* Gregory Orr, "Biography for Don Alvarado," Internet Movie Database, http://imdb.com/name/nm0023147/bio.

128 *"Don Page had a permanent job at Warners":* Jack Grinnage, authors' interview, 9/8/03.

128 *For the first time:* "Daily Production and Progress Report," 4/11/55, files on *Rebel Without a Cause,* Warner Bros. Archives.

128 *"We wrote some":* Beverly Long, authors' interview, 9/8/03.

128 *When Sidney sneezes:* Steffi Sidney, authors' interview, 9/5/03.

128 *As Ray once described it:* Dalton, *James Dean,* p. 243.

128 *At one point Ray:* Frank Mazzola, authors' interview, 9/16/03.

129 *Beverly Long remembers:* Beverly Long, authors' interview, 9/8/03.

129 *Wood's friend Mary Ann Brooks:* Mary Ann Brooks, authors' interview, 1/23/04.

129 *When the crew:* Beverly Long, authors' interview, 9/8/03.

129 *According to Long:* Beverly Long, authors' interview, 9/8/03.

129 *Although the call sheets:* "Daily Production and Progress Report," 4/11/55, files on *Rebel Without a Cause,* Warner Bros. Archives.

130 *Soon afterward, Ray went to Wood's mother:* Eisenschitz, *Nicholas Ray,* p. 246.

130 *Wood's mother complained to the studio:* Warner publicity memo, 4/6/55, files on *Rebel Without a Cause,* Warner Bros. Archives.

130 *"Nick snitched on me!":* Eisenschitz, *Nicholas Ray,* p. 246.

130 *"I resented this, and showed it":* Gavin Lambert, *Natalie Wood: A Life,* p. 98.

130 *"The infinite doom":* Dalton, *James Dean,* p. 239.

130 *If the students had attended:* Mike Eberts, "Griffith Observatory Goes to the Moon," *Griffith Park History Project,* http://english.glendale.cc.ca.us/ moonobs.html.

131 *According to Stewart Stern, this line was inspired:* Stewart Stern, "Interview with a Boy," undated manuscript, Papers of Stewart Stern, University of Iowa, Iowa City, Iowa.

131 *According to cast member Jack Grinnage:* Jack Grinnage, authors' interview, 9/8/03.

132 *Stewart Stern says that:* Stewart Stern, authors' interview, 9/6/03.

CHAPTER TEN. *Meet the Parents*

134 *Ray had conceived:* Stewart Stern, authors' interview, 9/6/03.

134 *The pamphlet recommended dispensing:* Charles G. Clarke, *Photographic Techniques of CinemaScope Pictures,* p. 6.

134 *The pamphlet also recommended:* Clarke, *Photographic Techniques,* p. 8.

134 *"They used a deep-focus lens":* Steffi Sidney, authors' interview, 9/5/03.

135 *According to Stern, it is just a coincidence:* Stewart Stern, authors' interview, 9/6/03.

135 *"She was scared to death":* Suzanne Finstad, *Natasha: The Biography of Natalie Wood,* p. 179.

135 *Crying scenes had been especially traumatic:* Finstad, *Natasha,* p. 38.

135 *"Whenever I did a movie":* Dick Moore, *Twinkle, Twinkle, Little Star: But Don't Have Sex or Take the Car,* p. 22.

135 *According to director Henry Jaglom:* Gavin Lambert, *Natalie Wood: A Life,* p. 232.

136 *Ray wanted to introduce Jim:* "Daily Production and Progress Report" and "Production Camera Sheet," 4/5/55, files on *Rebel Without a Cause,* Warner Bros. Archives, Cinema-Television Library, University of Southern California, Los Angeles.

136 *"Natalie had just gotten herself":* Jackie Perry, authors' interview, 12/10/03.

136 *By the time the crew had eaten lunch:* "Daily Production and Progress Report" and "Production Camera Sheet," 4/5/55, files on *Rebel Without a Cause,* Warner Bros. Archives.

136 *Beverly Long found her:* Beverly Long, authors' interview, 9/8/03.

136 *In an early draft of the script:* Stewart Stern, *Rebel Without a Cause* screenplay, 1/31/55, files on *Rebel Without a Cause,* Warner Bros. Archives.

136 *but censors nixed the implication she was arrested for soliciting:* memo from Geoffrey Shurlock to J. L. Warner, 3/31/55, files on *Rebel Without a Cause,* Warner Bros. Archives.

137 *To make sure those tears flowed:* Jackie Perry, authors' interview, 12/10/03.

137 *Desperate to finish the scene:* Frank Mazzola, authors' interview, 9/16/03.

137 *After seven takes:* "Production Camera Sheet," 4/5/55, files on *Rebel Without a Cause,* Warner Bros. Archives.

137 *And the Warners publicity department:* undated Warners publicity memo, files on *Rebel Without a Cause,* Warner Bros. Archives.

137 *A seasoned Hollywood professional:* Richard Valley, "Character Actress: Ann Doran," *Scarlet Street,* No. 17, Winter 1995, p. 48.

Notes

PAGE

138 *Although Doran had never met Ray or Dean:* Finstad, *Natasha,* pp. 184–85.

138 *Corey Allen, for one, was puzzled:* Corey Allen, authors' interview, 9/17/03.

139 *"We spent a lot of time":* Jim Backus, *Rocks on the Roof,* p. 153.

139 *Backus had actually met Dean:* Backus, *Rocks on the Roof,* p. 152.

139 *According to the screenplay: Rebel Without a Cause* screenplay, 3/25/55, p. A, Papers of Stewart Stern, University of Iowa, Iowa City, Iowa.

139 *"How in the world did they ever cast that woman?":* Stewart Stern, authors' interview, 9/6/03.

139 *He deliberately avoided using the word: I'm a Stranger Here Myself,* October Films, 1974.

139 *"We got a lot of flack":* Corey Allen, authors' interview, 9/17/03.

140 *Before going on set the first day:* Valley, "Character Actress: Ann Doran," pp. 48–49.

140 *At one point, in a take:* Beverly Long, authors' interview, 9/8/03.

140 *And Doran was also annoyed:* Valley, "Character Actress: Ann Doran," p. 49.

140 *House Peters Jr., who played the policeman:* House Peters Jr., authors' interview, 9/15/03.

140 *Dean's intensity was often startling:* Wayne Jones, "Marietta Canty Interview," *We Remember James Dean International Newsletter,* March 1982.

141 *He let Dean bar the cameraman:* David Dalton, *James Dean: The Mutant King,* p. 249.

141 *James Baird, who played Judy's little brother Beau:* James Baird, authors' interview, 12/8/03.

141 *Doran believed:* Finstad, *Natasha,* p. 185.

141 *Dean kept everyone waiting:* Backus, *Rocks on the Roof,* p. 155.

141 *The script called for:* Stewart Stern, *Rebel Without a Cause* screenplay, 3/25/55, p. 15.

141 *"We rehearsed that scene":* Susan Ray, ed., *I Was Interrupted: Nicholas Ray on Making Movies,* p. 131.

141 *He nailed the scene in one take:* Backus, *Rocks on the Roof,* p. 155.

142 *"Look, all you do is show":* Valley, "Character Actress: Ann Doran," p. 48.

142 *According to both Stern and Ray:* Adrian Aprá, Barry Boys, Ian Cameron, José Luis Guarner, Paul Mayersberg and V. F. Perkins, "Interview with Nicholas Ray," *Movie,* 9, May 1963, p. 17; Patrick McGilligan, *Backstory 2: Interviews with Screenwriters of the 1940s and 1950s,* p. 290.

142 *"contains all the Freudian theories":* memo from Jerry Wald to Steve Trilling, 11/14/49, files on *Rebel Without a Cause,* Warner Bros. Archives.

142 *"I was blaming my parents":* McGilligan, *Backstory 2,* p. 289.

142 *As Stern describes his own family:* Stewart Stern, authors' interview, 9/6/03.

143 *In fact, the Rebel scene that most strikingly illustrates:* Stewart Stern, authors' interview, 9/6/03.

143 *In an interview with a reporter:* Harrison Carroll, "Dean Terrorizes Film Set," *Los Angeles Herald-Examiner,* 5/21/55.

143 *In a best-selling book of the time:* Philip Wylie, *Generation of Vipers,* pp. 194–217.

143 *"If he had guts"*: Stewart Stern, *Rebel Without a Cause* screenplay, 3/25/55, p. 16, Papers of Stewart Stern, University of Iowa, Iowa City, Iowa.

144 *"When I first put the apron on"*: Dalton, *James Dean,* p. 250.

144 *"We knew we were walking a very thin line"*: Dalton, *James Dean,* p. 250.

145 *Ray and cinematographer Ernest Haller:* "Production Camera Sheet" and "Daily Production and Progress Report," 5/6/55, files on *Rebel Without a Cause,* Warner Bros. Archives.

145 *"The shot came to express"*: Susan Ray, *I Was Interrupted,* p. 115.

145 *At this point the screenplay's directions:* Stewart Stern, *Rebel Without a Cause* screenplay, 3/25/55, p. 75a.

145 *"Nick wanted the shock value of it"*: Jackie Perry, authors' interview, 12/10/03.

145 *The* Los Angeles Herald-Examiner's *Harrison Carroll:* Carroll, "Dean Terrorizes Film Set."

146 *"Backus was really shocked"*: Jackie Perry, authors' interview, 12/10/03.

146 *"I thought I was a goner"*: Carroll, "Dean Terrorizes Film Set."

146 *It demonstrated a key turning point:* Stewart Stern, authors' interview, 9/6/03.

146 *"Welcome to the Elia Kazan Hour"*: Army Archerd, "Just for Variety," *Daily Variety,* 5/2/55, p. 2.

146 *Asked why he did not give her a name:* Stewart Stern, authors' interview, 9/6/03.

146 *By the time Marietta Canty was cast in* Rebel: Constance Neyer, "Marietta Canty Dies; Actress Lived in City," *Hartford Courant,* 7/10/86, pp. A1, A12.

147 *"She was rather upset with those roles"*: Neyer, "Marietta Canty Dies," p. A1.

148 *At one point, Richard Dadier:* Richard Brooks, *Blackboard Jungle* screenplay.

148 *"How many times"*: James Baldwin, *The Devil Finds Work,* p. 87.

148 *"She would appear"*: Baldwin, *The Devil Finds Work,* p. 86.

149 *When Plato is called into a policeman's office:* Stewart Stern, *Rebel Without a Cause* screenplay, 3/25/55, p. 9.

149 *"They were nursing on their mother"*: Stewart Stern, *Rebel Without a Cause* screenplay, 3/25/55, p. 10.

149 *a line inspired:* Stewart Stern, authors' interview, 9/6/03.

149 *"It was probably"*: Jones, "Marietta Canty Interview."

149 *Yet in a 1990 book:* Leith Adams and Keith Burns, *James Dean: Behind the Scene,* p. 119.

150 *Rochelle Hudson, a onetime ingénue:* Ephraim Katz, *Film Encyclopedia,* p. 584.

150 *It was suggested:* Leon Uris, *Rebel Without a Cause #2,* 11/1/54, p. 8, files on *Rebel Without a Cause,* Warner Bros. Archives.

150 *Stern says that the relationship:* Stewart Stern, authors' interview, 9/6/03.

151 *In a memo to Jack Warner, Shurlock wrote:* Memo from Geoffrey Shurlock to J. L. Warner, 3/22/55, files on *Rebel Without a Cause,* Warner Bros. Archives.

151 *He offered a suggestion:* memo from Geoffrey Shurlock to J. L. Warner, 3/31/55, files on *Rebel Without a Cause,* Warner Bros. Archives.

151 *Warner Brothers' Code representative:* Jerold Simmons, "The Censoring of 'Rebel Without a Cause,'" *Journal of Popular Film and Television,* 6/1/95, p. 59.

Notes

151 *"I don't quite understand"*: memo from Finlay McDermid to Steve Trilling, 3/31/55, files on *Rebel Without a Cause,* Warner Bros. Archives.

151 *"The day I kissed my father"*: Harry Clein, "Natalie Wood: On Acting, Nudity, and Growing Up in Hollywood," *Entertainment World,* 1/30/70, pp. 7–9.

151 *It is also possible:* Simmons, "The Censoring of 'Rebel Without a Cause,'" p. 59.

151 *Stern's screenplay described the father:* Stern, *Rebel Without a Cause* screenplay, 3/25/55, p. A.

152 *But he also feels that Ray:* Kent Brown, *The Screenwriter as Collaborator: The Career of Stewart Stern,* p. 110.

CHAPTER ELEVEN. *A World of Their Own*

154 *his sense of the film:* David Dalton, *James Dean: The Mutant King,* p. 258.

154 *They brainstormed for only fifteen minutes:* Stewart Stern, authors' interview, 9/6/03.

154 *"We began to talk":* Brown, *The Screenwriter as Collaborator,* p. 104.

155 *"He had a notion":* Brown, *The Screenwriter as Collaborator,* p. 104.

155 *After their brief discussion:* Stewart Stern, authors' interview, 9/6/03.

155 *Built in 1924: Los Angeles Times,* "Wilshire Phantom House Soon to be Only Memory," 2/24/57, Part 2, p. 1.

155 *In 1936:* undated Warners publicity memo, files on *Rebel Without a Cause,* Warner Bros. Archives, Cinema-Television Library, University of Southern California, Los Angeles.

155 *Dubbed "the Phantom House": Los Angeles Times,* "Wilshire Phantom House," Part 2, p. 2.

155 *its status as a defining set:* Sam Staggs, *Close-Up on Sunset Boulevard,* pp. 84–85.

156 *Starting in mid-February:* memo from W. F. FitzGerald to W. L. Guthrie, 2/21/55, files on *Rebel Without a Cause,* Warner Bros. Archives.

156 *Meanwhile, they searched frantically:* memo from W. F. FitzGerald to W. L. Guthrie, 2/16/55, files on *Rebel Without a Cause,* Warner Bros. Archives.

156 *On February 21, Warner Brothers finally heard:* memo from W. F. FitzGerald to W. L. Guthrie, 2/21/55, files on *Rebel Without a Cause,* Warner Bros. Archives.

156 *By April 7 agreements were signed:* memo from W. F. FitzGerald to W. L. Guthrie, 4/7/55, files on *Rebel Without a Cause,* Warner Bros. Archives.

156 *Getty had recently won a lawsuit: Los Angeles Times,* "Wilshire Phantom House," Part 2, p. 1.

156 *But before filming could begin:* Jack Grinnage, authors' interview, 9/8/03.

156 *The Getty swimming pool:* Staggs, *Close-Up on Sunset Boulevard,* p. 85.

156 *The pool—which lacked a drain:* Jack Grinnage, authors' interview, 9/8/03.

157 *On the first day of shooting at the estate:* undated Warners publicity memo, files on *Rebel Without a Cause,* Warner Bros. Archives.

157 *But the crane was an hour late:* memo from Nicholas Ray to David Weisbart, 4/18/55, files on *Rebel Without a Cause,* Warner Bros. Archives.

157 *complicated fight choreography:* Frank Mazzola, authors' interview, 9/16/03.

157 *But in the middle of the boom shot:* memo from Nicholas Ray to David Weisbart, 4/18/55, files on *Rebel Without a Cause,* Warner Bros. Archives.

157 *Weisbart had been putting pressure:* memo from Nicholas Ray to David Weisbart, 4/18/55, files on *Rebel Without a Cause,* Warner Bros. Archives.

158 *the "Nick Ray 50-Hour Club":* "Interview with Nicholas Ray," *Camera Three,* CBS, 1977.

158 *"Nick was hassling with Ernie Haller":* Frank Mazzola, authors' interview, 9/16/03.

158 *Ray wanted to break away:* Susan Ray, ed., *I Was Interrupted: Nicholas Ray on Making Movies,* pp. 40–42.

158 *Vampira dropped by:* undated Warners publicity memo, files on *Rebel Without a Cause,* Warner Bros. Archives.

159 *Ray shot the scene three times:* "Production Camera Sheet," 4/18/55, files on *Rebel Without a Cause,* Warner Bros. Archives.

159 *pushing the scapegoated Hopper so hard:* undated Warners publicity memo, files on *Rebel Without a Cause,* Warner Bros. Archives.

159 *"I negotiated with Don Page":* Frank Mazzola, authors' interview, 9/16/03.

159 *All in all, Mazzola fell:* "Daily Production and Progress Report," 4/18/55, files on *Rebel Without a Cause,* Warner Bros. Archives.

159 *"Every time he fell":* Beverly Long, authors' interview, 9/8/03.

159 *Ray also shot a scene:* Frank Mazzola, authors' interview, 9/16/03.

159 *On that same day:* Frank Mazzola, authors' interview, 9/16/03.

160 *"When they weren't in front":* Jackie Perry, authors' interview, 12/10/03.

160 *"Boy, is he intent":* Natalie Wood, "You Haven't Heard the Half about Jimmy!," *Photoplay,* Nov. 1958, p. 84.

160 *"She was not happy with the way Jimmy":* Randall Riese, *The Unabridged James Dean: His Life and Legacy from A to Z,* p. 567.

160 *During her close-ups:* Suzanne Finstad, *Natasha: The Biography of Natalie Wood,* p. 182.

160 *"When he was off-camera":* Michael Goodwin and Naomi Wise, "Nicholas Ray: Rebel!," *Take One,* 5, Jan. 1977, p. 13.

160 *Actress Carroll Baker recalls:* Carroll Baker, *Baby Doll,* pp. 118–20.

161 *"Every time we'd get together":* Natalie Wood, "It's a Wonderful Whirl," *Motion Picture,* Aug. 1956, p. 62.

161 *Mineo "enjoyed horseplay":* Tom Hennesy, authors' interview, 9/18/03.

161 *"Honey, it's his way":* Finstad, *Natasha,* p. 196.

161 *Director Francis Ford Coppola:* Francis Ford Coppola, authors' interview, 6/1/04.

162 *black walnut: Los Angeles Times,* "Wilshire Phantom House," Part 2, p. 1.

162 *A Warners publicity memo states:* undated Warners publicity memo, files on *Rebel Without a Cause,* Warner Bros. Archives.

162 *This was the beginning:* H. Paul Jeffers, *Sal Mineo: His Life, Murder, and Mystery,* p. 32.

162 *Plato leads Judy and Jim:* Jack Grinnage, authors' interview, 9/8/03.

162 *As they make their way out into the garden:* Stewart Stern, *Rebel Without a Cause*

PAGE

   screenplay, 3/25/55, p. 92, Papers of Stewart Stern, University of Iowa, Iowa City, Iowa.

162 *Dean had been known:* Stewart Stern, authors' interview, 9/6/03.

163 *They suggested he substitute Mr. Magoo:* David Dalton, *James Dean: The Mutant King,* p. 257.

163 *"It's the lost boys":* Stewart Stern, authors' interview, 9/6/03.

163 *Stern saw the safe space:* Dalton, *James Dean,* p. 258.

164 *"The whole movement":* Stewart Stern, authors' interview, 9/6/03.

165 *"It was an accident":* Moss Mabry, authors' interview, 9/12/03.

165 *Many weeks later:* "Production Camera Sheet," 5/14/55, files on *Rebel Without a Cause,* Warner Bros. Archives.

165 *"Natalie was mad for James Dean":* Moss Mabry, authors' interview, 9/12/03.

165 *"I found myself constantly hoping to grow up":* Irene Thirer, "Screen Views," undated clipping, files on *Rebel Without a Cause,* Warner Bros. Archives.

165 *According to her friend Jackie Perry:* Jackie Perry, authors' interview, 12/10/03.

166 *Like many of Dean's other pals:* Lew Bracker, authors' interview, 12/4/03.

166 *But Wood's confidants understood:* Jackie Perry, authors' interview, 12/10/03; Mary Ann Brooks, authors' interview, 1/23/04.

166 *and according to Gavin Lambert:* Gavin Lambert, authors' interview, 9/19/03.

166 *On Monday:* undated Warners publicity memo, files on *Rebel Without a Cause,* Warner Bros. Archives.

166 *Censor Geoffrey Shurlock was concerned:* memo from Geoffrey Shurlock to J. L. Warner, 3/31/55, files on *Rebel Without a Cause,* Warner Bros. Archives.

167 *"Jim: There's something I should tell you, Judy":* Stewart Stern, *Rebel Without a Cause* screenplay, 3/25/55, p. 98.

167 *"I really wanted them both to be virgins":* Stewart Stern, authors' interview, 9/6/03.

167 *the claustrophobic ten-foot-square:* Los Angeles Times, "Wilshire Phantom House," Part 2, p. 1.

167 *"That was specifically copied":* Dennis Stock, authors' interview, 3/31/05.

167 *a short dolly shot:* "Production Camera Sheet" and "Daily Production and Progress Report," 4/21/55, files on *Rebel Without a Cause,* Warner Bros. Archives.

168 *"Natalie was so nervous":* Beverly Long, authors' interview, 9/8/03.

168 *According to Corey Allen:* Finstad, *Natasha,* p. 182.

168 *"They closed the set":* Jack Grinnage, authors' interview, 9/8/03.

168 *"terribly intimate exchanges":* Susan Ray, *I Was Interrupted,* p. 37.

168 *"When Nick had something to say":* Beverly Long, authors' interview, 9/8/03.

168 *Dean knew that Wood was jumpy:* Wood, "You Haven't Heard the Half About Jimmy!," p. 84.

169 *Their lips met:* Wood, "You Haven't Heard the Half About Jimmy!," p. 84.

169 *No wonder Wood:* undated Warners publicity memo, files on *Rebel Without a Cause,* Warner Bros. Archives.

169 *And, according to Ray, Wood had arrived:* Susan Ray, *I Was Interrupted,* pp. 87–88.

169 *In the future:* Susan Ray, *I Was Interrupted,* pp. 87–88.

170 *despite the sense of urgency: Los Angeles Times,* "Wilshire Phantom House," February 24, 1957, Part 2, p. 2

170 *In a memo:* memo from Eric Stacey to Don Page, 4/23/55, files on *Rebel Without a Cause,* Warner Bros. Archives.

CHAPTER TWELVE. *Jim Kisses Plato?*

171 *"Jim Kisses Plato?":* Steve Trilling, undated notes to screenplay, files on *Rebel Without a Cause,* Warner Bros. Archives, Cinema-Television Library, University of Southern California, Los Angeles.

171 *And Stern says he never wrote such a direction:* Stewart Stern, authors' interview, 9/6/03.

172 *"Warners didn't know":* "Interview with Nicholas Ray," *Camera Three,* CBS, 1977.

172 *"It is of course vital":* memo from Geoffrey M. Shurlock to Jack Warner, 3/22/55, files on *Rebel Without a Cause,* Warner Bros. Archives.

172 *In his four-page memo, Trilling proposed:* Steve Trilling, undated notes to screenplay, files on *Rebel Without a Cause,* Warner Bros. Archives.

172 *"Nick would always":* Gavin Lambert, authors' interview, 9/19/03.

173 *"I thought Lancaster":* Stewart Stern, authors' interview, 9/6/03.

173 *"I don't know why I had pictures":* Stewart Stern, authors' interview, 9/6/03.

173 *"Plato was the one":* Vito Russo, *The Celluloid Closet,* p. 110.

173 *"The gay community just wanted to own that movie":* Stewart Stern, authors' interview, 9/6/03.

174 *"I heard [Dean] explaining things to Sal":* Joe Hyams, *James Dean: Little Boy Lost,* p. 238.

174 *As Stern originally conceived it:* Stewart Stern, *Rebel Without a Cause* screenplay, 3/3/55, pp. 76–78, files on *Rebel Without a Cause,* Warner Bros. Archives; Stewart Stern, *Rebel Without a Cause* screenplay, 3/25/55, pp. 69–70, Papers of Stewart Stern, University of Iowa, Iowa City, Iowa.

174 *"This was an important scene":* Stewart Stern, authors' interview, 9/6/03.

175 *"I think that under no credible circumstances":* letter from Stewart Stern to Steve Trilling, 5/5/55, Papers of Stewart Stern, University of Iowa, Iowa City, Iowa.

175 *"Geez. I like that scene":* "Interview with Nicholas Ray," *Camera Three.*

175 *And in Hollywood, gays were hunted:* Sam Kashner and Jennifer MacNair, *The Bad and the Beautiful,* pp. 21, 47.

176 *even driving Rock Hudson:* Kashner and MacNair, *The Bad and the Beautiful,* pp. 148–50.

176 *Perhaps most importantly, in 1948, Alfred Kinsey:* Neil Miller, *Out of the Past,* pp. 250–51.

176 *Judd Marmor, an analyst:* Hyams, *James Dean,* p. 245.

176 *Ray biographer Bernard Eisenschitz reports:* Bernard Eisenschitz, *Nicholas Ray: An American Journey,* p. 20.

176 *Author Gavin Lambert had an intense affair:* Gavin Lambert, authors' interview, 9/19/03.

Notes

PAGE

177   *In his autobiography:* John Houseman, *Front and Center,* p. 178.

177   *Houseman also claimed:* Eisenschitz, *Nicholas Ray,* p. 71.

177   *But Ray's fourth and last wife, Susan:* Susan Ray, authors' interview, 12/29/03.

177   *"I'm not sure whether you mean":* "Interview with Nicholas Ray," *Camera Three.*

178   *"I didn't know whether":* Susan Ray, ed., *I Was Interrupted: Nicholas Ray on Making Movies,* p. 24.

178   *"I knew the approach":* Susan Ray, *I Was Interrupted,* p. 28.

178   *The Reverend James DeWeerd, who befriended Dean:* Hyams, *James Dean,* pp. 21–22.

178   *And while working in the parking lot of CBS:* Ronald Martinetti, *The James Dean Story,* pp. 35–37.

179   *"Well, I'm certainly not":* Hyams, *James Dean,* p. 90.

179   *In a 1980 slice of memoir:* Michael DeAngelis, *Gay Fandom and Crossover Stardom: James Dean, Mel Gibson, and Keanu Reeves,* pp. 113–14.

179   *"Gay, as a descriptive term":* Chris Huizenga, "William Bast: Portrait of Dean's Friend," *After Dark,* Feb. 1976, p. 34.

179   *According to actor Jack Larson:* Jack Larson, authors' interview, 12/4/03.

180   *"So I know he wasn't totally homosexual":* Beverly Long, authors' interview, 9/8/03.

180   *A number of women:* Hyams, *James Dean,* pp. 56, 216.

180   *Actress Betsy Palmer:* Betsy Palmer, authors' interview, 2/21/05.

180   *"James Dean was not gay":* Dennis Hopper, "James Dean," *Mirabella,* Nov. 1990, p. 186.

181   *Dean's good friend during that period:* Lew Bracker, authors' interview, 12/4/03.

181   *Ray's former boss Howard Hughes:* Hyams, *James Dean,* p. 240.

181   *But Bracker does believe:* Lew Bracker, authors' interview, 12/4/03.

181   *Director Elia Kazan thought:* Elia Kazan, *A Life,* p. 537.

181   *Gavin Lambert says:* Gavin Lambert, authors' interview, 9/19/03.

181   *"Some—most—will say":* H. Paul Jeffers, *Sal Mineo: His Life, Murder, and Mystery,* p. 27.

182   *"I was sitting":* Stewart Stern, authors' interview, 9/6/03.

182   *"We were all spoon-fed":* Ray Nielsen, "Corey Allen in 'Rebel Without a Cause,'" *Classic Images,* No. 216, June 1993, p. 56.

182   *"He said he had":* Hopper, "James Dean," p. 186.

182   *Critic Parker Tyler:* Parker Tyler, *Screening the Sexes: Homosexuality in the Movies,* pp. 143–44.

182   *In 1957, writer Jack Kerouac described:* Jack Kerouac, "America's New Trinity of Love: Dean, Brando, Presley," previously unpublished work read by Richard Lewis on *Kerouac: Kicks Joy Darkness,* CD, Rykodisc, 1997.

183   *Explaining his original conception of the Jim Stark character:* Eisenschitz, *Nicholas Ray,* pp. 254–55.

183   *"The army was built on the buddy system":* Stewart Stern, authors' interview, 9/6/03.

183   *Mel Ferrer's effete portrait painter:* Richard Barrios, *Screened Out: Playing Gay in Hollywood from Edison to Stonewall,* p. 205.

183 *the lesbian masseuse:* Barrios, *Screened Out,* p. 223.

184 *This dialogue does not appear in the final script by Stern:* Stewart Stern, authors' interview, 9/6/03.

184 *"I believe that I have been":* Susan Ray, *I Was Interrupted,* p. 28.

185 *a thick morning fog that would not lift:* undated Warners publicity memo, files on *Rebel Without a Cause,* Warner Bros. Archives.

185 *It's a well-written scene:* Stewart Stern, *Rebel Without a Cause* screenplay, 3/25/55, p. 21, Papers of Stewart Stern, University of Iowa, Iowa City, Iowa.

185 *In this scene, which was originally:* Stern, *Rebel Without a Cause* screenplay, 3/25/55, pp. 22–27.

186 *"What's that?":* Stern, *Rebel Without a Cause* screenplay, 3/25/55, p. 26.

186 *"We had hours":* Tom Bernard, authors' interview, 9/12/03.

186 *"against the law":* Beverly Long, authors' interview, 9/8/03.

186 *The cast made its way:* Steffi Sidney, authors' interview, 9/5/03.

186 *According to the script:* Stern, *Rebel Without a Cause* screenplay, 3/25/55, p. 2.

187 *"We shot way into dawn":* Steffi Sidney, authors' interview, 9/5/03.

187 *"They wouldn't do it today":* Jack Grinnage, authors' interview, 9/8/03.

187 *"We almost got into a fight":* Frank Mazzola, authors' interview, 9/16/03.

187 *It did not help:* Frank Mazzola, authors' interview, 9/16/03.

187 *"You're opening a keg of peas":* "Notes from Mr. Trilling," 3/24/55, files on *Rebel Without a Cause,* Warner Bros. Archives.

188 *But Dean told Ray:* Hyams, *James Dean,* p. 232.

188 *"We were all sitting":* Beverly Long, authors' interview, 9/8/03.

188 *"It summarized the themes of the film":* Stewart Stern, authors' interview, 9/5/03.

188 *According to author David Dalton:* David Dalton, *James Dean,* p. 235.

188 *"Jimmy did his opening scene":* Steffi Sidney, authors' interview, 9/5/03.

188 *"I was no further":* Beverly Long, authors' interview, 9/8/03.

188 *"Where did that come from?":* Dalton, *James Dean,* p. 235.

189 *"I don't know any other way":* Susan Ray, *I Was Interrupted,* p. 20.

189 *"Somebody reported it":* Steffi Sidney, authors' interview, 9/5/03.

189 *"It was a great day":* Tom Bernard, authors' interview, 9/12/03.

189 *"We'd only get":* Beverly Long, authors' interview, 9/08/03.

189 *"They had extra monkeys":* Steffi Sidney, authors' interview, 9/5/03.

CHAPTER THIRTEEN. *Chickie Run*

190 As Rebel *was about to enter its last month:* Val Holley, *James Dean: The Biography,* p. 268.

190 Giant, *which would begin production in less than four weeks:* Randall Riese, *The Unabridged James Dean: His Life and Legacy from A to Z,* p. 198.

190 Giant *director George Stevens had scheduled:* Holley, *James Dean,* p. 268.

190 *"If I thought I was risking my life":* Ronald Martinetti, *The James Dean Story,* p. 137.

Notes

PAGE

190   *But even the official program:* Bakersfield National Sports Car Races, Minter Field, 5/1/55, official program, p. 12.

190   *Four thousand fans:* Art Lauring, "Sports Car Racer Killed in Crash," *Los Angeles Times,* 5/2/55, Part I, p. 35.

191   *Von Neumann, the owner: Behind the Headlights: James Dean's Dark Destiny,* Speed Channel, 2004.

191   *"I encouraged his racing":* Martinetti, *The James Dean Story,* p. 123.

192   *"The war was over":* Joe Playan, authors' interview, 4/1/04.

192   *In 1947* Hot Rod *magazine:* Editors of *Hot Rod* Magazine, *50 Years of Hot Rod,* pp. 13–14.

192   *"They had cars in the script":* Frank Mazzola, authors' interview, 9/16/03.

192   *Years later, he would be immortalized:* Tom Wolfe, *The Kandy-Kolored Tangerine-Flake Streamline Baby,* p. 82.

193   *"Hot-rodders were militants":* George Barris, authors' interview, 3/18/04.

193   *In 1958* Motor Trend *magazine:* James E. Potter, "The Man Who Changes the Face of Detroit," *Motor Trend,* Aug. 1958, pp. 36–43.

193   *According to a March 28, 1955, memo:* memo from David Weisbart to Steve Trilling, 3/28/55, files on *Rebel Without a Cause,* Warner Bros. Archives, Cinema-Television Library, University of Southern California, Los Angeles.

193   *Mazzola says that every car in the film:* Frank Mazzola, authors' interview, 9/16/03.

193   *But the car was also a favorite:* George Barris, authors' interview, 3/18/04.

193   *"We were able to show that cars also could become stars":* George Barris, authors' interview, 3/18/04.

193   *In his song "Cadillac Ranch":* Bruce Springsteen, "Cadillac Ranch," *The River,* Columbia Records, 1980.

194   *According to Barris, the car was so admired:* George Barris, authors' interview, 3/18/04.

194   *Dean already knew:* George Barris, authors' interview, 3/18/04.

194   *A 1949* Life *magazine article: Life,* "The 'Hot-Rod' Problem: Teen-Agers Organize To Experiment with Mechanized Suicide," 11/7/49, pp. 122–28.

194   *A teenager and a baby: Washington Post,* "Juveniles Get Object Lesson in Perils of Playing 'Chicken,'" 7/7/50, p. 23.

195   *A Fort Pierce, Florida, man: Washington Post,* "1 Killed, 3 Hurt; Nobody 'Chicken,'" 10/27/52, p. 1.

195   *That same year: Traverse City (Mich.) Record Eagle,* "Play 'Chicken' Lose License," 1/15/52, p. 6.

195   *And in 1953: Los Angeles Times,* "Six Teen-agers Injured in Speed Dare Game as Cars Hit Head On," May 29, 1953, p. 9.

195   *"When we played 'chickie'":* David Dalton, *James Dean: The Mutant King,* p. 251.

195   *"Irving Shulman made a more dramatic suggestion":* Dalton, *James Dean,* p. 251.

195   *Warner Ranch, a 2,800-acre plateau:* Kevin Roderick, *The San Fernando Valley: America's Suburb,* p. 136.

195   *"It took a long time to prepare":* Ray Gosnell Jr., authors' interview, 12/15/03.

196 *"None of us had dressed warmly"*: Dalton, *James Dean*, p. 252.

196 *The next morning:* memo from Nicholas Ray to David Weisbart, 5/13/55, files on *Rebel Without a Cause*, Warner Bros. Archives.

196 *After arriving at the ranch:* "Production Camera Sheet," 5/13/55, files on *Rebel Without a Cause*, Warner Bros. Archives.

197 *At eleven o'clock, assistant director Don Page:* Faye Nuell Mayo, authors' interview, 9/15/03.

197 *Mayo had been working primarily:* Faye Nuell Mayo, authors' interview, 9/15/03.

197 *Mayo ended up shooting:* Faye Nuell Mayo, authors' interview, 9/15/03.

197 *"One of the reasons":* Tom Bernard, authors' interview, 9/12/03.

197 *Dean got along so well:* Faye Nuell Mayo, authors' interview, 9/15/03.

198 *While Wood may have been nervous:* Faye Nuell Mayo, authors' interview, 9/15/03.

198 *Mr. and Mrs. Gurdin:* Lana Wood, *Natalie: A Memoir by Her Sister Lana Wood*, pp. 1–2.

198 *When Hopper questioned Ray:* Gavin Lambert, *Natalie Wood: A Life*, p. 98.

198 *"Nick suddenly started yelling":* Suzanne Finstad, *Natasha: The Biography of Natalie Wood*, p. 187.

198 *Hopper decided to confront Ray:* Finstad, *Natasha* p. 187.

198 *Before walking away, Ray told Hopper:* Lambert, *Natalie Wood*, p. 98.

199 *"At that point":* Bernard Eisenschitz, *Nicholas Ray: An American Journey*, p. 246.

199 *"I grabbed Jimmy":* Aljean Harmetz, "Dangerous Rebel," *Premiere*, Feb. 2002, p. 39.

199 *Dean then asked Hopper:* Dennis Hopper, "James Dean," *Mirabella*, Nov. 1990, p. 185.

199 *"After hours, Frank was Buzz":* Corey Allen, authors' interview, 9/17/03.

200 *Years later:* Frank Mazzola, authors' interview, 9/16/03.

200 *"One of the things I wanted to show":* Vito Russo, *The Celluloid Closet*, p. 110.

200 *"I like you, you know?":* Stewart Stern, *Rebel Without a Cause* screenplay, 3/25/55, p. 60, Papers of Stewart Stern, University of Iowa, Iowa City, Iowa.

201 *"It was the best line in the picture":* Corey Allen, authors' interview, 9/17/03.

201 *"It was the sociological gift":* Corey Allen, authors' interview, 9/17/03.

201 *The cars, without drivers:* Steffi Sidney, authors' interview, 9/5/03; Beverly Long, authors' interview, 9/8/03.

201 *Ray yelled for everyone:* Jack Grinnage, authors' interview, 9/8/03.

201 *Dean had wanted to do his own stunts:* George Barris, authors' interview, 3/18/04.

202 *Bill Hickman:* George Barris, authors' interview, 3/18/04.

202 *Carey Loftin:* Carol Loftin, authors' interview, 8/5/04.

202 *After the film:* Paul Hendrickson, "Remembering James Dean Back Home in Indiana," *Los Angeles Times Calendar*, 7/22/73, p. 25; Carol Loftin, authors' interview, 8/5/04.

202 *Doubling for Dean:* Joe Hyams, *James Dean: Little Boy Lost*, p. 237.

202 *Among his many uncredited jobs:* Jon Olsen, "An Interview with Rod Amateau, director of The Garbage Pail Kids Movie," 10/26/02, *Angry Monkey Reader*, http://www.normalpeoplelikeyou.com/article_assets/garbagepailkidsinterview.htm.

Notes

PAGE

202   *"He was interested in anything":* Hyams, *James Dean,* p. 237.

202   *A prop man put down a mattress:* Holley, *James Dean,* p. 264.

202   *Shot with two cameras:* "Production Camera Sheet" and "Daily Production and Progress Report," 5/23/55, files on *Rebel Without a Cause,* Warner Bros. Archives.

202   *A second unit shot the footage:* "Daily Production and Progress Report," 5/17/55, files on *Rebel Without a Cause,* Warner Bros. Archives.

202   *Even though Dean was not required:* George Barris, authors' interview, 3/18/04.

202   *To shoot the scene, the studio first had to get permission:* memo from Eric Stacey to Nick Ray and David Weisbart, 4/11/55, files on *Rebel Without a Cause,* Warner Bros. Archives.

203   *Photographed from miles away:* "Daily Production and Progress Report," 5/17/55, files on *Rebel Without a Cause,* Warner Bros. Archives.

203   *As a time- and money-saving move:* memo from Eric Stacey to Don Page, 4/23/55, files on *Rebel Without a Cause,* Warner Bros. Archives.

203   *The first time they shot this scene:* Corey Allen, authors' interview, 9/17/03.

204   *"He couldn't relate":* Dalton, *James Dean,* p. 253.

204   *In fact, the chickie-run scenes were so troublesome:* "Daily Production and Progress Report," 6/23/55, files on *Rebel Without a Cause,* Warner Bros. Archives.

204   *In his history of game theory:* William Poundstone, *Prisoner's Dilemma: John Von Neumann, Game Theory and the Puzzle of the Bomb,* p. 197.

204   *Philosopher Bertrand Russell first made the analogy:* Bertrand Russell, *Common Sense and Nuclear Warfare,* p. 19.

205   *"It seemed for a while":* Robert Matthews, "Don't Get Even, Get Mad," *New Scientist,* 10/10/98, p. 26.

205   *Kahn, who believed the best strategy:* Herman Kahn, *On Thermonuclear War,* pp. 291–93.

205   *By having Jim and Buzz race:* Geoffrey Nunberg, "A Surge in Saber-Rattling at the Precipice," *New York Times,* 1/12/03, Section 4, p. 5.

205   *A 1954 study:* New York Times, "Youth Crime Rate in City Found High," 5/5/54, p. 33.

205   *On the day shooting of the chickie run began:* Washington Post, "European Reds Approve Military Pact Designed to Counter NATO Alliance," 5/14/55, p. 1.

205   *Meanwhile, Communist China and the United States:* Stephen Ambrose, *Eisenhower,* pp. 380–83.

205   *Tensions were so high:* Los Angeles Times, "False Air Raid Alert," 5/6/55, p. A1

206   *That same day: The American Experience: Race for the Superbomb,* PBS, 1999; *Operation Cue,* U.S. Civil Defense Administration film, 1955.

206   *Almost all the houses:* Marvin Miles, "Atom City Shows Few Could Have Survived Fury of the Blast," *Los Angeles Times,* 5/6/55, p. A1.

206   *"People may have known":* Beverly Long, authors' interview, 9/8/03.

206   *Stewart Stern would work:* Stewart Stern, authors' interview, 9/6/03.

206   *"I had no idea":* James Baird, authors' interview, 12/8/03.

206   *At five in the morning of May 15:* "Daily Production and Progress Report" and

"Production Camera Sheet," dated 5/14/55, files on *Rebel Without a Cause*, Warner Bros. Archives.

206 *"Everybody was bewildered"*: Beverly Long, authors' interview, 9/8/03.

207 *Sidney remembers seeing the flash*: Steffi Sidney, authors' interview, 9/5/03.

207 *Code-named "Zucchini"*: Defense Nuclear Agency, Department of Defense, *Operation Teapot, 1955—United States Atmospheric Nuclear Weapons Tests, Nuclear Test Personnel Review*, p. 8.

CHAPTER FOURTEEN. *Last Good-bye*

208 *"We were running way over"*: Faye Nuell Mayo, authors' interview, 9/15/03.

208 *"I believe every effort"*: Randall Riese, *The Unabridged James Dean: His Life and Legacy from A to Z*, p. 208.

209 *"It is neither possible or practical"*: memo from Eric Stacey to Steve Trilling, 5/11/55, files on *Rebel Without a Cause*, Warner Bros. Archives, Cinema-Television Library, University of Southern California, Los Angeles.

209 *"To lose the momentary isolation"*: memo from Nicholas Ray to David Weisbart, 5/23/55, files on *Rebel Without a Cause*, Warner Bros. Archives.

209 *Wood tripped and fell*: undated Warners publicity memo, files on *Rebel Without a Cause*, Warner Bros. Archives.

210 *Dean blamed weariness*: David Dalton, *James Dean: The Mutant King*, p. 266; Val Holley, *James Dean: The Biography*, p. 268.

210 *"I warned you"*: memo from Nicholas Ray to David Weisbart, 5/23/55, files on *Rebel Without a Cause*, Warner Bros. Archives.

210 *At one point, he loudly spat on the ground*: Beverly Long, authors' interview, 9/8/03.

210 *Finally, Ray approached Frank Mazzola*: Frank Mazzola, authors' interview, 9/16/03.

211 *Ann Doran had been nagging*: Richard Valley, "Character Actress: Ann Doran," *Scarlet Street*, Winter 1995, No. 17, p. 48.

211 *Stewart Stern found these lines*: Patrick McGilligan, *Backstory 2: Interviews with Screenwriters of the 1940s and 1950s*, p. 289.

211 *In the scene, as Stern wrote it*: Stewart Stern, *Rebel Without a Cause* screenplay, 3/25/55, p. 110, Papers of Stewart Stern, University of Iowa, Iowa City, Iowa.

211 *Stern says that this scene*: Stewart Stern, authors' interview, 9/6/03.

212 *During the making of* Rebel, *Dean's fan mail*: production notes on *Rebel Without a Cause*, p. 5, files on *Rebel Without a Cause*, Warner Bros. Archives.

212 *So many fans had shown up*: undated Warners publicity memo, files on *Rebel Without a Cause*, Warner Bros. Archives.

212 *"Genius or Jerk?"*: Jan Jamison, "Genius or Jerk?," *Silver Screen*, Dec. 1955, p. 21.

212 *"Maybe publicity"*: Richard Moore, "Lone Wolf," *Modern Screen*, Aug. 1955, p. 28.

212 *"very shrewd or very honest"*: Ruth C. Rowland, "What Jimmy Dean Has Done to Hollywood," *Movie Stars Parade*, Sept. 1955.

212 *"He saw his picture on the wall"*: Nick Adams, "Jimmy's Happiest Moments," *Modern Screen*, Oct. 1956.

Notes

PAGE

212 *During the last weeks on the film:* "Interview with Nicholas Ray," *Camera Three,* CBS, 1977.

213 *"Today my emotional apparatus":* "James Dean Discusses His Craft on the Set of *Rebel Without a Cause,*" *Great Moments of the 20th Century,* Rhino CD, 2000.

213 *Dean's friend Lew Bracker:* Lew Bracker, authors' interview, 12/4/03.

213 *Chuck Hicks, who played the ambulance driver:* Chuck Hicks, authors' interview, 9/12/04.

213 *"I wanted to do that scene":* Michael DeAngelis, *Gay Fandom and Crossover Stardom: James Dean, Mel Gibson, and Keanu Reeves,* p. 115.

214 *"He was very protective":* H. Paul Jeffers, *Sal Mineo: His Life, Murder, and Mystery,* p. 34.

214 *"In Plato's death scene":* Jeffers, *Sal Mineo,* p. 34.

214 *"[Jim] had the hots":* Boze Hadleigh, *Conversations with My Elders,* p. 12.

214 *In his landmark book:* Vito Russo, *The Celluloid Closet,* p. 110.

214 *Filmmaker Eric Rohmer wrote:* Eric Rohmer, "Ajax or the Cid?," in Jim Hillier, ed., *Cahiers du Cinéma: The 1950s: Neo-Realism, Hollywood, New Wave,* p. 114.

214 *Ray was instructed:* memo from David Weisbart to Nicholas Ray, 5/18/55, files on *Rebel Without a Cause,* Warner Bros. Archives.

214 *In his notes to Ray:* Steve Trilling, undated notes to screenplay, files on *Rebel Without a Cause,* Warner Bros. Archives.

214 *Surprisingly, Stewart Stern says that originally:* Stewart Stern, authors' interview, 9/6/03.

215 *As Ray would note:* Michael Goodwin and Naomi Wise, "Nicholas Ray: Rebel!," *Take One,* Jan. 1977, p. 13.

215 *After he finished shooting the night scenes:* Wayne Jones, "Marietta Canty Interview," *We Remember James Dean International Newsletter,* March 1982.

215 *Chuck Hicks says Ray:* Chuck Hicks, authors' interview, 9/12/04.

216 *When Ray told Stewart Stern:* Stewart Stern, authors' interview, 9/6/03.

216 *Just a few days before:* Stewart Stern, authors' interview, 9/6/03.

216 *and so alarming local residents:* undated Warners publicity memo, files on *Rebel Without a Cause,* Warner Bros. Archives.

217 *It was 6:55 on the morning of May 25:* "Daily Production and Progress Report," 5/24/55, files on *Rebel Without a Cause,* Warner Bros. Archives.

217 *"awaiting," as filmmaker Mark Rappaport:* Mark Rappaport, "The Picture in Sal Mineo's Locker," *Senses of Cinema,* July-Aug. 2001, http://www.sensesofcinema.com/contents/02/21/sd_sal_mineo.html.

217 *As the film began to wind down, Lew Bracker:* Lew Bracker, authors' interview, 12/4/03.

218 *"Everyone was kind of sad":* Bernard Eisenschitz, *Nicholas Ray: An American Journey,* p. 252.

218 *the two formed a bond with their dueling Mr. Magoos:* undated Warners publicity memo, files on *Rebel Without a Cause,* Warner Bros. Archives.

218 *"squared off":* Suzanne Finstad, *Natasha: The Biography of Natalie Wood,* p. 185.

218 *Dean would visit her home:* Holley, *James Dean,* p. 264.

218 *One night, he even showed up:* Donald Spoto, *Rebel: The Life and Legend of James Dean,* p. 224.

218 *Ray spent a large portion of the last production day:* "Production Camera Sheet" and "Daily Production and Progress Report," 5/26/55, files on *Rebel Without a Cause,* Warner Bros. Archives.

218 *Ray realized that he still needed a close-up: A&E Biography: Natalie Wood,* A&E television documentary, 2003.

218 *Ray got his close-up:* "Production Camera Sheet" and "Daily Production and Progress Report," 5/26/55, files on *Rebel Without a Cause,* Warner Bros. Archives.

218 *But during these last moments:* Faye Nuell Mayo, authors' interview, 9/15/03.

219 *"We didn't really want to admit":* John Howlett, *James Dean: The Biography,* p. 113.

219 *Ray, Wood, Dennis Hopper:* Eisenschitz, *Nicholas Ray,* p. 252.

219 *"like a flying angel":* Howlett, *James Dean,* p. 113.

219 *"That should be the end of the film!":* Eisenschitz, *Nicholas Ray,* p. 252.

CHAPTER FIFTEEN. *Crash*

220 *Mineo had to redo some dialogue:* cutting notes, 7/12/55, files on *Rebel Without a Cause,* Warner Bros. Archives, Cinema-Television Library, University of Southern California, Los Angeles.

220 *Other lines had to be dubbed:* memo from David Weisbart to William A. Mueller, 9/6/55, files on *Rebel Without a Cause,* Warner Bros. Archives.

221 *"Dean was a mumbler":* Tom Bernard, authors' interview, 9/12/03.

221 *In an April 1 memo to Ray:* memo from David Weisbart to Nicholas Ray, 4/1/55, files on *Rebel Without a Cause,* Warner Bros. Archives.

221 *and a month later he reiterated his concerns:* memo from David Weisbart to Nicholas Ray, 4/28/55, files on *Rebel Without a Cause,* Warner Bros. Archives.

221 *Weisbart was especially concerned:* undated memo from David Weisbart to George Groves, files on *Rebel Without a Cause,* Warner Bros. Archives.

221 *On June 7, Ray sent a letter:* memo from Nicholas Ray to J. L. Warner, 6/7/55, files on *Rebel Without a Cause,* Warner Bros. Archives.

222 *On July 12, with the starting date on* Hot Blood: memo from Nicholas Ray to David Weisbart, 7/12/55, files on *Rebel Without a Cause,* Warner Bros. Archives.

222 *Sometime during this period:* Gavin Lambert, authors' interview, 9/19/03; Gavin Lambert, *Natalie Wood: A Life,* p. 107.

222 *One night, while Ray was out:* Jackie Perry, authors' interview, 12/10/03.

223 *"The picture itself is excellent":* memo from Jack Warner to Steve Trilling, 7/1/55, files on *Rebel Without a Cause,* Warner Bros. Archives.

223 *the first twelve-tone score:* Sabine M. Feisst, "Serving Two Masters: Leonard Rosenman Music for Films and the Concert Hall," *21st Century Music,* Vol. 7, No. 5, May 2000, p. 20.

223 *Dean took director Elia Kazan: Conversations with Robert Clary,* Jewish Television Network, 1992.

223 *But his ex-wife, Adele Essman:* Adele Essman, authors' interview, 9/13/03.

Notes

PAGE

223 *Rosenman ultimately took: Leonard Rosenman: Hollywood Beginnings,* Henderson Film Industries, 1999.

224 *Rosenman wrote much of his music:* Adele Essman, authors' interview, 9/13/03.

224 *According to Rosenman: Leonard Rosenman: Hollywood Beginnings.*

224 *"In many cases, I tell filmmakers":* Feisst, "Serving Two Masters," p. 20.

224 *Rosenman was flexible enough: Leonard Rosenman: Hollywood Beginnings.*

225 *Ray had wanted Rosenman:* David Dalton, *James Dean: The Mutant King,* p. 243.

225 *His music was so complex:* production notes, p. 4, files on *Rebel Without a Cause,* Warner Bros. Archives.

225 *polytonalities, fractured rhythms:* John Adams, conductor, liner notes to *The Film Music of Leonard Rosenman,* Nonesuch Records, 1997.

225 *Rosenman's Rebel score would also be a great influence:* Christopher Palmer, *The Composer in Hollywood,* p. 320.

226 *Dean had been excited:* Randall Riese, *The Unabridged James Dean: His Life and Legacy from A to Z,* p. 198.

226 *"I sat there for three days":* Hedda Hopper, *The Whole Truth and Nothing But,* p. 175.

226 *When Dean showed up:* Dalton, *James Dean,* pp. 267–68.

226 *"It was really depressing":* Dalton, *James Dean,* p. 268.

226 *He was especially anxious:* Steffi Sidney, authors' interview, 9/5/03.

227 *Meanwhile, Natalie Wood was also having a miserable time:* Lambert, *Natalie Wood,* pp. 104–6.

227 *"I only want to make pictures with kids":* Eisenschitz, *Nicholas Ray,* pp. 257–58.

227 *Ray had planned to do:* Eisenschitz, *Nicholas Ray,* pp. 258–59.

227 *He tried to re-create:* Eisenschitz, *Nicholas Ray,* p. 260.

227 *"The tragedy and the flaws in the film":* Eisenschitz, *Nicholas Ray,* p. 258.

228 *"Audience reaction on sight of his name":* telegram from Steve Trilling to Jack Warner, 9/2/55, files on *Rebel Without a Cause,* Warner Bros. Archives.

228 *While the audience's reaction was encouraging:* Stewart Stern, authors' interview, 9/6/03.

228 *Editing notes dated September 18, 1955:* cutting notes, 9/18/55, files on *Rebel Without a Cause,* Warner Bros. Archives.

228 *The Villa had become Dean's new hangout:* Val Holley, *James Dean: The Biography,* p. 265.

229 *Dean noticed that Wood was crying:* Nick Adams, "Jimmy Dean—Why We Loved Him," *Movie Life,* Sept. 1956.

229 *a brief moment in the alley:* Jeff Freedman, "Natalie Wood," *Interview,* Oct. 1978, p. 34.

229 *Dean comforted Wood:* Adams, "Jimmy Dean."

229 *Later in the evening:* Lew Bracker, authors' interview, 12/4/03.

229 *"I'm sorry that I allowed Nick Ray":* letter from Arthur S. Abeles Jr. to Wolfe Cohen, 11/28/55, files on *Rebel Without a Cause,* Warner Bros. Archives.

229 *In the end, the British censors cut:* Eisenschitz, *Nicholas Ray,* p. 267.

230 *Before Ray left for Europe:* John Howlett, *James Dean: The Biography,* pp. 134–36.

230 *"I had a secret fantasy":* Derek Marlowe, "Soliloquy on James Dean's Forty-Fifth Birthday," *New York,* 11/8/76, p. 46.

230 *On the evening of September 30:* Natalie Wood, "It's a Wonderful Whirl," *Motion Picture,* Aug. 1956, p. 62.

231 *The* Los Angeles Herald-Examiner *reported:* Riese, *The Unabridged James Dean,* p. 311.

231 *When a reporter asked Dean:* Holley, *James Dean,* p. 276.

231 *One day in September:* Lew Bracker, authors' interview, 12/4/03.

231 *Von Neumann and Joe Playan:* Joe Playan, authors' interview, 4/1/04.

231 *The only way Von Neumann would sell:* George Barris, authors' interview, 3/18/04.

231 *Dean agreed, trading in his Speedster:* Riese, *The Unabridged James Dean,* p. 396.

231 *Dean was proud: Memories of Giant,* Warner Bros. Film, 1998.

232 *Dean's friends:* George Barris, authors' interview, 3/18/04.

232 *Perhaps the oddest encounter:* Alec Guinness, *Blessings in Disguise,* pp. 34–35.

232 *Of Guinness's Obi-Wan Kenobi–like premonition:* Lew Bracker, authors' interview, 12/4/03.

232 *Customizer George Barris also says:* George Barris, authors' interview, 3/18/04.

232 *"In those final days":* Paul Hendrickson, "Remembering James Dean Back Home in Indiana," *Los Angeles Times Calendar,* 7/22/73, p. 25.

232 *Before Dean left:* Joe Hyams, *James Dean: Little Boy Lost,* p. 276.

232 *"Nowadays [Jim] lives":* Richard Moore, "Lone Wolf," *Modern Screen,* Aug. 1955, p. 75.

233 *Dean offered to take his father:* Hyams, *James Dean,* p. 276.

233 *Wütherich, Hickman and photographer Sanford Roth:* George Barris, authors' interview, 3/18/04.

233 *According to a persistent:* Hyams, *James Dean,* p. 277.

233 *As they sped down Highway 99:* Rolf Wütherich, "Death Drive: The Last Story About Jimmy," *Modern Screen,* Oct. 1957.

233 *At 3:30 p.m. Dean was stopped:* Hyams, *James Dean,* pp. 278–80.

233 *At 5:45, at the intersection:* Hyams, *James Dean,* pp. 278–80.

233 *Although an investigator would conclude:* Warren Beath, *The Death of James Dean,* p. 95.

233 *From the station wagon trailing the Spyder:* Hendrickson, "Remembering James Dean," p. 25.

234 *Roth got his camera:* Beath, *The Death of James Dean,* pp. 50–51.

234 *Suffering from a broken neck:* Riese, *The Unabridged James Dean,* p. 384.

234 *There was shocked silence:* Eisenschitz, *Nicholas Ray,* p. 267.

234 *Sal Mineo learned of Dean's death:* Lambert, *Natalie Wood,* p. 108.

235 *"Everyone was in hysterics":* Freedman, "Natalie Wood," p. 34.

235 *After the taping:* Lambert, *Natalie Wood,* p. 108.

235 *Steffi Sidney had just received:* Steffi Sidney, authors' interview, 9/5/03.

235 *Corey Allen had just gotten back:* Corey Allen, authors' interview, 9/17/03.

Notes

PAGE

235 *Beverly Long was planning to elope:* Beverly Long, authors' interview, 9/8/03.

235 *Frank Mazzola was driving:* Frank Mazzola, authors' interview, 9/16/03.

235 *Dennis Hopper and his agent were:* Dennis Hopper, "James Dean," *Mirabella,* Nov. 1990, p. 188.

235 *Stewart Stern was staying at Arthur Loew Jr.'s:* Patrick McGilligan, *Backstory 2: Interviews with Screenwriters of the 1940s and 1950s,* p. 291.

236 *Dean's childhood mentor:* Paul Alexander, *Boulevard of Broken Dreams: The Life, Times, and Legend of James Dean,* p. 257.

236 *On the train back to Los Angeles:* Stewart Stern, authors' interview, 9/6/03.

237 *"Nobody will come and see a corpse":* Wes D. Gehring, "Hollywood's Dilemma About Posthumous Releases: Audience's Reactions to Films Distributed After the Death of Their Stars Have Reflected Mixed Results," *USA Today Magazine,* May 2003, p. 64.

237 *"What's going to happen to the film?":* Jack Grinnage, authors' interview, 9/8/03.

237 *"Death of James Dean in an auto accident":* Variety, "Death of James Dean, Promising Star of 24, Not Affecting 'Rebel,'" 10/5/55, p. 7.

237 *On October 25, Ray returned to New York:* Eisenschitz, *Nicholas Ray,* p. 267.

237 *At a press screening:* Suzanne Finstad, *Natasha: The Biography of Natalie Wood,* p. 204.

237 *In Los Angeles,* Rebel *premiered:* Frank Mazzola, authors' interview, 9/16/03.

237 *The Los Angeles premiere:* Tom Bernard, authors' interview, 9/12/03.

238 *"JAMES DEAN CHEATS CAR DEATH IN BIT OF FILM IRONY":* Phillip Scheuer, "James Dean Cheats Car Death in Bit of Film Irony," *Los Angeles Times,* October 30, 1955, Part IV, p. 2.

238 Variety *called it:* Robert J. Landry, "Rebel Without a Cause," *Variety,* 10/26/55, p. 6.

238 *The* New York Times*'s stodgy critic:* Bosley Crowther, "The Screen: Delinquency; 'Rebel Without Cause' Has Debut at Astor," *New York Times,* 10/27/55, p. 28.

238 *"the cult of the dead teenager":* Geoffrey O'Brien, *Sonata for Jukebox,* p. 234.

238 *"To us teenagers":* Margaret Moran, "Letters to the Editor," *Life,* 10/15/56, p. 19.

238 *A year after* Rebel's *release:* Ezra Goodman, "Delirium Over Dead Star," *Life,* 9/24/56, p. 75.

238 *He received more letters: Washington Post,* "Fan Mail Pours in for a Dead Actor," 8/12/56, p. H2.

238 *Even Jim Backus:* Charles Denton, "Jimmy Dean Legend Swells," *Washington Post,* 4/15/56, p. J13.

239 Life *magazine called the obsession with Dean:* Goodman, "Delirium Over Dead Star," p. 75.

239 *Author Jack Kerouac:* Jack Kerouac, "America's New Trinity of Love: Dean, Brando, Presley," previously unpublished work read by Richard Lewis on *Kerouac: Kicks Joy Darkness* CD, Rykodisc, 1997.

239 *Fan magazines helped: Photoplay,* "The Truth Behind the Rumors That James Dean Committed Suicide," Nov. 1956, pp. 52–112.

239 *There were rumors that Dean's death:* Nell Blythe, "Jimmy Dean Fights Back from the Grave," *Movie Life,* June 1956, pp. 68–69.

239 *Some fans even believed:* Blythe, "Jimmy Dean Fights Back from the Grave," p. 24.

239 *Jack Grinnage contends:* Jack Grinnage, authors' interview, 9/8/03.

239 *The scandal magazine* Inside Story *claimed:* Lisette Dufy, "The Amazing James Dean Hoax," *Inside Story,* Feb. 1957, pp. 45–49.

239 *There were also stories that Warners: Washington Post,* "Fan Mail Pours In for a Dead Actor," p. H2.

239 *A mere two days after Dean died: Los Angeles Times,* "Death Premonition By Dean Recalled," 10/2/55, p. A-1.

239 *"The way he died":* Hendrickson, "Remembering James Dean," p. 25.

240 *In its first year of release:* Cobbett Steinberg, *Reel Facts: The Movie Book of Records,* p. 347.

240 *Screenwriter Irving Shulman protested:* Stewart Stern, authors' interview, 9/6/03.

240 *"When we were shooting* Rebel*":* Ron Smith, "The Car, the Star—and the Curse That Linked Them," *Robb Report,* Aug. 1990, p. 41.

CHAPTER SIXTEEN. *The Leading Lady*

241 *It wasn't long after finishing* Rebel: Faye Nuell Mayo, authors' interview, 9/15/03.

241 *"It's a gruesome thought":* Suzanne Finstad, *Natasha: The Biography of Natalie Wood,* p. 204.

242 *"I was embarrassed":* Finstad, *Natasha,* p. 204.

242 *"When Jimmy died":* Faye Nuell Mayo, authors' interview, 9/15/03.

242 *According to Jack Grinnage:* Jack Grinnage, authors' interview, 9/8/03.

242 *"We were always envious":* Finstad, *Natasha,* pp. 190–91.

242 *Meanwhile, Wood was:* Finstad, *Natasha,* p. 201.

243 *"They were just good friends":* Jackie Perry, authors' interview, 12/10/03.

243 *"He knew I was a friend":* David Dalton, *James Dean: The Mutant King,* p. 332.

243 *Louella Parsons demanded:* Gavin Lambert, *Natalie Wood: A Life,* p. 120.

243 *"He didn't drink":* Albert Goldman, *Elvis,* pp. 219–20.

243 *Wood made a pilgrimage to Graceland:* Finstad, *Natasha,* p. 231.

243 *"He felt he had been given this gift":* Goldman, *Elvis,* p. 220.

243 *Presley-mania was too much for Wood to handle:* Finstad, *Natasha,* p. 231.

243 *Walter Winchell reported:* Walter Winchell, ". . . Chatter from Broadway," *Washington Post and Times Herald,* 10/2/56, p. J6.

244 *Hennesy says that he would sometimes:* Tom Hennesy, authors' interview, 9/12/04.

244 *The long list of other men Wood reportedly dated:* Finstad, *Natasha,* pp. 208–11, 238.

244 *By the end of 1956:* Finstad, *Natasha,* p. 235.

244 *"She was running around with Jimmy Dean":* Mark Goodman, "Robert Wagner Heart to Heart," *GQ,* March 1986, p. 369.

244 *And she was bitterly betrayed by Nick Adams:* Lambert, *Natalie Wood,* p. 154.

244 *On February 7, 1968, Adams died:* Peter L. Winkler, "Nick Adams: His Hollywood Life and Death," *Crime Magazine,* 8/15/03, http://crimemagazine.com/03/nickadams,0815.htm.

Notes

PAGE

245 *On the first anniversary of their first date:* Lambert, *Natalie Wood*, p. 138.

245 *They bought a mansion in Beverly Hills:* Lambert, *Natalie Wood*, pp. 149–59.

245 *When she found out:* Finstad, *Natasha*, p. 213.

245 *One suspension lasted eighteen months:* Harry Clein, "Natalie Wood: On Acting, Nudity, and Growing Up in Hollywood," *Entertainment World*, 1/30/70, p. 8.

246 *"Later in life she often described":* Lambert, *Natalie Wood*, pp. 98–99.

246 *For the public, Wood would be able:* Lambert, *Natalie Wood*, pp. 232–233.

246 *"Natalie knew she had made":* Clein, "Natalie Wood," p. 8.

246 *"I put paint remover on her":* *Newsweek*, "Movie Star into Actress: The Story of Natalie Wood," 2/26/62, p. 56.

246 *In fact, working on* Splendor: Dick Moore, *Twinkle, Twinkle, Little Star: But Don't Have Sex or Take the Car*, p. 173.

246 *"When the persona fitted the role":* Lambert, *Natalie Wood*, p. 329.

247 *At first, Kazan was an insightful:* Lambert, *Natalie Wood*, p. 335.

247 *"Kazan showed me different ways to play a scene":* Moore, *Twinkle, Twinkle, Little Star*, p. 174.

247 *Not all of his lessons stuck:* Moore, *Twinkle, Twinkle, Little Star*, p. 173.

247 *"I always had a bit of inner resistance":* Moore, *Twinkle, Twinkle, Little Star*, p. 228.

247 *Reportedly Elizabeth Taylor was so upset:* Thomas Thompson, "Natalie Wood," *Cosmopolitan*, Aug. 1975, p. 124.

248 *Wood rehearsed the role with obsessive tenacity:* Finstad, *Natasha*, p. 268.

248 *In fact, even at this late date, her mother:* Lambert, *Natalie Wood*, p. 185.

248 *"I think* Love With the Proper Stranger*":* Lambert, *Natalie Wood*, p. 339.

249 *Finding herself once again swinging:* Finstad, *Natasha*, pp. 289, 292, 294.

249 *One night in the midst of shooting:* Lambert, *Natalie Wood*, pp. 215–16.

249 *In the mid-1960s, Wood finally broke her contract:* Clein, "Natalie Wood," p. 8.

250 *"Now is the most exciting period of film":* Clein, "Natalie Wood," p. 8.

250 *Though she had taken a cut in salary:* Clein, "Natalie Wood," p. 7.

250 *When she was offered:* Lana Wood, "Making Peace with Natalie Two Years After Her Death," *People*, 10/10/83, p. 93.

251 *"Right before a scene would start":* Finstad, *Natasha*, p. 390.

251 *"In spite of her love for RJ":* Lambert, *Natalie Wood*, p. 304.

251 *Reportedly, Wagner had been hearing rumors:* Sam Kashner, "Natalie Wood's Fatal Voyage," *Vanity Fair*, March 2000, p. 228.

251 *The day before Thanksgiving:* Faye Nuell Mayo, authors' interview, 9/15/03.

251 *The sea was rough:* Kashner, "Natalie Wood's Fatal Voyage," pp. 228–29.

251 *But by the next day:* Finstad, *Natasha*, pp. 408–9.

252 *When they were back on board:* Gavin Lambert, *Natalie Wood: A Life*, p. 311.

252 *Walken later told police:* Kashner, "Natalie Wood's Fatal Voyage," p. 231.

252 *Wood went down to bed:* Lambert, *Natalie Wood*, pp. 312–13.

252 *As soon as her body was found:* *Time*, "The Last Hours of Natalie Wood," 12/14/81, p. 40.

252 *Later, in the 1986 biography:* Kashner, "Natalie Wood's Fatal Voyage," p. 230.

253 *"There was no indication":* *Time*, "The Last Hours of Natalie Wood," p. 40.

253 *In an article about her death: Time,* "The Last Hours of Natalie Wood," p. 40.

253 *Years after she died:* Stewart Stern, authors' interview, 9/6/03.

CHAPTER SEVENTEEN. *The Erotic Politician*

254 *As he once quipped:* Boze Hadleigh, *Conversations with My Elders,* p. 12.

254 *In fact, having taken Mineo under his wing: A&E Biography: Sal Mineo: Hollywood's Forgotten Rebel,* A&E television documentary, 1999.

254 *Warners had agreed to lend:* Randall Riese, *The Unabridged James Dean: His Life and Legacy from A to Z,* p. 500.

255 *According to actor Ken Miller:* Ken Miller, authors' interview, 12/9/03.

255 *Throughout the mid-1950s, Mineo was constantly featured: Photoplay,* "TNT," Aug. 1958, p. 38.

255 *"Win a Date with Sal Mineo": Photoplay,* "Win a Date with Sal Mineo," Dec. 1956, p. 73.

255 *"He doesn't like to date the same girl": Photoplay,* "TNT," p. 39.

255 *Between films, Mineo continued: A&E Biography: Sal Mineo.*

256 Photoplay *magazine reported: Photoplay,* "TNT," p. 39.

256 *He recorded two singles:* H. Paul Jeffers, *Sal Mineo: His Life, Murder, and Mystery,* p. 59.

256 *The press book:* Jeffers, *Sal Mineo,* pp. 53–55.

257 *"There are a lot of things Sal did":* H. Paul Jeffers, authors' interview, 11/1/03.

257 *One of those incidents:* George Carpozi Jr., "Is Sal Mineo Too Fast for His Own Good?," *Photoplay,* Feb. 1962, p. 50.

257 *"Sal told me that he realized":* H. Paul Jeffers, authors' interview, 11/1/03.

257 *Although Jeffers does not feel:* H. Paul Jeffers, authors' interview, 11/1/03.

258 *"He was gung-ho in this picture":* Ray Gosnell Jr., authors' interview, 12/15/03.

258 *"He helped end movie censorship":* Hadleigh, *Conversations with My Elders,* p. 11.

259 *"The word* homosexual *had hardly been mentioned":* Hadleigh, *Conversations with My Elders,* p. 11.

259 *"wheat-flour dumpling":* Hadleigh, *Conversations with My Elders,* p. 8.

259 *On Oscar night:* Ruthe Stein, "50 Years of Oscar Viewing Start with a Splash," *San Francisco Chronicle,* 2/25/05, p. E-2.

259 *Years later, Joe Bonelli:* Joe Bonelli, authors' interview, 12/3/03.

259 *Mineo would often tell:* H. Paul Jeffers, authors' interview, 11/1/03.

260 *A particularly ludicrous* Rebel *myth:* Hadleigh, *Conversations with My Elders,* p. 24.

261 *"I found myself on the weirdo list":* Jeffers, *Sal Mineo,* p. 119.

261 *"You see, in some of the shots":* Jeremy Hughes, "Sal Mineo: The Eternal Original," *In Touch,* May/June 1976, p. 23.

261 *"Fortune and Men's Eyes was originally set":* H. Paul Jeffers, authors' interview, 11/1/03.

261 *The New York program for the play:* Jeffers, *Sal Mineo,* p. xii.

262 *"I don't consider the play to be about homosexuality":* Dustin Halliday, "Interview: Sal Mineo," *Avanti,* p. 7, http://salmineo.com/news/avanti.html.

PAGE

262   *The production was blasted:* Clive Barnes, "Theater: Question Marks on Stage 73," *New York Times,* 10/23/69, p. 55.

262   *"When I first met him he had a Bentley":* A&E Biography: Sal Mineo.

262   *In 1974, Mineo was momentarily reunited with his old director:* Susan Ray, authors' interview, 12/29/03.

263   *At one point, he was interested in buying:* Hadleigh, *Conversations with My Elders,* p. 20.

263   *He even talked about resuscitating his old music career:* Hughes, "Sal Mineo," p. 25.

263   *Eventually, he would comically refer to the film:* Hadleigh, *Conversations with My Elders,* p. 17.

263   *Joe Bonelli remembers:* Joe Bonelli, authors' interview, 12/3/03.

264   *In a 1978 article in* Esquire: Peter Bogdanovich, "The Murder of Sal Mineo," *Esquire,* 3/1/78, p. 118.

264   *According to former L.A. detective Dan Tankersley:* A&E Biography: Sal Mineo.

265   *In fact, the crime might have remained unsolved:* Tom Morgenthau, with Martin Kasindorf, "The Sal Mineo Case," *Newsweek,* 2/26/79, p. 54.

265   *On February 14, 1979:* New York Daily News, "An Ex-Pizza Deliveryman Guilty in Mineo's Slaying," 2/14/79, p. 17.

265   *"Three witnesses":* New York Daily News, "An Ex-Pizza Deliveryman Guilty in Mineo's Slaying," p. 17.

265   *Williams was sentenced to serve fifty-one years to life:* Jeffers, *Sal Mineo,* p. 202.

265   *He was paroled in 1994:* A&E Biography: Sal Mineo.

265   *The day after Mineo's stabbing:* New York Times, "250 Attend Sal Mineo Funeral; Actor is Called 'Gentle Person,'" 2/18/76, p. 40.

266   *"It meant a lot to him to be a gay icon":* Joe Bonelli, authors' interview, 12/3/03.

266   *"He was proud to say he was the first gay teenager in the movies":* H. Paul Jeffers, authors' interview, 11/1/03.

CHAPTER EIGHTEEN. *Elegy for a Director*

267   *"Jimmy was the key":* Frank Mazzola, authors' interview, 9/16/03.

267   *"We would have done both feature pictures and a TV series":* Bob Thomas, Associated Press, *Los Angeles Mirror-News,* 11/16/55, files on *Rebel Without a Cause,* Warner Bros. Archives, Cinema-Television Library, University of Southern California, Los Angeles.

267   *Dean and Ray discussed plans to adapt various projects:* Bernard Eisenschitz, *Nicholas Ray: An American Journey,* p. 266.

267   *a novella by Italian author Alberto Moravia titled* Agostino: Gavin Lambert, authors' interview, 9/19/03.

268   *"indisputable records of a very personal anguish":* Andrew Sarris, *The American Cinema,* pp. 108–9.

268   *"If* Rebel *has been playing":* David Dalton, *James Dean: The Mutant King,* p. 260.

269   *In the last writings:* Susan Ray, ed., *I Was Interrupted: Nicholas Ray on Making Movies,* p. 54.

269 *"I could see him":* Gavin Lambert, *Mainly About Lindsay Anderson,* p. 134.

269 *Just before beginning work on one of his slightest projects:* Lambert, *Mainly About Lindsay Anderson,* p. 138.

269 *For the lead, he hoped to hire Elvis Presley:* Eisenschitz, *Nicholas Ray,* p. 283.

269 *According to Lambert:* Gavin Lambert, "Good-bye to Some of All That," *Film Quarterly,* vol. 12, Fall 1958, p. 27.

270 *"I'd do it entirely as a ballad":* Eisenschitz, *Nicholas Ray:* p. 284.

270 *During a rare golden moment:* Lambert, *Mainly About Lindsay Anderson,* p. 142.

270 *The shoot was plagued by money problems:* Eisenschitz, *Nicholas Ray,* p. 297.

270 *After a stormy two years:* Lambert, *Mainly About Lindsay Anderson,* p. 144.

270 *"He was a very dear man":* Gavin Lambert, authors' interview, 9/19/03.

271 *"There were people in high places who believed in him":* Eisenschitz, *Nicholas Ray,* p. 348.

271 *Reportedly, upon hearing the news, the director threw up:* Vincent Curcio, *Suicide Blonde,* p. 103.

271 *Years later, Ray would pour out his unresolved anger:* Nicholas Ray, *The Cain and Abke Stiry* [sic], undated manuscript, Tom Farrell personal collection.

271 *at Betty Utey's urging:* Curcio, *Suicide Blonde,* p. 102.

271 *Ray taught Tim about filmmaking:* Vincent Canby, "A Fine Director Unemployed," *New York Times,* 6/8/69, Sec. 2, p. 18.

271 *But things did not work out well:* Curcio, *Suicide Blonde,* p. 102.

272 *A former executive at Columbia Pictures:* Ephraim Katz, *Film Encyclopedia,* p. 168.

272 *"I Was a Teenage Jesus":* Time, "Cinema: Sign of the Cross," 10/27/61, p. 55.

272 *"The flaming red garments":* Jonathan Rosenbaum, "Nicholas Ray," in Richard Roud, *Cinema: A Critical Dictionary,* p. 809.

272 *"I made the mistake":* Michael Goodwin and Naomi Wise, "Nicholas Ray: Rebel!," *Take One,* Vol. 5, Jan. 1977, p. 19.

273 *Then on September 11, 1962, Ray had a heart attack:* Eisenschitz, *Nicholas Ray,* p. 386.

273 *At one point:* John Houseman, *Front and Center,* p. 179.

274 *He would be called the theory's "test case":* David Thomson, "The Poet of Nightfall," *Guardian,* 12/27/03, p. 16.

274 *"cause célèbre":* Andrew Sarris, *The American Cinema,* p. 107.

274 *François Truffaut would dub him:* François Truffaut, "A Wonderful Certainty," in Jim Hillier, ed., *Cahiers du Cinéma: The 1950s: Neo-Realism, Hollywood, New Wave,* pp. 107–8.

274 *Jacques Rivette:* Jacques Rivette, "On Imagination," in Hillier, *Cahiers du Cinéma,* pp. 104–5.

274 *But most famously of all:* Jean-Luc Godard, "Beyond the Stars," in Hillier, *Cahiers du Cinéma,* p. 118.

274 *"dream-like, magical":* Truffaut, "A Wonderful Certainty," pp. 107–8.

274 *"ingrowing sickness":* David Thomson, *A Biographical Dictionary of Film,* p. 615.

275 *He came to know:* Eisenschitz, *Nicholas Ray,* p. 403.

275 *His embrace by young filmmakers:* Houseman, *Front and Center,* p. 179.

Notes

PAGE

275 *In 1957, Jean-Luc Godard had:* Jean-Luc Godard, "Nothing But Cinema," in Hillier, *Cahiers du Cinéma,* p. 116.

275 *At Cannes:* Susan Ray, *I Was Interrupted,* p. xv.

275 *"You know, instead of drinking yourself to death":* Hubert Cornfield, authors' interview, 5/25/04.

275 *It began as a project called* The Defendant: Eisenschitz, *Nicholas Ray,* p. 409.

276 *As critic David Thomson would write:* Thomson, *The Biographical Dictionary of Film,* p. 615.

276 *He called the trial "the greatest circus of bigotry":* I'm a Stranger Here Myself, October Films, 1974.

276 *"We were all . . . well, honored":* Eisenschitz, *Nicholas Ray,* p. 413.

276 *Using what he described:* Goodwin and Wise, "Nicholas Ray: Rebel!," p. 19.

276 *"We couldn't get cameras into the court":* Goodwin and Wise, "Nicholas Ray: Rebel!," p. 19.

276 *"The three great pornographers of the United States":* Goodwin and Wise, "Nicholas Ray: Rebel!," p. 21.

276 *"The money was withdrawn":* Susan Ray, authors' interview, 12/29/03.

277 *a point of view backed up:* James Leahy, "Breathing Together: The Author in Search of Inventors," *Senses of Cinema,* July–August 2003, http://www.sensesofcinema.com/contents/03/27/nicholas_ray_leahy.html.

277 *When the Chicago Seven project:* Susan Ray, authors' interview, 12/29/03.

277 *"My eye was kind of heavy":* Goodwin and Wise, "Nicholas Ray: Rebel!," p. 21.

277 *"He would buy eye patches":* Susan Ray, authors' interview, 12/29/03.

277 *"There's some question":* Susan Ray, authors' interview, 12/29/03.

278 *Shooting speed at this point:* Eisenschitz, *Nicholas Ray,* p. 410.

278 *Then in 1970 at a Grateful Dead concert:* Susan Ray, *I Was Interrupted,* p. xxvii.

278 *"Nick was unemployed":* Susan Ray, *I Was Interrupted,* p. xxvii.

278 *"big falling out":* Patrick McGilligan, *Backstory 2: Interviews with Screenwriters of the 1940s and 1950s,* p. 293.

278 *The film was being financed in part by Universal:* Peter Biskind, *Easy Riders, Raging Bulls,* p. 125.

279 *"With him living at the house":* Eisenschitz, *Nicholas Ray,* p. 427.

279 *"I was sure as hell going to get them":* Goodwin and Wise, "Nicholas Ray: Rebel!," p. 20.

279 *"It describes a psychological state":* Susan Ray, authors' interview, 12/29/03.

279 *"I dreamed for years about breaking the rectangular frame":* Eisenschitz, *Nicholas Ray,* p. 433.

280 *"still very much a part of our culture":* Tom Farrell, authors' interview, 9/20/04.

280 *"I play the part of a betrayer":* Goodwin and Wise, "Nicholas Ray: Rebel!," p. 21.

280 *"Nick was very manipulative":* Leslie Levinson, authors' interview, 5/9/05.

281 *"Nick taught us that acting is living":* Tom Farrell, authors' interview, 9/20/04.

281 *"Some people had dropped out":* Tom Farrell, authors' interview, 9/20/04.

281 *In the spring of 1972:* Tom Farrell, authors' interview, 9/20/04.

281 *After the school year ended:* Tom Farrell, authors' interview, 9/20/04.

282 *He called Gene Kelly:* Tom Farrell, authors' interview, 9/20/04.

282 *and even tried:* Canby, "A Fine Director, Unemployed," Sec. 2, p. 18.

282 *The bungalow still looked as it did in 1955:* Tom Farrell, authors' interview, 9/20/04.

282 *"The simple fact that this guy":* Eisenschitz, *Nicholas Ray,* p. 445.

282 *To get around town, Ray borrowed a car:* Frank Mazzola, authors' interview, 9/16/03.

282 *For the last time, Ray would organize:* Eisenschitz, *Nicholas Ray,* p. 445; Tom Farrell, authors' interview, 9/20/04.

283 *"It was hell":* Susan Ray, authors' interview, 12/29/03.

283 *Within a week of Susan's leaving:* Susan Ray, authors' interview, 12/29/03.

283 *Then, in early 1977, the newly sober Ray:* Susan Ray, *I Was Interrupted,* p. xxxiv.

283 *While at NYU, he would teach:* Eisenschitz, *Nicholas Ray,* p. 476.

284 *"Of course there was a kind of denial":* Susan Ray, authors' interview, 12/29/03.

284 *Ray would undergo:* Eisenschitz, *Nicholas Ray,* pp. 474–75.

284 *Ray wanted to make a film that centered on illness:* Eisenschitz, *Nicholas Ray,* p. 477.

284 *According to Wenders:* Director's commentary, *Lightning Over Water,* DVD, Anchor Bay Entertainment, 1980.

284 *At one point Ray suggested:* Eisenschitz, *Nicholas Ray,* p. 480.

285 *"I don't think Nick thought":* Susan Ray, authors' interview, 12/29/03.

285 *According to Tom Farrell:* Tom Farrell, authors' interview, 9/20/04.

285 *Susan Ray felt that, ultimately, Wenders:* Susan Ray, authors' interview, 12/29/03.

285 *John Houseman called the film:* Lambert, *Mainly About Lindsay Anderson,* p. 317.

285 *Elia Kazan was shocked:* Elia Kazan, *A Life,* p. 789.

286 *He remained estranged:* Curcio, *Suicide Blonde,* pp. 219–22.

286 *"Nick always seemed hard on him":* Tom Farrell, authors' interview, 9/20/04.

286 *"To his own sons":* Susan Ray, authors' interview, 12/29/03.

286 *"I think he felt guilty for his gifts":* Susan Ray, authors' interview, 12/29/03.

287 *"He didn't give in":* Kazan, *A Life,* p. 792.

287 *"He went 'all the way'":* Kazan, *A Life,* p. 790.

287 *In a fragment titled "I Am Concerned with the State":* Susan Ray, *I Was Interrupted,* p. 9.

AFTERWORD. *The* Rebel *Effect*

288 *"a worldwide cult phenomenon":* Elliott Stein, "Hello Stranger," *Village Voice,* 3/12–18/03, p. 116.

288 *According to Brewer's:* *Brewer's Twentieth-Century Dictionary of Phrase and Fable,* p. 512.

288 *Columnist George Will:* George Will, "The Roaring '50s," *Washington Post,* 6/20/93, p. C7.

289 *Director Peter Bogdanovich believes:* Peter Bogdanovich, authors' interview, 2/11/05.

289 *"It gave voice to something":* Arthur Penn, authors' interview, 5/25/04.

Notes

PAGE

289 *"It was ten years in advance":* Bernardo Bertolucci, authors' interview, 7/10/04.

289 *"Maybe teenager land":* Richard Linklater, *Dazed and Confused: Inspired by the Screenplay,* p. 6.

289 *Ironically, psychologist Robert Lindner:* Robert Lindner, *Must You Conform?,* p. 40.

289 *Sociologist Orrin Klapp:* Alvin Toffler, *Future Shock,* p. 308.

289 *According to writer David Dalton:* "Friends, Family and Co-Stars Remember Actor James Dean," *Larry King Live,* CNN, 1/11/04.

290 *"Clyde would have been a perfect part for James Dean":* J. Hoberman, *The Dream Life: Movies, Media, and the Mythology of the Sixties,* p. 184.

290 *"Ray's most forceful heir":* Anthony Lane, "Only the Lonely," *New Yorker,* 3/24/03, p. 89.

291 *The industry trade magazine:* Randall Riese, *The Unabridged James Dean: His Life and Legacy from A to Z,* p. 461.

291 *Growing up in the 1950s, Bob Dylan:* Marcus Winslow, authors' interview, 5/5/05.

292 *On their car-culture concept album:* Beach Boys, "A Young Man Is Gone," *Little Deuce Coupe,* Capitol Records, 1962.

292 *In England, where Rebel was banned for teens until 1968:* John Francis Kreidl, *Nicholas Ray,* pp. 155–61.

292 *Even John Lennon said:* Terry Cunningham, *James Dean: The Way It Was,* p. 38.

292 *"a '50s hood in the James Dean mold":* Jay Cocks, "Rock's New Sensation: The Backstreet Phantom of Rock," *Time,* 10/22/75, pp. 48–58.

292 *reportedly carried a biography of Dean:* Riese, *The Unabridged James Dean,* p. 503.

292 *"James Dean with a guitar":* Bruce Harris, "Review: David Bowie's *Rise and Fall of Ziggy Stardust and the Spiders From Mars*," *Words & Music,* Sept. 1972.

293 *"the James Dean of our times":* Quincy Jones, foreword to *Tupac Shakur,* p. 152.

293 *"I have to go back to James Dean":* Andrew Sarris, "Eminem Made Me a Believer: He's James Dean, Not Elvis," *New York Observer,* 11/25/02, p. 23.

293 *Eric Rohmer wrote:* Eric Rohmer, "Ajax or the Cid?" in Jim Hillier, ed., *Cahiers du Cinéma: The 1950s: Neo-Realism, Hollywood, New Wave,* p. 114.

293 *At one time, France even had a cable channel:* Interview, "Canal Jimmy," March 1991, p. 52.

293 *In postwar West Germany:* Kreidl, *Nicholas Ray,* pp. 165–67.

293 *"Every time I go to Europe":* Dennis Hopper, "James Dean," *Mirabella,* Nov. 1990, p. 188.

293 *In Brazil:* Caetano Veloso, *Tropical Truth: A Story of Music and Revolution in Brazil,* p. 33.

293 *There is a Japanese brand of cigarettes called "Dean":* James Hopgood, "Another Japanese Version: An American Actor in Japanese Hands," in Joan Ferrante and Prince Brown, eds., *The Social Construction of Race and Ethnicity in the United States,* p. 471.

294 *Cruel Story of Youth has been called:* Stephen Holden, "Film: Young Japanese Rebels Adrift in Neon Nihilism," *New York Times,* 8/13/99, p. E24.

294 *The word teenager, coined originally as a marketing term:* Thomas Hine, *The Rise and Fall of the American Teenager,* p. 8.

294 *After an Ace comb showed up:* Gary Maddox, "Movies That Try to Make You Buy Are Stealing the Show," *Sydney Morning Herald,* 1/14/03, p. 10.

294 Forbes *magazine ranked Dean:* Lisa DiCarlo, "Top-Earning Dead Celebrities," *Forbes.com,* 10/23/03, http://www.forbes.com/2003/10/23/cx_ld_deadcelebtear_17.html.

295 *Although costume designer Moss Mabry:* Moss Mabry, authors' interview, 9/12/03.

295 *Another friend of Dean's, performer Sammy Davis Jr.:* Joe Bills, *James Dean Collectors Guide,* p. 33.

295 *After Dean's accident:* George Barris, authors' interview, 3/18/04.

295 *A fire broke out:* William Beath, *The Death of James Dean,* p. 106.

295 *A man who bought the car's transmission:* Ron Smith, "The Car, the Star—and the Curse That Linked Them," *Robb Report,* Aug. 1990, p. 39.

295 *At one show, the car rolled off the platform:* George Barris, authors' interview, 3/18/04.

295 *James Hopgood, an anthropologist:* James F. Hopgood, "Back Home in Indiana: The Semiotics of Pilgrimage and Belief in Honor of an American Icon," in Walter R. Adams and Frank A. Salamone, eds., *Anthropology and Theology: Gods, Icons and God-talk,* pp. 343–44.

296 *"James Dean was the perfect embodiment":* Graham McCann, *Rebel Males: Clift, Brando and Dean,* p. 125.

296 *"The James Dean necrophilia":* Turner Cassity, "Letters to the Editors," *Life,* 10/15/56, p. 19.

296 *In 1983,* Rolling Stone *put Sean Penn on its cover:* Christopher Connelly, "Bad Boy, Slab Boy, Every Boy," *Rolling Stone,* 5/26/83, pp. 26–31.

296 *"James Dean's acting":* François Truffaut, *The Films in My Life,* p. 297.

296 *Johnny Depp once stayed in the room:* Neal Travis, "Neal Travis' New York," *New York Post,* 3/5/98, p. 9.

296 *just as Dean once stayed:* Riese, *The Unabridged James Dean,* pp. 46–47.

296 *"If Marlon Brando changed the way people acted":* Riese, *The Unabridged James Dean,* p. 488.

297 *"I grew up with the Dean* thing": Riese, *The Unabridged James Dean,* p. 377.

297 *"50 Greatest Movies":* TV Guide, "TV Guide's 50 Greatest Movies on TV and Video," 8/8–14/98, p. 21.

297 Entertainment Weekly, *whose critic called it:* Ty Burr, *The 100 Greatest Movies of All Time,* 1999, p. 139.

297 *When asked to explain:* Patrick McGilligan, *Backstory 2: Interviews with Screenwriters of the 1940s and 1950s,* p. 308.

297 New Yorker *critic Anthony Lane wrote:* Anthony Lane, "Only the Lonely," *New Yorker,* 3/24/03, p. 89.

Bibliography

BOOKS

Adams, Leith, and Keith Burns. *James Dean: Behind The Scene.* New York: Carol Publishing Group, 1990.

Adams, Walter R., and Frank A. Salamone, eds. *Anthropology and Theology: Gods, Icons and God-talk.* Lanham, Md.: University Press of America, 2000.

Alexander, Paul. *Boulevard of Broken Dreams: The Life, Times and Legend of James Dean.* New York: Penguin Books, 1994.

Ambrose, Stephen E. *Eisenhower.* New York: Simon & Schuster, 1991.

American Business Consultants, Inc. *Red Channels: The Report of Communist Influence in Radio and Television.* New York: Counterattack, 1950.

Aristotle. *Poetics.* Translated by S. H. Butcher. New York: Hill & Wang, 1961.

Andrew, Geoff. *The Films of Nicholas Ray: The Poet of Nightfall.* London: British Film Institute, 2004.

Backus, Jim. *Rocks on the Roof.* New York: Putnam, 1958.

Balazs, Andre. *Hollywood Handbook: Chateau Marmont.* New York: Universe Publishing, 1996.

Baker, Carroll. *Baby Doll.* New York: Dell, 1985.

Baldwin, James. *The Devil Finds Work.* New York: Dell, 1976.

Barrios, Richard. *Screened Out: Playing Gay in Hollywood from Edison to Stonewall.* New York and London: Routledge, 2002.

Bast, William. *James Dean: A Biography.* New York: Ballantine Books, 1956.

Beath, Warren. *The Death of James Dean.* New York: Grove Press, 1986.

Bills, Joe. *James Dean Collectors Guide.* Gas City, Ind.: L-W Book Sales, 1999.

Biskind, Peter. *Easy Riders, Raging Bulls.* New York: Simon & Schuster, 1998.

Blaine, Allan. *Nicholas Ray: A Guide to References and Resources.* Boston: G. K. Hall, 1984.

Blair, Betsy. *The Memory of All That: Love and Politics in New York, Hollywood, and Paris.* New York: Alfred A. Knopf, 2003.

Bogdanovich, Peter. *Who the Hell's in It?* New York: Alfred A. Knopf, 2004.

Bosworth, Patricia. *Marlon Brando.* New York: Viking Penguin, 2001.

Brando, Marlon. *Songs My Mother Taught Me.* New York: Random House, 1994.

Brewer's Twentieth-Century Dictionary of Phrase and Fable. Boston: Houghton Mifflin, 1992.

Brown, Kent R. *The Screenwriter as Collaborator: The Career of Stewart Stern.* New York: Arno Press, 1980.

Buñuel, Luis. *My Last Sigh.* New York: Alfred A. Knopf, 1983.

Burr, Ty. *The 100 Greatest Movies of All Time.* New York: Time-Life Inc., 1999.

Bibliography

Chaplin, Saul. *The Golden Age of Movie Musicals and Me.* Norman, Okla.: University of Oklahoma Press, 1994.

Ciment, Michel. *Conversations with Losey.* London: Routledge & Kegan Paul, 1985.

Clarke, Charles G. *Photographic Techniques of CinemaScope Pictures.* Los Angeles: Twentieth Century Fox, 1955.

Collins, Joan. *Second Act: An Autobiography.* New York: St. Martin's Press, 1997.

Cunningham, Terry. *James Dean: The Way It Was.* Philadelphia: Electric Reader, 1983.

Curcio, Vincent. *Suicide Blonde: The Life of Gloria Grahame.* New York: William Morrow, 1989.

Dalton, David. *James Dean: The Mutant King.* New York: St. Martin's, 1974.

DeAngelis, Michael. *Gay Fandom and Crossover Stardom: James Dean, Mel Gibson, and Keanu Reeves.* Durham, N.C.: Duke University Press, 2001.

Defense Nuclear Agency, Department of Defense. *Operation Teapot, 1955—United States Atmospheric Nuclear Weapons Tests, Nuclear Test Personnel Review.* Washington, D.C.: Defense Nuclear Agency, 1981.

Editors of *Hot Rod* magazine. *50 Years of Hot Rod.* Osceola, Wis.: Motorbooks International, 1998.

Eisenschitz, Bernard. *Nicholas Ray: An American Journey.* London: Faber & Faber, 1993.

Ferrante, Joan, and Prince Brown, eds. *The Social Construction of Race and Ethnicity in the United States.* New York: Longman, 1998.

Finstad, Suzanne. *Natasha: The Biography of Natalie Wood.* New York: Harmony Books, 2001.

Fried, Richard M. *Nightmare in Red: The McCarthy Era in Perspective.* London: Oxford University Press, 1991.

Gelb, Arthur and Barbara. *O'Neill: Life with Monte Cristo.* New York: Applause Theatre & Cinema Book Publishers, 2000.

Gilmore, John. *Live Fast—Die Young: My Life with James Dean.* New York: Thunder's Mouth Press, 1997.

Goldman, Albert. *Elvis.* New York: McGraw-Hill, 1984.

Guinness, Alec. *Blessings in Disguise.* New York: Alfred A. Knopf, 1986.

Guralnick, Peter. *Last Train to Memphis: The Rise of Elvis Presley, Vol. 1.* New York: Little Brown, 1994.

Hadleigh, Boze. *Conversations with My Elders.* New York: St. Martin's Press, 1987.

Hajdu, David. *Positively 4th Street: The Lives and Times of Joan Baez, Bob Dylan, Mimi Baez Fariña and Richard Fariña.* New York: North Point Press, 2002.

Hillier, Jim, ed. *Cahiers du Cinéma: The 1950s: Neo-Realism, Hollywood, New Wave.* Cambridge, Mass.: Harvard University Press, 1985.

Hine, Thomas. *The Rise and Fall of the American Teenager.* New York: HarperCollins, 1999.

Hoberman, J. *The Dream Life: Movies, Media, and the Mythology of the Sixties.* New York: New Press, 2003.

Holley, Val. *James Dean: The Biography.* New York: St. Martin's Griffin, 1995.

Hopper, Hedda. *The Whole Truth and Nothing But.* New York: Doubleday, 1963.

Houseman, John. *Front and Center.* New York: Simon & Schuster, 1979.

Howlett, John. *James Dean: A Biography.* London: Plexus, 1975.

Hyams, Joe. *James Dean: Little Boy Lost.* New York: Warner Books, 1991.

Jeffers, H. Paul. *Sal Mineo: His Life, Murder, and Mystery.* New York: Carroll & Graf, 2002.

Jones, Quincy. Foreword to *Tupac Shakur,* by *Vibe* Magazine. Three Rivers, Mich.: Three Rivers Press, 1998.

Kael, Pauline. *I Lost It at the Movies.* Boston: Little, Brown, 1965.

Kahn, Herman. *On Thermonuclear War.* Princeton, N.J.: Princeton University Press, 1961.

Kashner, Sam, and Jennifer MacNair. *The Bad and the Beautiful.* New York: W. W. Norton, 2002.

Katz, Ephraim. *Film Encyclopedia.* New York: Harper & Row, 1979.

Kazan, Elia. *A Life.* New York: Alfred A. Knopf, 1988.

Kreidl, John Francis. *Nicholas* Ray. Boston: Twayne Publishers, 1977.

Lambert, Gavin. *Mainly About Lindsay Anderson.* London: Faber & Faber, 2000.

———. *Natalie Wood: A Life.* New York: Alfred A. Knopf, 2004.

Levy, Shawn. *Rat Pack Confidential: Frank, Dean, Sammy, Peter, Joey and the Last Great Show Biz Party,* New York: Main Street Books, 1999.

Lindner, Robert M. *Must You Conform?* New York: Rinehart & Co., 1956.

———. *Rebel Without a Cause: The Story of a Criminal Psychopath.* New York: Grune & Stratton, 1944. Reprint, New York: Grove Press, 1956.

Linklater, Richard. *Dazed and Confused: Inspired by the Screenplay.* New York: St. Martin's Press, 1993.

Lüscher, Max. *The Lüscher Color Test.* New York: Random Library, 1980.

Martinetti, Ronald. *The James Dean Story.* New York: Carol/Birch Lane, 1995.

McCann, Graham. *Rebel Males: Clift, Brando and Dean.* New Brunswick, N.J.: Rutgers University Press, 1993.

McDougal, Dennis. *The Last Mogul: Lew Wasserman, MCA, and the Hidden History of Hollywood.* New York: Random House, 1998.

McGilligan, Patrick. *Backstory 2: Interviews with Screenwriters of the 1940s and 1950s.* Berkeley: University of California Press, 1997.

McGilligan, Patrick, and Paul Buhle. *Tender Comrades:* New York: St. Martin's Griffin, 1999.

Miller, Neil. *Out of the Past.* New York: Vintage Books, 1995.

Moore, Dick. *Twinkle, Twinkle Little Star: But Don't Have Sex or Take the Car.* New York: HarperCollins, 1984.

Morrissey, Steven. *James Dean Is Not Dead.* London: Babylon Books, 1983.

Navasky, Victor. *Naming Names.* New York: Viking Press, 1983.

O'Brien, Geoffrey. *Hardboiled America: Lurid Paperbacks and the Masters of Noir.* New York: Da Capo Press, 1997.

———. *Sonata for Jukebox.* New York: Counterpoint, 2004.

O'Hara, Maureen. *'Tis Herself.* New York: Simon & Schuster, 2004.

Palmer, Christopher. *Composer in Hollywood.* London: Marion Boyars, 1990.

Poundstone, William. *Prisoner's Dilemma: John Von Neumann, Game Theory and the Puzzle of the Bomb.* New York: Anchor Books, 1993.

Ray, Susan, ed. *I Was Interrupted: Nicholas Ray on Making Movies.* Berkeley: University of California Press, 1993.

Riese, Randall. *The Unabridged James Dean: His Life and Legacy from A to Z.* New York: Wings Books, 1994.

Roderick, Kevin. *The San Fernando Valley: America's Suburb.* Los Angeles: Los Angeles Times Books, 2001.

Roud, Richard, *Cinema: A Critical Dictionary.* New York: Penguin, 1982.

Russell, Bertrand. *Common Sense and Nuclear Warfare.* London: Routledge, 2001.

Russo, Vito. *The Celluloid Closet.* New York: Perennial, 1987.

Sarlot, Raymond R., and Fred E. Basten. *Life at the Marmont.* Malibu, Calif.: Roundtable Publishing, 1987.

Sarris, Andrew. *The American Cinema.* New York: Da Capo Press, 1996.

Schrecker, Ellen. *Many Are the Crimes: McCarthyism in America.* New York: Little, Brown, 1998.

Schuster, Mel. *Motion Picture Performers: A Bibliography of Magazine and Periodical Articles 1900–1969.* Metuchen, N.J.: Scarecrow Press, 1971.

———. *Motion Picture Performers: A Bibliography of Magazine and Periodical Articles 1970–1974.* Metuchen, N.J.: Scarecrow Press, 1976.

Spoto, Donald. *Rebel: The Life and Legend of James Dean.* New York: HarperCollins, 1996.

Staggs, Sam. *Close-Up on Sunset Boulevard.* New York: St. Martin's Press, 2002.

Steinberg, Cobbett. *Reel Facts: The Movie Book of Records.* New York: Vintage, 1978.

Sugarman, Danny, and Jerry Hopkins. *No One Here Gets Out Alive.* New York: Warner Books, 1995.

Thomson, David. *The Biographical Dictionary of Film.* New York: Alfred A. Knopf, 1994.

Toffler, Alvin. *Future Shock.* New York: Bantam, 1984.

Truffaut, François. *The Films in My Life.* Paris: Flammarion, 1975.

Tyler, Parker. *Screening the Sexes: Homosexuality in the Movies.* New York: Anchor Books, 1972.

Veloso, Caetano. *Tropical Truth: A Story of Music and Revolution in Brazil.* New York: Alfred A. Knopf, 2002.

Vidal, Gore. *Palimpsest.* New York: Penguin Books, 1995.

Wallace, David. *Hollywoodland.* New York: St. Martin's Griffin, 2003.

Winters, Shelley. *Shelley II.* New York: Simon & Schuster, 1989.

Wolfe, Tom. *The Kandy-Kolored Tangerine-Flake Streamline Baby.* New York: Bantam, 1999.

Wood, Lana. *Natalie: A Memoir by Her Sister Lana Wood.* New York: Putnam 1986.

Wylie, Philip. *Generation of Vipers.* Normal, Ill.: Dalkey Archive Press, 1996.

ARTICLES

Adams, Nick. "The Girl Who Grew Up Too Fast." *Modern Screen,* May 1956, pp. 42, 96–98.

———. "Jimmy's Happiest Moments." *Modern Screen,* October 1956.

———. "Jimmy Dean—Why We Loved Him." *Movie Life,* September 1956.

Archerd, Army. "Just for Variety." *Daily Variety*, May 2, 1955, p. 2.

———. "Just for Variety." *Daily Variety*, November 23, 1954, p. 2.

Aprá, Adrian, and Barry Boys, Ian Cameron, José Luis Guarner, Paul Mayersberg, and V. F. Perkins. "Interview With Nicholas Ray." *Movie*, Vol. 9, May 1963, pp. 14–24.

Bakersfield National Sports Car Races, Minter Field. Official program. May 1, 1955.

Barnes, Anthony. "*Rebel Without a Cause* Named Most Stylish Film Ever." *Irish Examiner*, May 2, 2003, http://archives.tcm.ie/irishexaminer/2003/05/02/story437776418.asp

Barnes, Clive. "Theater: Question Marks on Stage 73 (Review of *Fortune and Men's Eyes*)." *New York Times*, October 23, 1969, p. 55.

Blythe, Nell. "Jimmy Dean Fights Back from the Grave." *Movie Life*, June 1956, pp. 23–26, 67–69.

Bogdanovich, Peter. "The Murder of Sal Mineo." *Esquire*, March 1, 1978, pp. 116–18.

Canby, Vincent. "A Fine Director, Unemployed." *New York Times*, June 8, 1969, Sec. 2, pp. 1, 18.

Capote, Truman. "The Duke in His Domain." *New Yorker*, November 9, 1957, pp. 53–100.

Carpozi, George Jr. "Is Sal Mineo Too Fast for His Own Good?" *Photoplay*, February 1962, pp. 50–51, 90–91.

Carroll, Harrison. "Dean Terrorizes Film Set." *Los Angeles Herald-Examiner*, May 21, 1955.

Cassity, Turner. "Letters to the Editor." *Life*, October 15, 1956, p. 19.

Clein, Harry. "Natalie Wood: On Acting, Nudity, and Growing Up in Hollywood." *Entertainment World*, January 30, 1970, pp. 7–9.

Clendenen, Richard. "Why Teen-Agers Go Wrong." *U.S. News and World Report*, September 17, 1954.

Cocks, Jay. "Rock's New Sensation: The Backstreet Phantom of Rock." *Time*, October 27, 1975, pp. 48–58.

Cole, K. C. "Ed Krupp's Star-Studded Cosmic Extravaganza." *Los Angeles Times*, February 14, 1999, p. 10.

Connelly, Christopher. "Bad Boy, Slab Boy, Every Boy." *Rolling Stone*, May 26, 1983, pp. 26–31.

Connelly, Mike. "Rambling Reporter." *Hollywood Reporter*, December 24, 1955, p. 2.

———. "This Was My Friend, Jimmy Dean." *Modern Screen*, December 1955, p. 80.

Crowther, Bosley. "The Screen: Delinquency; 'Rebel Without Cause' Has Debut at Astor." *New York Times*, October 27, 1955, p. 28.

Denton, Charles. "Jimmy Dean Legend Swells." *Washington Post*, April 15, 1956, p. J13.

Dufy, Lisette. "The Amazing James Dean Hoax." *Inside Story*, February 1957, pp. 45–49.

Feisst, Sabine M. "Serving Two Masters: Leonard Rosenman Music for Films and the Concert Hall." *21st Century Music*, Vol. 7, No. 5, May 2000, pp. 19–24.

Freedman, Jeff. "Natalie Wood." *Interview*, October 1978, p. 34.

Gehring, Wes D. "Hollywood's Dilemma About Posthumous Releases: Audience's Reactions to Films Distributed After the Death of Their Stars Have Reflected Mixed Results." *USA Today Magazine*, May 2003, pp. 64–69.

Goodman, Ezra. "Delirium Over Dead Star." *Life*, September 24, 1956, pp. 75–86.

Bibliography

Goodman, Mark. "Robert Wagner Heart to Heart." *GQ,* March 1986, pp. 268–69, 366–71.

Goodwin, Michael, and Naomi Wise. "Nicholas Ray: Rebel!" *Take One,* Vol. 5, January 1977, pp. 7–21.

Halliday, Dustin. "Interview: Sal Mineo." *Avanti,* pp. 6–11, 56–58, http://salmineo.com/news/avanti.html.

Harmetz, Aljean. "Dangerous Rebel." *Premiere,* February 2002, pp. 36–39.

Harris, Bruce. "Review: David Bowie's *Rise and Fall of Ziggy Stardust and the Spiders From Mars.*" *Words & Music,* September 1972.

Hendrickson, Paul. "Remembering James Dean Back Home in Indiana." *Los Angeles Times Calendar,* July 22, 1973, pp. 22–23, 25.

Holden, Stephen. "Film: Young Japanese Rebels Adrift in Neon Nihilism." *New York Times,* August 13, 1999, p. E24.

Hollowell, John. "I'm Going to Live My Life." *New York Times,* March 9, 1969, p. D13.

Hopper, Dennis. "James Dean." *Mirabella,* November 1990, pp. 184–88.

Houston, Penelope, and John Gillet. "Conversations with Nicholas Ray and Joseph Losey." *Sight and Sound,* Vol. 30, Autumn 1961, pp. 182–87.

Hughes, Jeremy. "Sal Mineo: The Eternal Original." *In Touch,* No. 23, May/June 1976, pp. 22–25.

Huizenga, Chris. "William Bast: Portrait of Dean's Friend." *After Dark,* February 1976, p. 34.

Interview. "Canal Jimmy." March 1991, p. 52.

Jamison, Jan. "Genius or Jerk?" *Silver Screen,* December 1955, pp. 21–25.

Jones, Wayne. "Marietta Canty Interview." *We Remember James Dean International Newsletter,* March 1982.

Kashner, Sam. "Natalie Wood's Fatal Voyage." *Vanity Fair,* March 2000, pp. 214–33.

Lambert, Gavin. "Good-bye to Some of All That." *Film Quarterly,* Vol. 12, Fall 1958, pp. 25–29.

Landry, Robert J. "Rebel Without a Cause." *Variety,* October 26, 1955, p. 6.

Lane, Anthony. "Only the Lonely." *New Yorker,* March 24, 2003, pp. 88–89.

Lardine, Bob. "A Star Is Born Again." *New York Sunday News Magazine,* February 11, 1979, pp. 22–36.

Lauring, Art. "Sports Car Racer Killed in Crash." *Los Angeles Times,* May 2, 1955, Part I, p. 35.

Life. "The 'Hot-Rod' Problem: Teen-Agers Organize to Experiment with Mechanized Suicide." November 7, 1949, pp. 122–28.

Los Angeles Times. "Death Premonition By Dean Recalled." October 2, 1955, p. A-1.

———. "False Air Raid Alert." May 6, 1955, Part I, pp. 1, 3, 18.

———. "Six Teen-agers Injured in Speed Dare Game as Cars Hit Head On," May 29, 1953, p. 9.

———. "Wilshire Phantom House Soon to be Only Memory." February 24, 1957, Part 2, pp. 1, 2.

Maddox, Gary. "Movies That Try to Make You Buy Are Stealing the Show." *Sydney Morning Herald,* January 14, 2003, p. 10.

Marlowe, Derek. "Soliloquy on James Dean's Forty-Fifth Birthday." *New York,* November 8, 1976, pp. 41–46.

Matthews, Robert. "Don't Get Even, Get Mad." *New Scientist,* October 10, 1998, p. 26.

McKinley, Jesse. "Helmut Newton Is Dead at 83." *New York Times,* January 25, 2004, p. 1.

Miles, Marvin. "Atom City Shows Few Could Have Survived Fury of Blast." *Los Angeles Times,* May 7, 1955, Part I, pp. 1, 4.

Mineo, Vic, and Sarina Mineo. "My Brother's Tough—He Is Not." *Motion Picture,* 1956, http://salmineo.com/news/tough.html.

Moore, Dick. "A Last Visit with Natalie Wood." *McCall's,* October 1984, pp. 52–56, 167.

Moore, Richard. "Lone Wolf." *Modern Screen,* August 1955, pp. 28–29, 75.

Moran, Margaret. "Letters to the Editor." *Life,* October 15, 1956, p. 19.

Morganthau, Tom, with Martin Kasindorf. "The Sal Mineo Case." *Newsweek,* February 26, 1979, p. 54.

Nafus, Charles. "Writing Rebel." *Austin Chronicle,* June 16, 2000, http://www.austinchronicle.com/issues/dispatch/2000-06-16/screens_feature2.html.

Nathan, Jean. "What's Up with the Old Hotel." *New York Times,* August 1, 1993, pp. V1–V9.

Newsweek. "Movie Star Into Actress: The Story of Natalie Wood." February 26, 1962, pp. 54–57.

———. "Our Vicious Young Hoodlums: Is There Any Hope?" September 6, 1954, p. 43.

New York Daily News. "An Ex-Pizza Deliveryman Guilty in Mineo's Slaying." February, 14, 1979, p. 17.

New York Times. "Flores Succumbs to Ring Injuries." September 3, 1951, p. 18.

———. "250 Attend Sal Mineo Funeral; Actor is Called 'Gentle Person.'" February 18, 1976, p. 40.

———. "Youth Crime Rate in City Found High." May 5, 1954, p. 33.

Neyer, Constance. "Marietta Canty Dies; Actress Lived in City." *Hartford Courant,* July 10, 1986, pp. A1, A12.

Nielsen, Ray. "Corey Allen in 'Rebel Without a Cause.'" *Classic Images,* No. 216, June 1993, pp. 42–43, 56.

Nunberg, Geoffrey. "Ideas & Trends: A Surge in Saber-Rattling at the Precipice." *New York Times,* January 12, 2003, Sec. 4, p. 5.

Photoplay. "TNT." August 1958, pp. 37–39.

———. "The Truth Behind the Rumors That James Dean Committed Suicide." November 1956, pp. 52, 112.

———. "Win a Date with Sal Mineo." December 1956, p. 73.

Potter, James E. "The Man Who Changes the Face of Detroit." *Motor Trend,* August 1958, pp. 36–43.

Pryor, Thomas. "Busy Hollywood." *New York Times,* September 15, 1957, p. X7.

———. "Color Is Required For CinemaScope." *New York Times,* April 5, 1955, p. 33.

———. "Columbia to Film Poems by Jeffers." *New York Times,* March 17, 1955, p. 28.

———. "Film Assignment for Jane Russell." *New York Times,* January 4, 1955, p. 24.

———. "Warners to Seek Fresh Film Faces." *New York Times,* February 4, 1955, p. 17.

Rau, Neil. "The Fight Was for Blood—and They Got It." *Los Angeles Examiner,* May 22, 1955, p. 15.

Ray, Nicholas. "Story into Script." *Sight and Sound,* Autumn 1956, pp. 70–74.

Bibliography

Reynolds, Patricia. "Natalie Wood's Own Story." *Pageant,* July 1971, pp. 47–58.

Rosenman, Leonard. "Jimmy Dean: Giant Legend, Cult Rebel." *Los Angeles Times Calendar,* December 18, 1977, p. 70.

Rowland, Ruth C. "What Jimmy Dean Has Done to Hollywood." *Movie Stars Parade,* September 1955.

Sarris, Andrew. "Eminem Made Me a Believer: He's James Dean, Not Elvis." *New York Observer,* November 25, 2002, p. 23.

Scheuer, Phillip. "James Dean Cheats Car Death in Bit of Film Irony." *Los Angeles Times,* October 30, 1955, Part IV, p. 2.

Simmons, Jerold. "The Censoring of 'Rebel Without a Cause.'" *Journal of Popular Film and Television,* June 1, 1995, pp. 57–63.

Skolsky, Sidney. "Demon Dean." *Photoplay,* July 1955, pp. 38, 77–78.

Smith, Ron. "The Car, the Star—and the Curse That Linked Them." *Robb Report,* August 1990, pp. 34–41.

Stein, Elliott. "Hello Stranger." *Village Voice,* March 12–18, 2003, p. 116.

Stein, Ruthe. "50 Years of Oscar Viewing Start with a Splash." *San Francisco Chronicle,* February 25, 2005, p. E-2.

Thompson, Howard. "Another Dean Hits the Big League." *New York Times,* March 13, 1955, Section II, p. 5.

Thompson, Thomas. "Natalie Wood." *Cosmopolitan,* August 1975, pp. 123–25.

Thomson, David. "The Poet of Nightfall." *Guardian,* December 27, 2003, p. 16.

Time. "Cinema: Sign of the Cross." October 27, 1961, p. 55.

———. "The Last Hours of Natalie Wood." December 14, 1981, p. 40.

Traverse City (Mich.) Record Eagle. "Play 'Chicken' Lose License." January 15, 1952, p. 6.

Travis, Neal. "Neal Travis' New York," *New York Post,* March 5, 1998, p. 9.

TV Guide. "TV Guide's 50 Greatest Movies on TV and Video." August 8–14, 1998, pp. 14–33.

Valley, Richard. "Character Actress: Ann Doran." *Scarlet Street,* No. 17, Winter 1995, pp. 44–49, 104–5.

Variety. "Death of James Dean, Promising Star of 24, Not Affecting 'Rebel.'" October 5, 1955 p. 7.

Washington Post. "European Reds Approve Military Pact Designed to Counter NATO Alliance." May 14, 1955, p. 1.

———. "Juveniles Get Object Lesson in Perils of Playing 'Chicken.'" July 7, 1950, p. 23.

———. "1 Killed, 3 Hurt; Nobody 'Chicken.'" October 27, 1952, p. 1.

———. "Fan Mail Pours in for a Dead Actor." August 12, 1956, p. H2.

Walters, Richard H., and Edward Llewellyn Thomas and C. William Acker. "Enhancement of Punitive Behavior by Audio-Visual Displays." *Science,* June 8, 1962, pp. 872–73.

Will, George. "The Roaring '50s." *Washington Post,* June 20, 1993, p. C7.

Winchell, Walter. ". . . Chatter from Broadway." *Washington Post and Times Herald,* October 2, 1955, p. J6.

Wood, Lana. "Making Peace with Natalie Two Years After Her Death." *People,* October 10, 1983, pp. 83–102.

Wood, Natalie. "It's a Wonderful Whirl." *Motion Picture*, August 1956, pp. 43, 61–62.

———. "You Haven't Heard the Half About Jimmy!" *Photoplay*, November 1955, pp. 55, 82–84.

Wütherich, Rolf. "Death Drive: The Last Story About Jimmy." *Modern Screen*, October 1957.

ARCHIVAL DOCUMENTS

Esther McCoy Papers. Archives of American Art, Smithsonian Institution, Washington, D.C.

Files on Nicholas Ray. United States Department of Justice, Federal Bureau of Investigation, Washington, D.C.

Files on *Rebel Without a Cause*. Warner Bros. Archives, Cinema-Television Library, University of Southern California, Los Angeles.

House Un-American Activities Committee Files. Records of the U.S. House of Representatives, Center for Legislative Archives, National Archives, Washington, D.C.

Irving Shulman Collection. Ohio University, Athens, Ohio.

Papers of Stewart Stern. University of Iowa, Iowa City, Iowa.

RECORDINGS

The Beach Boys. "A Young Man Is Gone." *Little Deuce Coupe.* Capitol Records, 1962.

The Film Music of Leonard Rosenman. Conducted by John Adams. Nonesuch Records, 1997.

"James Dean Discusses His Craft on the Set of *Rebel Without a Cause*." *Great Moments of the 20th Century.* Rhino Records, 2000.

Kerouac, Jack. "America's New Trinity of Love: Dean, Brando, Presley." Read by Richard Lewis. *Kerouac: Kicks Joy Darkness.* Rykodisc, 1997.

Springsteen, Bruce, "Cadillac Ranch." *The River,* Columbia Records, 1980.

FILM AND VIDEO

A&E Biography: Natalie Wood. A&E, 2003.

A&E Biography: Sal Mineo: Hollywood's Forgotten Rebel. A&E, 1999.

American Experience: Race for the Superbomb. PBS, 1999.

Behind the Headlights: James Dean's Dark Destiny. Speed Channel, 2004.

Blackboard Jungle. MGM, 1955.

Camera Three. "Interview with Nicholas Ray." CBS, 1977.

Conversations with Robert Clary. Jewish Television Network, 1992.

East of Eden. Warner Brothers, 1955.

Giant. Warner Brothers, 1956.

Hollywood on Trial. October Films, 1976,

I'm a Stranger Here Myself. October Films, 1974.

Intimate Portrait: Natalie Wood. Lifetime Television, 1996.

James Dean: The First American Teenager. ZIV International, 1975.

The James Dean Story. Warner Brothers, 1957.

Larry King Live. "Friends, Family and Co-Stars Remember Actor James Dean." CNN, January 11, 2004.

Leonard Rosenman: Hollywood Beginnings. Henderson Film Industries, 1999.

Lightning Over Water. Anchor Bay Entertainment, 1980.

Los Olvidados. Ultramar Films, 1950.

Memories of Giant. Warner Brothers, 1998.

Operation Cue. U.S. Civil Defense Administration, 1955.

Rebel Without a Cause. Warner Brothers, 1955.

WEB SITES

DiCarlo, Lisa. "Top-Earning Dead Celebrities." *Forbes.com,* October 23, 2003, http://www.forbes.com/2003/10/23/cx_ld_deadcelebtear_17.html.

Eberts, Mike. "Griffith Observatory Goes to the Moon." *Griffith Park History Project,* http://english.glendale.cc.ca.us/moonobs.html.

Leahy, James. "Breathing Together: The Author in Search of Investors." *Senses of Cinema,* July–August 2003, http://www.sensesofcinema.com/contents/03/27/nicholas_ray_leahy.html.

Olsen, Jon. "An Interview with Rod Amateau, director of The Garbage Pail Kids Movie." *Angry Monkey Reader,* October 26, 2002, http://www.normalpeoplelikeyou.com/article_assets/garbagepailkidsinterview.htm.

Orr, Gregory. "Biography for Don Alvarado." *Internet Movie Database,* http://imdb.com/name/nm0023147/bio.

Rappaport, Mark. "The Picture in Sal Mineo's Locker." *Senses of Cinema,* July–August 2002, http://www.sensesofcinema.com/contents/02/21/sd_sal_mineo.html.

Winkler, Peter L. "Nick Adams: His Hollywood Life and Death." *Crime Magazine,* August 15, 2003, http://crimemagazine.com/03/nickadams,0815.htm.

Acknowledgments

The credits that roll at the end of a film make it clear that no movie could be made without the help of numerous people. Even though the cover of *Live Fast, Die Young* displays our names only, the truth is that, as with *Rebel* or any movie, there are many who deserve a huge debt of gratitude for this book's existence.

Live Fast, Die Young would not have been possible without the *Rebel* cast and crew members who took time out of their lives, opened their homes and their hearts and reached far back in their memories to help us tell this story. We will never forget the moments we spent with Corey Allen, Tom Bernard, Jack Grinnage, Tom Hennesy, Beverly Long, Moss Mabry, Faye Nuell Mayo, Frank Mazzola, House Peters Jr. and Steffi Sidney. Just getting the chance to share in their personal histories made writing this book a pleasure. It was as if we had entered the movie—a movie we've loved since childhood—and become part of it. There is something miraculous about that.

In addition, James Baird, Ray Gosnell Jr., Chuck Hicks, Marsha Hunt, Mitzi McCall, Ken Miller, Jim and Gary Nelson, Dennis Stock and Henry Vilardo were also extremely helpful. We were very touched that despite the illness of her husband, Leonard, Judie Rosenman went out of her way to help us, even taking us to the house of her husband's ex-wife Adele Essman, where we spent an amazing afternoon listening to them reminisce about this extraordinary man. And we will never forget the moment that Leonard Rosenman sat down at his piano and, despite his illness, played a moving, note-perfect version of *Rebel*'s tender musical themes. Gavin Lambert was gracious and insightful in discussing his friends Natalie Wood and Nicholas Ray, and we are grateful for the time he took to speak with us. Susan Ray was extremely generous, candid, funny and moving when talking about her husband, and she was very kind in granting us access to her archives. Her compilation of her husband's writings and lectures—*I Was Interrupted*—was invaluable in helping us to understand Ray and create an immediate portrait of him. Tom Farrell not only provided an honest and touching picture of Nick in his later years, he also selflessly went out of his way to aid us in any way he could, helping us to contact people and providing material from his archives. And finally, our book would have suffered greatly if not for the eloquence, thoughtfulness, intelligence and sensitivity of Stewart Stern. The time we spent with him and his charming wife, Marilee, are memories we will never forget as long as we live. We hope that his spirit—which is infused in many of *Rebel*'s best scenes—guided us, at least in small part, as we were writing this book.

A number of others were also very generous with their time in speaking with us, contributing many details about the people and the times covered in our book. H. Paul Jeffers was invaluable in helping us to put together the puzzle of Sal Mineo. Betsy Blair painted a remarkably idiosyncratic portrait of Nicholas Ray. We also received fresh and invaluable information from George Barris, Bernardo Bertolucci, Peter Bogdanovich, Joe Bonelli, Lew Bracker, Mary Ann Brooks, Roydon Clark, Francis Ford Coppola, Hubert Cornfield, Syd Field, Bob Heller, Maggie Hickman, Jack Larson, Leslie Levinson, Norman Lloyd, Carol Loftin, Maureen O'Hara, Betsy Palmer, Arthur Penn, Jackie Perry, Joe Playan, William Self, Phil Stern and Marcus Winslow. Without the aide of Marietta Canty's nephew Kyle Anderson and journalist Constance Neyer, we would never have been able to give the actress her due. And it would have been very difficult to discuss some of the more specialized fields our book touches on—from linguistics to anthropology to game theory—were it not for the scholars who patiently guided us or referred us to those who could help us, including Bob Aumann, Steven Brams, Tom Dalzell, Morton Davis, James Hopgood, Harold Kuhn, Jonathan Lighter, Jonathan Morduch, Jay Newell, Geoffrey Nunberg, Barry O'Neill, Thomas Schelling and Martin Shubik.

A great number of people also made researching the book much easier than it might have been. We owe special thanks to Jennifer Prindiville, curator, USC Warner Bros. Archives; Kathryn Hodson, special collections reader services liaison, University of Iowa Libraries; George Bain, head of the Robert E. and Jean R. Mahn Center for Archives & Special Collections, Ohio University Libraries; River Skybetter, Danny Kahn and Katherine Rosenwink at Warner Studios; James Quandt, senior programmer, Cinematheque Ontario; Bill Davis, researcher, Center for Legislative Archives, National Archives; Roberta Gordon, *Palisadian-Post*; Ann Swaney, Mark & Helen Osterlin Library, Northwestern Michigan College; Charlie Coates, Turner Classic Movies; Charles Silver, Museum of Modern Art; Kim Fraser, *Ladies' Home Journal*; David Loehr at The James Dean Gallery; John Seger, Salmineo.com; and the staffs of the Calabasas Library in California, the New York Public Library for the Performing Arts and the Library of Congress. Maria Dwight and Sue Coliton were more than kindhearted in allowing us to share their homes while we were researching in L.A. and Seattle.

We are very grateful to Mark Goldstein and Paul Newman for letting us use their wonderful photographs and to Howard Mandelbaum at Photofest and Michael Shulman at Magnum Photos, who were extremely helpful in researching and securing pictures that would illustrate the story.

Of course, this book would not have existed at all were it not for the efforts and advice of our agents, Martha Kaplan and Drew Nederpelt; and our editor at Simon & Schuster, Amanda Patten, whose comments and suggestions helped us along the way. We would also like to thank production editor Jonathon Brodman for getting the book out on a tight schedule; jacket designer/illustrator Richie Fahey for his beautiful cover; book designer Joy O'Meara for her stylish work; copyeditor Tom Pitoniak for his meticulous and careful read of our manuscript; publicist Shida Carr for getting the word out; and Amanda's hardworking assistant, Cathy Erway. And a special thanks to Jean Brown, who aided us in transcribing some of the taped interviews we accrued.

Writing this book would have been especially difficult if not for the support of our family. We are especially grateful for the help of Mimi Weisel, Sue Douglas and Diane Weisel, whose love and support began years before this book was even conceived. Boundless love goes out to Laura Mecca and future rebels Sarah, Anna and Lawrence Mecca. Our dear friends were always willing to act as sounding boards and give us thoughtful advice: special thanks to Maurice Berger, Anthony DeCurtis, Kathy Heintzelman, John McAlley, Guy Nicolucci, Marion Osmun, Tom Rapp, Roman Schreiner, Champe Smith, Brian Thompson and Richard and Sherry Zucker. Finally, we want to express our love and eternal gratitude to our partners Alan Richardson, who was extremely helpful in allowing us to exploit the resources of his photo studio throughout the development of the book, as well as offering his advice on text and photography; and Alejandro Molano-Bernal, whose input, support and endless reserves of patience helped us get through this sometimes trying process.

Index

Abdul, Paula, 291
Abeles, Arthur S., Jr., 229
Academy Awards, 72, 110, 229, 240, 245, 247, 248, 250, 259, 260
Actors Lab (Los Angeles), 73
Actors Studio (New York), 18–19, 36, 73, 88, 113
Adams, Leith, 149–50
Adams, Nick, 34, 106, 114, 125, 185–86, 201, 212, 228, 229; cast in *Rebel*, 75; Dean's death and, 230–31, 234, 242; Dean's jocular behavior with, 108, 124; death of, 244–45; lines and screen time grabbed by, 123–24; Wood's relationship with, 242, 243, 244
Affair, The, 250
Agostino (Moravia), 267
Allen, Corey, 84, 98, 109, 117, 119, 126, 128, 131, 138, 139, 168, 185–86, 187, 290; cast in *Rebel,* 68–72, 74; chickie-run scene and, 191, 196, 199–200, 201, 203, 204; Dean's death and, 235; family background of, 69; knife-fight scene and, 112–16, 123; Mazzola's feud with, 71–72, 199–200, 210; name changed, 68–69; planetarium set left by Hopper and, 129–30; preparation ritual of, 126
Allen, Rose, 138
Alter, Dinsmore, 130
Altman, Robert, 6, 240
Amateau, Rodney, 116, 202
Amboy Dukes, The (Shulman), 25, 48
American Friend, The, 284
American Graffiti, 290
Anderson, Edward, 6
Anderson, Emily, 147
Anderson, Sherwood, 32
Andress, Ursula, 180, 181, 232
Androcles and the Lion, 101
Angeli, Pier, 51, 180–81

Anniversary Waltz, 98–99
anti-Communism, 2, 120, 239; Hollywood blacklist and, 4, 98–102; HUAC hearings on, 44–45, 98, 100, 101–2
Archerd, Army, 25
Aristotle, 56
Ashley, Frederick M., 107
Athenians (gang), 62–67, 187
Austin, John C., 107
auteur theory, 274–75
Avanti, 262
Axmann, Hanna, 234

Bacall, Lauren, 24, 244
Backus, Jim, 117, 135, 138–46, 218, 238–39; apron scene and, 143–44; Dean's imitation of Mr. Magoo and, 162–63, 218
Back Where I Come From, 6
Bad and the Beautiful, The, 156
Badlands, 291
Baiano, Solly, 76
Baird, James, 141, 206
Baker, Carroll, 36, 76, 89, 160–61, 244
Baldwin, James, 148, 176
Barnes, Clive, 262
Barrios, Richard, 183
Barris, George, 192–94, 202, 232, 233, 295
Bast, William, 179
Battle Cry, 45
Beach Boys, 292
Beatles, 292
Beatty, Warren, 246–47, 249, 296
Beavers, Louise, 150
Belushi, John, 89, 121
Bernard, Tom, 74, 75, 118, 123, 126, 185, 186, 189, 197–98, 221, 237
Bernhardt, Sarah, 296
Bernstein, Leonard, 1, 225
Bert, Malcolm, 118, 133, 156
Bertolucci, Bernardo, 289
Beymer, Richard, 85–86
Bigger Than Life, 43, 268, 269, 274

Bitter Victory, 43, 184, 268, 270, 274
Blackboard Jungle, 103, 116, 117, 148, 225, 229, 256, 289
Blair, Betsy, 1–2, 3, 51, 53, 287
"Blind Run, The," 11–14, 42, 43–44, 48, 53, 59, 187, 191, 216
Bob & Carol & Ted & Alice, 250
Bock, Richie, 280
Bogart, Humphrey, 7, 228, 244
Bogdanovich, Peter, 262, 264, 289, 290
Bonelli, Joe, 259, 263, 266
Bonnie and Clyde, 290
Bornstein, Charles, 282
Born to Be Bad, 183, 202
Bowers, Hoyt, 62, 68
Bowie, David, 292
Boyar, Ann, 128
Boys in the Band, 264
Bracker, Lew, 166, 181, 213, 217, 228, 229, 231, 232, 236
Brackett, Rogers, 178
Brainstorm, 250–51
Brando, Marlon, 13, 19, 21, 24, 55, 99, 113, 182, 185, 214, 221, 240, 289, 296; Adams's impression of, 108; Dean's emulation of, 19, 22, 26, 81, 258
Brissac, Virginia, 135, 139
British Board of Film Censors, 229, 234
Bronston, Sam, 272, 273
Brooks, Mary Ann Marinkovich, 34, 35, 38, 91, 129
Bruskin, Perry, 99
Buchholz, Horst, 293
Buckley, Lord, 66
Buñuel, Luis, 10, 46, 55
Burning Hills, 245
Burr, Courtney, 263
Burr, Raymond, 244
Butler, Michael, 276

"Cadillac Ranch," 193–94
Cahiers du Cinéma, 274
Cain and Abel Story, The, 271
Cain and Mabel, 204
Callahan, Mushy, 113
Cannes Film Festival, 282–83
Canty, Marietta, 135, 140–41, 146–50, 215
Carroll, Harrison, 145, 146
Carson, Jeannie, 235
Cassavetes, John, 76
Cassity, Turner, 296
Castillo, Gloria, 76
Cates, Joseph, 260

Cat on a Hat Tin Roof, 184, 250
Cavell, Marc, 65, 78–79
Celluloid Closet, The (Russo), 214
censorship, 258; *Rebel* and, 136, 150, 151, 166–67, 172, 229–30, 234
Chakiris, George, 259
Chapman, Michael, 261
Charisse, Cyd, 271
Chateau Marmont (Los Angeles), 88–89; as Ray's base of operations, 9, 23, 25, 36, 37, 84–85, 88–90, 91, 93–98, 102, 176, 222, 227, 269, 282
Chicago Seven, 276–77
chicken races: chickie-run scene in *Rebel* and, 12, 48, 49, 54, 71, 157, 174, 191–207, 230, 238; Cold War tensions and, 204–7; game theory and, 204–5; hot-rod culture and, 194–95, 204
Children of the Dark (Shulman), 53
Chuck D, 293
CinemaScope, 36, 110–11, 137, 238, 268, 270; Ray's achievements with, 197, 203; switch to color and, 116–18; technical difficulties of, 110, 111, 134, 195–96
civil rights movement, 147–48
Clark, Larry, 291
Clendenen, Richard, 9
Clift, Montgomery, 182
Cobain, Kurt, 292–93
Cobweb, The, 24, 76, 223, 224
Cochran, Eddie, 291
Cohen, Carl, 69
Cohn, Harry, 88
Cold War, 204–7; atomic tests and, 206–7; chickie-run scene as metaphor for, 204–5
Collins, Joan, 35
Confidential, 175–76
Continental Divide, 121
Coppola, Francis Ford, 161, 290
Cornfield, Hubert, 275
Crawford, Cheryl, 18, 83
Crawford, Joan, 7, 8, 183
Crowley, Mart, 264
Crime in the Streets, 256, 290
Crowther, Bosley, 238
Cukor, George, 25
Curtiz, Michael, 17

Daily News (New York), 265
Dalton, David, 188, 289
Damone, Perry, 181

Damone, Vic, 180–81
Davalos, Richard, 160, 230
Davies, Marion, 204
Davis, Bette, 29, 110–11, 118, 137
Davis, Bill, 102
Davis, Sammy, Jr., 295
Dawson's Creek, 291
Dead Toreador (Manet), 188
Dean, James, 4, 15–28, 35, 59, 75, 88, 90,
    219, 249, 258, 261, 279; acting skills
    and technique of, 18–20, 73, 141,
    144, 162–63, 188–89, 199, 210–11,
    213–14, 296–97; auto racing of, 104,
    108, 190–91, 201–2, 231–33; casting
    of Judy and, 36, 76; casting of Plato
    and, 78, 79–81, 84–86; cast in *Rebel,*
    15–16, 23–28, 29, 42, 61, 75–76, 280;
    celebrity status of, 107, 212; chickie-
    run scene and, 191, 193–94,
    197–202; conceptions of masculinity
    and, 182–83; as cultural icon, viii,
    238–40, 288–97; death of, vii–viii,
    230–40, 241–42, 267–68;
    disappearance of, at start of *Rebel*
    shoot, 103–6; early career of, 17–21,
    45; *East of Eden* and, 16, 21–22, 24,
    53, 64–65, 103, 104–5, 107, 109, 113,
    138, 191, 212, 223, 237, 238, 240,
    293; family background of, 17, 141,
    199; finale sequence and, 212–15;
    first preview of *Rebel* and, 228–29;
    funeral of, 236; *Giant* and, 24, 36,
    60–61, 105–6, 123, 181, 190, 208,
    210, 212, 220, 226, 228, 230, 231,
    237, 238, 239, 254; glasses worn by,
    106, 109, 121; homosexuality and,
    172–75, 176, 184; Hopper's acting
    influenced by, 199; independent
    production company planned by Ray
    and, 212, 220, 230, 235, 267–68;
    Kazan and, 15–16, 18, 19, 21–22, 24,
    104–5, 108, 109, 191; knife-fight
    scene and, 111–16; L.A. gang life
    experienced by, 66–67; mansion
    sequence and, 154, 158, 161–70, 184;
    Mayo's relationship with, 197–98;
    Mazzola's first encounter with,
    64–65; Mazzola's police station scene
    with, 210–11; Mineo's relationship
    with, 84–85, 109, 125, 160–61, 254,
    257, 263; monkey scene and, 186–89;
    mumbling of, 97, 109, 221; New York
    apartment of, 26; older actors' scenes
    with, 138–46; on-set behavior of,
71–72, 107–9, 124, 140–41, 160;
    opening police station scene and,
    135, 136, 139–42, 224–25; Oscar
    nomination for, 240; planetarium
    sequence and, 107–9, 111–16, 128,
    130–32; Porsche Spyder of, 191, 194,
    231–34, 295; Presley's obsession
    with, 243, 291; Ray's relationship
    with, 17, 23–28, 61, 93–96, 104–6,
    109, 111, 115, 125–26, 140–41, 191,
    212, 213, 220, 230, 267–68, 278–79,
    297; *Rebel* cast members' bonds with,
    217–18; red jacket worn by, 119–21,
    218, 233, 288, 295; rock music
    influenced by, 291–93; Rosenman's
    score assignments and, 223, 224;
    scrapbook of, 165; sexuality of, 85,
    166, 176, 178–82; Simmons's
    relationship with, 79–81, 179–80;
    Stern's relationship with, 52–53, 58;
    Walken compared to, 250–51;
    Wood's first encounters with, 29,
    31–33; Wood's relationship with, 33,
    109, 154, 160–61, 165–66, 218,
    241–42; writing of *Rebel* screenplay
    and, 48, 50–51, 94–96
Dean, Winton, 17, 232–33
Deaners, 295–96
Death Is My Neighbor, 19–20
Defendant, The, 275–77
"Demon Dean" (Skolsky), 79–80
Depp, Johnny, 296
Derek, John, 181, 184
De Sica, Vittorio, 46
DeWeerd, Rev. James, 21, 178, 236
Dietrich, Marlene, 147
Dino, 255, 256
Donen, Josh, 251
Donoghue, Roger, 93, 113, 218, 219, 227,
    234, 237
Doran, Ann, 98, 135, 137–38, 140, 141,
    142, 146, 161, 211, 218
Dreamers, The, 289
Drummond, Jack, 190–91
Dullea, Keir, 264
Dunham, Katherine, 113
Dylan, Bob, 120, 292

Eagles, 292
East of Eden, vii, 8, 15–16, 31, 52, 53,
    64–65, 109, 113, 118, 191, 230,
    233, 235, 237, 238, 293; Oscar
    nominations for, 240; responses
    to, 24, 103, 107, 117, 138, 212;

East of Eden (cont.)
　　Rosenman's score for, 223–24;
　　tensions between Dean and Kazan
　　during making of, 21–22, 104–5
Easy Rider, 278, 290
Edwards, Blake, 249
Eisenschitz, Bernard, 49, 102, 176
Elephant, 291
Eminem, 293
Emmy Awards, 250
Entertainment Weekly, 297
Escape from the Planet of the Apes, 262
Essex, David, 292
Essman, Adele, 91, 223
Evans, Gene, 97
Evans, Jean, 2, 5, 100, 102, 176
Exodus, 258–59

Faith, Adam, 292
Farrell, Tom, 280, 281–82, 285, 286
FBI, 100
Ferber, Edna, 24, 60
Ferrer, Mel, 183
Field, Syd, 62, 63, 64, 67
55 Days at Peking, 57, 272–73, 284
Finstad, Suzanne, 38
"Five O'Clock Whistle," 225
FitzGerald, W. F., 156
Fletcher, Louise, 251
Flying Leathernecks, 202
Flynn, Errol, 52
Forbes, 294
Ford, Glenn, 148
Ford, John, 75, 127, 220, 227
Forman, Milos, 284
Fortune and Men's Eyes, 261–62, 263–64
Foulk, Robert, 149
French New Wave, 274, 275
Freudianism, 142
From Here to Eternity, 250
Front and Center (Houseman), 177
Fuchs, Daniel, 240
Fuller, Sam, 17
Fury, Billy, 292

Garbo, Greta, 1
Garfein, Jack, 36
Garland, Judy, 1, 52
Geisel, Theodor, 43
Gene Krupa Story, The, 258
Generation of Vipers (Wylie), 143
George, George W., 240
G.E. Theater, 79
Getty, J. Paul, 155, 156

Getty Mansion (Los Angeles), 155–56;
　　Rebel sequence filmed at, 153–70
Giant, 181, 182, 210, 220, 226–27, 228,
　　231, 238, 254; casting of, 24, 36, 37;
　　Dean's death and, 237, 239; Oscar
　　nominations for, 240; *Rebel* shooting
　　schedule and, 60–61, 123, 190, 208,
　　212; tensions between Dean and
　　Stevens during making of, 105–6,
　　226, 230
Gide, Andre, 21
Gilmore, John, 179
Ginsberg, Allen, 176, 235, 236
Godard, Jean-Luc, 274, 275, 293
Golden Globe awards, 244, 259
Googie's (Los Angeles), 31, 39; as Dean's
　　hangout, 31–32, 79–80, 179, 219,
　　228, 236
Gosnell, Ray, Jr., 111, 195–96, 258
Graduate, The, 290
Graetz, Paul, 270
Grahame, Gloria, 1–3, 4, 7, 24, 27, 73, 91,
　　151, 271, 284, 286
Granger, Farley, 183
Grant, Kathryn, 76
Gray, Billy, 81–82
Great Race, The, 249
Green Promise, The, 31
Gregson, Natasha, 250, 251
Gregson, Richard, 250
Griffith, Griffith J., 107
Griffith Observatory (Los Angeles),
　　106–7; finale sequence shot at,
　　157, 208–17; planetarium sequence
　　shot at, 106–16, 128–32, 133, 174,
　　220
Grinnage, Jack, 110, 119, 127, 128,
　　129, 131, 154, 156, 158, 168, 187,
　　237, 239, 242, 290; cast in *Rebel,*
　　71, 74
Group Theatre, 118
Grove Press, 276
Guinness, Alec, 232
Gurdin, Maria, 30–31, 32, 34, 35, 37, 38,
　　39, 41, 92, 130, 135, 136, 198, 218,
　　248
Guys and Dolls, 240
Gypsy, 248

Hair, 284
Haley, Bill, and His Comets, 103
Haller, Ernest, 110–11, 134, 145, 157–58,
　　188
Hallyday, Johnny, 293

Hamburger Hamlet, 116
Hambleton, John, 118
Harlow, Jean, 88, 237, 242
Harpur College of Arts and Sciences, 279–82
Hathaway, Henry, 244
Haworth, Jill, 260
Hayes, Helen, 34
Hays Office, 113–14
Hearst, William Randolph, 204
Heart to Heart with Robert Wagner, 252–53
Hefner, Hugh, 276
Heidi, 234–35
Heindorf, Ray, 224
Heller, Bob, 27
Hennesy, Tom, 109, 124–25, 130, 136, 161, 197, 244
Herbert, John, 261
Herlihy, James Leo, 263
Heroic Love (Loomis), 230, 267
Hickman, Bill, 202, 232, 233–34, 239
Hicks, Chuck, 213, 215
High Green Wall, 110
Hilton, Nicky, 244
Hitchcock, Alfred, 89, 216, 261, 274
Hoberman, J., 290
Hoffman, Abbie, 276
Holliday, Judy, 90
Hollywood Fights Back, 98, 99
homosexuality, 171–84, 289; allusions in *Rebel* to, 78, 80–81, 86–87, 171–75, 177, 184, 214, 259–66, 289; as viewed in 1950s, 175–76
Hoover, J. Edgar, 100
Hopgood, James, 295–96
Hopper, Dennis, 38, 85–86, 131, 154, 180–81, 182, 185, 188–89, 219, 228, 293, 296; after *Rebel,* 220, 242–43, 278–79, 284, 290; in car crash, 39–40, 41; casting of *Rebel* and, 36–37, 39, 74, 75–76, 78; Dean's death and, 235, 242; Dean's impact on acting of, 199; *Giant* and, 37, 220, 226–27; mansion sequence and, 158–59; Ray's relationship with, 37, 40, 97, 110, 129–30, 198–99, 227, 278–79; Wood's affair with, 37, 40, 78, 110, 125, 129, 130, 166, 198, 242–43, 244
Hopper, Hedda, 73, 150, 226, 245
Hopper, William, 73, 135, 150, 151
Hot Blood, 220, 222, 227, 240, 268, 274
hot-rod culture, 192–95; chicken games and, 194–95, 204
Houseman, John, 2, 3, 5–6, 7, 44, 52, 58, 147, 177, 273, 275, 283, 285
House Un-American Activities Committee (HUAC), 44–45, 98, 100, 101–2
Hudson, Rochelle, 150
Hudson, Rock, 60, 176, 226
Hughes, Howard, 2, 7, 69, 99, 101, 181, 282
Hunt, Marsha, 97–99, 138
Hunter, Jeffrey, 184, 272
Hunter, Tab, 15, 45, 76, 244, 245
Hyams, Joe, 115, 178

I'm a Fool, 29, 32–33, 79, 168
I Married a Communist, 100–101
Immoralist, The, 21
In a Lonely Place, 4, 7, 43, 96, 183, 202, 268, 274
Inside Daisy Clover, 249
Inside Story, 239

Jackson, Michael, 295
Jaglom, Henry, 135–36
James Dean: Behind the Scene (Adams), 149–50
James Dean Story, The, 240
Jarmusch, Jim, 283–84, 291
Jeffers, H. Paul, 257, 260, 266
Jenkins, William O., 155
Jessel, George, 229
Joey Bishop Show, The, 263
Johnny Guitar, 4, 7–8, 57, 102, 183, 184, 274
Johnson, Ray, 296
Jour de Fête, 26
juvenile delinquency, 48, 49, 145, 248, 287; *Blackboard Jungle* and, 103; chicken games and, 194–95, 204; Cold War tensions and, 204–5; hot-rod culture and, 192–95; Kefauver Committee's hearings on, 9, 10, 112, 221; L.A. gangs and, 61–68; Lindner's book and lectures on, 10–11, 13–14; media reports on, 8–9; Ray's interest in, 9–11; Ray's research on, 45–47; teensploitation films and, 290–91
Juvenile Story, 49–50

Kael, Pauline, 107
Kahn, Herman, 205
Kardell, Lili, 180
Kauffman, Stanley, 241–42

Kazan, Elia, 4, 12, 13, 55, 70, 181, 283, 285, 287; Dean and, 15–16, 18, 19, 21–22, 24, 104–5, 108, 109, 191; *East of Eden* and, 8, 15–16, 21–22, 103, 118, 191, 223–24, 293; HUAC hearings and, 44–45, 99; Ray's relationship with, 5, 6, 22–23, 85, 99, 126; *Rebel* script read by, 58; *Splendor in the Grass* and, 246–47

Kefauver, Estes, 9, 10, 112, 221

Kelley, Douglas, 56

Kelly, Gene, 1, 3, 51, 53, 282

Kendall, Kenneth, 107

Kerouac, Jack, 182–83, 239

Kerr, John, 15, 76

Kesey, Ken, 282

King and I, The, 83

King of Kings, 57, 184, 272

Kinsey, Alfred, 176

Kirkwood, James, 264

Kitt, Eartha, 232

Klapp, Orrin, 289

Knock on Any Door, 7, 10, 184, 292

Knox, Mickey, 44

Krupa, Gene, 258

Kubrick, Stanley, 205

Kunstle, John, 190

Ladd, Alan, 118, 173

Ladies' Home Journal, 167

Lambert, Gavin, 2, 3, 4, 8, 13, 35, 41, 43, 57–58, 84, 85, 90, 101, 126, 166, 222, 245, 249, 269, 270; homosexuality and, 172–73, 176–77, 178, 181

Lancaster, Burt, 173

Lane, Anthony, 290, 297

Langlois, Henri, 275

Larson, Jack, 80, 127, 179–80

Last Movie, The, 278–79

Last Picture Show, The, 290

Leahy, James, 277

Led Zeppelin, 89

Lee Strasberg Institute, 283

Lemmon, Jack, 240

Lennon, John, 292

Levant, Oscar, 52

Levinson, Leslie, 280

Lewis, Robert, 18

Life, 118, 194, 238, 239, 296

Lightning Over Water, 284–86

Lindner, Robert, 10–11, 13–14, 42, 142, 289

Linklater, Richard, 289

Little Prince, The, 35

"Live fast, die young, and have a good-looking corpse," origin of phrase, 10

Live Fast—Die Young: My Life with James Dean (Gilmore), 179

Living Newspaper, The, 102

Lloyd, Norman, 3, 99, 100

Loew, Arthur, Jr., 51–52, 53, 54, 58, 106, 180, 182, 235, 249

Loftin, Carey, 202

Lomax, Alan, 5, 6, 67

Lombard, Carole, 237

Long, Beverly, 68, 80, 98, 106, 107–8, 113, 123, 124, 125, 127, 128, 129, 136, 158, 159, 168, 180, 206–7, 210; cast in *Rebel,* 72, 75; Dean's death and, 235; 24-Hour Day and, 185, 186, 188, 189

Long Time Till Dawn, A, 20

Loomis, Edward, 230, 267

Lopez, Perry, 69, 71, 219, 244

Loren, Sophia, 247

Los Angeles Herald-Examiner, 231

Los Angeles Juvenile Hall, 134

Los Angeles Mirror-News, 58

Los Angeles Times, 195, 206, 238

Losey, Joseph, 4

Love Me or Leave Me, 240

Love Me Tender, 243, 269

"Love Story" (Stock), 167

Love With the Proper Stranger, 248–49

Lucas, George, 290

Lüscher Color Test, 118–19

Lusty Men, The, 7, 183, 184, 274

Mabry, Moss, 118, 165; Dean's red jacket and, 119–21, 295; Wood's makeover and, 91–92, 109–10

Macao, 2, 101

Main Street, Heaventown, 49

Malick, Terrence, 290–91

Manet, Edouard, 188

Mansfield, Jayne, 39, 90, 97, 244

Marlowe, Scott, 38

Marmont, Percy, 89

Marmor, Judd, 176

Marton, Andrew, 273

Matthau, Walter, 44

Matthews, Robert, 205

Mattson's, 119

Mayo, Faye Nuell, 38–39, 73, 197–98, 208, 241, 242, 251

Mazursky, Paul, 250, 286

Mazzola, Anthony, 79

Mazzola, Frank, 62–68, 97, 110, 119, 128, 137, 154, 185, 187, 267, 282; Allen's feud with, 71–72, 199–200, 210; Big Bear brawl and, 62–64; casting of *Rebel* and, 65–66, 70, 71–72, 74, 78–79; chickie-run scene and, 192, 193, 195, 199–200; Dean's death and, 235, 237; Dean's entry into L.A. gang life and, 66–67; Dean's first encounter with, 64–65; Dean's police station scene with, 210–11; family background of, 64; mansion sequence and, 158, 159; as Ray's gang advisor, 66–68, 112, 113, 159, 192, 193

MCA, 2, 7

McCall, Mitzi, 97

McCambridge, Mercedes, 183

McCoy, Esther, 49

McDermid, Finlay, 151

McDowall, Roddy, 262

McKenzie, Benjamin, 291

McLaren, Malcolm, 292

McLean, Don, 292

McQueen, Steve, 248–49, 296

Medford, Don, 33, 79

Medic, 37

Meehan, John, 155

Mercury (1949), 192–94, 196

Method acting, 5, 18–19, 97, 108, 138, 139, 140, 142, 221, 226

MGM, 24, 52, 76, 103, 156, 254, 271

Midnight Cowboy, 263

Miller, Ken, 75, 123, 255

Milner, Martin, 244

Mineo, Sal, viii, 82–87, 96, 97, 122, 169, 224, 240; acting style of, 254–57; after *Rebel,* 220, 254–66, 290; casting of, 82, 83–87; chickie-run scene and, 191; Dean's death and, 230–31, 234, 235; Dean's relationship with, 84–85, 109, 125, 160–61, 254, 257, 263; death of, 264–65; early career of, 82–83; family background of, 82, 255–56; finale sequence and, 213–14; *Giant* and, 220, 226, 254; mansion sequence and, 154, 157, 158–59, 161–65; on-set behavior of, 124–25; Oscar nominations for, 240, 259, 260; packaged as teen idol, 224, 255–57; Plato's homosexuality and, 86–87, 172–75; Ray's relationship with, 90; sexuality of, 86–87, 125, 254, 256, 259–66; theater projects of, 83, 261–62, 263–64; Wood's relationship with, 161

Minnelli, Vincente, 24, 31, 156, 223, 268, 274

Mintz, Elliot, 261

Mr. Roberts, 240

Modern Screen, 244

Moise, Nina, 92

momism, 143

Monroe, Marilyn, 3, 51, 90, 93, 288

Moon Is Blue, The, 258

Moravia, Alberto, 267

Morris, Clifford, 75

Morrison, Jim, 89

Morrissey, 292

Murphy, Fae, 11, 12, 65, 96

Murray, Jan, 261

My Own Private Idaho, 291

Nash, John, 205

Nelson, Gary, 36–37, 125, 127

Nelson, Jim, 36–37

Newman, Paul, 29, 254, 296

Newsweek, 9

Newton, Helmut, 89

New York Times, 18, 116–17, 121, 238, 262, 265

New York University, 283–84

Nixon, Marni, 248

Noguchi, Thomas, 252, 253

Nunberg, Geoffrey, 205

Nurmi, Maila. *See* Vampira

O'Brien, Geoffrey, 9, 118

O'Brien, Margaret, 31–32, 34

O.C., The, 291

Odets, Clifford, 25, 44–45, 89, 99, 213

Office of War Information (OWI), 6, 101, 177

O'Hara, Frank, 180, 296

Ohnishi, Seita, 293–94

Olivier, Laurence, 250

Olken, Jerry, 75

Olvidados, Los, 10, 46, 55

On Dangerous Ground, 7, 45, 92, 268

One Desire, 33–34

On the Waterfront, 8, 55, 70, 113, 120, 214

Operation Teapot, 206, 207

Oshima, Nagisa, 294

Pacino, Al, 297

Page, Don, 128, 129, 159, 170, 197

Paik, Nam June, 279

Palmer, Betsy, 19–20, 180

Parsons, Louella, 243

Party Girl, 271, 272, 274
Penn, Arthur, 20, 289
Penn, Sean, 296
Perry, Jackie Eastes, 35, 36, 38, 39–40, 41, 91, 94, 135, 136, 145, 146, 160, 165–66, 243
Peter Pan, 57, 163
Peters, House, Jr., 140
Photoplay, 79–80, 255, 256
Pickford, Mary, 52
Planer, Franz, 110
Platt, Edward, 97, 135
Playan, Marion "Joe," 190, 192, 231
Poetics (Aristotle), 56
Poitier, Sidney, 148
Porsche Spyder 550, 191, 194, 231–34, 295
Poundstone, William, 204
Preminger, Otto, 258–59
Presley, Elvis, 193, 243, 269, 288, 290, 291
Presnell, Robert, Jr., 98
Privilege, 263
Production Code, 176, 258
Prowse, Juliet, 261
psychoanalysis, 142
P.S. Your Cat Is Dead, 263–64

Race With Destiny, 232
Racket, The, 2, 101
RAND Corporation, 205
Rappaport, Mark, 61, 217
Rau, Neil, 115–16
Ray, Julie Christina, 271
Ray, Nicca, 271
Ray, Nicholas, viii–ix, 1–17, 226, 241, 243, 246, 254, 265, 292, 297; after *Rebel,* 267–87; allusions to homosexuality in films of, 171–75, 177, 183–84; blacklist and, 4, 99–102; casting of *Rebel* and, 15–16, 23–28, 34–37, 39–42, 60, 61–62, 65, 68–79, 81, 84–87, 91–93, 99, 139, 280; censors and, 136, 150, 151, 166–67, 172, 229–30, 234; Chateau Marmont quarters of, 88–90, 102; chickie-run scene and, 191–99, 201–5; CinemaScope and, 110–11, 117–18, 134, 197, 203, 268; cinematic style of, 134, 144–45, 158, 161, 238, 268; Dean's death and, 234, 237, 267–68; Dean's relationship with, 17, 23–28, 61, 93–96, 104–6, 109, 111, 115, 125–26, 140–41, 191, 212, 213, 220, 230, 267–68, 278–79, 297; on Dean's sexuality, 181; Dean's vanishing act and, 103–5; directorial style of, 6, 22–23, 27, 125–30, 137, 141, 159, 168, 169, 188–89, 238, 281; early career of, 5–8; eye patch of, 277–78; family background of, 4–5, 152, 286; as father, 2–5, 9, 27, 49, 54, 94, 105, 152, 271–72, 286; in final shot of *Rebel,* 215–17; Grahame's relationship with, 1–3, 4, 7, 91; homosexuality and, 176–78, 281–82; Hopper's relationship with, 37, 40, 97, 110, 129–30, 198–99, 227, 278–79; illness and death of, 284–86; inarticulateness and, 44, 54; independent production company planned by Dean and, 212, 220, 230, 235, 267–68; influence of, 291; Kazan's relationship with, 5, 6, 22–23, 85, 99, 126; knife-fight scene and, 111–16; last days of shooting and, 217–19; mansion sequence and, 153–59, 161–70, 184; Mineo's relationship with, 90; Mineo's reunion with (1974), 262–63; mumbling of actors and, 221; older actors' scenes and, 137–39, 142, 145, 151, 152, 211; original treatment by ("Blind Run"), 11–14, 42, 43–44, 48, 53, 59, 187, 191, 216; Oscar nomination for, 240; passion of, for story of *Rebel,* 3–4, 8–11; planetarium sequence and, 49, 107, 109–16, 128–32, 225; police station scene and, 133–37, 140–41, 147; postproduction work and, 220–25, 228; race issue and, 147–49; research conducted by, 45–47, 54, 61, 65–66, 67–68, 112, 134, 135; resurgence in reputation of (1960s), 273–75; script changes during shooting and, 43, 122–23, 128, 171–72, 175, 184, 211, 218; self-destructive behavior of, 1, 7, 268, 269, 270, 271–72, 273, 275, 277–78, 283; shooting of finale sequence and, 208–11, 215–17; studio control and, 102, 170, 172, 208, 267–68; switch to color and, 116–21; as teacher, 279–82, 283–84; womanizing of, 3, 90–91, 101, 176–78; Wood's makeover and, 91–92, 109–10; Wood's sexual relationship with, 35, 37, 90, 91, 130, 166, 198, 222, 282; writing of *Rebel* screenplay and, 42–59, 94–96

Ray, Susan, 5, 44, 95, 101, 119, 177, 178, 262–63, 276–79, 283, 284, 285, 286

Ray, Timothy, 2, 3, 152, 271, 284, 285, 286

Ray, Tony, 5, 84, 269; Dean's relationship with, 27; father's relationship with, 2, 3–4, 9, 54, 94, 105, 286; Grahame's relationship with, 2, 3, 151, 271, 284, 286

"Rayfield" sketch, 47

Reagan, Ronald, 79

Rebel, The (television series), 244

Rebel Without a Cause: adolescence as portrayed in, viii–ix, 152, 153, 238, 288–90; alley scene in, 172, 174–75, 184–85; apron scene in, 57, 143–44; box-office success of, 238, 240, 294; casting of, 15–16, 23–30, 34–42, 60, 61–62, 65–66, 68–87, 91–93, 98–99, 139, 280; censors and, 136, 150, 151, 166–67, 172, 229–30, 234; chickie-run scene in, 12, 48, 49, 54, 71, 157, 174, 191–207, 230, 238; CinemaScope process and, 36, 110–11, 117–18, 134, 195, 238; cinematic style of, 134, 144–45, 158, 161, 238; Dean's death and, vii–viii, 230–40; Dean's disappearance at start of shooting of, 103–6; fantasy scenes cut from, 55–56; finale of, 45, 50, 53, 157, 208–17; first day of shooting of, 103; first preview of, 228–29; garden and gazebo scenes in, 161–65; going-to-school scene in, 185–86; homosexuality in, 78, 80–81, 86–87, 171–75, 177, 184, 214, 289; incestuous tensions in, 48, 150–51; knife-fight scene in, 12, 106, 111–16, 123, 224, 230; last days of shooting for, 217–19; legacy of, 275–76, 288–97; love scene in, 154, 158, 165–70, 184; mansion sequence in, 49, 85–86, 153–70, 174, 184; milk-bottle scene in, 95, 169; monkey scene in, 186–89; mumbling of cast in, 97, 109, 221; official premieres of, 237; official read-through of script for, 96–98; older actors' scenes in, 137–52, 211; Oscar nominations for, 229, 240, 245; planetarium sequence in, 49, 56, 58, 106–16, 128–32, 133, 157, 174, 224, 225; Plato character in, 78–81, 86–87, 119, 173–75; Plato's nanny in, 146–50, 215; police station scene in, 133–37, 139–42, 147, 149, 167, 169, 224–25, 230; portrayal of Judy's family in, 150–52; portrayal of Stark's parents in, 142–46, 211; postproduction work on, 220–25, 228; producer chosen for, 12–13; race issue and, 147–48; Ray's appearance in final shot of, 215–17; Ray's original treatment for ("Blind Run"), 11–14, 42, 43–44, 48, 53, 59, 187, 191, 216; Ray's passion for story of, 3–4, 8–11; red jacket worn by Dean in, 119–21, 218, 233, 295; rehearsals for, 70–74, 96–98, 109, 123, 164; research for, 45–47, 48, 54–55, 61–68, 112, 134, 135; reviews of, 237–38; rough cut of, 221–22, 223; script changes during shooting and, 122–24, 128, 171–72, 175, 184, 211, 228; shooting schedule for, 60–61, 123, 156, 170, 196, 208; Shulman's screenplay for, 49–50, 53, 58, 132, 195, 214; soundstage work in, 203–4, 209, 210–11, 217–18; soundtrack of, 223–25; studio's control over shooting of, 170, 203; switch to color and, 116–21, 122; title chosen for, 13–14; tutoring of underage actors in, 124–25; 24-Hour Day and, 172, 184–89; twenty-four-hour structure of, 56–57, 132, 154, 209, 216; Uris's treatments for, 47–48, 53, 58, 150; writing credits for, 59, 216, 240; writing of screenplay for, 42–59, 65–66, 94–96, 103, 132

Rebel Without a Cause: The Story of a Criminal Psychopath (Lindner), 10–11, 13–14, 42, 142

"rebel without a cause," as phrase, 288

Red Channels, 98

Reed, Lou, 292

Reeves, Keanu, 291

Republic Pictures, 8

Reynolds, Debbie, 76, 249

Richard, Cliff, 292

Richards, Silvia, 49

Ride of the Valkyries, 141

Rivette, Jacques, 274

RKO Pictures, 2, 6–7, 100–101, 268

Robbins, Jerome, 248

Roberts, Monty, 233

"Rock Around the Clock," 103

Rock, Pretty Baby, 256–57, 290

Index

rock music, 103; *Rebel*'s influence on, 291–92
Rogers, Will, 237
Rohmer, Eric, 112, 293
Romeo and Juliet, 49
Roseanna McCoy, 101
Rosenbaum, Jonathan, 272
Rosenman, Leonard, 17, 26, 51, 53, 58, 91, 96, 295; as Dean's mentor, 20–21; *East of Eden* score by, 15–16, 223–24; *Rebel* soundtrack by, 131, 186, 223–25
Rose Tattoo, The, 83
Roth, Sanford, 233–34
Run for Cover, 4, 7, 8, 9, 102, 184, 274
Rushmore, Howard, 175–76
Russell, Bertrand, 204–5
Russell, Jane, 227
Russo, Vito, 214
Ryan, Robert, 92

Sackler, Howard, 20
Sarris, Andrew, 268, 293
Savage Innocents, The, 271, 272
Saxon, John, 256
Schary, Dore, 6–7
Scheuer, Phillip, 238
Schulberg, Budd, 99, 271
Schwab's, 72
Scorsese, Martin, 290
Screen Facts, 91
Searchers, The, 127, 220, 227, 240
"Secret Doorway," 224
See the Jaguar, 19
Segal, George, 248
Senate Subcommittee to Investigate Juvenile Delinquency, 9, 10, 112, 221
Serling, Rod, 20
Sex and the Single Girl, 249
Sexual Behavior in the Human Male (Kinsey), 176
Shakur, Tupac, 293
Sheen, Martin, 291, 297
Sheridan, Dizzy, 180
Shoeshine, 46
Shulman, Irving, 25, 48–51, 53, 57, 58, 59, 94, 132, 195, 214, 216, 240
Shurlock, Geoffrey, 113–14, 151, 166–67, 172
Sidney, Steffi, 31, 76, 110, 111, 116, 118, 120, 122, 125, 128, 129, 134, 201, 207, 227, 290; cast in *Rebel*, 72–75; Dean's death and, 235; family background of, 72–73; lines and

screen time lost by, 123–24; 24-Hour Day and, 185, 187, 188, 189
Silver, Jeff, 78
Simmons, Jack, 23, 79–81, 84, 86, 97, 158, 179–80, 185, 186, 236, 280
Sinatra, Frank, 39, 69, 193, 228, 244
Sirk, Douglas, 17, 268, 271
Six Bridges to Cross, 82, 83
Skolsky, Sidney, 72–73, 79–80
Smith, John, 32
Solt, Andrew, 93
Somebody Up There Likes Me, 113, 254–55
Splendor in the Grass, 246–47, 248, 251
Springsteen, Bruce, 193–94, 291, 292
Stacey, Eric, 76, 209
Stanislavsky, Konstantin, 18
Stein, Elliott, 288
Stern, Phil, 80
Stern, Stewart, viii, 4, 51–59, 70, 88, 94, 95, 120, 180, 185, 188, 191, 206, 240, 253, 278, 297; absent from set during shooting, 106; chickie-run scene and, 191, 200; conceptions of masculinity and, 183, 200; Dean's death and, vii, 235–36; Dean's relationship with, 52–53, 58; on Dean's sexuality, 181–82; Dean's vanishing act and, 104–5; family background of, 51–52, 142–43, 146; fantasy sequence and, 55–56; finale sequence and, 209, 214, 216; homosexuality in *Rebel* and, 171, 172, 173–75; Judy's relationship with her father and, 150–52; mansion sequence and, 86, 154–55, 162, 163–64, 167; planetarium sequence and, 131, 132; Plato character and, 78, 80–81; Plato's nanny and, 146, 149; portrayal of Stark's parents and, 139, 142–43, 145, 146, 211; research of, 54–55, 66, 134, 135; script changes during shooting and, 122–23, 175, 184, 211, 228; twenty-four-hour structure and, 56–57; writing credits and, 59, 216; writing process of, 53–59, 96, 103
Stevens, George, 24, 37, 60, 190, 208, 210, 231, 232, 233, 239, 254; tensions between Dean and, 105–6, 226, 230
Stock, Dennis, 12, 97, 126, 167, 236
Stranger Than Paradise, 284, 291
Strasberg, Lee, 18
Strasberg, Paula, 73
Strasberg, Susan, 73

Streetcar Named Desire, A, 8, 12, 13, 19, 81, 85, 185
Stritch, Elaine, 261
Sunset Boulevard, 154–55, 156
Sutcliffe, Stuart, 292

Taliesin Fellowship, 5, 176
Tankersley, Dan, 264–65
Tati, Jacques, 26
Taylor, Elizabeth, 60, 61, 226, 230, 236, 247, 249, 254
"teenager," origin of word, 9, 294
teensploitation films, 290–91
Teresa, 51, 52, 143, 180
Theatre of Action (New York), 5, 6, 44, 99, 100
They Live by Night (1948), 6, 183, 268, 269, 278
Thieves Like Us (Anderson), 6
This Property Is Condemned, 249
Thomas, Shirley, 213
Thomson, David, 96, 274, 276
Thoulouze, Michel, 293
Time, 253, 272, 292
To Be or Not to Be, 237
Todd, Thelma, 74
Tomorrow Is Forever, 30, 135, 136
Tree Grows in Brooklyn, A, 6
Trilling, Steve, 11, 51, 76, 92, 116, 117, 129, 151, 175, 187, 214, 228, 234; homosexuality in *Rebel* and, 171, 172, 174
True Story of Jesse James, The, 184, 269–70
Truffaut, François, 274, 293, 296
Trumbull, Douglas, 250, 251
Tsai Ming Liang, 294
Turnupseed, Donald, 233
TV Guide, 297
Twentieth Century Fox, 110, 116–17, 134
Two Women, 247
Tyler, Parker, 182

Ugly American, The, 183
Universal, 83, 256, 278–79
Uris, Leon, 45, 46, 47, 53, 54, 58, 150
U.S. News & World Report, 9
Ustinov, Peter, 259
Utey, Betty, 271, 273

Valentino, Rudolph, 239
Vampira (Maila Nurmi), 23, 24, 61, 79, 94, 158, 280
Van Dien, Casper, 232
Van Fleet, Jo, 235, 240

Van Sant, Gus, 291
Variety, 229, 237, 238
Vartan, Sylvie, 293
Vaughn, Robert, 244
Vidal, Gore, 89, 90, 176
Viertel, Peter, 42–43
Vilardo, Henry, 115, 125, 127
Villa Capri (Los Angeles), 39, 181, 228–29, 232, 235
Vincent, Gene, 291
Von Neumann, Johnnie, 191, 231
von Sternberg, Josef, 2, 127

Wagner, Courtney, 250, 251
Wagner, Robert, 15, 76, 184, 244, 245, 247, 249, 250, 269, 282; Wood's death and, 251–53
Wald, Jerry, 13, 42, 48, 142
Walken, Christopher, 250–53
Wallace, William, 156
Warhol, Andy, 296
Warner, Jack, 11, 16, 24, 128, 204, 224, 226; Dean's death and, 237; HUAC hearings and, 44; *Rebel* and, 13, 65–66, 76, 92, 114, 116, 117, 151, 172, 208, 221–22, 223, 228, 229; Wood's contract and, 92–93, 245, 249
Warner Brothers, 53, 54, 60, 104, 127, 128, 142, 149–50, 173, 190, 241, 244, 254; casting of *Rebel* and, 15, 24, 27, 28, 34, 37, 41, 61, 62, 65, 68–69, 73, 76, 91–93, 99; control exerted over *Rebel* shoot by, 170, 203, 208; Dean's contract with, 24, 231; Dean's death and, 237, 239, 240; Dean's imitation of Mr. Magoo and, 162–63; Dean's red jacket and, 119, 121; Dean's reputation at, 16; development of *Rebel* project and, 10–14, 42; Getty Mansion set and, 156, 167–68; homosexuality in *Rebel* and, 171, 172; postproduction work on *Rebel* and, 220; publicity of, 111, 114, 137, 162, 166; shooting of finale sequence and, 214, 217, 219; Stage 7 (now Stage 16) of, 203–4; switch to color and, 116–18; Wood's contract with, 92–93, 245, 249; writing of *Rebel* screenplay and, 42–43, 45, 51
WarnerColor, 122
Warner Ranch (Calabasas, Calif.), shooting of chickie-run scene at, 195–202, 206–7

Wasserman, Edie, 9, 90
Wasserman, Lew, 7, 8, 9–10, 11, 12, 90, 99, 279
Watkins, Arthur, 234
Watkins, Peter, 263
Wavy Gravy, 282
We Can't Go Home Again, 279–83, 284, 285, 286
Weisbart, David, 51, 66, 92, 111, 117, 155, 157, 196, 243; casting and, 37, 78; cast's mumbling and, 221; chosen to produce *Rebel*, 12–13; editing and, 204, 222, 223; finale sequence and, 209, 210, 219; script development and, 46, 47, 49, 53, 56
Wenders, Wim, 284–86
West Side Story, 225, 248
Westwood, Vivienne, 292
Whitmore, James, 18
Who Killed Teddy Bear?, 260–61
Wilde, Cornel, 227
Wilder, Billy, 155, 158
Wild One, The, 229, 289, 290
Will, George, 288–89
Williams, Lionel, 265
Williams, Sumner, 46
Williams, Tennessee, 19, 83, 176, 249
Williamson, Kevin, 291
Winchell, Walter, 243–44
Wind Across the Everglades, 99, 271, 272
Winslow, Marcus, 236
Winters, Shelley, 90, 93–94, 97
Wise, Robert, 248, 254
Wolfe, Ian, 130–31
Wolfe, Tom, 193
Woman's Secret, A, 6–7, 91
Wong Kar-Wai, 294
Wood, Natalie, viii, 29–41, 42, 58, 75, 79, 85–86, 88, 96, 118, 119, 126, 128, 138, 219, 225, 238, 278, 290; after *Rebel*, 220, 227, 241–53, 282; in car crash, 39–41; cast in *Rebel*, 29–30, 34–41, 76, 91–93; chickie-run scene and, 191, 196–98; crying scenes and, 135–36, 247; Dean's death and, 230–31, 234–35, 237, 241–42; Dean's first encounters with, 29, 31–33; Dean's relationship with, 33, 109, 154, 160–61, 165–66, 218, 241–42; death of, 251–53; early career of, 29, 30–31, 32–34; finale sequence and, 209–10; first preview of *Rebel* and, 228–29; Hopper's affair with, 37, 40, 78, 110, 125, 129, 130, 166, 198, 242–43, 244; makeover of, 91–92, 109–10; mansion sequence and, 154, 158, 161–70, 184; Mayo as double for, 197–98; Mineo's relationship with, 161; on-set behavior of, 124–25, 136; Oscar nominations for, 240, 245, 247, 248, 249; police station scene and, 133–34, 135–37, 169; Presley's affair with, 243; rape of, 38–39; Ray's sexual relationship with, 35, 37, 90, 91, 130, 166, 198, 222, 282; rebellious behavior of, 31, 32, 37, 40–41; red jacket given to, 218, 295; in scenes with father character, 150–52; *The Searchers* and, 220, 227, 240; *Splendor in the Grass* and, 246–47, 248; suicide attempt of, 249; time limits for minors and, 76, 124, 136, 196–97, 218; voice of, 92; Wagner's relationship with, 244, 245, 247, 249, 250, 251; Warners' contract with, 92–93, 245, 249
WPA Theater Project, 102
Wright, Frank Lloyd, 5, 118, 176
Wütherich, Rolf, 231, 233
Wylie, Philip, 143
Wynn, Keenan, 139

Yordan, Philip, 57–58, 272
You Are There, 19
Young Don't Cry, The, 256, 290
Young Go First, The, 5

Ziegler, William, 204, 210, 222, 223
Zukor, Adolph, 51, 52, 146